PREPARE!

An Ecumenical
Music and Worship Planner

2016–2017

David L. Bone
and
Mary J. Scifres

Abingdon Press
Nashville

PREPARE! AN ECUMENICAL MUSIC AND WORSHIP PLANNER 2016–2017

Copyright © 2016 by Abingdon Press

This book is printed on acid-free, recycled paper.

ISBN 978-1-5018-1099-2

All scripture quotations are taken from the Common English Bible. Copyright 2011 by the Common English Bible. Used by permission. All rights reserved. www.CommonEnglishBible.com.

16 17 18 19 20 21 22 23 24 25—10 9 8 7 6 5 4 3 2 1

MANUFACTURED IN CHINA

Do you have the book you need?

We want you to have the best planner, designed to meet your specific needs. How do you know if you have the right resource? Simply complete this one-question quiz:

Do you lead worship in a United Methodist congregation?

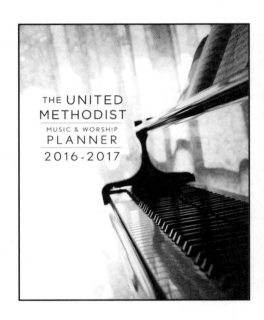

Yes.

Use *The United Methodist Music and Worship Planner, 2016–2017* (ISBN: 9781501810978)

No.

Use *Prepare! An Ecumenical Music and Worship Planner, 2016–2017* (ISBN: 9781501810992)

To order these resources, call Cokesbury toll free at 1-877-877-8674, or shop online at www.cokesbury.com. Do you find yourself rushing at the last minute to order your new planner? Subscribe today and receive your new *The United Methodist Music and Worship Planner* or *Prepare!* automatically next year and every year. Call toll free 1-800-672-1789 to request a subscription.

Abingdon Press™

USING PREPARE!

How We Organize the Resource Lists

Prepare! is designed to give you as many ideas as possible about a given worship service. Use it alongside a worship plan notebook that you create, a copy of your church's hymnal, and other supplements you use such as *The Faith We Sing, Sing the Faith, Songs for Praise and Worship,* or *Worship & Song.* New this year are selections from *The Africana Hymnal* (AH), a new collection of black sacred music from Abingdon Press (ISBN #9781426776441), available on a flash drive. Features of *Prepare!* include:

- The lectionary verses found on left-hand pages of *Prepare!* come from the Common English Bible (CEB), published through Abingdon Press in 2011. In order to provide the full lectionary text in the space available, all psalms are presented in "run-in" style; slashes indicate line breaks in the poetry. NOTE: The CEB italicizes Old Testament quotations in the New Testament. Where available, we have added psalter numbers from standard hymnals, including New Century, Presbyterian, United Methodist, and the new Presbyterian Hymnal, *Glory to God.*

- Each week **Primary Hymns and Songs for the Day** are suggested first. These suggestions include various helps for singing the hymns. These hymns and songs have the closest relationship to the scriptures and are widely known. The lengthier lists of **Additional Hymn Suggestions** and **Additional Contemporary Suggestions** will add variety to your musical selections.

- The musical suggestions are chosen to suggest a wide variety of styles.

- Each item is referenced to scripture or occasion.

- **Opening (O)** and **Closing (C)** hymns are suggested for each worship service.

- At least one **Communion (Comm.)** hymn is recommended for the first Sunday of each month and liturgical season. When appropriate, Communion hymns related to the scriptures are noted on other days as well.

- **Additional Contemporary Suggestions** include not only praise choruses but also global and ethnic music, folk music, and meditative music from traditions such as Taizé. Information about resources referenced in this section can be found on page 7. Please note that contemporary songs may also be listed under **Additional Hymn Suggestions, Vocal Solos,** or **Other Suggestions**.

- **Vocal Solos** and **Anthems** provide ideas for vocal music "performance" offerings, and may also inspire ideas for additional congregational selections.

- The recommended **Vocal Solos** are taken from a group of eleven collections that range from contemporary settings of hymn texts and praise choruses to spirituals to well-known classics (see page 7). Augment these suggestions from your own library.

- The **Anthem** suggestions include new works as well as generally known works that are already in many church choral libraries. Your study of the scripture and hymn texts will lead you to anthems in your church library that are appropriate. Some anthems in this planner are taken from the collection *St. Olaf Choirbook for Men* (SOCM; Augsburg ISBN #9781451499032).

- **One word of advice:** Be sure to consult all the music suggestions regardless of the type of service you are planning. In the changing world of worship, no one style defines a song or a worship service. Many items appropriate for contemporary and emergent styles are listed under the **Additional Hymn Suggestions** and many resources for traditional and blended services can be found in the **Additional Contemporary Suggestions** list. **Vocal Solos, Anthems,** and **Other Suggestions** may be appropriate for congregational use as well. Don't let the "category" here deter you from using any item that will enhance your worship service. Planners should consult all lists when choosing congregational music.

- Suggestions for "**Visuals**" are offered for each service. See the article "Visuals in Worship" (page 4) for discussion of these suggestions. Visual ideas are found in the **Other Suggestions** lists. They have been compiled by Ashley M. Calhoun and supplemented by our authors. Ashley is known for his inventive use of "found" items in creating visual worship settings. Worship committees, visual artists, dancers, and altar guilds can use these ideas to create their own unique worship centers, altar pieces, banners, and dance images. Screen visual artists can use these themes to select appropriate background and theme screens for worship.

- **Other Suggestions** also include words for worship, suggestions for choral introits and sung benedictions, and ideas for musical responses related to the spoken liturgy.

- A two-year, at-a-glance **2016–2017 Calendar** follows the **Worship Planning Sheets** (see page 144). It includes a note on the lectionary years covered in this edition of *Prepare!*

- *Prepare!* uses the *Revised Common Lectionary.* From the Second Sunday after Pentecost to Christ the King Sunday, the lectionary includes two patterns of readings. One pattern includes semi-continuous readings from the Hebrew Scriptures, Epistles, and Gospels. These readings are not necessarily related but allow for a sequential experience of the biblical narrative. **This is the pattern used to determine the scripture texts included in *Prepare!*** It is the pattern followed by most users of the hymnals referenced. In the second pattern, the Hebrew scripture is chosen to relate to the Gospel passage. This pattern is used primarily in traditions where Communion is celebrated at every service of worship. These **Alternate Lections** may be found in *The Revised Common Lectionary* (Abingdon Press, 1992) or online at http://lectionary.library.vanderbilt.edu/. Worship planners may certainly choose to follow the pattern that best serves the needs and traditions of your church. Neither pattern is necessarily better than the other; they are simply different ways of offering scripture in the worship setting over a three-year cycle in the church.

Planning Worship with These Resources

When planning any worship service, it is always best to start with the scripture and let it guide your thoughts and plans. If your church is not using the *Revised Common Lectionary*, but you do know what the scripture text will be for a service, look up that text in the **Index of Scriptures Referenced** on page 136.

As you read and study the scripture passages, read all of the suggested hymn texts. The hymns may remind you of anthems, solos, or keyboard selections. It is wise to mark your hymnal with the dates individual hymns are sung to avoid singing some too frequently. The **Hymn Resources** (see page 7) can enhance congregational singing, but should be used sparingly.

Use a three-ring binder to organize your plans. For each service of worship, include a copy of one of the **Worship Planning Sheets** found on pages 141-43 (or design your own!) along with blank paper for listing further ideas. Do not simply "fill in the blanks" for each service, but use the Planning Sheet to guide your work.

Use the suggestions in *Prepare!* along with your own page of ideas to begin making decisions about worship. Will the choir sing a "Call to Worship"? Can a hymn verse serve as a prayer response? Can a particular anthem or vocal solo give direction to the sermon? What prayers will be used? Once your decisions are made, complete the **Worship Planning Sheet**. Make a separate list of tasks related to that service. Planning worship is an awesome responsibility, but one that can be accomplished with an organized effort along with spiritual guidance.

VISUALS IN WORSHIP
Ashley M. Calhoun

The suggestions for visuals in this planner are meant to help worship leaders use objects and images to increase the impact of the gospel on a people who are increasingly visually oriented. These suggestions can be incorporated into many visual elements: hanging and processional banners, worship settings (whether on the altar or in the chancel or narthex), worship folder covers, and bulletin boards. The ideas can also be used to suggest ways to use classical and contemporary works of art, sculpture, needlework, and photography in worship services

With more churches incorporating screens and video walls into their worship spaces, there is tremendous potential for the use of still or moving imagery. Also, interpretive movement and drama can be very strong in visual impact.

The visual suggestions in this *Planner* have several characteristics:

- The suggestions are not meant to give detailed plans, but to spark your imagination and creativity.
- Some are drawn literally from the lessons; others are thematic.
- The suggestions are organized by reference to the lectionary passages:

O	Old Testament or Easter season, Acts reading
P	Psalm reading or Canticle
E	Epistle or New Testament reading
G	Gospel reading

- Chapter and verse numbers are sometimes given to indicate actual phrases in the scripture passage that can serve as visual elements.
- Themes such as "forgiveness," "love," or "rejoicing" are offered to encourage creative use of video and photographic images of people engaged in demonstrating those themes.

So much about worship is visual and intended to strengthen the proclamation of the gospel. The worship space is filled with visual elements that send a message. The church year is a treasure trove of color, texture, symbolism, and visual imagery. Special Sundays and special days in the cultural and denominational calendars also offer opportunities for visual expression. Evaluate the visual aspects of your worship services and find ways to enhance the worship experience with thoughtful, intentional use of visual elements and images.

CAN THE LECTIONARY STILL LIBERATE?
Reasons to Keep Using the *Revised Common Lectionary* in Worship Planning

Mary J. Scifres

The question arises for worship leaders and ordained ministers, "How does one prepare worship services that allow the flexibility necessary for the work of the Holy Spirit while also ordering the life of prayer and meditation to encourage disciplined growth?" Even in a world enamored with theme-based planning, new lectionaries like *Seasons of Creation* and the *Narrative Lectionary*, the *Revised Common Lectionary* can be one of the best liberators for organizing and designing creative, meaningful worship. Although my writing partner David Bone and I use many resources in our creative planning and respect the diversity of resources available, we still see the lectionary as a helpful tool on which to base inspired worship planning to encourage growth in the life of the church.

Attempting to coordinate the message of the musical selections, the visual images, and the words of worship with the message of the pulpit is a time-consuming and important task for church staff and worship leaders. Time and again, we hear from worship leaders who find lectionary use frees them for creative design time that otherwise would need to be spent in coordination meetings and individualized research. Church musicians, artists, laypersons, worship coordinators, and pastors give many hours each week to plan worship services that proclaim the Word, strengthen and challenge the community, and deepen the participants' faith. Ordained and diaconal ministers face the challenge of writing and choosing texts, prayers, and sermons for worship each week; musicians select, plan, and rehearse a variety of vocal and instrumental music to enhance and facilitate the worship experience of the churches they serve; and, church artists and lay worship leaders pursue means of leading worship, preparing the sanctuary for worship, designing additional creative elements, and devising other aspects of the worshiping experience.

The preacher can ease this task significantly by using the *Revised Common Lectionary* and communicating on a regular basis with other worship leaders regarding worship service needs. A church can find both freedom and unity when the pastoral leadership uses this lectionary as the basis for planning worship and its individual aspects (sermon, hymns, anthems, prayers) without exalting it to a level of sole importance. First, lectionary use prevents the abusive appeal to a limited number of scriptures and topics, toward which some preachers are tempted. Regarding the concern for local needs, the lectionary need not be used to ignore specific spiritual, emotional, or physical needs of a congregation. Rather, the lectionary can provide a means for integrating such needs into the worship service by relating scriptural messages to the current needs and situation of the community. While interpreting the lections for worship, both planners and preachers can find ways of exploring the historical meanings of the texts and bringing such historical understandings into the present.

Second, the pedagogical advantage of using the lectionary to acquaint Christians with the broad tradition of which we are a part can deepen worship and learning experiences of the community of faith. As pastors in the twenty-first century face growing concern regarding the types of "burn out" that result from remaining static in a setting that has become routine instead of a challenge, following the lectionary cycle can open up opportunities for growth and support in a number of ways. Being forced to grapple with difficult texts in addition to familiar passages enlivens the mind and encourages the preacher to look to new exegetical resources and homiletic aids. Support can also come from an ecumenical community of pastors in one's city or county who are studying the same text during the cycle. Study groups within the local church can wrestle with the lectionary scriptures, growing their biblical and theological knowledge in the process.

Likewise, church musicians who wade through piles of contemporary and classical music every season to choose the anthems, organ selections, hymns, responsive psalms, and other musical contributions to the worship service can find a common guide to that selection when the lectionary is used. In the local church, the musician finds the opportunity to be a minister of music *and* Word when the lections provide the core of the worship service. In a time when the shortage of church musicians affects many churches, a church musician may be able to serve several churches and use the same musical selections in each setting. If a church musician, called to full-time ministry of music, can be employed by two or three local congregations who agree to use the same anthems and hymns each week and to schedule worship services at different times, both musician and congregation can benefit from this new approach to music ministry, which supports full-time service and receives music of high quality. The possibilities for providing equitable salaries for ministers of music as well as nurturing several local church communities through Spirit-filled, well-performed music are enhanced when the unifying elements of ecumenical cooperation and common lections are available.

In terms of teaching, the lectionary can provide a helpful method of coordinating the community worship experience with church school, weekly Bible study groups, prayer and devotional groups, music rehearsals, singing and praise gatherings, and other small groups in the life of the church. Small groups, which sometimes seem to go off in their own directions, away from the Sunday morning community, would more easily feel a part of the fold with the integrative element of the lectionary. And the educational system of the church, which so often leaves teachers and students feeling excluded and separated from the worshiping body, can find inclusion in the integrative element of the lectionary. How much more easily a child would sit through a sermon and find meaning in mysterious hymns when the basic scriptural text has been heard and discussed in church school prior to worship or explored in church school after worship!

Overall, lectionary use can provide an integrative and unifying element to the entire life of the church, when used in its various dimensions through curriculum, worship resources, music selections, and local cooperative church events. Where proclamation of the Word is central, that Word can and should be the integrative element of a holistic worship service. In churches that seek to reach people with a message that is unified thematically, lectionary use provides a scriptural base that all planners know well in advance and can use when choosing and developing the themes or topics for the Sundays of any given season. When the lectionary is used in this way, choirs or music teams have adequate time to rehearse appropriate music, liturgists or worship facilitators have sufficient time to write or find liturgy and prayers for the service, and other church artists (actors, dancers, composers, visual artists, banner makers, arts guilds, and screen programmers) may plan and prepare their contributions to the service and the season.

Frequent lectionary use need not limit other options during the year. When preaching pastors are called to address a pressing congregational or community issue, lectionary scriptures can provide a starting point to keep the conversation biblically based in worship. When the Spirit calls a preacher or worship team to focus in a different direction, taking a short or even seasonal break from lectionary use is another option. When a sermon series or a church theme pulls worship designers toward different scriptures, the vast indices in lectionary resources can help you reference scriptures even when used on non-lectionary schedules. Even as a preacher who is led by the Spirit, I find myself returning to the *Revised Common Lectionary* to ease the burden on my staff and create a cohesive conversation as we plan not only worship but also the focused life and ministry of the churches we serve.

With this book, we invite your congregation and its worship leaders to begin the process of integrating your various aspects of worship planning by means of the *Revised Common Lectionary*. As thematic ideas begin to emerge in each week's worship service and as the various scriptures provide diverse bases for worship planning, we hope that you will find worship becoming an increasingly growth-filled and exciting aspect of your congregation's life.

RESOURCE KEY

AH   *The Africana Hymnal.* Nashville: Abingdon Press, 2015. ISBN #9781426776441.

B   Forbis, Wesley, ed. *The Baptist Hymnal.* Nashville: Convention Press, 1991.

C   Merrick, Daniel and Polk, David, ed. *Chalice Hymnal.* St. Louis: Chalice Press, 1996.

E   *The Hymnal 1982.* New York: The Church Hymnal Corporation, 1985.

EL   *Evangelical Lutheran Worship.* Minneapolis: Augsburg Fortress, 2006.

F   Bock, Fred, ed. *Hymns for the Family of God.* Nashville: Paragon Associates, Inc., 1976.

G   *Glory to God: The Presbyterian Hymnal.* Louisville: Presbyterian Publishing Corporation, 2013.

L   *Lutheran Book of Worship.* Minneapolis: Augsburg Publishing House, 1978.

N   Clyde, Arthur G., ed. *The New Century Hymnal.* Cleveland, OH: The Pilgrim Press, 1995.

P   McKim, LindaJo, ed. *The Presbyterian Hymnal.* Louisville: Westminster/John Knox Press, 1990.

S   Hickman, Hoyt L., ed. *The Faith We Sing.* Nashville: Abingdon Press, 2000. Cokesbury Ord. #090547 (Pew Edition).

SF   Hickman, Hoyt L., ed. *Sing the Faith.* Louisville: Westminster/John Knox Press, 2003.

UM   Young, Carlton R., ed. *The United Methodist Hymnal.* Nashville: The United Methodist Publishing House, 1989. ISBN #9780687431328.

VU   Ambrose, John E., ed. *Voices United.* Etobicoke, Ontario, Canada: The United Church Publishing House, 1996.

W   Batastini, Robert J., ed. *Worship.* Chicago: GIA Publications, Inc., 1986.

WS   Smith, Gary Alan, ed. *Worship & Song.* Nashville: Abingdon Press, 2011. Accompaniment, singer, guitar, and planning editions available. Cokesbury Ord. #090547

WSL   Smith, Gary Alan, ed. *Worship & Song Leader's Edition.* Nashville: Abingdon Press, 2011. #9781426709944 (Leader's edition). *These resources WSL1-WSL222 refer to the written words for worship (prayers, litanies, benedictions) available in worship resource editions of Worship & Song.*

HYMN RESOURCES

S-1   Smith, Gary Alan, ed. *The United Methodist Hymnal: Music Supplement.* Nashville: Abingdon Press, 1991. Cokesbury Ord. #431476.

S-2   Bennett, Robert C., ed. *The United Methodist Hymnal: Music Supplement II.* Nashville: Abingdon Press, 1993. Cokesbury Ord. #430135.

H-3   Hopson, Hal H. *The Creative Church Musician Series.* Carol Stream, IL: Hope Publishing Co.
        Hbl Vol. 1. *The Creative Use of Handbells in Worship.* 1997. Cokesbury Ord. #921992.
        Chr Vol. 2. *The Creative Use of Choirs in Worship.* 1999. Cokesbury Ord. #732807.
        Desc *The Creative Use of Descants in Worship.* 1999. Cokesbury Item #732864.
        Org *The Creative Use of the Organ in Worship.* 1997. Cokesbury Ord. #323904.

VOCAL SUGGESTION RESOURCES

V-1   Kimbrough, Steven, ed. *Sweet Singer: Hymns of Charles Wesley.* Chapel Hill, NC: Hinshaw Music, 1987. Catalogue #CV-1 Cokesbury Ord. #811712 V-2 Handel, George Frederic. *Messiah.* Various editions available.

V-3   Hayes, Mark. *The Mark Hayes Vocal Solo Collection*
        V-3 (1) *Ten Spirituals for Solo Voice.* Van Nuys, CA: Alfred Music Publishing, 2007. ISBN #9780882848808
        V-3 (2) *Seven Praise and Worship Songs for Solo Voice.* Van Nuys, CA: Alfred Music Publishing, 2010. ISBN #9780739037249

V-3 (3) *Ten Hymns and Gospel Songs for Solo Voice.* ISBN#9780739006979

V-4   Scott, K. Lee. *Sing a Song of Joy.* Minneapolis, MN: Augsburg Fortress, 1989. ISBN #9780800647889 (Medium High Voice) (Medium Low Voice) ISBN #9780800652821.

V-5   Various Editors. *With All My Heart: Contemporary Vocal Solos.* Minneapolis, MN: Augsburg Fortress, 2004.
        V-5 (1) Volume 1: Autumn and Winter. ISBN # 9780800676841
        V-5 (2) Volume 2: Spring and Summer. ISBN # 9780800676858
        V-5 (3) Volume 3: Baptisms, Weddings, Funerals. ISBN # 9780800679460

V-6   Walters, Richard, arr. *Hymn Classics: Concert Arrangements of Traditional Hymns for Voice and Piano.* Milwaukee, WI: Hal Leonard Publishing, 1993. ISBN #9780793560080. High Voice: Cokesbury Ord. #811290. Low Voice: Cokesbury Order #811233.

V-7   Johnson, Hall, arr. *Thirty (30) Spirituals.* New York: G. Schirmer, Inc., 1949. ISBN #9780793548033.

V-8   Wilson, John F., Don Doig, and Jack Schrader, eds. *Everything for the Church Soloist.* Carol Stream, IL: Hope Publishing Company, 1980. Cokesbury Ord. #810103.

V-9   Scott, K. Lee. *Rejoice Now My Spirit: Vocal Solos for the Church Year.* Minneapolis, MN: Augsburg Fortress, 1992. ISBN #9780800651084

V-10   Hayes, Mark et al. *From the Manger to the Cross—Seasonal Solos for Medium Voice.* Dayton, OH: The Lorenz Corporation, 2006. Cokesbury Ord. #526369.

V-11   Pote, Allen. *A Song of Joy.* Carol Stream, IL: Hope Publishing, 2003. Cokesbury Ord. #505068.

ANTHEM RESOURCE

SOCM   Aspaas, Christopher, ed. *St. Olaf Choirbook for Men.* Minneapolis, MN: Augsburg Fortress, 2015. ISBN #9781451499032.

CONTEMPORARY RESOURCES

SP   Various. *Songs for Praise and Worship Singalong Edition.* Waco, TX: Word Music, 1992. ISBN #9783010203494.

M1-M55 Barker, Ken, ed. *More Songs for Praise and Worship Choir/Worship Team Edition.* Waco, TX: Word Music, 2000. Cokesbury Ord. #509802 (*Keyboard Edition:* Cokesbury Ord. #509776. *Piano/Guitar/Vocal Edition:* Cokesbury Ord. #509764).M56-M115

        Barker, Ken, ed. *More Songs for Praise and Worship 2 Choir/Worship Team Edition.* Waco, TX: Word Music, 2002. Cokesbury Ord. #512053 (*Keyboard Edition:* Cokesbury Ord. #512075. *Piano/Guitar/Vocal Edition:* Cokesbury Ord. #080689314186).

M116-   Barker, Ken, ed. *More Songs for Praise and Worship 3 Choir/Worship Team Edition.* Waco, TX: Word Music, 2005. Cokesbury Ord. #523357 (*Keyboard Edition:* Cokesbury Ord. # 523418. *Piano/Guitar/Vocal Edition:* Cokesbury Ord. #523369).
M168

M169-   Barker, Ken, ed. *More Songs for Praise and Worship 4 Choir/Worship Team Edition.* Waco, TX: Word Music, 2006. Cokesbury Ord. # 529198 (*Keyboard Edition:* Cokesbury Ord. # 529244. *Piano/Guitar/Vocal Edition:* ISBN #9785557996822).
M219

M220-   McClure, Mark and Sarah G. Huffman, eds. *More Songs for Praise and Worship 5.* Waco, TX: Word Music, 2011. (*Piano/Guitar/Vocal Edition.* ISBN#978-1458418807. *Choir/Worship Team Edition.* ISBN#9781458418814; *Keyboard/SATB Edition.* Catalogue #0-80689-50087-9).
M279

See also Vocal Solo suggestions from V-3 and V-5.

Jeremiah 18:1-11

[1]Jeremiah received the LORD's word: [2]Go down to the potter's house, and I'll give you instructions about what to do there. [3]So I went down to the potter's house; he was working on the potter's wheel. [4]But the piece he was making was flawed while still in his hands, so the potter started on another, as seemed best to him. [5]Then the LORD's word came to me: [6]House of Israel, can't I deal with you like this potter, declares the LORD? Like clay in the potter's hand, so are you in mine, house of Israel! [7]At any time I may announce that I will dig up, pull down, and destroy a nation or kingdom; [8]but if that nation I warned turns from its evil, then I'll relent and not carry out the harm I intended for it. [9]At the same time, I may announce that I will build and plant a nation or kingdom; [10]but if that nation displeases and disobeys me, then I'll relent and not carry out the good I intended for it. [11]Now say to the people of Judah and those living in Jerusalem: This is what the LORD says: I am a potter preparing a disaster for you; I'm working out a plan against you. So each one of you, turn from your evil ways; reform your ways and your actions.

Psalm 139:1-6, 13-18 (G28/29, N715, P248, UM854)

[1]LORD, you have examined me. / You know me. / [2]You know when I sit down and when I stand up. / Even from far away, you comprehend my plans. / [3]You study my traveling and resting. / You are thoroughly familiar with all my ways. / [4]There isn't a word on my tongue, LORD, / that you don't already know completely. / [5]You surround me—front and back. / You put your hand on me. / [6]That kind of knowledge is too much for me; / it's so high above me that I can't fathom it. . . .

[13]You are the one who created my innermost parts; / you knit me together while I was still in my mother's womb. / [14]I give thanks to you that I was marvelously set apart. / Your works are wonderful—I know that very well. / [15]My bones weren't hidden from you / when I was being put together in a secret place, / when I was being woven together in the deep parts of the earth. / [16]Your eyes saw my embryo, / and on your scroll every day was written what was being formed for me, / before any one of them had yet happened. / [17]God, your plans are incomprehensible to me! / Their total number is countless! / [18]If I tried to count them—they outnumber grains of sand! / If I came to the very end—I'd still be with you.

Philemon 1-21

[1]From Paul, who is a prisoner for the cause of Christ Jesus, and our brother Timothy.

To Philemon our dearly loved coworker, [2]Apphia our sister, Archippus our fellow soldier, and the church that meets in your house.

[3]May the grace and peace from God our Father and the Lord Jesus Christ be with you.

[4]Philemon, I thank my God every time I mention you in my prayers [5]because I've heard of your love and faithfulness, which you have both for the Lord Jesus and for all God's people. [6]I pray that your partnership in the faith might become effective by an understanding of all that is good among us in Christ. [7]I have great joy and encouragement because of your love, since the hearts of God's people are refreshed by your actions, my brother.

[8]Therefore, though I have enough confidence in Christ to command you to do the right thing, [9]I would rather appeal to you through love. I, Paul—an old man, and now also a prisoner for Christ Jesus—[10]appeal to you for my child Onesimus. I became his father in the faith during my time in prison. [11]He was useless to you before, but now he is useful to both of us. [12]I'm sending him back to you, which is like sending you my own heart. [13]I considered keeping him with me so that he might serve me in your place during my time in prison because of the gospel. [14]However, I didn't want to do anything without your consent so that your act of kindness would occur willingly and not under pressure. [15]Maybe this is the reason that Onesimus was separated from you for a while so that you might have him back forever—[16]no longer as a slave but more than a slave—that is, as a dearly loved brother. He is especially a dearly loved brother to me. How much more can he become a brother to you, personally and spiritually in the Lord!

[17]So, if you really consider me a partner, welcome Onesimus as if you were welcoming me. [18]If he has harmed you in any way or owes you money, charge it to my account. [19]I, Paul, will pay it back to you(I'm writing this with my own hand). Of course, I won't mention that you owe me your life.

[20]Yes, brother, I want this favor from you in the Lord! Refresh my heart in Christ. [21]I'm writing to you, confident of your obedience and knowing that you will do more than what I ask.

Luke 14:25-33

[25]Large crowds were traveling with Jesus. Turning to them, he said, [26]"Whoever comes to me and doesn't hate father and mother, spouse and children, and brothers and sisters—yes, even one's own life—cannot be my disciple. [27]Whoever doesn't carry their own cross and follow me cannot be my disciple.

[28]"If one of you wanted to build a tower, wouldn't you first sit down and calculate the cost, to determine whether you have enough money to complete it? [29]Otherwise, when you have laid the foundation but couldn't finish the tower, all who see it will begin to belittle you. [30]They will say, 'Here's the person who began construction and couldn't complete it!' [31]Or what king would go to war against another king without first sitting down to consider whether his ten thousand soldiers could go up against the twenty thousand coming against him? [32]And if he didn't think he could win, he would send a representative to discuss terms of peace while his enemy was still a long way off. [33]In the same way, none of you who are unwilling to give up all of your possessions can be my disciple."

Primary Hymns and Songs for the Day
"Take Up Thy Cross" (Luke) (O)
  B494, E675, EL667, G718, L398, N204, P393, UM415, VU561, W634
        H-3   Chr-178, 180; Org-44
        S-1   #141-43 Various treatments
"Change My Heart, O God" (Jer)
  EL801, G695, S2152, SF2152, SP195,
"I Was There to Hear Your Borning Cry" (Pss, Baptism)
  C75, EL732, G488, N351, S2051, SF2051, VU644
"All My Days" (Pss)
  WS3011
"Help Us Accept Each Other" (Phlm)
  C487, G754, N388, P358, UM560, W656
"When I Survey the Wondrous Cross" (Luke)
  B144, C195, EL803, F258, G223, N224, P101, UM298
        H-3   Hbl-6, 102; Chr-213; Desc-49; Org-49
        S-1   #155. Desc.
  E474, L482, G224, P100, UM299 (PD), VU149 (Fr.)
        H-3   Hbl-47; Chr-214; Desc-90; Org-127
        S-1   #288. Transposition to E-flat major
"I Have Decided to Follow Jesus" (Luke)
  B305, C344, S2129, SF2129
"Have Thine Own Way, Lord" (Jer, Luke) (C)
  B294, C588, F400, UM382 (PD)
        S-2   #2. Instrumental desc.

Additional Hymn Suggestions
"Spirit of the Living God" (Jer)
  B244, C259, G288, N283, P322, SP131, UM393, VU376
"As a Fire Is Meant for Burning" (Jer)
  S2237, SF2237, VU578
"God the Sculptor of the Mountains" (Jer, Pss)
  EL736, G5, S2060, SF2060
"Womb of Life" (Pss, Comm.)
  C14, G3, N274, S2046, SF2046
"Mothering God, You Gave Me Birth" (Pss, Comm.)
  C83, EL735, G7, N467, S2050, SF2050, VU320
"In Christ There Is No East or West" (Phlm)
  B385, C687, E529, EL650 (PD), F685, G317/318, L359, N394/N395, P439/P440, UM548, VU606, W659
"Since Jesus Came into My Heart" (Phlm)
  B441, F639, S2140, SF2140
"Together We Serve" (Phlm)
  G767, S2175, SF2175
"Called as Partners in Christ's Service" (Phlm)
  C453, G761, N495, P343
"A Place at the Table" (Phlm, Comm.)
  G769, WS3149
"In the Cross of Christ I Glory" (Phlm, Luke)
  B554, C207, E441, EL324, F251, G213, L104, N193, P84, UM295
"Where He Leads Me" (Luke)
  B288, C346, F607, UM338 (PD)
"Must Jesus Bear the Cross Alone" (Luke)
  B475, F504, SF2112, UM424 (PD)
"This Little Light of Mine" (Luke)
  N525, UM585 (See also AH4150, EL677, N524)
"For the Bread Which You Have Broken" (Luke, Comm.)
  C411, E340/E341, EL494, G516, L200, P508/P509, UM614/UM615, VU470
"Living for Jesus" (Luke)
  B282, C610, F462, S2149, SF2149

Additional Contemporary Suggestions
"Praise You" (Jer, Stewardship)
  M84, S2003, SF2003
"Water, River, Spirit, Grace" (Jer, Baptism)
  C366, N169, S2253, SF2253
"The Potter's Hand" (Jer, Pss, Stewardship)
  M85
"Oh, I Know the Lord's Laid His Hands on Me" (Pss)
  S2139, SF2139
"He Knows My Name" (Pss)
  M109
"These Hands" (Pss, Stewardship)
  M101
"You Are Mine" (Pss, Luke)
  EL581, G177, S2218, SF2218
"Cry of My Heart" (Luke)
  M39, S2165, SF2165
"Let It Be Said of Us" (Luke)
  M53
"Every Move I Make" (Luke)
  M122
"Everyday" (Luke)
  M150
"One Way" (Luke)
  M248

Vocal Solos
"Have Thine Own Way, Lord!" (Jer)
  V-8   p. 191
"Here I Am" (Jer, Luke)
  V-11   p. 19
"Sing a Song of Joy" (Pss)
  V-4   p. 2
"Christ Living Within You" (Luke)
  V-8   p. 177

Anthems
"The Image of God" (Pss)
Craig Courtney; Beckenhorst BP2054
SATB, piano and opt. C instrument

"Follow Jesus" (Luke)
Anne Organ; Augsburg 0800677420
Two-part, organ

Other Suggestions
Visuals:
  O   Potter's wheel/clay, hands/clay, building, planting
  P   Sitting/standing, open mouth, hand on shoulder
  E   Letter, old man writing. manacles, heart
  G   Carrying crosses, tower, calculator, document, dove
Opening Prayer: N826 (Jer) or C771 (Pss)
Prayer: C262. You Are the Work of God (Jer)
Sung Response: UM98 and WS3015. "How Great" (Pss)
Create a choral medley or praise band song set, using the traditional "How Great Thou Art" (B10, C33, EL856, F2, G625, L532, N35, P467, UM77, VU238) and the new "How Great You Are"(WS3015).
Blessing: WSL158. "Here in this sanctuary" (Phlm, Luke)
Sung Benediction: M87. "Let the Peace of God Reign" (Phlm)
Alternate Lessons (see p. 4): Deut 30:15-20, Ps 1

Jeremiah 4:11-12, 22-28

[11]At that time, this people and Jerusalem will be told:
A blistering wind from the bare heights;
    it rages in the desert toward my people,
        not merely to winnow or cleanse.
    [12]This wind is too devastating for that.
Now I, even I, will pronounce my sentence against them.
....

[22]My people are foolish.
    They don't even know me!
They are thoughtless children
    without understanding;
        they are skilled at doing wrong,
        inept at doing right.
[23]I looked at the earth,
    and it was without shape or form;
        at the heavens
        and there was no light.
[24]I looked at the mountains
    and they were quaking;
    all the hills were rocking back and forth.
[25]I looked and there was no one left;
    every bird in the sky had taken flight.
[26]I looked and the fertile land was a desert;
    all its towns were in ruins
        before the LORD,
        before his fury.
[27]The LORD proclaims:
    The whole earth
        will become a desolation,
        but I will not destroy it completely.
[28]Therefore, the earth will grieve
    and the heavens grow dark
        because I have declared my plan
        and will neither change my mind
            nor cancel the plan.

Psalm 14:1-7 (G335, N626, UM746)

[1]Fools say in their hearts, There is no God. / They are corrupt and do evil things; / not one of them does anything good.

[2]The LORD looks down from heaven on humans / to see if anyone is wise, / to see if anyone seeks God, / [3]but all of them have turned bad. / Everyone is corrupt. / No one does good— / not even one person!

[4]Are they dumb, all these evildoers, / devouring my people / like they are eating bread / but never calling on the LORD?

[5]Count on it: they will be in utter panic / because God is with the righteous generation. / [6]You evildoers may humiliate / the plans of those who suffer, / but the LORD is their refuge.

[7]Let Israel's salvation come out of Zion! / When the LORD changes / his people's circumstances for the better, / Jacob will rejoice; / Israel will celebrate!

1 Timothy 1:12-17

[12]I thank Christ Jesus our Lord, who has given me strength because he considered me faithful. So he appointed me to ministry [13]even though I used to speak against him, attack his people, and I was proud. But I was shown mercy because I acted in ignorance and without faith. [14]Our Lord's favor poured all over me along with the faithfulness and love that are in Christ Jesus. [15]This saying is reliable and deserves full acceptance: "Christ Jesus came into the world to save sinners"—and I'm the biggest sinner of all. [16]But this is why I was shown mercy, so that Christ Jesus could show his endless patience to me first of all. So I'm an example for those who are going to believe in him for eternal life. [17]Now to the king of the ages, to the immortal, invisible, and only God, may honor and glory be given to him forever and always! Amen.

Luke 15:1-10

[1]All the tax collectors and sinners were gathering around Jesus to listen to him. [2]The Pharisees and legal experts were grumbling, saying, "This man welcomes sinners and eats with them."

[3]Jesus told them this parable: [4]"Suppose someone among you had one hundred sheep and lost one of them. Wouldn't he leave the other ninety-nine in the pasture and search for the lost one until he finds it? [5]And when he finds it, he is thrilled and places it on his shoulders. [6]When he arrives home, he calls together his friends and neighbors, saying to them, 'Celebrate with me because I've found my lost sheep.' [7]In the same way, I tell you, there will be more joy in heaven over one sinner who changes both heart and life than over ninety-nine righteous people who have no need to change their hearts and lives.

[8]"Or what woman, if she owns ten silver coins and loses one of them, won't light a lamp and sweep the house, searching her home carefully until she finds it? [9]When she finds it, she calls together her friends and neighbors, saying, 'Celebrate with me because I've found my lost coin.' [10]In the same way, I tell you, joy breaks out in the presence of God's angels over one sinner who changes both heart and life."

Primary Hymns and Songs for the Day

"Immortal, Invisible, God Only Wise" (1 Tim) (O)
B6, C66, E423, EL834, F319, G12, L526, N1, P263, UM103
(PD), VU264, W512
- H-3   Hbl-15, 71; Chr-65; Desc-93; Org-135
- S-1   #300. Harm.

"O for a Closer Walk with God" (Jer)
E684, G739, N450, P396

"My Lord, What a Morning" (Jer, Pss, Luke)
C708, EL438 (PD), G352, P449, UM719, VU708

"Praise, My Soul, the King of Heaven" (1 Tim)
B32, C23, E410, EL864/865, F339, G619/620, L549,
P478/479, UM66 (PD), VU240, W530
- H-3   Hbl-88; Chr-162; Desc-67; Org-75
- S-1   #205. Harm.
         #206. Desc.

"Grace Alone" (1 Tim)
M100, S2162, SF2162

"Amazing Grace" (1 Tim, Luke)
AH4091, B330, C546, E671, EL779, F107, G649, L448, N547
and N548, P280, UM378 (PD), VU266 (Fr.), W583
- H-3   Hbl-14, 46; Chr-27; Desc-14; Org-4
- S-2   #5-7. Various treatments
- V-8, p. 56. Vocal solo

"To God Be the Glory" (1 Tim) (C)
B4, C72, F363, G634, P485, UM98 (PD)

Additional Hymn Suggestions

"Steal Away to Jesus" (Jer, Pss, Luke)
C644, G358, N599, UM704

"O Day of God, Draw Nigh" (Jer, Pss)
B623, C700, E601, N611, P452, UM730 (PD), VU688 and
VU689 (Fr.)

"Alas! And Did My Savior Bleed" (1 Tim)
AH4067, B139/145, C204, EL337, F274, G212, L98, N199/
N200, P78, UM294/UM359

"There Are Some Things I May Not Know" (1 Tim)
N405, S2147, SF2147

"In the Singing" (1 Tim, Comm.)
EL466, G533, S2255, SF2255

"The First Song of Isaiah" (1 Tim, Luke)
G71, S2030, SF2030

"Come, Thou Fount of Every Blessing" (1 Tim, Luke)
AH4086, B15/18, C16, E686, EL807, F318, G475, L499,
N459, P356, UM400 (PD), VU559

"Just as I Am, Without One Plea" (Luke)
B303/307, C339, E693, EL592, F417, G442, L296, N207,
P370, UM357 (PD), VU508

"Savior, Like a Shepherd Lead Us" (Luke)
B61, C558, E708, EL789, F601, G187, L481, N252, P387,
UM381 (PD)

"Come, We That Love the Lord" (Luke)
B525, E392, N379, UM732, VU715, W552

"Marching to Zion" (Luke)
AH4153, B524, C707, EL625, F550, N382, UM733 (PD),
VU714

"A Woman and a Coin" (Luke)
C74, G173, VU360

"I'm So Glad Jesus Lifted Me" (Luke)
C529, EL860 (PD), N474, S2151, SF2151

"Just a Closer Walk with Thee" (Luke)
B448, C557, EL697, F591, G835, S2158, SF2158

"Lord of All Hopefulness" (Luke)
E482, EL765, G683, L469, S2197, SF2197, W568

Additional Contemporary Suggestions

"Mighty to Save" (Jer, Luke, Pss)
M246, WS3038

"Holy Spirit, Come to Us" (Pss)
EL406, G281, S2118, SF2118, W473

"My Tribute" ("To God Be the Glory") (1 Tim)
B153, C39, F365, N14, SP118, UM99; V-8 p. 5 Vocal Solo

"God Is Good All the Time" (1 Tim)
AH4010, M45, WS3026

"Shout to the North" (1 Tim)
G319, M99, WS3042

"Amazing Grace" ("My Chains Are Gone") (1 Tim)
M205, WS3104

"Sing Alleluia to the Lord" (1 Tim, Comm.)
B214, C32, S2258, SF2258, SP93

"Here Is Bread, Here Is Wine" (1 Tim, Comm.)
EL483, S2266, SF2266

"God Is So Good" (1 Tim, Luke)
B23, G658, S2056, SF2056

"We Fall Down" (1 Tim)
G368, M66, WS3187

"When It's All Been Said and Done" (1 Tim, Luke)
M115

"Grace Like Rain" (1 Tim, Luke)
M251

"You Are My All in All" (Luke)
G519, SP220, WS3040

"Take, O Take Me as I Am" (Luke)
EL814, G698, WS3119

Vocal Solos

"Redeeming Grace" (1 Tim)
- V-4   p. 47

"Strength to My Soul" (1 Tim, Luke)
- V-8   p. 352

Anthems

"A Debtor to Mercy Alone" (1 Tim)
John Hudson; Beckenhorst BP1941
SATB, keyboard

"Savior, Like a Shepherd Lead Us" (Luke)
Arr. Lloyd Larson; Lorenz 10/4688L
SATB a cappella

Other Suggestions

Visuals:
- **O**   Desert, wind, mountains, earthquake, birds, ruins, mourning, darkness
- **P**   Stray sheep, eating bread, Ps. 14:6, poor, joy
- **E**   Christ, 1 Tim 1:15, Paul, glory, crown
- **G**   One sheep, Jesus carrying lost sheep, ten coins, lamp, broom, woman rejoicing, one coin

If your congregation is remembering the 15-year anniversary of 9/11 today, intertwine the broken world theme of Jeremiah 4 with the theme of God's commitment to the lost in Luke 15.

Introit: C583, EL768, G740, S2214, SF2214. "Lead Me, Guide Me" (Luke)

Opening Prayer: N830 (2 Tim) and Confession: N838 (Pss)

Affirmation of Faith: WSL76 or UM889 (1 Tim)

Alternate Lessons (see p. 4): Exod 32:7-14, Ps 51:1-10

Jeremiah 8:18–9:1

[18]No healing,
    only grief;
        my heart is broken.
[19]Listen to the weeping of my people
    all across the land:
    "Isn't the LORD in Zion?
    Is her king no longer there?"
Why then did they anger me
    with their images,
    with pointless foreign gods?
[20]"The harvest is past,
    the summer has ended,
        yet we aren't saved."
[21]Because my people are crushed,
    I am crushed;
    darkness and despair overwhelm me.

[22]Is there no balm in Gilead?
    Is there no physician there?
Why then have my people
    not been restored to health?
9If only my head were a spring of water
    and my eyes a fountain of tears,
I would weep day and night
    for the wounds of my people.

Psalm 79:1-9 (G430, N671)

[1]The nations have come into your inheritance, God! / They've defiled your holy temple. / They've made Jerusalem a bunch of ruins. / [2]They've left your servants' bodies / as food for the birds; / they've left the flesh of your faithful / to the wild animals of the earth. / [3]They've poured out the blood of the faithful / like water all around Jerusalem, / and there's no one left to bury them. / [4]We've become a joke to our neighbors, / nothing but objects of ridicule / and disapproval to those around us.
[5]How long will you rage, LORD? Forever? / How long will your anger burn like fire? / [6]Pour out your wrath on the nations / who don't know you, / on the kingdoms / that haven't called on your name. / [7]They've devoured Jacob / and demolished his pasture. / [8]Don't remember the iniquities of past generations; / let your compassion hurry to meet us / because we've been brought so low. / [9]God of our salvation, help us / for the glory of your name! / Deliver us and cover our sins / for the sake of your name!

1 Timothy 2:1-7

[1]First of all, then, I ask that requests, prayers, petitions, and thanksgiving be made for all people. [2]Pray for kings and everyone who is in authority so that we can live a quiet and peaceful life in complete godliness and dignity. [3]This is right and it pleases God our savior, [4]who wants all people to be saved and to come to a knowledge of the truth. [5]There is one God and one mediator between God and humanity, the human Christ Jesus, [6]who gave himself as a payment to set all people free. This was a testimony that was given at the right time. [7]I was appointed to be a preacher and apostle of this testimony—I'm telling the truth and I'm not lying! I'm a teacher of the Gentiles in faith and truth.

Luke 16:1-13

[1]Jesus also said to the disciples, "A certain rich man heard that his household manager was wasting his estate. [2]He called the manager in and said to him, 'What is this I hear about you? Give me a report of your administration because you can no longer serve as my manager.'
[3]"The household manager said to himself, What will I do now that my master is firing me as his manager? I'm not strong enough to dig and too proud to beg. [4]I know what I'll do so that, when I am removed from my management position, people will welcome me into their houses.
[5]"One by one, the manager sent for each person who owed his master money. He said to the first, 'How much do you owe my master?' [6]He said, 'Nine hundred gallons of olive oil.' The manager said to him, 'Take your contract, sit down quickly, and write four hundred fifty gallons.' [7]Then the manager said to another, 'How much do you owe?' He said, 'One thousand bushels of wheat.' He said, 'Take your contract and write eight hundred.'
[8]"The master commended the dishonest manager because he acted cleverly. People who belong to this world are more clever in dealing with their peers than are people who belong to the light. [9]I tell you, use worldly wealth to make friends for yourselves so that when it's gone, you will be welcomed into the eternal homes.
[10]"Whoever is faithful with little is also faithful with much, and the one who is dishonest with little is also dishonest with much. [11]If you haven't been faithful with worldly wealth, who will trust you with true riches? [12]If you haven't been faithful with someone else's property, who will give you your own? [13]No household servant can serve two masters. Either you will hate the one and love the other, or you will be loyal to the one and have contempt for the other. You cannot serve God and wealth."

Primary Hymns and Songs for the Day

"Dear Lord and Father of Mankind" (Jer, Pss, Luke) (O)
(Alternate Text: "Dear God, Embracing Humankind")
B267, C594, E652/563, F422, G169, L506, N502, P345,
UM358 (PD), VU608

"There Is a Balm in Gilead" (Jer)
AH4110, B269, C501, E676, EL614 (PD), F48, G792, N553,
P394, UM375, VU612, W608
     S-2   #21. Desc.

"How Long, O Lord" (Pss)
G777, S2209, SF2209

"This Is My Song" (1 Tim)
C722, EL887, G340, N591, UM437

"More Precious than Silver" (Luke)
S2065, SF2065, SP99

"We Give Thee but Thine Own" (Luke)
B609, C382, EL686, F515, G708, L410, N785, P428, VU543

"Forth in Thy Name, O Lord" (Luke) (C)
L505, UM438 (PD), VU416
     H-3   Hbl-29, 57, 58; Chr-117; Desc-31; Org-31
     S-1   #100-103. Various treatments

Additional Hymn Suggestions

"O Master, Let Me Walk with Thee" (Jer) (O)
B279, C602, E659/E660, EL818, F442, G738, L492, N503,
P357, UM430 (PD), VU560

"Lord of All Hopefulness" (Jer)
E482, EL765, G683, L469, S2197, SF2197, W568

"O for a Closer Walk with God" (Jer, Pss)
E684, G739, N450, P396

"Why Stand so Far Away, My God" (Jer, Pss)
C671, G786, S2180, SF2180

"Dust and Ashes" (Jer, Pss)
N186, VU105, WS3098

"Forgive Our Sins as We Forgive" (Jer, Pss)
E674, EL605, G444, L307, P347, UM390, VU364

"I Love the Lord" (Jer, Pss, Luke)
G799, P362, N511, VU617, WS3142

"For the Healing of the Nations" (Jer, 1 Tim)
C668, G346, N576, UM428, VU678, W643

"What Does the Lord Require of You?" (Jer, Luke)
C661, G70, S2174, SF2174, VU701

"All Who Love and Serve Your City" (Pss, Luke)
C670, E570/E571, EL724, G351, L436, P413, UM433, W621

"To God Be the Glory" (1 Tim)
B4, C72, F363, G634, P485, UM98 (PD)

"Take My Life, and Let It Be" (1 Tim)
B277/B283, C609, E707, EL583/EL685, G697, L406, P391,
N448, UM399 (PD), VU506

"Make Me a Channel of Your Peace" (1 Tim)
G753, S2171, SF2171, VU684

"Baptized in Water" (1 Tim, Baptism)
B362, EL456, G482, P492, S2248, W720

"Jesús Es Mi Rey Soberano" ("O Jesus, My King") (Luke)
C109, P157, UM180

"Jesus Calls Us" (Luke)
B293, C337, E549/551, EL696, G720, L494, N171/172,
UM398, VU562

"What Does the Lord Require?" (Luke)
C659, E605, P405, UM441, W624

"More Love to Thee, O Christ" (Luke)
B473, C527, F476, G828, N456, P359, UM453 (PD)

"Living for Jesus" (Luke)
B282, C610, F462, S2149, SF2149

"I'm Gonna Live So God Can Use Me" (Luke)
C614, G700, P369, S2153, VU575

"We Are Called" (Luke) (C)
EL720, G749, S2172, SF2172

"Somebody's Knockin' at Your Door" (Luke)
G728, P382, W415, WS3095

"Take, Oh, Take Me As I Am" (Luke)
EL814, G698, WS3119

Additional Contemporary Suggestions

"Trading My Sorrows" (Jer, Pss)
M75, WS3108

"Hear Us from Heaven" (Jer, Pss)
M267

"Jesus Messiah" (1 Tim)
M253

"Jesus, Name above All Names" (1 Tim)
S2071, SF2071, SP76

"Praise You" (Luke, Praise)
M84, S2003, SF2003

"As the Deer" (Luke)
G626, S2025, SF2025, SP200, VU766 *(See also G778)*

"Make Me a Servant" (Luke)
S2176, SF2176, SP193

"Seek Ye First" (Luke)
B478, C354, E711, G175, P333, UM405, SP182, VU356

"Take This Life" (Luke, Stewardship)
M98

"These Hands" (Luke, Stewardship)
M101

"Lord, Be Glorified" (Luke, Stewardship)
B457, EL744, G468, S2150, SF2150, SP196

Vocal Solos

"There Is a Balm in Gilead" (Jer)
  V-3 (1)   p. 29
  V-7   p. 44

"Seek First" (Luke)
  V-8   p. 145

"Here I Am" (Luke, Stewardship)
  V-11   p. 19

Anthems

"Prayer for Today" (Jer)
Margaret Tucker; Choristers Guild CGA-358
Unison, keyboard (opt. flute)

"Refuge" (Jer, Pss, 1 Tim)
Keith Christopher; Hope C5893
SATB, piano

Other Suggestions

Visuals:
  O   Grief, heart, reaching, harvest, poor, heal, spring
  P   Ruins, blood, fire, Ps. 79:9
  E   Praying hands, judge, hand of God, Christ, cross
  G   Ledger, shovel, ten cup, 100/50, oil, wheat, 100/80,
      darkness/light, symbols of wealth

A stewardship focus relates well to today's Luke reading.
Prayer: N851. Guidance (Jer) or N854 (Pss) or N863 (Pss)
Offertory Prayer: WSL146 or WSL147 (Luke)
Alternate Lessons (see p. 4): Amos 8:4-7, Ps 113

Jeremiah 32:1-3a, 6-15

[1]Jeremiah received the LORD's word in the tenth year of Judah's King Zedekiah, which was the eighteenth year of Nebuchadnezzar's rule. [2]At that time, the army of the Babylonian king had surrounded Jerusalem, and the prophet Jeremiah was confined to the prison quarters in the palace of Judah's king. [3]Judah's King Zedekiah had Jeremiah sent there after questioning him. . . .

[6]Jeremiah said, The LORD's word came to me: [7]Your cousin Hanamel, Shallum's son, is on his way to see you; and when he arrives, he will tell you: "Buy my field in Anathoth, for by law you are next in line to purchase it." [8]And just as the LORD had said, my cousin Hanamel showed up at the prison quarters and told me, "Buy my field in Anathoth in the land of Benjamin, for you are next in line and have a family obligation to purchase it." Then I was sure this was the LORD's doing.

[9]So I bought the field in Anathoth from my cousin Hanamel, and weighed out for him seventeen shekels of silver. [10]I signed the deed, sealed it, had it witnessed, and weighed out the silver on the scales. [11]Then I took the deed of purchase—the sealed copy, with its terms and conditions, and the unsealed copy— [12]and gave it to Baruch, Neriah's son and Mahseiah's grandson, before my cousin Hanamel and the witnesses named in the deed, as well as before all the Judeans who were present in the prison quarters. [13]I charged Baruch before all of them: [14]"The LORD of heavenly forces, the God of Israel, proclaims: Take these documents—this sealed deed of purchase along with the unsealed one—and put them into a clay container so they will last a long time. [15]The LORD of heavenly forces, the God of Israel, proclaims: Houses, fields, and vineyards will again be bought in this land."

Psalm 91:1-6, 14-16 (G43/168, N681, P212, UM810)

[1]Living in the Most High's shelter, / camping in the Almighty's shade, / [2]I say to the LORD, "You are my refuge, my stronghold! / You are my God—the one I trust!"

[3]God will save you from the hunter's trap / And from deadly sickness. / [4]God will protect you with his pinions; / You'll find refuge under his wings. / His faithfulness is a protective shield. / [5]Don't be afraid of terrors at night, / Arrows that fly in daylight, / [6]Or sickness that prowls in the dark, / Destruction that ravages at noontime. . . .

[14]God says, "Because you are devoted to me, / I'll rescue you. / I'll protect you because you know my name. / [15]Whenever you cry out to me, I'll answer. / I'll be with you in troubling times. / I'll save you and glorify you. / [16]I'll fill you full with old age. / I'll show you my salvation."

1 Timothy 6:6-19

[6]Actually, godliness is a great source of profit when it is combined with being happy with what you already have. [7]We didn't bring anything into the world and so we can't take anything out of it: [8]we'll be happy with food and clothing. [9]But people who are trying to get rich fall into temptation. They are trapped by many stupid and harmful passions that plunge people into ruin and destruction. [10]The love of money is the root of all kinds of evil. Some have wandered away from the faith and have impaled themselves with a lot of pain because they made money their goal.

[11]But as for you, man of God, run away from all these things. Instead, pursue righteousness, holy living, faithfulness, love, endurance, and gentleness. [12]Compete in the good fight of faith. Grab hold of eternal life—you were called to it, and you made a good confession of it in the presence of many witnesses. [13]I command you in the presence of God, who gives life to all things, and Christ Jesus, who made the good confession when testifying before Pontius Pilate. [14]Obey this order without fault or failure until the appearance of our Lord Jesus Christ. [15]The timing of this appearance is revealed by God alone, who is the blessed and only master, the King of kings and Lord of lords. [16]He alone has immortality and lives in light that no one can come near. No human being has ever seen or is able to see him. Honor and eternal power belong to him. Amen.

[17]Tell people who are rich at this time not to become egotistical and not to place their hope on their finances, which are uncertain. Instead, they need to hope in God, who richly provides everything for our enjoyment. [18]Tell them to do good, to be rich in the good things they do, to be generous, and to share with others. [19]When they do these things, they will save a treasure for themselves that is a good foundation for the future. That way they can take hold of what is truly life.

Luke 16:19-31

[19]"There was a certain rich man who clothed himself in purple and fine linen, and who feasted luxuriously every day. [20]At his gate lay a certain poor man named Lazarus who was covered with sores. [21]Lazarus longed to eat the crumbs that fell from the rich man's table. Instead, dogs would come and lick his sores.

[22]"The poor man died and was carried by angels to Abraham's side. The rich man also died and was buried. [23]While being tormented in the place of the dead, he looked up and saw Abraham at a distance with Lazarus at his side. [24]He shouted, 'Father Abraham, have mercy on me. Send Lazarus to dip the tip of his finger in water and cool my tongue because I'm suffering in this flame.' [25]But Abraham said, 'Child, remember that during your lifetime you received good things whereas Lazarus received terrible things. Now Lazarus is being comforted and you are in great pain. [26]Moreover, a great crevasse has been fixed between us and you. Those who wish to cross over from here to you cannot. Neither can anyone cross from there to us.'

[27]"The rich man said, 'Then I beg you, Father, send Lazarus to my father's house. [28]I have five brothers. He needs to warn them so that they don't come to this place of agony.' [29]Abraham replied, 'They have Moses and the Prophets. They must listen to them.' [30]The rich man said, 'No, Father Abraham! But if someone from the dead goes to them, they will change their hearts and lives.' [31]Abraham said, 'If they don't listen to Moses and the Prophets, then neither will they be persuaded if someone rises from the dead.'"

Primary Hymns and Songs for the Day

"Ye Servants of God" (1 Tim) (O)
   B589, C110, E535, EL825 (PD), F360, G299, N305, P477,
   UM181 (PD), VU342
         H-3   Hbl-90, 105; Chr-221; Desc-49; Org-51
         S-2   #71-74. Intro. and harm.
"God Will Take Care of You" (Pss)
   B64, F56, N460, UM130 (PD)
"On Eagle's Wings" (Pss)
   B71, C77, EL787, G43, N775, UM143, VU807/808
   V-3 (2) p. 2 Vocal solo OR S-2 #143. Stanzas for soloist
"Give Thanks" (Luke)
   C528, G647, S2036, SF2036, SP170
"Where Cross the Crowded Ways of Life" (Luke) (C)
   C665, E609, EL719, F665, G343, L429, N543, P408, UM427
   (PD), VU681

Additional Hymn Suggestions

"Hope of the World" (Jer)
   C538, E472, G734, L493, N46, P360, UM178, VU215
"O Day of Peace That Dimly Shines" (Jer)
   C711, E597, EL711, G373, P450, UM729, VU682, W654
"Immortal, Invisible, God Only Wise" (1 Tim)
   B6, C66, E423, EL834, F319, G12, L526, N1, P263, UM103
   (PD), VU264, W512
"Take My Life, and Let It Be" (1 Tim)
   B277/B283, C609, E707, EL583/EL685, G697, L406, P391,
   N448, UM399 (PD), VU506
"Stand Up, Stand Up for Jesus" (1 Tim)
   B485/B487, C613, E561, F616, L389, UM514 (PD)
"He Is King of Kings" (1 Tim)
   G273, P153, W498
"We Give Thee but Thine Own" (1 Tim)
   B609, C382, EL686, F515, G708, L410, N785, P428, VU543
"Fight the Good Fight" (1 Tim)
   E552, F613, G846, L461, P307 (PD), VU674
"Fairest Lord Jesus" (1 Tim, Luke)
   B176, C97, E383, EL838, F240, G630, L518, N44, P306,
   UM189 (PD), VU341
"I Sing a Song of the Saints of God" (1 Tim, Luke)
   E293, G730, N295, P364, UM712 (PD)
"Pues Si Vivimos" ("When We Are Living") (1 Tim, Luke)
   C536, EL639, G822, N499, P400, UM356, VU581
"O Christ, the Healer" (Luke)
   C503. EL610, G793, L360, N175, P380, UM265, W747
"Cuando el Pobre" ("When the Poor Ones") (Luke)
   C662, EL725, G762, P407, UM434, VU702
"The Church of Christ, in Every Age" (Luke)
   B402, C475, EL729, G320, L433, N306, P421, UM589,
   VU601, W626
"The Voice of God Is Calling" (Luke)
   C666, UM436 (PD)
"We Are Called" (Luke)
   EL720, G749, S2172, SF2172
"What Does the Lord Require of You?" (Luke)
   C661, G70, S2174, SF2174, VU701
"Here Am I" (Luke)
   C654, S2178, SF2178

Additional Contemporary Suggestions

"I Have a Hope" (Jer)
   M265
"You Are My Hiding Place" (Pss)
   C554, S2055, SF2055

"Nothing Can Trouble" ("Nada Te Turbe") (Pss)
   G820, S2054, SF2054, VU290
"I've Got Peace Like a River" (Pss)
   B418, C530, G623, N478, P368, S2145, VU577
"Still" (Pss)
   M216, WS3134
"Crown Him King of Kings" (1 Tim)
   M22
"When It's All Been Said and Done" (1 Tim)
   M115
"King of Kings" (1 Tim)
   B234, S2075, SF2075, SP94, VU167
"We Will Glorify" (1 Tim)
   B213, S2087, SF2087, SP68
"He Who Began a Good Work in You" (1 Tim)
   S2163, SF2163, SP180
"Majesty" (1 Tim)
   B215, SP73, UM176
"Forevermore" (1 Tim)
   M229
"I Will Boast" (1 Tim, Luke)
   M227
"You Are My All in All" (1 Tim, Luke)
   G519, SP220, WS3040
"Jesus, Remember Me" (Luke)
   C569, EL616, G227, P599, UM488, VU148, W423

Vocal Solos

"It Is Well with My Soul" (Pss)
   V-5 (2)   p. 35
"Jesus Is Lord of All" (1 Tim)
   V-8   p. 254
"Sinner-Man So Hard to Believe" (Luke)
   V-7   p. 48

Anthems

"Beautiful Savior" (SOCM4) (1 Tim, Luke)
Christiansen/Wycisk; Augsburg 9781451499032
TTBB a cappella

"Poor Man Lazarus" (Luke)
Arr. Jester Hairston; Bourne 2653-7
SATB a cappella (other voicings available)

Other Suggestions

Visuals:
   O   War, field, scales, earthen jar, house
   P   Shadow, refuge, fort, eagle, snare, shield/arrow
   E   Newborn, coffin, money, 1 Tim. 6:11b, Jesus/Pilate,
        cross/ crown, generosity, treasure
   G   Purple robe/linen, feast, sores, dogs, five men, angels,
        flames, water, Bible open to Exodus
Stewardship emphasis relates to New Testament lessons today.
Introit: EL406, G281, S2118, SF2118, W473. "Holy Spirit, Come
   to Us" (Pss)
Prayer: N830 (2 Tim), N863 (Jer, Luke) or F88 (Luke)
Prayers: WSL204, WSL92, or WSL93 (Luke)
Response: C299, S2277, SF2277. "Lord, Have Mercy" (Luke)
Offertory Prayer: WSL104. "O God, may our use" (Luke)
Communion Prayer: C774 (Luke)
Alternate Lessons (see p. 4): Amos 6:1a, 4-7, Ps 146

Lamentations 1:1-6

¹Oh, no!
She sits alone,
　　the city that was once full of people.
Once great among nations,
　　she has become like a widow.
Once a queen over provinces,
　　she has become a slave.

²She weeps bitterly in the night,
　　her tears on her cheek.
None of her lovers comfort her.
All her friends lied to her;
　　they have become her enemies.

³Judah was exiled after suffering
　　and hard service.
She lives among the nations;
　　she finds no rest.
All who were chasing her caught her—
　　right in the middle of her distress.

⁴Zion's roads are in mourning;
　　no one comes to the festivals.
All her gates are deserted.
　　Her priests are groaning,
her young women grieving. She is bitter.

⁵Her adversaries have become rulers;
　　her enemies relax.
Certainly the LORD caused her grief
　　because of her many wrong acts.
Her children have gone away,
　　captive before the enemy.

⁶Daughter Zion lost all her glory.
Her officials are like deer
　　that can't find pasture.
They have gone away, frail,
　　before the hunter.

Psalm 137 (G72, N713, P246, UM852)

¹Alongside Babylon's streams, / there we sat down, / crying because we remembered Zion. / ²We hung our lyres up / in the trees there / ³because that's where our captors asked us to sing; / our tormentors requested songs of joy: / "Sing us a song about Zion!" they said. / ⁴But how could we possibly sing / the LORD's song on foreign soil? / ⁵Jerusalem! If I forget you, / let my strong hand wither! / ⁶Let my tongue stick to the roof of my mouth / if I don't remember you, / if I don't make Jerusalem my greatest joy. / ⁷LORD, remember what the Edomites did / on Jerusalem's dark day: / "Rip it down, rip it down! / All the way to its foundations!" they yelled. / ⁸Daughter Babylon, you destroyer, / a blessing on the one who pays you back / the very deed you did to us! / ⁹A blessing on the one who seizes your children / and smashes them against the rock!

2 Timothy 1:1-14

¹From Paul, an apostle of Christ Jesus by God's will, to promote the promise of life that is in Christ Jesus.

²To Timothy, my dear child.

Grace, mercy, and peace from God the Father and Christ Jesus our Lord.

³I'm grateful to God, whom I serve with a good conscience as my ancestors did. I constantly remember you in my prayers day and night. ⁴When I remember your tears, I long to see you so that I can be filled with happiness. ⁵I'm reminded of your authentic faith, which first lived in your grandmother Lois and your mother Eunice. I'm sure that this faith is also inside you. ⁶Because of this, I'm reminding you to revive God's gift that is in you through the laying on of my hands. ⁷God didn't give us a spirit that is timid but one that is powerful, loving, and self-controlled.

⁸So don't be ashamed of the testimony about the Lord or of me, his prisoner. Instead, share the suffering for the good news, depending on God's power. ⁹God is the one who saved and called us with a holy calling. This wasn't based on what we have done, but it was based on his own purpose and grace that he gave us in Christ Jesus before time began. ¹⁰Now his grace is revealed through the appearance of our savior, Christ Jesus. He destroyed death and brought life and immortality into clear focus through the good news. ¹¹I was appointed a messenger, apostle, and teacher of this good news. ¹²This is also why I'm suffering the way I do, but I'm not ashamed. I know the one in whom I've placed my trust. I'm convinced that God is powerful enough to protect what he has placed in my trust until that day. ¹³Hold on to the pattern of sound teaching that you heard from me with the faith and love that are in Christ Jesus. ¹⁴Protect this good thing that has been placed in your trust through the Holy Spirit who lives in us.

Luke 17:5-10

⁵The apostles said to the Lord, "Increase our faith!"

⁶The Lord replied, "If you had faith the size of a mustard seed, you could say to this mulberry tree, 'Be uprooted and planted in the sea,' and it would obey you.

⁷"Would any of you say to your servant, who had just come in from the field after plowing or tending sheep, 'Come! Sit down for dinner'? ⁸Wouldn't you say instead, 'Fix my dinner. Put on the clothes of a table servant and wait on me while I eat and drink. After that, you can eat and drink'? ⁹You won't thank the servant because the servant did what you asked, will you? ¹⁰In the same way, when you have done everything required of you, you should say, 'We servants deserve no special praise. We have only done our duty.'"

Primary Hymns and Songs for the Day

"Standing on the Promises" (2 Tim) (O)
  AH4057, B335, C552, F69, G838, UM374 (PD)
      H-3   Chr-177; Org-117
"By the Babylonian Rivers" (Pss)
  G72, P246, S2217, VU859, W426
"I Know the Lord's Laid His Hands on Me" (2 Tim)
  S2139, SF2139
"I Bind unto Myself Today" (2 Tim)
  E370, EL450 (PD), G6, L188, VU317
"One Bread, One Body" (World Comm.)
  C393, EL496, G530, UM620, VU467
      H-3   Chr-156
"Forth in Thy Name, O Lord" (1 Tim, Luke) (C)
  L505, UM438 (PD), VU416
      H-3   Hbl-29, 57, 58; Chr-117; Desc-31; Org-31
      S-1   #100-103. Various treatments

Additional Hymn Suggestions

"It's Me, It's Me, O Lord" (Lam)
  C579, N519, UM352
"My Song Is Love Unknown" (2 Cor)
  E458, EL343, G209, L94, N222, P76, S2083, SF2083, VU143,
  W439
"In the Midst of New Dimensions" (Lam, Pss, World Comm.)
  G315, N391, S2238, SF2238
"I Love Thy Kingdom, Lord" (Pss, 2 Tim)
  B354, C274, E524, F545, G310, L368, N312, P441, UM540
"Holy Spirit, Truth Divine" (2 Tim)
  C241, EL398, L257, N63, P321, UM465 (PD), VU368
"O Thou Who Camest from Above" (2 Tim)
  E704, UM501 (PD)
"God of Grace and God of Glory" (2 Tim)
  B395, C464, E594/595, EL705, F528, G307, L415, N436,
  P420, UM577, VU686
"I Come with Joy" (2 Tim, World Comm.)
  B371, C420, E304, EL482, G515, N349, P507, UM617,
  VU477, W726
"Draw Us in the Spirit's Tether" (2 Tim, Comm.)
  C392, EL470, G529, N337, P504, UM632, VU479, W731
"In the Singing" (2 Tim, Comm.)
  EL466, G533, S2255, SF2255
"Here Is Bread, Here Is Wine" (2 Tim, Comm.)
  EL483, S2266, SF2266
"Give Me Jesus" (2 Tim)
  EL770, N409, WS3140
"My Faith Looks Up to Thee" (2 Tim, Luke)
  B416, C576, E691, EL759, G829, L479, P383, UM452, VU663
"By Gracious Powers" (2 Tim, Luke)
  E695/696, EL626, G818, N413, P342, UM517, W577
"All Who Love and Serve Your City" (Luke)
  C670, E570/E571, EL724, G351, L436, P413, UM433, W621
"We Walk by Faith" (2 Cor, Matt)
  E209, EL635, G817, N256, P399, S2196, SF2196, W572
"Lord, When I Came Into This Life" (Luke)
  N354, G691, P522
"Bread of the World" (World Comm.)
  C387, E301, G499, N346, P502, UM624, VU461
"Become to Us the Living Bread" (Comm.)
  C423, P500, UM630
"A Place at the Table" (World Comm.)
  G769, WS3149

Additional Contemporary Suggestions

"I Have a Hope" (Lam, Pss)
  M265
"By the Waters of Babylon" (Pss)
  G784, P245
"Come and Fill Our Hearts" (Pss)
  EL538, G466, S2157, SF2157, W561
"Trading My Sorrows" (Pss)
  M75, WS3108
"Come to the Table of Grace" (Pss, 2 Tim, Comm.)
  G507, WS3168
"He Who Began a Good Work in You" (2 Tim)
  S2163, SF2163, SP180
"Cry of My Heart" (2 Tim)
  M39, S2165, SF2165
"He Is Able" (2 Tim)
  M37
"These Hands" (2 Tim)
  M101
"Grace Like Rain" (2 Tim)
  M251
"Sing Alleluia to the Lord" (2 Tim, Comm.)
  B214, C32, S2258, SF2258, SP93
"Make Us One" (World Comm.)
  AH4142, S2224, SF2224, SP137
"Bind Us Together" (World Comm.)
  S2226, SF2226, SP140

Vocal Solos

"Here I Am" (2 Tim, Luke)
  V-11   p. 19
"One Bread, One Body" (World Comm.)
  V-3 (2)   p. 40

Anthems

"Glory to His Name" (1 Tim)
Arr. Bob Burroughs; Alfred 44221
SATB, piano, opt. flute

"Bread of the World" (Comm.)
Greg Scheer; Augsburg 0-8006-7793-5
SATB, piano

Other Suggestions

Visuals:
  O   Empty city, widow, tiara/chains, weeping, stag
  P   River, sitting/weeping, harp on willow
  E   Letter, praying hands, tears/joy, women, flame, risen
        Christ, trumpet, treasure, Spirit
  G   Mustard/mulberry trees, sea, plow, sheep, table/meal,
        chain/manacles
  World Communion: Flags, nationalities, breads
Reading: C412. The Miracle of Communion (World Comm.)
Prayer: F549 or N848 or WSL67 (World Comm.)
Prayer: WSL151. "O God, we are so grateful" (2 Tim)
Offertory Prayer: WSL151. "O God" (World Comm.)
Communion Prayers: C774 (World Comm.)
Communion Response: N786 or N787 (World Comm.)
Blessing: WS40. "May the Spirit of God" (2 Tim)
Blessing: N875 (2 Tim.)
Alternate Lessons (see p. 4): Hab 1:1-4, 2:1-4, Ps 37:1-9

Jeremiah 29:1, 4-7

[1]The prophet Jeremiah sent a letter from Jerusalem to the few surviving elders among the exiles, to the priests and the prophets, and to all the people Nebuchadnezzar had taken to Babylon from Jerusalem. . . .

[4]The LORD of heavenly forces, the God of Israel, proclaims to all the exiles I have carried off from Jerusalem to Babylon: [5]Build houses and settle down; cultivate gardens and eat what they produce. [6]Get married and have children; then help your sons find wives and your daughters find husbands in order that they too may have children. Increase in number there so that you don't dwindle away. [7]Promote the welfare of the city where I have sent you into exile. Pray to the LORD for it, because your future depends on its welfare.

Psalm 66:1-12 (G54, N662)

[1]Shout joyfully to God, all the earth! / [2]Sing praises to the glory of God's name! / Make glorious his praise! / [3]Say to God: / "How awesome are your works! / Because of your great strength, / your enemies cringe before you. / [4]All the earth worships you, / sings praises to you, / sings praises to your name!" *[Selah]* / [5]Come and see God's deeds; / his works for human beings are awesome: / [6]He turned the sea into dry land / so they could cross the river on foot. / Right there we rejoiced in him! / [7]God rules with power forever; / keeps a good eye on the nations. / So don't let the rebellious exalt themselves. *[Selah]* / [8]All you nations, bless our God! / Let the sound of his praise be heard! / [9]God preserved us among the living; / he didn't let our feet slip a bit.

[10]But you, God, have tested us— / you've refined us like silver, / [11]trapped us in a net, / laid burdens on our backs, / [12]let other people run right over our heads— / we've been through fire and water.

But you brought us out to freedom!

---

2 Timothy 2:8-15

[8]Remember Jesus Christ, who was raised from the dead and descended from David. This is my good news. [9]This is the reason I'm suffering to the point that I'm in prison like a common criminal. But God's word cannot be imprisoned. [10]This is why I endure everything for the sake of those who are chosen by God so that they too may experience salvation in Christ Jesus with eternal glory. [11]This saying is reliable:

"If we have died together, we will also live together.

[12]If we endure, we will also rule together.

If we deny him, he will also deny us.

[13]If we are disloyal, he stays faithful"

because he can't be anything else than what he is.

[14]Remind them of these things and warn them in the sight of God not to engage in battles over words that aren't helpful and only destroy those who hear them. [15]Make an effort to present yourself to God as a tried-and-true worker, who doesn't need to be ashamed but is one who interprets the message of truth correctly.

Luke 17:11-19

[11]On the way to Jerusalem, Jesus traveled along the border between Samaria and Galilee. [12]As he entered a village, ten men with skin diseases approached him. Keeping their distance from him, [13]they raised their voices and said, "Jesus, Master, show us mercy!"

[14]When Jesus saw them, he said, "Go, show yourselves to the priests." As they left, they were cleansed. [15]One of them, when he saw that he had been healed, returned and praised God with a loud voice. [16]He fell on his face at Jesus' feet and thanked him. He was a Samaritan. [17]Jesus replied, "Weren't ten cleansed? Where are the other nine? [18]No one returned to praise God except this foreigner?" [19]Then Jesus said to him, "Get up and go. Your faith has healed you."

Primary Hymns and Songs for the Day

"I'll Praise My Maker While I've Breath" (Luke, Pss) (O)
    B35, C20, E429 (PD), G806, P253, UM60, VU867
        H-3   Chr-109; Org-105
        S-2   #141. Harm.
"When God Restored Our Common Life" (Jer)
    G74, S2182, SF2182
        H-3   Chr-139; Desc-90; Org-123
"O Christ, the Healer" (Luke)
    C503. EL610, G793, L360, N175, P380, UM265, W747
"An Outcast among Outcasts" (Luke)
    N201, S2104, SF2104
        H-3   Hbl-80; Chr-142; Desc-69; Org-78
        S-1   #215. Harm.
"Give Thanks" (Luke)
    C528, G647, S2036, SF2036, SP170
"All Who Love and Serve Your City" (Jer) (C)
    C670, E570/E571, EL724, G351, L436, P413, UM433, W621
        H-3   Chr-26, 65; Org-19
        S-1   #62. Desc.

Additional Hymn Suggestions

"Great Is Thy Faithfulness" (Jer, Pss, Luke) (O)
    B54, C86, EL733, F98, G39, N423, P276, UM140, VU288
"Lift Every Voice and Sing" (Jer, Pss)
    AH4055, B627, C631, E599, EL841, G339, L562, N593, P563,
    UM519, W641
"*Heleluyan*" (Pss)
    EL171, G642, P595, UM78
"Joyful, Joyful, We Adore Thee" (Pss, 2 Tim)
    B7, C2, E376, EL836, F377, G611, L551, N4, P464, UM89
    (PD), VU232, W525
"Praise, My Soul, the King of Heaven" (Pss, Luke)
    B32, C23, E410, EL864/865, F339, G619/620, L549,
    P478/479, UM66 (PD), VU240, W530
"Jesus Shall Reign" (Pss, Luke)
    B587, C95, E544, EL434, F238, G265, L530, N157, P423,
    UM157 (PD), VU330, W492
"Jesus, the Very Thought of Thee" (2 Tim)
    C102, E642, EL754, G629, L316, N507, P310, UM175
"In the Cross of Christ I Glory" (2 Tim)
    B554, C207, E441, EL324, F251, G213, L104, N193, P84,
    UM295
"*Pues Si Vivimos*" ("When We Are Living") (2 Tim)
    C536, EL639, G822, N499, P400, UM356, VU581
"O Jesus, I Have Promised" (2 Tim)
    B276, C612, E655, EL810, F402, G724/725, L503, N493,
    P388/389, UM396 (PD), VU120
"Take Up Thy Cross" (2 Tim)
    B494, E675, EL667, G718, L398, N204, P393, UM415, VU561,
    W634
"How Clear Is Our Vocation, Lord" (2 Tim)
    EL580, G432, P419, VU504
"God, Whose Giving Knows No Ending" (2 Tim)
    C606, F513, G716, L408, N565, P422, W631
"We Know That Christ Is Raised" (2 Tim, Baptism)
    E296, EL449, G485, L189, P495, UM610, VU448, W721
"O For a Thousand Tongues to Sing" (Luke)
    B216, C5, E493, EL886, F349, G610, L559, N42, P466, UM57
    (PD), VU326 (See also WS3001)
"God of the Sparrow, God of the Whale" (Luke)
    C70, EL740, G22, N32, P272, UM122, VU229
"Lord of the Dance" (Luke)
    G157, P302, UM261, VU352, W636

"We Cannot Measure How You Heal" (Luke)
    G797, VU613, WS3139
"Live into Hope" (Luke)
    G772, P332, VU699

Additional Contemporary Suggestions

"Song of Hope" ("*Canto de Esperanza*") (Jer)
    G765, P432, S2186, VU424
"Your Grace Is Enough" (Jer, Pss, Luke)
    M191, WS3106
"My Tribute" ("To God Be the Glory") (Pss)
    B153, C39, F365, N14, SP118, UM99; V-8 p. 5 Vocal solo
"Awesome God" (Pss)
    G616, S2040, SF2040, SP11
"Refiner's Fire" (Pss)
    M50
"Sing, Sing, Sing" (Pss, Luke)
    M235
"All Hail King Jesus" (2 Tim)
    S2069, SF2069, SP63
"Through It All" (2 Tim, Luke)
    C555, F43, UM507
"Thank You, Lord" (Luke)
    AH4081, C531, UM84
"I'm So Glad Jesus Lifted Me" (Luke)
    C529, EL860 (PD), N474, S2151, SF2151
"People Need the Lord" (Luke)
    B557, S2244, SF2244
"I Thank You, Jesus" (Luke)
    AH4079, C116, N41, WS3037
"Jesus Paid It All" (Luke)
    B134, F273, M244, WS3100

Vocal Solos

"Bright and Beautiful" (Pss, Luke)
    V-3 (3)   p. 10
"I Just Came to Praise the Lord" (Luke)
    V-8   p. 294

Anthems

"Psalm 146: I'll Praise My Maker While I've Breath" (Pss, Luke)
Hal H. Hopson; MorningStar MSM-50- 3901
SATB divisi, organ

"If I Forget, Yet God Remembers" (Luke)
Daniel Pederson; Augsburg 0-8006-7805-2
SATB a cappella

Other Suggestions

Visuals:
    O   Letter, houses, garden, marriage, prayer/chain
    P   Praise, nations, awe, sea/desert, river, feet, refining,
         net, full backpack, fire/water, open space
    E   Christus Rex, chain, open manacles, cross
    G   Lepers, one prostrate, feet, praise, walking
Greeting or Litany: WSL158. "Here in This Sanctuary" (Jer)
Response: EL152, S2275, SF2275, WS3133. "*Kyrie*" or C299,
    G576, S2277, SF2277. "Lord, Have Mercy" (Luke)
Prayer: C549. Thoughtful Silence (2 Tim.)
Prayer of Thanksgiving: N859. Thankfulness and Hope (Luke)
Closing Prayer: WSL171. "Thank You, God" (Jer, Comm.)
Alternate Lessons (see p.4): 2 Kgs 5:1-3, 7-15c; Ps 111

Jeremiah 31:27-34

[27]The time is coming, declares the LORD, when I will plant seeds in Israel and Judah, and both people and animals will spring up. [28]Just as I watched over them to dig up and pull down, to overthrow, destroy, and bring harm, so I will watch over them to build and plant, declares the LORD. [29]In those days, people will no longer say:

Sour grapes eaten by parents
leave a bitter taste
in the mouths of their children.

[30]Because everyone will die
for their own sins:
whoever eats sour grapes
will have a bitter taste
in their own mouths.

[31]The time is coming, declares the LORD, when I will make a new covenant with the people of Israel and Judah. [32]It won't be like the covenant I made with their ancestors when I took them by the hand to lead them out of the land of Egypt. They broke that covenant with me even though I was their husband, declares the LORD. [33]No, this is the covenant that I will make with the people of Israel after that time, declares the LORD. I will put my Instructions within them and engrave them on their hearts. I will be their God, and they will be my people. [34]They will no longer need to teach each other to say, "Know the LORD!" because they will all know me, from the least of them to the greatest, declares the LORD; for I will forgive their wrongdoing and never again remember their sins.

Psalm 119:97-104 (G64, N701, UM840)

[97]I love your Instruction! / I think about it constantly. / [98]Your commandment makes me wiser than my enemies / because it is always with me. / [99]I have greater insight than all my teachers / because I contemplate your laws. / [100]I have more understanding than the elders / because I guard your precepts. / [101]I haven't set my feet on any evil path / so I can make sure to keep your word. / [102]I haven't deviated from any of your rules / because you are the one who has taught me. / [103]Your word is so pleasing to my taste buds— / it's sweeter than honey in my mouth! / [104]I'm studying your precepts— / that's why I hate every false path.

2 Timothy 3:14–4:5

[14]But you must continue with the things you have learned and found convincing. You know who taught you. [15]Since childhood you have known the holy scriptures that help you to be wise in a way that leads to salvation through faith that is in Christ Jesus. [16]Every scripture is inspired by God and is useful for teaching, for showing mistakes, for correcting, and for training character, [17]so that the person who belongs to God can be equipped to do everything that is good.

4 I'm giving you this commission in the presence of God and of Christ Jesus, who is coming to judge the living and the dead, and by his appearance and his kingdom. [2]Preach the word. Be ready to do it whether it is convenient or inconvenient. Correct, confront, and encourage with patience and instruction. [3]There will come a time when people will not tolerate sound teaching. They will collect teachers who say what they want to hear because they are self-centered. [4]They will turn their back on the truth and turn to myths. [5]But you must keep control of yourself in all circumstances. Endure suffering, do the work of a preacher of the good news, and carry out your service fully.

Luke 18:1-8

[1]Jesus was telling them a parable about their need to pray continuously and not to be discouraged. [2]He said, "In a certain city there was a judge who neither feared God nor respected people. [3]In that city there was a widow who kept coming to him, asking, 'Give me justice in this case against my adversary.' [4]For a while he refused but finally said to himself, I don't fear God or respect people, [5]but I will give this widow justice because she keeps bothering me. Otherwise, there will be no end to her coming here and embarrassing me." [6]The Lord said, "Listen to what the unjust judge says. [7]Won't God provide justice to his chosen people who cry out to him day and night? Will he be slow to help them? [8]I tell you, he will give them justice quickly. But when the Human One comes, will he find faithfulness on earth?"

Primary Hymns and Songs for the Day

"Love Divine, All Loves Excelling" (Jer) (O)
  B208, C517, E657, EL631, F21, G366, N43, P376, UM384
  (PD), VU333, W588
      H-3   Chr-134; Desc-18; Org-13
      S-1   #41-42. Desc. and harm.
"Change My Heart, O God" (Jer)
  EL801, G695, S2152, SF2152, SP195,
"Spirit of God, Descend upon My Heart" (Jer, Luke)
  B245, C265, EL800, F147, G688, L486, N290, P326, UM500
  (PD), VU378
"Thy Word Is a Lamp" (Pss, 2 Tim)
  C326, G458, SP183, UM601
"It's Me, It's Me, O Lord" (Luke)
  C579, N519, UM352
      H-3   Chr-177
"Lord, Listen to Your Children" (Luke)
  C305, G469, S2193, SF2193, VU400
"Lord, Speak to Me" (2 Tim, Luke) (C)
  B568, EL676, F625, G722, L403, N531, P426, UM463 (PD),
  VU589

Additional Hymn Suggestions

"This Is a Day of New Beginnings" (Jer)
  B370, C518, N417, UM383, W661
"O Love That Wilt Not Let Me Go" (Jer)
  B292, C540, G833, L324, N485, P384, UM480 (PD), VU658
"Here I Am, Lord" (Jer) (C)
  C452, EL574, G69, P525, UM593, VU509
"O Day of Peace That Dimly Shines" (Jer)
  C711, E597, EL711, G373, P450, UM729, VU682, W654
"God the Sculptor of the Mountains" (Jer)
  EL736, G5, S2060, SF2060
"Wonder of Wonders" (Jer, Baptism)
  C378, G489, N328, P499, S2247
"Holy Spirit, Truth Divine" (Jer, 2 Tim, Luke)
  C241, EL398, L257, N63, P321, UM465 (PD), VU368
"Blessed Jesus, at Thy Word" (Jer, Pss, 2 Tim)
  E440, EL520, G395, N74, P454, UM596 (PD), VU500
"Wonderful Words of Life" (Pss, 2 Tim)
  B261, C323, F29, N319, UM600 (PD)
"O Master, Let Me Walk with Thee" (Pss, 2 Tim)
  B279, C602, E659/E660, EL818, F442, G738, L492, N503,
  P357, UM430 (PD), VU560
"Break Thou the Bread of Life" (Pss, 2 Tim, Comm.)
  B263, C321, EL515, F30, G460, L235, N321, P329, UM599
  (PD), VU501
"Immortal, Invisible, God Only Wise" (2 Tim)
  B6, C66, E423, EL834, F319, G12, L526, N1, P263, UM103
  (PD), VU264, W512
"Lord, You Give the Great Commission" (2 Tim) (C)
  C459, E528, EL579, G298, P429, UM584, VU512, W470
"Deep in the Shadows of the Past" (2 Tim)
  G50, N320, P330, S2246
"Lord of All Good" (2 Tim)
  G711, L411, P375, VU539
"Seek Ye First" (Luke)
  B478, C354, E711, G175, P333, UM405, SP182, VU356
"Be Thou My Vision" (Luke)
  B60, C595, E488, EL793, G450, N451, P339, UM451, VU642
"What a Friend We Have in Jesus" (Luke)
  B182, C585, EL742, F466, G465, L439, N506, P403, UM526
  (PD), VU661

"The Lord's Prayer" (Luke)
  B462, C307-C310, F440, G464, P589, S2278, SF2278. UM271,
  WS3068-WS3071
"Hear My Prayer, O God" (Luke)
  G782, WS3131
"Give Me Jesus" (Luke)
  EL770, N409, WS3140

Additional Contemporary Suggestions

"Refresh My Heart" (Jer)
  M49
"The Potter's Hand" (Jer)
  M85
"You Have Saved Us" (Jer)
  M266
"Knowing You" ("All I Once Held Dear") (Pss)
  M30
"In the Secret" ("I Want to Know You") (Pss)
  M38
"Breathe" (Pss)
  M61, WS3112
"Ancient Words" (Pss)
  M149
"More Precious than Silver" (Pss)
  S2065, SF2065, SP99
"As the Deer" (Pss)
  G626, S2025, SF2025, SP200, VU766 (*See also G778*)
"Cry of My Heart" (Pss)
  M39, S2165, SF2165
"He Who Began a Good Work in You" (2 Tim)
  S2163, SF2163, SP180
"Lord, Listen to Your Children" (Luke)
  EL752, S2207, SF2207

Vocal Solos

"God Will Make a Way" (with "He Leadeth Me") (Jer)
  V-3 (2)   p. 9
"Lord, Listen to Your Children" (Luke)
  V-8   p. 168

Anthems

"Thy Word Is Like a Garden, Lord" (Pss, 2 Tim)
Dan Forrest; Hal Leonard 08745683
SATB, piano

"Believer's Prayer" (Luke)
Joel Raney; Hope C-5510
SATB, piano

Other Suggestions

Visuals:
  O   Sowing seeds, destruction, build/plant, torn
         document, Jer. 31:33b, heart, all ages, eraser
  P   Bible, meditation, feet, Ps 119:103, honey
  E   Child, Bible, Christ, teacher, 2 Tim 3:16, tools, gavel
  G   Prayer, gavel, scales of justice, woman pleading
Introit: WS3047, st. 3. "God Almighty, We Are Waiting" (Jer)
Greeting: N823. "My heart is ready" (Jer)
Prayer of Preparation: WSL75 or UM602 (2 Tim)
Response: EL751, G471, S2200, SF2200. "O Lord, Hear My
  Prayer" (Luke)
Benediction: C268. Sarum Blessing (Jer, Pss)
Alternate Lessons (see p. 4): Gen 32:22-31, Ps 121

Joel 2:23-32

²³Children of Zion,
　　rejoice and be glad in the LORD your God,
　because he will give you the early rain as a sign of
　　righteousness;
　　he will pour down abundant rain for you,
　　　the early and the late rain, as before.
²⁴The threshing floors will be full of grain;
　　the vats will overflow with new wine and fresh oil.
²⁵I will repay you for the years
　　that the cutting locust,
　the swarming locust, the hopping locust, and the devour-
　　ing locust have eaten—
　　my great army, which I sent against you.
²⁶You will eat abundantly and be satisfied,
　　and you will praise the name of the LORD your God,
　who has done wonders for you;
　　and my people will never again be put to shame.
²⁷You will know that I am in the midst of Israel,
　　and that I am the LORD your God—no other exists;
　　never again will my people be put to shame.
²⁸After that I will pour out my spirit upon everyone;
　　your sons and your daughters will prophesy,
　　your old men will dream dreams,
　　and your young men will see visions.
²⁹In those days, I will also pour out my
　　spirit on the male and female slaves.
　³⁰I will give signs in the heavens and on the earth—blood and fire and columns of smoke. ³¹The sun will be turned to darkness, and the moon to blood before the great and dreadful day of the LORD comes. ³²But everyone who calls on the LORD's name will be saved; for on Mount Zion and in Jerusalem there will be security, as the LORD has promised; and in Jerusalem, the LORD will summon those who survive.

Psalm 65 (G38, N661, P200/201, UM789)

¹God of Zion, to you even silence is praise. / Promises made to you are kept— / ²you listen to prayer— / and all living things come to you. / ³When wrongdoings become too much for me, / you forgive our sins. / ⁴How happy is the one you choose to bring close, / the one who lives in your courtyards! / We are filled full by the goodness of your house, / by the holiness of your temple.

⁵In righteousness you answer us, / by your awesome deeds, / God of our salvation— / you, who are the security / of all the far edges of the earth, / even the distant seas; / ⁶you establish the mountains by your strength; / you are dressed in raw power; / ⁷you calm the roaring seas; / calm the roaring waves, / calm the noise of the nations. / ⁸Those who dwell on the far edges / stand in awe of your acts. / You make the gateways / of morning and evening sing for joy. / ⁹You visit the earth and make it abundant, / enriching it greatly / by God's stream, full of water. / You provide people with grain / because that is what you've decided. / ¹⁰Drenching the earth's furrows, / leveling its ridges, / you soften it with rain showers; / you bless its growth. / ¹¹You crown the year with your goodness; / your paths overflow with rich food. / ¹²Even the desert pastures drip with it, / and the hills are dressed in pure joy. / ¹³The meadowlands are covered with flocks, / the valleys decked out in grain— / they shout for joy; / they break out in song!

2 Timothy 4:6-8, 16-18

⁶I'm already being poured out like a sacrifice to God, and the time of my death is near. ⁷I have fought the good fight, finished the race, and kept the faith. ⁸At last the champion's wreath that is awarded for righteousness is waiting for me. The Lord, who is the righteous judge, is going to give it to me on that day. He's giving it not only to me but also to all those who have set their heart on waiting for his appearance.
. . .
¹⁶No one took my side at my first court hearing. Everyone deserted me. I hope that God doesn't hold it against them! ¹⁷But the Lord stood by me and gave me strength, so that the entire message would be preached through me and so all the nations could hear it. I was also rescued from the lion's mouth! ¹⁸The Lord will rescue me from every evil action and will save me for his heavenly kingdom. To him be the glory forever and always. Amen.

Luke 18:9-14

⁹Jesus told this parable to certain people who had convinced themselves that they were righteous and who looked on everyone else with disgust. ¹⁰"Two people went up to the temple to pray. One was a Pharisee and the other a tax collector. ¹¹The Pharisee stood and prayed about himself with these words, 'God, I thank you that I'm not like everyone else—crooks, evildoers, adulterers—or even like this tax collector. ¹²I fast twice a week. I give a tenth of everything I receive.' ¹³But the tax collector stood at a distance. He wouldn't even lift his eyes to look toward heaven. Rather, he struck his chest and said, 'God, show mercy to me, a sinner.' ¹⁴I tell you, this person went down to his home justified rather than the Pharisee. All who lift themselves up will be brought low, and those who make themselves low will be lifted up."

Primary Hymns and Songs for the Day

"I Sing the Almighty Power of God" (Joel) (O)
  C64, G32, N12, P288 (PD)
        H-3   Hbl-16, 22, 68; Chr-101; Desc-37
        S-1   #115. Harm.
  B42, E398, UM152 (PD)
        H-3   Hbl-44; Chr-21; Desc-40; Org-40
        S-1   #131-32. Intro. and desc.
  VU231 (PD), W502 (PD)
"Guide My Feet" (2 Tim) (O)
  G741, N497, P354, S2208
        H-3   Hbl-66; Chr-89
"We've Come This Far by Faith" (2 Tim)
  AH4042, C533, EL633, G656
"Just As I Am, Without One Plea" (Luke)
  B303/307, C339, E693, EL592, F417, G442, L296, N207,
  P370, UM357 (PD), VU508
        H-3   Chr-120; Org-186
"Humble Thyself in the Sight of the Lord" (Luke)
  S2131, SF2131, SP223
"The Trees of the Field" (Pss) (C)
  G80, S2279, SF2279, SP128, VU884

Additional Hymn Suggestions

"Be Thou My Vision" (Joel)
  B60, C595, E488, EL793, G450, N451, P339, UM451, VU642
"Spirit of God, Descend upon My Heart" (Joel)
  B245, C265, EL800, F147, G688, L486, N290, P326, UM500
  (PD), VU378
"Spirit, Spirit of Gentleness" (Joel)
  C249, EL396, G291, N286, P319, S2120, VU375 (Fr.)
"Healer of Our Every Ill" (Joel)
  C506, EL612, G795, S2213, SF2213, VU619
"How Great Thou Art" (Pss, Luke)
  AH4015, B10, C33, EL856, F2, G625, L532, N35, P467,
  UM77, VU238 (Fr.)
"Fight the Good Fight" (2 Tim)
  E552, F613, G846, L461, P307 (PD), VU674
"He Leadeth Me" (2 Tim)
  B52, C545, F606, L501, UM128 (PD), VU657
"Leaning on the Everlasting Arms" (2 Tim)
  AH4100, B333, C560, EL774 (PD), G837, N471, UM133
"Jesus, Lover of My Soul" (2 Tim, Luke)
  B180 (PD), C542, E699, G440, N546, P303, UM479, VU669
"Before I Take the Body of My Lord" (Luke, Comm.)
  C391, G428, VU462
"There's a Wideness in God's Mercy" (Luke)
  B25, C73, E470, EL587/88, F115, G435, L290, N23, P298,
  UM121, VU271, W595
"Pass Me Not, O Gentle Savior" (Luke)
  AH4107, B308, F416, N551, UM351 (PD), VU665
"Depth of Mercy" (Luke)
  B306, UM355, WS3097
"Have Thine Own Way, Lord" (Luke)
  B294, C588, F400, UM382 (PD)
"Lord, I Want to Be a Christian" (Luke)
  B489, C589, F421, G729, N454, P372 (PD), UM402
"I Am Thine, O Lord" (Luke)
  AH4087, B290, C601, F455, N455, UM419 (PD)
"Forgive Us, Lord" ("Perdón, Señor") (Luke)
  G431, S2134, SF2134
"Gather Us In" (Luke)
  C284, EL532, G401, S2236, SF2236, W665

Additional Contemporary Suggestions

"Open the Eyes of My Heart" (Joel)
  G452, M57, WS3008
"Open Our Eyes, Lord" (Joel)
  B499, S2086, SF2086, SP199
"Shout to the Lord" (Pss)
  EL821, M16, S2074, SF2074; V-3 (2) p. 32 Vocal solo
"Awesome God" (Pss)
  G616, S2040, SF2040, SP11
"How Great Is Our God" (Pss)
  M117, WS3003
"He Who Began a Good Work in You" (2 Tim)
  S2163, SF2163, SP180
"You Are My All in All" (2 Tim)
  G519, SP220, WS3040
"Shout to the North" (2 Tim)
  G319, M99, WS3042
"I Will Never Be (the Same Again)" (2 Tim, Luke)
  M34
"I Will Boast" (2 Tim, Luke)
  M227
"Came to My Rescue" (2 Tim, Luke)
  M257
"Grace Alone" (2 Tim, Luke)
  M100, S2162, SF2162
"I'm So Glad Jesus Lifted Me" (Luke)
  C529, EL860 (PD), N474, S2151, SF2151
"Falling on My Knees" ("Hungry") (Luke)
  M155, WS3099
"Take, O Take Me As I Am" (Luke)
  EL814, G698, WS3119

Vocal Solos

"Spirit of God" (Joel)
  V-8   p. 170
"Stan'in' In De Need of Prayer" (Luke)
  V-7   p. 40

Anthems

"Rise Up, O Saints of God" (SOCB70) (Luke)
Arr. Kenneth Jennings; Augsburg 9781451499032
TTBB a cappella

"O, My God, Bestow Thy Tender Mercy" (Luke)
Pergolesi/Hopson; Carl Fischer CM7974
Two-part mixed, keyboard

Other Suggestions

Visuals:
  O   Rain, thresh/grain, wine/oil, locusts, plenty, people,
          manacles, blood/fire/smoke, eclipse, red moon
  P   Praise, worship, sea/mountain, storm/calm, sunrise/
          set, rain, river, harvest/wagon tracks, hills, flocks
  E   Spilled wine, boxing gloves, open Bible, scales
  G   Two men (proud/humble), hands (raised/beating
          chest), Luke 18:14b
Introit: WS3046. "Come, O Redeemer, Come" (Luke)
Call to Confession and Prayer: N833 and N834 or C772 (Luke)
Prayer: WSL37 or WSL38 (Joel)
Response: EL152, S2275, SF2275, WS3133 or C299, G576, S2277,
  SF2277. "Lord, Have Mercy" (Luke)
Alternate Lessons (see p. 4): Jer 14:7-10, 19-22, Ps 84:1-7

Habakkuk 1:1-4; 2:1-4

The oracle that Habakkuk the prophet saw.
²Lord, how long will I call for help and you not listen?
   I cry out to you, "Violence!"
      but you don't deliver us.
³Why do you show me injustice and look at anguish
   so that devastation and violence are before me?
There is strife, and conflict abounds.
   ⁴The Instruction is ineffective;
      justice does not endure
      because the wicked surround the righteous.
   Justice becomes warped.
....

2 I will take my post;
   I will position myself on the fortress.
   I will keep watch to see what the Lord says to me
   and how he will respond to my complaint.

²Then the Lord answered me and said,
   Write a vision, and make it plain upon a tablet
      so that a runner can read it.
         ³There is still a vision for the appointed time;
            it testifies to the end;
               it does not deceive.
   If it delays, wait for it;
      for it is surely coming;
         it will not be late.
⁴Some people's desires are truly audacious;
      they don't do the right thing.
   But the righteous person will live honestly.

Psalm 119:137-144 (G64, N701, UM840)

¹³⁷Lord, you are righteous, / and your rules are right. / ¹³⁸The laws you commanded are righteous, / completely trustworthy. / ¹³⁹Anger consumes me / because my enemies have forgotten what you've said. / ¹⁴⁰Your word has been tried and tested; / your servant loves your word! / ¹⁴¹I'm insignificant and unpopular, / but I don't forget your precepts. / ¹⁴²Your righteousness lasts forever! / Your Instruction is true! / ¹⁴³Stress and strain have caught up with me, / but your commandments are my joy! / ¹⁴⁴Your laws are righteous forever. / Help me understand so I can live!

2 Thessalonians 1:1-4, 11-12

From Paul, Silvanus, and Timothy:
To the church of the Thessalonians, which is in God our Father, and in the Lord Jesus Christ.
²Grace and peace to all of you from God our Father and the Lord Jesus Christ.
³Brothers and sisters, we must always thank God for you. This is only right because your faithfulness is growing by leaps and bounds, and the love that all of you have for each other is increasing. ⁴That's why we ourselves are bragging about you in God's churches. We tell about your endurance and faithfulness in all the harassments and trouble that you have put up with. . . .
¹¹We are constantly praying for you for this: that our God will make you worthy of his calling and accomplish every good desire and faithful work by his power. ¹²Then the name of our Lord Jesus will be honored by you, and you will be honored by him, consistent with the grace of our God and the Lord Jesus Christ.

Luke 19:1-10

Jesus entered Jericho and was passing through town. ²A man there named Zacchaeus, a ruler among tax collectors, was rich. ³He was trying to see who Jesus was, but, being a short man, he couldn't because of the crowd. ⁴So he ran ahead and climbed up a sycamore tree so he could see Jesus, who was about to pass that way. ⁵When Jesus came to that spot, he looked up and said, "Zacchaeus, come down at once. I must stay in your home today." ⁶So Zacchaeus came down at once, happy to welcome Jesus.
⁷Everyone who saw this grumbled, saying, "He has gone to be the guest of a sinner."
⁸Zacchaeus stopped and said to the Lord, "Look, Lord, I give half of my possessions to the poor. And if I have cheated anyone, I repay them four times as much."
⁹Jesus said to him, "Today, salvation has come to this household because he too is a son of Abraham. ¹⁰The Human One came to seek and save the lost."

Primary Hymns and Songs for the Day
"O God of Every Nation" (Hab) (O)
  C680, E607, EL713, G756, L416, P289, UM435, VU677
    H-3   Chr-63, 145; Org-102
"A Mighty Fortress Is Our God" (Reformation) (O)
  B8, C65, E687/E688, EL503/504/505, F118, G275, L228/
  L229, N439/N440, P259/P260, UM110 (PD), VU261/
  VU262/VU263, W575/W576
"Be Thou My Vision" (Hab)
  B60, C595, E488, EL793, G450, N451, P339, UM451, VU642
    H-3   Hbl-15, 48; Chr-36; Org-153
    S-1   #319. Arr. for organ/voices in canon
"Lord, Be Glorified" (2 Thess)
  B457, EL744, G468, S2150, SF2150, SP196
"I Am Thine, O Lord" (Luke) (C)
  AH4087, B290, C601, F455, N455, UM419 (PD)

Additional Hymn Suggestions
"Be Still, My Soul" (Hab)
  C566, F77, G819, N488, UM534, VU652
"Let All Mortal Flesh Keep Silence" (Hab)
  B80, C124, E324, EL490, F166, G347, L198, N345, P5,
  UM626 (PD), VU473 (Fr.), W523
"I Love Thy Kingdom, Lord" (2 Thess)
  B354, C274, E524, F545, G310, L368, N312, P441, UM540
"Blest Be the Tie That Binds" (2 Thess)
  B387, C433, EL656, F560, G306, L370, N393, P438, UM557
  (PD), VU602
"O Jesus, I Have Promised" (2 Thess, Luke)
  B276, C612, E655, EL810, F402, G724/725, L503, N493,
  P388/389, UM396 (PD), VU120
"Lord Jesus, Think on Me" (Luke)
  E641, EL599 (PD), G417, L309, P301, VU607
"Come, Ye Sinners, Poor and Needy" (Luke)
  B323 (PD), G415, UM340, W756
"Amazing Grace" (Luke)
  AH4091, B330, C546, E671, EL779, F107, G649, L448, N547
  and N548, P280, UM378 (PD), VU266 (Fr.), W583
"This Is a Day of New Beginnings" (Luke, Comm.)
  B370, C518, N417, UM383, W661
"Jesus Calls Us" (Luke)
  B293, C337, E549/551, EL696, G720, L494, N171/172,
  UM398, VU562
"Take My Life, and Let It Be" (Luke)
  B277/B283, C609, E707, EL583/EL685, G697, L406, P391,
  N448, UM399 (PD), VU506
"*Cuando el Pobre*" ("When the Poor Ones") (Luke)
  C662, EL725, G762, P407, UM434, VU702
"I Come with Joy" (Luke, Comm.)
  B371, C420, E304, EL482, G515, N349, P507, UM617,
  VU477, W726
"The Summons" ("Will You Come and Follow Me") (Luke)
  EL798, G726, S2130, SF2130, VU567
"Somebody's Knockin' at Your Door" (Luke)
  G728, P382, W415, WS3095

Additional Contemporary Suggestions
"Falling on My Knees" ("Hungry") (Hab, Pss, Luke)
  M155, WS3099
"Thy Word Is a Lamp" (Pss)
  C326, G458, SP183, UM601
"Show Me Your Ways" (Pss)
  M107
"Ancient Words" (Pss)
  M149

"Cry of My Heart" (Pss, Luke)
  M39, S2165, SF2165
"He Who Began a Good Work in You" (2 Thess)
  S2163, SF2163, SP180
"Lord, Be Glorified" (2 Thess)
  B457, EL744, G468, S2150, SF2150, SP196
"Be Glorified" (2 Thess)
  M13
"Be Glorified" (2 Thess)
  M152
"Take My Life" (2 Thess, Luke)
  M91
"Give Thanks" (2 Thess, Luke)
  C528, G647, S2036, SF2036, SP170
"I'm So Glad Jesus Lifted Me" (Luke)
  C529, EL860 (PD), N474, S2151, SF2151
"Shout to the North" (Luke)
  G319, M99, WS3042
"Amazing Grace" ("My Chains Are Gone") (Luke)
  M205, WS3104
"We Fall Down" (Luke, All Saints)
  G368, M66, WS3187
"I Will Never Be (the Same Again)" (Luke)
  M34
"Stronger" (Luke)
  M228
"Salvation Is Here" (Luke)
  M242
"Grace Like Rain" (Luke)
  M251

Vocal Solos
"Be Thou My Vision" (Hab)
  V-6   p. 13
"Lost in the Night" (Hab, Luke)
  V-5 (1)   p. 18
"Here I Am" (1 Thess, Luke)
  V-11   p. 19
"Where Shall My Wondering Soul Begin?" (Luke)
  V-1   p. 59

Anthems
"Amazing Grace" (Luke)
Arr. Sandra Eithun; Choristers Guild CGA-1269
Unison, piano

"Zacchaeus" (Luke)
John D. Horman; Choristers Guild CGA1073
Unison/two-part, piano

Other Suggestions
Visuals:
  O   Praying hands, overturned scales, tower, tablets
  P   Open Bible, Ten Commandments
  E   Letter, embrace, love, persecution, prayer
  G   Tax form, small man (running, climbing tree), 1/2,
       4x, Jesus, Luke 19:9*a*
  Reformation Sunday: Luther, reformers, 95 Theses
Introit: WS3047, st. 3 "God Almighty, We Are Waiting" (Hab)
Prayers: WSL189 and WSL163 (Luke)
Sung Benediction: M87. "Let the Peace of God Reign" (2 Thess)
Alternate Lessons (see p. 4): Isa 1:10-18, Ps 32:1-7

Daniel 7:1-3, 15-18

[1]In the first year of Babylon's King Belshazzar, Daniel had a dream—a vision in his head as he lay on his bed. He wrote the dream down. Here is the beginning of the account:

[2]I am Daniel. In the vision I had during the night I saw the four winds of heaven churning the great sea. [3]Four giant beasts emerged from the sea, each different from the others.
. . .

[15]Now this caused me, Daniel, to worry. My visions disturbed me greatly. [16]So I went to one of the servants who was standing ready nearby. I asked him for the truth about all this.

He spoke to me and explained to me the meaning of these things. [17]"These four giant beasts are four kings that will rise up from the earth, [18]but the holy ones of the Most High will receive the kingship. They will hold the kingship securely forever and always."

Psalm 149 (G550, N722, P257)

[1]Praise the LORD!

Sing to the LORD a new song; / sing God's praise in the assembly of the faithful! / [2]Let Israel celebrate its maker; / let Zion's children rejoice in their king! / [3]Let them praise God's name with dance; / let them sing God's praise with the drum and lyre! / [4]Because the LORD is pleased with his people, / God will beautify the poor with saving help. / [5]Let the faithful celebrate with glory; / let them shout for joy on their beds. / [6]Let the high praises of God be in their mouths / and a double-edged sword in their hands, / [7]to get revenge against the nations / and punishment on the peoples, / [8]binding their rulers in chains / and their officials in iron shackles, / [9]achieving the justice / written against them. / That will be an honor for all God's faithful people.

Praise the LORD!

Ephesians 1:11-23

[11]We have also received an inheritance in Christ. We were destined by the plan of God, who accomplishes everything according to his design. [12]We are called to be an honor to God's glory because we were the first to hope in Christ. [13]You too heard the word of truth in Christ, which is the good news of your salvation. You were sealed with the promised Holy Spirit because you believed in Christ. [14]The Holy Spirit is the down payment on our inheritance, which is applied toward our redemption as God's own people, resulting in the honor of God's glory.

[15]Since I heard about your faith in the Lord Jesus and your love for all God's people, this is the reason that [16]I don't stop giving thanks to God for you when I remember you in my prayers. [17]I pray that the God of our Lord Jesus Christ, the Father of glory, will give you a spirit of wisdom and revelation that makes God known to you. [18]I pray that the eyes of your heart will have enough light to see what is the hope of God's call, what is the richness of God's glorious inheritance among believers, [19]and what is the overwhelming greatness of God's power that is working among us believers. This power is conferred by the energy of God's powerful strength. [20]God's power was at work in Christ when God raised him from the dead and sat him at God's right side in the heavens, [21]far above every ruler and authority and power and angelic power, any power that might be named not only now but in the future. [22]God put everything under Christ's feet and made him head of everything in the church, [23]which is his body. His body, the church, is the fullness of Christ, who fills everything in every way.

Luke 6:20-31

[20]Jesus raised his eyes to his disciples and said:

"Happy are you who are poor,
because God's kingdom is yours.

[21]Happy are you who hunger now,
because you will be satisfied.

Happy are you who weep now,
because you will laugh.

[22]Happy are you when people hate you, reject you, insult you, and condemn your name as evil because of the Human One. [23]Rejoice when that happens! Leap for joy because you have a great reward in heaven. Their ancestors did the same things to the prophets.

[24]But how terrible for you who are rich,
because you have already received your comfort.

[25]How terrible for you who have plenty now,
because you will be hungry.

How terrible for you who laugh now,
because you will mourn and weep.

[26]How terrible for you when all speak well of you.
Their ancestors did the same things to the false prophets.

[27]"But I say to you who are willing to hear: Love your enemies. Do good to those who hate you. [28]Bless those who curse you. Pray for those who mistreat you. [29]If someone slaps you on the cheek, offer the other one as well. If someone takes your coat, don't withhold your shirt either. [30]Give to everyone who asks and don't demand your things back from those who take them. [31]Treat people in the same way that you want them to treat you."

Primary Hymns and Songs for the Day

"Come, Thou Almighty King" (Dan) (O)
    B247, C27, E365, EL408, F341, G2, L522, N275, P139, UM61
    (PD), VU314, W487
                    H-3 Hbl-28, 49, 53; Chr-56; Desc-57; Org-63
        S-1   #185-86. Desc. and harm.

"My Hope Is Built" (Eph)
    B406, C537, EL596/597, F92, G353, L293/ 294, N368, P379,
    UM368 (PD)
        H-3   Chr-191
        S-2   #171-72. Trumpet and vocal descs.

"We Are God's People" (Eph)
    B383, F546, S2220, SF2220

"For All the Saints" (Eph, Luke)
    S2283, SF2283
        H-3   Chr-200; Org-45

"Blest Are They" (Luke)
    EL728, G172, S2155, SF2155, VU896

"I Sing a Song of the Saints of God" (All Saints)
    E293, G730, N295, P364, UM712 (PD)

"For All the Saints" (Dan, Eph) (C)
    B355, C637, E287, EL422, F614, G326, L174, N299, P526,
    UM711 (PD), VU705, W705
        H-3   Hbl-58; Chr-65; Org-152
        S-1   #314-18. Various treatments

Additional Hymn Suggestions

"Immortal, Invisible, God Only Wise" (Dan) (O)
    B6, C66, E423, EL834, F319, G12, L526, N1, P263, UM103
    (PD), VU264, W512

"The God of Abraham Praise" (Dan)
    B34, C24, E401, EL831, F332, G49, L544, N24, P488, UM116
    (PD), VU255, W537

"*Cantad al Señor*" ("O Sing to the Lord") (Pss)
    EL822, G637, P472, VU241

"All People That on Earth Do Dwell" (Pss)
    B5, C18, E377/378, EL883, F381, G385, L245, N7, P220,
    UM75 (PD), VU822 (Fr.), W669/670

"Open My Eyes, That I May See" (Pss, Eph)
    B502, C586, F486, G451, P324, UM454, VU371

"Holy, Holy, Holy" (Eph)
    B2, C4, E362, F323, EL413, G1, L165, N277, P138, UM64/65,
    VU315, W485

"Holy God, We Praise Thy Name" (Eph)
    E366, F385, EL414 (PD), G4, L535, N276, P460, UM79,
    VU894 (Fr.), W524

"At the Name of Jesus" (Eph)
    B198, E435, EL416, F351, G264, L179, P148, UM168, VU335,
    W499

"Take, O Take Me as I Am" (Eph)
    EL814, G698, WS3119

"Give Me Jesus" (Eph, All Saints)
    EL770, N409, WS3140

"Lift Every Voice and Sing" (Eph, Luke)
    AH4055, B627, C631, E599, EL841, G339, L562, N593, P563,
    UM519, W641

"Lord, I Want to Be a Christian" (Luke, All Saints)
    B489, C589, F421, G729, N454, P372 (PD), UM402

"*Kum Ba Yah*" ("Come By Here") (Luke)
    C590, G472, P338, UM494

"Holy" ("*Santo*") (Luke)
    EL762, G594, S2019, SF2019

"Goodness Is Stronger than Evil" (Luke)
    EL721, G750, S2219, SF2219

"How Lovely, Lord, How Lovely" (All Saints)
    C285, G402, P207, S2042, VU801

"As We Gather at Your Table" (All Saints, Comm.)
    EL522, N332, S2268, SF2268, VU457

"For the Bread Which You Have Broken" (All Saints, Comm.)
    C411, E340/E341, EL494, G516, L200, P508/P509, UM614/
    UM615, VU470

Additional Contemporary Suggestions

"There's Something about That Name" (Dan)
    B177, C115, F227, SP89, UM171

"I Could Sing of Your Love Forever" (Pss)
    M63

"I Will Enter" ("He Has Made Me Glad") (Pss)
    S2270, SF2270, SP168

"I Will Celebrate" (Pss)
    M46, SP147

"He Who Began a Good Work in You" (Eph)
    S2163, SF2163, SP180

"Open the Eyes of My Heart" (Eph)
    G452, M57, WS3008

"Holy Is the Lord" (Eph)
    WS3028, M131

"In Christ Alone" (Eph)
    M138, WS3105

"Above All" (Eph)
    M77; V-3 (2) p. 17 Vocal solo

"Forever" (Eph)
    M68, WS3023

"Give Thanks" (Luke)
    C528, G647, S2036, SF2036, SP170

"We Fall Down" (All Saints)
    G368, M66, WS3187

Vocal Solos

"Deep River" (All Saints)
    V-3 (1)   p. 4

"In Bright Mansions Above" (All Saints)
    V-4   p. 39

Anthems

"In Christ an Inheritance Is Ours" (Eph)
Michael D. Costello; MorningStar MSM-60-6010
SATB, organ, flute and oboe

"Neither Angels, Nor Demons, Nor Powers" (All Saints)
Timothy C. Takach; www.GraphitePublishing.com GP-T010
SSATBB a cappella

Other Suggestions

Visuals:
    O   Storm, bed, dreamscape, four beasts, terror, four
               crowns
    P   Praise, new song, assembly, dance, instruments
    E   Will, Christ, Bible, seal, flames/dove, jewelry box
    G   Feeding/poor, smile through tears, leaping, prayer,
               turned cheek, shirt/coat, giving, warning
    All Saints Day: Pictures of deceased members
All Saints scriptures and ideas may be used on Oct. 30 or Nov. 6.
Greeting: C825 (Luke)
Litany: C488 or WSL49 (Luke, All Saints)

Haggai 1:15b–2:9

. . . [15b]in the second year of Darius the king.

2 On the twenty-first day of the seventh month, the Lord's word came through Haggai the prophet: [2]Say to Judah's Governor Zerubbabel, Shealtiel's son, and to the Chief Priest Joshua, Jehozadak's son, and to the rest of the people:

[3]Who among you is left who saw this house in its former
glory?
How does it look to you now?
Doesn't it appear as nothing to you?
[4]So now, be strong, Zerubbabel, says the Lord.
Be strong, High Priest Joshua, Jehozadak's son,
and be strong, all you people of the land, says the
Lord.
Work, for I am with you, says the Lord of heavenly forces.
[5]As with our agreement when you came out of Egypt,
my spirit stands in your midst.
Don't fear.
[6]This is what the Lord of heavenly forces says:
In just a little while, I will make the heavens, the earth,
the sea, and the dry land quake.
[7]I will make all the nations quake.
The wealth of all the nations will come.
I will fill this house with glory, says the Lord of heavenly
forces.
[8]The silver and the gold belong to me, says the Lord of
heavenly forces.
[9]This house will be more glorious than its predecessor,
says the Lord of heavenly forces.
I will provide prosperity in this place,
says the Lord of heavenly forces.

Psalm 145:1-5, 17-21 (G42/270/622, N718, P251/252, UM857)

[1]I will lift you up high, my God, the true king. / I will bless your name forever and always. / [2]I will bless you every day. / I will praise your name forever and always. / [3]The Lord is great and so worthy of praise! / God's greatness can't be grasped. / [4]One generation will praise your works to the next one, / proclaiming your mighty acts. / [5]They will talk all about the glorious splendor of your majesty; / I will contemplate your wondrous works. . . .

[17]The Lord is righteous in all his ways, / faithful in all his deeds. / [18]The Lord is close to everyone who calls out to him, / to all who call out to him sincerely. / [19]God shows favor to those who honor him, / listening to their cries for help and saving them. / [20]The Lord protects all who love him, / but he destroys every wicked person. / [21]My mouth will proclaim the Lord's praise, / and every living thing will bless God's holy name / forever and always.

2 Thessalonians 2:1-5, 13-17

[1]Brothers and sisters, we have a request for you concerning our Lord Jesus Christ's coming and when we are gathered together to be with him. [2]We don't want you to be easily confused in your mind or upset if you hear that the day of the Lord is already here, whether you hear it through some spirit, a message, or a letter supposedly from us. [3]Don't let anyone deceive you in any way. That day won't come unless the rebellion comes first and the person who is lawless is revealed, who is headed for destruction. [4]He is the opponent of every so-called god or object of worship and promotes himself over them. So he sits in God's temple, displaying himself to show that he is God. [5]You remember that I used to tell you these things while I was with you, don't you? . . .

[13]But we always must thank God for you, brothers and sisters who are loved by God. This is because he chose you from the beginning to be the first crop of the harvest. This brought salvation, through your dedication to God by the Spirit and through your belief in the truth. [14]God called all of you through our good news so you could possess the honor of our Lord Jesus Christ. [15]So then, brothers and sisters, stand firm and hold on to the traditions we taught you, whether we taught you in person or through our letter. [16]Our Lord Jesus Christ himself and God our Father loved us and through grace gave us eternal comfort and a good hope. [17]May he encourage your hearts and give you strength in every good thing you do or say.

Luke 20:27-38

[27]Some Sadducees, who deny that there's a resurrection, came to Jesus and asked, [28]"Teacher, Moses wrote for us that *if a man's brother dies* leaving a widow *but no children, the brother must marry the widow and raise up children for his brother.* [29]Now there were seven brothers. The first man married a woman and then died childless. [30]The second [31]and then the third brother married her. Eventually all seven married her, and they all died without leaving any children. [32]Finally, the woman died too. [33]In the resurrection, whose wife will she be? All seven were married to her."

[34]Jesus said to them, "People who belong to this age marry and are given in marriage. [35]But those who are considered worthy to participate in that age, that is, in the age of the resurrection from the dead, won't marry nor will they be given in marriage. [36]They can no longer die, because they are like angels and are God's children since they share in the resurrection. [37]Even Moses demonstrated that the dead are raised—in the passage about the burning bush, when he speaks of the Lord as *the God of Abraham, the God of Isaac, and the God of Jacob.* [38]He isn't the God of the dead but of the living. To him they are all alive."

Primary Hymns and Songs for the Day

"Come, Ye Faithful, Raise the Strain" (2 Thess, Luke) (O)
C215, E199, EL363, G234, L132, N230, P115, UM315 (PD),
VU165, W456
    H-3   Hbl-53; Chr-57; Desc-94; Org-141
    S-2   #161. Desc.

"God Is Here" (2 Thess, Luke) (O)
C280, EL526, G409, N70, P461, UM660, VU389, W667
    H-3   Hbl-61; Chr-132; Org-2
    S-1   #4-5. Instrumental and vocal descs.

"Standing on the Promises" (Hag, Luke)
AH4057, B335, C552, F69, G838, UM374 (PD)
    H-3   Chr-177; Org-117

"Great Is the Lord" (Pss)
B12, G614, S2022, SF2022, SP30

"*Pues Si Vivimos*" ("When We Are Living") (Luke) (C)
C536, EL639, G822, N499, P400, UM356, VU581

"Sent Forth by God's Blessing" (Luke) (C)
EL547, L221, N76, UM664, VU481
    H-3   Chr-125; Desc-; Org-9
    S-1   #327. Desc.

Additional Hymn Suggestions

"Come, Thou Long-Expected Jesus" (Hag) (O)
B77, C125, E66, EL254, F168, G82/83, L30, N122, P1/2,
UM196 (PD), VU2, W364

"God of the Ages" (Hag, Luke)
B629, C725, E718, G331, L567, N592, P262, UM698 (PD)

"My Lord, What a Morning" (Hag, 2 Thess)
C708, EL438 (PD), G352, P449, UM719, VU708

"O God, Our Help in Ages Past" (Hag, Pss) (O)
B74, C67, E680, EL632, F370, G687, L320, N25, P210,
UM117 (PD), VU806, W579

"Taste and See" (Pss, Comm.)
EL493, G520, S2267, SF2267

"I Love the Lord" (Pss)
G799, P362, N511, VU617, WS3142

"Let All Things Now Living" (Pss, Luke)
B640, C717, EL881, F389, G37, L557, P554, S2008, VU242

"Now Thank We All Our God" (2 Thess)
B638, C715, E396/397, EL839/840, F525, G643, L533 or
L534, N419, P555, UM102 (PD), VU236 (Fr.), W560

"Holy God, We Praise Thy Name" (2 Thess)
E366, F385, EL414 (PD), G4, L535, N276, P460, UM79,
VU894 (Fr.), W524

"I Want Jesus to Walk with Me" (2 Thess)
B465, C627, EL325, G775, N490, P363, UM521

"Loving Spirit" (2 Thess)
C244, EL397, G293, P323, S2123, VU387

"In the Singing" (2 Thess, Comm.)
EL466, G533, S2255, SF2255

"The God of Abraham Praise" (Luke)
B34, C24, E401, EL831, F332, G49, L544, N24, P488, UM116
(PD), VU255, W537

"Sing Praise to God Who Reigns Above" (Luke)
B20, C6, E408, EL871, F343, G645, N6, P483, UM126 (PD),
VU216, W528

"Thine Be the Glory" (Luke)
B163, C218, EL376, F291, G238, L145, N253, P122, UM308,
VU173 (Fr.)

"Sing with All the Saints in Glory" (Luke) (C)
EL426, UM702 (PD), W467

"Praise the Source of Faith and Learning" (Luke) (O)
N411, S2004, SF2004

Additional Contemporary Suggestions

"Hosanna" (Hag)
M268, WS3188

"Famous One" (Hag, Pss)
M126

"Be Bold, Be Strong" (Hag)
SP207

"God Is Good All the Time" (Pss)
AH4010, M45, WS3026

"You Are Good" (Pss)
AH4018, M124, WS3014

"Lord, I Lift Your Name on High" (Pss, Luke)
AH4071, EL857, M2, S2088, SF2088

"Lord, Be Glorified" (2 Thess)
B457, EL744, G468, S2150, SF2150, SP196

"Give Thanks" (2 Thess)
C528, G647, S2036, SF2036, SP170

"Sing Alleluia to the Lord" (2 Thess, Comm.)
B214, C32, S2258, SF2258, SP93

"Here Is Bread, Here Is Wine" (2 Thess, Comm.)
EL483, S2266, SF2266

"Wait for the Lord" (2 Thess)
EL262, G90, VU22, WS3049

"Today Is the Day" (2 Thess)
M223

"Grace Like Rain" (2 Thess)
M251

"Spirit of the Living God" (2 Thess, Luke)
B244, C259, G288, N283, P322, SP131, UM393, VU376

"Alive Forever, Amen" (Luke)
M201

Vocal Solos

"Come, Thou Long-Expected Jesus" (Hag)
    V-10   p. 11

"Courage, My Heart" (Hag, 2 Thess)
    V-9   p. 20

Anthems

"Great Is the Lord" (Pss)
Rosephanye Powell; Gentry 00145523
SATB, percussion

"Children of the Heavenly Father" (Luke)
Arr. Daniel Kallman; Morningstar 50-8431
SATB, organ and children's choir

Other Suggestions

Visuals:
    O   Church in ruins/restored, Exodus, quake, sea/desert
    P   Crown, teach/learn, light, natural wonders, praise
    E   Second Coming, fruit, preaching, letter, 2 Thess 2:16-17
    G   Coffin, wedding, seven brothers, bride, resurrection, children in white robes, burning bush, Luke 20:38a

All Saints scriptures and ideas may be used today.
Opening Prayer: N831 (Hag, Pss)
Prayer: UM721. Christ the King (Hag, 2 Thess)
Blessing: N872 (Hag) or C776 (2 Thess)
Alternate Lessons (see p. 4): Job 19:23-27a, Ps 17:1-9

Isaiah 65:17-25

[17]Look! I'm creating
    a new heaven and a new earth:
    past events won't be remembered;
    they won't come to mind.
[18]Be glad and rejoice forever
    in what I'm creating,
    because I'm creating Jerusalem as a joy
    and her people as a source of gladness.
[19]I will rejoice in Jerusalem
    and be glad about my people.
    No one will ever hear the sound
       of weeping or crying in it again.
[20]No more will babies live only a few days,
    or the old fail to live out their days.
The one who dies at a hundred
    will be like a young person,
    and the one falling short of a hundred
       will seem cursed.
[21]They will build houses and live in them;
    they will plant vineyards
       and eat their fruit.
[22]They won't build for others to live in,
    nor plant for others to eat.
Like the days of a tree
    will be the days of my people;
    my chosen will make full use
       of their handiwork.
[23]They won't labor in vain,
    nor bear children to a world of horrors,
    because they will be people
       blessed by the LORD,
    they along with their descendants.
[24]Before they call, I will answer;
    while they are still speaking, I will hear.
[25]Wolf and lamb will graze together,
    and the lion will eat straw like the ox,
    but the snake—its food will be dust.
They won't hurt or destroy
    at any place on my holy mountain,
    says the LORD.

Isaiah 12

You will say on that day:
"I thank you, LORD.
Though you were angry with me,
    your anger turned away and you comforted me.
[2]God is indeed my salvation;
    I will trust and won't be afraid.
Yah, the LORD, is my strength and my shield;
    he has become my salvation."
[3]You will draw water with joy from the springs of salvation.
[4]And you will say on that day:
"Thank the LORD; call on God's name;
    proclaim God's deeds among the peoples;
    declare that God's name is exalted.
[5]Sing to the LORD, who has done glorious things;
    proclaim this throughout all the earth."
[6]Shout and sing for joy, city of Zion,
    because the holy one of Israel is great among you.

2 Thessalonians 3:6-13

[6]Brothers and sisters, we command you in the name of our Lord Jesus Christ to stay away from every brother or sister who lives an undisciplined life that is not in line with the traditions that you received from us. [7]You yourselves know how you need to imitate us because we were not undisciplined when we were with you. [8]We didn't eat anyone's food without paying for it. Instead, we worked night and day with effort and hard work so that we would not impose on you. [9]We did this to give you an example to imitate, not because we didn't have a right to insist on financial support. [10]Even when we were with you we were giving you this command: "If anyone doesn't want to work, they shouldn't eat." [11]We hear that some of you are living an undisciplined life. They aren't working, but they are meddling in other people's business. [12]By the Lord Jesus Christ, we command and encourage such people to work quietly and put their own food on the table. [13]Brothers and sisters, don't get discouraged in doing what is right.

Luke 21:5-19

[5]Some people were talking about the temple, how it was decorated with beautiful stones and ornaments dedicated to God. Jesus said, [6]"As for the things you are admiring, the time is coming when not even one stone will be left upon another. All will be demolished."

[7]They asked him, "Teacher, when will these things happen? What sign will show that these things are about to happen?"

[8]Jesus said, "Watch out that you aren't deceived. Many will come in my name, saying, 'I'm the one!' and 'It's time!' Don't follow them. [9]When you hear of wars and rebellions, don't be alarmed. These things must happen first, but the end won't happen immediately."

[10]Then Jesus said to them, "Nations and kingdoms will fight against each other. [11]There will be great earthquakes and wide-scale food shortages and epidemics. There will also be terrifying sights and great signs in the sky. [12]But before all this occurs, they will take you into custody and harass you because of your faith. They will hand you over to synagogues and prisons, and you will be brought before kings and governors because of my name. [13]This will provide you with an opportunity to testify. [14]Make up your minds not to prepare your defense in advance. [15]I'll give you words and wisdom that none of your opponents will be able to counter or contradict. [16]You will be betrayed by your parents, brothers and sisters, relatives, and friends. They will execute some of you. [17]Everyone will hate you because of my name. [18]Still, not a hair on your heads will be lost. [19]By holding fast, you will gain your lives."

Primary Hymns and Songs for the Day

"My Hope Is Built" (Luke) (O)
  B406, C537, EL596/597, F92, G353, L293/294, N368, P379,
  UM368 (PD)
"O Day of Peace That Dimly Shines" (Isa 65, Luke)
  C711, E597, EL711, G373, P450, UM729, VU682, W654
"The First Song of Isaiah" (Isa 12)
  G71, S2030, SF2030
"Soon and Very Soon" (2 Thess, Luke)
  B192, EL439, G384, UM706
         S-2   #187. Piano arr.
"My Lord, What a Morning" (Luke)
  C708, EL438 (PD), G352, P449, UM719, VU708
"O Master, Let Me Walk with Thee" (Luke) (C)
  B279, C602, E659/E660, EL818, F442, G738, L492, N503,
  P357, UM430 (PD), VU560

Additional Hymn Suggestions

"Joy Comes with the Dawn" (Isa 65)
  S2210, SF2210, VU166
"Joy in the Morning" (Isa 65)
  S2284, SF2284
"I'll Fly Away" (Isa 65)
  N595, S2282, SF2282
"Isaiah the Prophet Has Written of Old" (Isa 65)
  G77, N108, P337, VU680
"For the Healing of the Nations" (Isa, 2 Thess, Luke)
  C668, G346, N576, UM428, VU678, W643
"On Jordan's Stormy Banks I Stand" (Isa 65, Luke)
  B521, EL437, N598, UM724 (PD)
"Sing Praise to God Who Reigns Above" (Isa 12)
  B20, C6, E408, EL871, F343, G645, N6, P483, UM126 (PD),
  VU216, W528
"The Trees of the Field" (Isa 12) (C)
  G80, S2279, SF2279, SP128, VU884
"Together We Serve" (2 Thess)
  G767, S2175, SF2175
"You, Lord, Are Both Lamb and Shepherd" (2 Thess)
  G274, SF2102, VU210. WS3043
"Go to the World" (2 Thess)
  G295, VU420, WS3158
"Come, Labor On" (2 Thess)
  E541, G719, N532, P415
"Today We All Are Called to Be Disciples" (2 Thess)
  G757, P434, VU507
"Called as Partners in Christ's Service" (2 Thess)
  C453, G761, N495, P343
"It Is Well with My Soul" (2 Thess, Luke)
  B410, C561, EL785, F495, G840, L346, N438, UM377
"All Who Love and Serve Your City" (2 Thess, Luke)
  C670, E570/E571, EL724, G351, L436, P413, UM433, W621
"I Want to Be Ready" (2 Thess, Luke)
  N616, UM722
"Where Cross the Crowded Ways of Life" (Luke)
  C665, E609, EL719, F665, G343, L429, N543, P408, UM427
  (PD), VU681
"Lord, Speak to Me" (Luke)
  B568, EL676, F625, G722, L403, N531, P426, UM463 (PD),
  VU589
"O Day of God, Draw Nigh" (Luke) (C)
  B623, C700, E601, N611, P452, UM730 (PD), VU688 and
  VU689 (Fr.)

Additional Contemporary Suggestions

"I Will Enter" ("He Has Made Me Glad") (Isa 65) (O)
  S2270, SF2270, SP168
"Give Thanks" (Isa 65)
  C528, G647, S2036, SF2036, SP170
"There's Something about That Name" (Isa 65)
  B177, C115, F227, SP89, UM171
"Forever" (Isa 65)
  M68, WS3023
"Trading My Sorrows" (Isa 65)
  M75, WS3108
"Days of Elijah" (Isa 65)
  M139, WS3186
"Someone Asked the Question" (Isa 65, Isa 12)
  N523, S2144
"Hear Our Praises" (Isa 65, Isa 12)
  M64
"He Is Exalted" (Isa 12)
  S2070, SF2070, SP66
"Shout to the Lord" (Isa 12)
  EL821, M16, S2074, SF2074; V-3 (2) p. 32 Vocal solo
"In the Lord I'll Be Ever Thankful" (Isa 12)
  G654, S2195, SF2195
"You Are My All in All" (Isa 12)
  G519, SP220, WS3040
"I See the Lord" (Isa 12, Luke)
  M31
"Rule of Life" (2 Thess)
  AH4056, WS3117
"Freedom Is Coming" (Luke)
  G359, S2192, SF2192
"Hosanna" (Luke)
  M268, WS3188
"The Battle Belongs to the Lord" (Luke)
  SP158

Vocal Solos

"Turn My Heart to You" (Isa, Luke)
  V-5 (2)   p. 14
"My Lord, What a Mornin'" (Luke)
  V-3 (1)   p. 39
  V-7   p. 68

Anthems

"I Saw the Cross of Jesus" (Col, Luke 23)
Victor C. Johnson; Choristers Guild CGA-1346
SATB, piano

"*Sizohamba Naye*" ("We Will Walk with God") (Luke 1)
Arr. Terry Taylor; Choristers Guild CGA-1250
Unison choir, opt. SATB, piano, opt. percussion

Other Suggestions

Visuals:
  O   Space/earth, joy, building, grapes, work, wolf/lamb
  P   Worship, anger/comfort, arm, water/well, joy
  E   Idleness, bread, work, food
  G   Temple, toppled rock, Jesus, war, whip/chain,
          betrayal, hair
Introit: WS3047, st. 2. "God Almighty, We Are Waiting" (Isa)
Canticle: UM734. "Canticle of Hope" (Isa, Luke)
Confession: WSL90. "You asked for my hands" (2 Thess)
Prayer: N857 (Isa) and N856 (Luke)
Alternate Lessons (see p. 4): Mal 4:1-2a, Ps 98

Jeremiah 23:1-6

¹Watch out, you shepherds who destroy and scatter the sheep of my pasture, declares the LORD. ²This is what the LORD, the God of Israel, proclaims about the shepherds who "tend to" my people: You are the ones who have scattered my flock and driven them away. You haven't attended to their needs, so I will take revenge on you for the terrible things you have done to them, declares the LORD. ³I myself will gather the few remaining sheep from all the countries where I have driven them. I will bring them back to their pasture, and they will be fruitful and multiply. ⁴I will place over them shepherds who care for them. Then they will no longer be afraid or dread harm, nor will any be missing, declares the LORD.

⁵The time is coming, declares the LORD, when I will raise up a righteous descendant from David's line, and he will rule as a wise king. He will do what is just and right in the land. ⁶During his lifetime, Judah will be saved and Israel will live in safety. And his name will be The LORD is Our Righteousness.

Luke 1:68-79

⁶⁸"Bless the Lord God of Israel
   because he has come to help and has delivered his
      people.
⁶⁹He has raised up a mighty savior for us in his servant
      David's house,
⁷⁰   just as he said through the mouths of his holy prophets
      long ago.
⁷¹He has brought salvation from our enemies
   and from the power of all those who hate us.
⁷²He has shown the mercy promised to our ancestors,
   and remembered his holy covenant,
⁷³   the solemn pledge he made to our ancestor Abraham.
He has granted ⁷⁴that we would be rescued
      from the power of our enemies
   so that we could serve him without fear,
⁷⁵   in holiness and righteousness in God's eyes,
         for as long as we live.
⁷⁶You, child, will be called a prophet of the Most High,
   for you will go before the Lord to prepare his way.
⁷⁷You will tell his people how to be saved
   through the forgiveness of their sins.
⁷⁸Because of our God's deep compassion,
   the dawn from heaven will break upon us,
⁷⁹   to give light to those who are sitting in darkness
   and in the shadow of death,
      to guide us on the path of peace."

Colossians 1:11-20

[¹⁰We're praying this so that you can live lives that are worthy of the Lord and pleasing to him in every way: by producing fruit in every good work and growing in the knowledge of God;] ¹¹by being strengthened through his glorious might so that you endure everything and have patience; ¹²and by giving thanks with joy to the Father. He made it so you could take part in the inheritance, in light granted to God's holy people. ¹³He rescued us from the control of darkness and transferred us into the kingdom of the Son he loves. ¹⁴He set us free through the Son and forgave our sins.

¹⁵   The Son is the image of the invisible God,
      the one who is first over all creation,

¹⁶   Because all things were created by him:
      both in the heavens and on the earth,
      the things that are visible and the things that are
         invisible.
      Whether they are thrones or powers,
      or rulers or authorities,
   all things were created through him and for him.

¹⁷   He existed before all things,
      and all things are held together in him.

¹⁸   He is the head of the body, the church,
      who is the beginning,
         the one who is firstborn from among the dead
         so that he might occupy the first place in
            everything.

¹⁹   Because all the fullness of God was pleased to live in him,
²⁰   and he reconciled all things to himself through him—
      whether things on earth or in the heavens.
         He brought peace through the blood of his cross.

Luke 23:33-43

³³When they arrived at the place called The Skull, they crucified him, along with the criminals, one on his right and the other on his left. ³⁴Jesus said, "Father, forgive them, for they don't know what they're doing." They drew lots as a way of dividing up his clothing.

³⁵The people were standing around watching, but the leaders sneered at him, saying, "He saved others. Let him save himself if he really is the Christ sent from God, the chosen one."

³⁶The soldiers also mocked him. They came up to him offering him sour wine ³⁷and saying, "If you really are the king of the Jews, save yourself." ³⁸Above his head was a notice of the formal charge against him. It read "This is the king of the Jews."

³⁹One of the criminals hanging next to Jesus insulted him, "Aren't you the Christ? Save yourself and us!"

⁴⁰Responding, the other criminal spoke harshly to him, "Don't you fear God, seeing that you've also been sentenced to die? ⁴¹We are rightly condemned, for we are receiving the appropriate sentence for what we did. But this man has done nothing wrong." ⁴²Then he said, "Jesus, remember me when you come into your kingdom."

⁴³Jesus replied, "I assure you that today you will be with me in paradise."

Primary Hymns and Songs for the Day

"Immortal, Invisible, God Only Wise" (Col) (O)
  B6, C66, E423, EL834, F319, G12, L526, N1, P263, UM103
  (PD), VU264, W512
      H-3   Hbl-15, 71; Chr-65; Desc-93; Org-135
      S-1   #300. Harm.
"Blessed Be the God of Israel" (Luke 1)
  C135, E444, EL250/552, G109, P602, UM209, VU901
"Jesus, Remember Me" (Luke)
  C569, EL616, G227, P599, UM488, VU148, W423
"Above All" (Luke, Christ the King)
  M77; V-3 (2) p. 17 Vocal solo
"Jesus Shall Reign" (Christ the King) (C)
  B587, C95, E544, EL434, F238, G265, L530, N157, P423,
  UM157 (PD), VU330, W492
      H-3   Hbl-29, 57, 58; Chr-117; Desc-31; Org-31
      S-1   #100-103. Various treatments
"Crown Him with Many Crowns" (Christ the King) (C)
  B161, C234, E494, EL855, F345, G268, L170, N301, P151,
  UM327 (PD), VU211

Additional Hymn Suggestions

"How Great Thou Art" (Jer)
  AH4015, B10, C33, EL856, F2, G625, L532, N35, P467,
  UM77, VU238 (Fr.)
"How Firm a Foundation" (Jer)
  B338, C618, E636/637, EL796, F32, G463, L507, N407, P361,
  UM529 (PD), VU660, W585
"O Worship the King" (Luke 1)
  B16, C17, E388, EL842, F336, G41, L548, N26, P476, UM73
  (PD), VU235
"We Are Called" (Luke 1, Christ the King)
  EL720, G749, S2172, SF2172
"Gather Us In" (Luke 1, Comm.)
  C284, EL532, G401, S2236, SF2236, W665
"You, Lord, Are Both Lamb and Shepherd" (Luke 1, Col)
  G274, SF2102, VU210. WS3043
"Holy God, We Praise Thy Name" (Col)
  E366, F385, EL414 (PD), G4, L535, N276, P460, UM79,
  VU894 (Fr.), W524
"To God Be the Glory" (Col)
  B4, C72, F363, G634, P485, UM98 (PD)
"In the Cross of Christ I Glory" (Col)
  B554, C207, E441, EL324, F251, G213, L104, N193, P84,
  UM295
"God of Grace and God of Glory" (Col)
  B395, C464, E594/595, EL705, F528, G307, L415, N436,
  P420, UM577, VU686
"I've Got Peace Like a River" (Col)
  B418, C530, G623, N478, P368, S2145, VU577
"Blessed Quietness" (Col, Luke 23)
  F145, C267, N284, S2142, SF2142
"Sing, My Tongue, the Glorious Battle" (Col, Luke 23)
  E165/166, EL355/356, G225, L118, N220, UM296, W437
"Beneath the Cross of Jesus" (Col, Luke 23)
  B291, C197, E498, EL338, F253, G216, L107, N190, P92,
  UM297 (PD), VU135
"Jesus, Keep Me Near the Cross" (Col, Luke 23)
  AH4135, B280, C587, EL335, N197, UM301 (PD), VU142

Additional Contemporary Suggestions

"We Are Marching" ("Siyahamba") (Luke 1)
  C442, EL866, G853, N526, S2235-ab, SF2235-ab, VU646
"Here Is Bread, Here Is Wine" (Luke 1, Comm.)
  EL483, S2266, SF2266

"Shine, Jesus, Shine" (Luke 1)
  B579, EL671, G192, S2173, SF2173, SP142;
  V-3 (2) p. 48 Vocal solo
"How Great Is Our God" (Luke 1)
  M117, WS3003
"God Is Good All the Time" (Luke 1)
  AH4010, M45, WS3026
"Here I Am to Worship" (Luke 1, Christ the King)
  M116, WS3177
"Marvelous Light" (Luke 1, Col)
  M249
"Came to My Rescue" (Col, Luke 23)
  M257
"Lamb of God" (Luke 23)
  EL336, G518, S2113, SF2113
"Awesome God" (Luke 23, Christ the King)
  G616, S2040, SF2040, SP11
"King of Kings" (Christ the King)
  B234, S2075, SF2075, SP94, VU167
"The King of Glory Comes" (Christ the King)
  B127, S2091, SF2091, W501
"The Power of the Cross" (Luke 23, Christ the King)
  M222, WS3085
"Hosanna" (Christ the King)
  M268, WS3188
"Blessing, Honour, Glory" (Luke 23, Christ the King)
  M21
"My Savior Lives" (Luke 23, Christ the King)
  M237
"Forever Reign" (Luke 23, Christ the King)
  M256

Vocal Solos

"King of Glory, King of Peace" (Christ the King)
  V-9   p. 24
"Holy Is the Lamb" (Luke, Christ the King)
  V-5 (1)   p. 5

Anthems

"There Shall a Star Come Out of Jacob" (Jer)
Felix Mendelssohn; Schmitt, Hall, & McCreary SCHCH 1903
SATB, keyboard

"*Sizohamba Naye*" ("We Will Walk with God") (Luke 1)
Arr. Terry Taylor; Choristers Guild CGA-1250
Unison choir, opt. SATB, piano, opt. percussion

Other Suggestions

Visuals:
  O   Scattered/herding sheep, today's shepherds, branch
  P   Christus Rex, rescue, service, child, dawn, feet
  E   Glory, joy, light/dark, rescue, creation, Christ
  G   Skull, blood/lots/cross/clothes, INRI, wine, Luke
             23:42
  Christ the King: Crown, Christus Rex
Canticle: C137, F191, UM208, VU900. "Zechariah" (Luke 1)
Prayer: N853. Peace (Luke 1, Col)
Affirmation of Faith: WSL76. "We Believe in One God" (Col)
Sung Confession: WS3084. "O Christ, You Hang upon a Cross"
  (Luke 23)
Prayer: UM466, UM721, WSL63, (Christ the King)
Prayers of the People: WSL26. "Jesus, Remember Us" (Luke 23)
Alternate Lessons (see p. 4): Jer 23:1-6, Ps 46

Deuteronomy 26:1-11

[1]Once you have entered the land the LORD your God is giving you as an inheritance, and you take possession of it and are settled there, [2]take some of the early produce of the fertile ground that you have harvested from the land the LORD your God is giving you, and put it in a basket. Then go to the location the LORD your God selects for his name to reside. [3]Go to the priest who is in office at that time and say to him: "I am declaring right now before the LORD my God that I have indeed arrived in the land the LORD swore to our ancestors to give us."

[4]The priest will then take the basket from you and place it before the LORD your God's altar. [5]Then you should solemnly state before the LORD your God:

"My father was a starving Aramean. He went down to Egypt, living as an immigrant there with few family members, but that is where he became a great nation, mighty and numerous. [6]The Egyptians treated us terribly, oppressing us and forcing hard labor on us. [7]So we cried out for help to the LORD, our ancestor's God. The LORD heard our call. God saw our misery, our trouble, and our oppression. [8]The LORD brought us out of Egypt with a strong hand and an outstretched arm, with awesome power, and with signs and wonders. [9]He brought us to this place and gave us this land—a land full of milk and honey. [10]So now I am bringing the early produce of the fertile ground that you, LORD, have given me."

Set the produce before the LORD your God, bowing down before the LORD your God. [11]Then celebrate all the good things the LORD your God has done for you and your family—each one of you along with the Levites and the immigrants who are among you.

Psalm 100 (G385, N688, P220, UM821)

[1]Shout triumphantly to the LORD, all the earth! / [2]Serve the LORD with celebration! / Come before him with shouts of joy! / [3]Know that the LORD is God— / he made us; we belong to him. / We are his people, / the sheep of his own pasture. / [4]Enter his gates with thanks; / enter his courtyards with praise! / Thank him! Bless his name! / [5]Because the LORD is good, / his loyal love lasts forever; / his faithfulness lasts generation after generation.

Philippians 4:4-9

[4]Be glad in the Lord always! Again I say, be glad! [5]Let your gentleness show in your treatment of all people. The Lord is near. [6]Don't be anxious about anything; rather bring up all of your requests to God in your prayers and petitions, along with giving thanks. [7]Then the peace of God that exceeds all understanding will keep your hearts and minds safe in Christ Jesus.

[8]From now on, brothers and sisters, if anything is excellent and if anything is admirable, focus your thoughts on these things: all that is true, all that is holy, all that is just, all that is pure, all that is lovely, and all that is worthy of praise. [9]Practice these things: whatever you learned, received, heard, or saw in us. The God of peace will be with you.

John 6:25-35

[25]When they found him on the other side of the lake, they asked him, "Rabbi, when did you get here?"

[26]Jesus replied, "I assure you that you are looking for me not because you saw miraculous signs but because you ate all the food you wanted. [27]Don't work for the food that doesn't last but for the food that endures for eternal life, which the Human One will give you. God the Father has confirmed him as his agent to give life."

[28]They asked, "What must we do in order to accomplish what God requires?"

[29]Jesus replied, "This is what God requires, that you believe in him whom God sent."

[30]They asked, "What miraculous sign will you do, that we can see and believe you? What will you do? [31]Our ancestors ate manna in the wilderness, just as it is written, *He gave them bread from heaven to eat.*"

[32]Jesus told them, "I assure you, it wasn't Moses who gave the bread from heaven to you, but my Father gives you the true bread from heaven. [33]The bread of God is the one who comes down from heaven and gives life to the world."

[34]They said, "Sir, give us this bread all the time!"

[35]Jesus replied, "I am the bread of life. Whoever comes to me will never go hungry, and whoever believes in me will never be thirsty."

Primary Hymns and Songs for the Day

"Come, Ye Thankful People, Come" (Deut, Pss) (O)
B637, C718, E290, EL693, F392, G367, L407, N422, P551, UM694 (PD), VU516, W759
    H-3   Hbl-54; Chr-58; Desc-94; Org-137
    S-1   #302-303. Harms. with desc.

"All People That on Earth Do Dwell" (Pss)
B5, C18, E377/378, EL883, F381, G385, L245, N7, P220, UM75 (PD), VU822 (Fr.), W669/670
    H-3   Hbl-45; Chr-24; Desc-84, 85; Org-107
    S-1   #257-59. Various treatments
    S-2   #140. Desc.

"Now Thank We All Our God" (Pss)
B638, C715, E396/397, EL839/840, F525, G643, L533 or L534, N419, P555, UM102 (PD), VU236 (Fr.), W560
    H-3   Hbl-78; Chr-140; Desc-81; Org-98
    S-1   #252-54. Various treatments

"Rejoice, Ye Pure in Heart" (Phil)
B39, C15, E556/557, EL873/874, F394, G804, N55/71, P145/146, UM160/161
    H-3   Hbl-17, 90; Chr-166; Desc-73; Org-85
    S-1   #228. Desc.

"For the Beauty of the Earth" (John)
B44, C56, E416, EL879, F1, G14, L561, P473, N28, UM92 (PD), VU226, W557

"Guide Me, O Thou Great Jehovah" (Deut, John) (C)
B56, C622, E690, EL618, F608, G65, L343, N18/19, P281, UM127 (PD), VU651 (Fr.)
    H-3   Hbl-25, 51, 58; Chr-89; Desc-26; Org-23
    S-1   #76-77. Desc. and harm.

Additional Hymn Suggestions

"God Be with You till We Meet Again" (Deut) (C)
C434, EL536, F523, G541/542, N81, P540, UM672/673, VU422/423

"O God Beyond All Praising" (Deut)
EL880, S2009, SF2009, VU256, W541

"O Worship the King" (Pss)
B16, C17, E388, EL842, F336, G41, L548, N26, P476, UM73 (PD), VU235

"Sing Praise to God Who Reigns Above" (Pss)
B20, C6, E408, EL871, F343, G645, N6, P483, UM126 (PD), VU216, W528

"Take My Life, and Let It Be" (Phil) (C)
B277/B283, C609, E707, EL583/EL685, G697, L406, P391, N448, UM399 (PD), VU506

"Kum Ba Yah" ("Come By Here") (Phil)
C590, G472, P338, UM494

"Rejoice, the Lord Is King" (Phil)
B197, C699, E481, EL430, F374, G363, L171, N303, P155, UM715 (PD), VU213, W493

"Lord of All Hopefulness" (Phil)
E482, EL765, G683, L469, S2197, SF2197, W568

"My Life Flows On" (Phil, Thanks)
C619, EL763, G821, N476, S2212, SF2212, VU716

"You Are Mine" (Phil, John)
EL581, G177, S2218, SF2218

"As Those of Old Their First Fruits Brought" (John)
B639, E705, G712, P414, VU518

"For the Fruits of This Creation" (John)
B643, C714, E424, EL679, G36, L563, N425, P553, UM97, VU227, W562

"For the Healing of the Nations" (John)
C668, G346, N576, UM428, VU678, W643

"Gather Us In" (John, Thanks,)
C284, EL532, G401, S2236, SF2236, W665

"Eat This Bread" (John, Comm.)
C414, EL472, G527, N788, UM628, VU466, W734

"You Satisfy the Hungry Heart" (John, Comm.)
C429, EL484, G523, P521, UM629, VU478, W736

"Let All Things Now Living" (Thanks.)
B640, C717, EL881, F389, G37, L557, P554, S2008, VU242

Additional Contemporary Suggestions

"We Bring the Sacrifice of Praise" (Deut)
S2031, SF2031, SP1

"Blessed Be Your Name" (Deut, Thanks.)
M163, WS3002

"You Are Good" (Pss)
AH4018, M124, WS3014

"In the Lord I'll Be Ever Thankful" (Pss)
G654, S2195, SF2195

"Hallelujah" ("Your Love Is Amazing") (Pss, John)
M118, WS3027

"Wait for the Lord" (Phil)
EL262, G90, VU22, WS3049

"Alleluia" (John)
B223, C106, F361, N765, SP108, UM186

"Eat This Bread" (John, Comm.)
C414, EL472, G527, N788, UM628, VU466, W734

"Halle, Halle, Halleluja" (John, Thanks.)
C41, EL172, G591, N236, S2026, SF2026, VU958

"Let Us Be Bread" (John, Comm.)
S2260, SF2260

"Fill My Cup, Lord" (John, Comm.)
C351, F481, UM641 (refrain only), WS3093

"I Thank You, Jesus" (Thanks.)
AH4079, C116, N41, WS3037

Vocal Solos

"Maybe the Rain" (Deut, John)
    V-5 (2)   p. 27

"Thanks to God" (Thanks.)
    V-8   p. 296

Anthems

"Jubilate Deo" (Pss)
Dan R. Edwards; Choristers Guild CGA-1278
SAT, piano and opt. Orff instrument

"Think on These Things" (Phil)
Beth A. Elston; Choristers Guild CGA-1387
SATB, piano

Other Suggestions

Visuals:
   O   Produce, harvest, basket, altar, bricks, manacles
   P   Praise, singing, sheep, gates
   E   Rejoicing, Phil. 4:6, praying hands, Christ, Phil. 4:7
   G   Jesus teaching, loaves, John 6:27, manna, John 6:35
Call to Worship: WS3148. "There's a Spirit of Love" (Phil)
Prayers: WSL55, WSL169, and C771 (John)
Prayer: N858 or WSL203 (Deut., Thanks.)
Offertory Prayer: WSL153. "Exalted one, we joyfully" (Pss)

COMMON ENGLISH BIBLE
STUDY BIBLES FOR EVERY AGE

The Common English Bible translation is the most readable and reliable available. It is not a revision or a paraphrase; it is a translation from the original biblical languages.

Our study Bibles provide readers with age-appropriate resources, informed by the best in modern biblical scholarship, inviting people to engage with scripture as they grow in their faith.

The CEB Study Bible

With hundreds of articles and thousands of notes—all written by leading biblical scholars—plus 21 full-color, indexed maps; cross-references; and other in-text maps, charts, and pictures, The CEB Study Bible gives you the tools, illustrations, and explanations to make informed decisions about the meaning of the Bible.

INTRODUCING

The CEB Student Bible is by and for young people and invites them into deeper forms of personal and social holiness. The book introductions, more than 400 articles, and group activities were written by biblical scholars with experience in youth ministry. Prayers written by teens are also included throughout.

Deep Blue Kids Bible

Ideal for children 7 to 12, this interactive Bible includes four-color icons, notes and devotionals, and illustrations throughout. Three life-like characters—Edgar, Kat, and Asia—walk readers through the Bible as kids discover what it means to their lives.

Readable, Reliable, Relevant

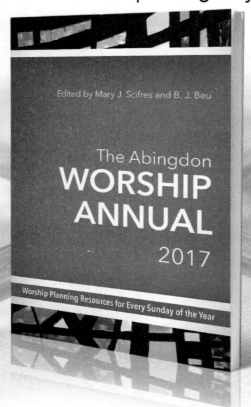

2013

Isaiah 2:1-5

[1]This is what Isaiah, Amoz's son, saw concerning Judah and Jerusalem.

[2] In the days to come
   the mountain of the LORD's house
   will be the highest of the mountains.
   It will be lifted above the hills;
      peoples will stream to it.

[3] Many nations will go and say,
   "Come, let's go up to the LORD's mountain,
      to the house of Jacob's God
         so that he may teach us his ways
         and we may walk in God's paths."
   Instruction will come from Zion;
      the LORD's word from Jerusalem.

[4] God will judge between the nations,
      and settle disputes of mighty nations.
   Then they will beat their swords into iron plows
      and their spears into pruning tools.
   Nation will not take up sword against nation;
      they will no longer learn how to make war.

[5] Come, house of Jacob,
      let's walk by the LORD's light.

Psalm 122 (G400, N705, P235, UM845)

[1]I rejoiced with those who said to me, / "Let's go to the LORD's house!" / [2]Now our feet are standing / in your gates, Jerusalem!

[3]Jerusalem is built like a city / joined together in unity. / [4]That is where the tribes go up— / the LORD's tribes! / It is the law for Israel / to give thanks there to the LORD's name / [5]because the thrones of justice are there— / the thrones of the house of David!

[6]Pray that Jerusalem has peace: / "Let those who love you have rest. / [7]Let there be peace on your walls; / let there be rest on your fortifications." / [8]For the sake of my family and friends, / I say, "Peace be with you, Jerusalem." / [9]For the sake of the / LORD our God's house / I will pray for your good.

Romans 13:11-14

[11]As you do all this, you know what time it is. The hour has already come for you to wake up from your sleep. Now our salvation is nearer than when we first had faith. [12]The night is almost over, and the day is near. So let's get rid of the actions that belong to the darkness and put on the weapons of light. [13]Let's behave appropriately as people who live in the day, not in partying and getting drunk, not in sleeping around and obscene behavior, not in fighting and obsession. [14]Instead, dress yourself with the Lord Jesus Christ, and don't plan to indulge your selfish desires.

Matthew 24:36-44

[36]"But nobody knows when that day or hour will come, not the heavenly angels and not the Son. Only the Father knows. [37]As it was in the time of Noah, so it will be at the coming of the Human One. [38]In those days before the flood, people were eating and drinking, marrying and giving in marriage, until the day Noah entered the ark. [39]They didn't know what was happening until the flood came and swept them all away. The coming of the Human One will be like that. [40]At that time there will be two men in the field. One will be taken and the other left. [41]Two women will be grinding at the mill. One will be taken and the other left. [42]Therefore, stay alert! You don't know what day the Lord is coming. [43]But you understand that if the head of the house knew at what time the thief would come, he would keep alert and wouldn't allow the thief to break into his house. [44]Therefore you also should be prepared, because the Human One will come at a time you don't know."

Primary Hymns and Songs for the Day
"We Are Called" (Isa) (O)
  EL720, G749, S2172, SF2172
"You, Lord, Are Both Lamb and Shepherd" (Isa)
  G274, SF2102, VU210, WS3043
"I Want to Walk as a Child of the Light" (Isa, Rom)
  E490, EL815, G377, UM206, W510
    S-2   #91. Desc.
"Watchman, Tell Us of the Night" (Rom)
  E640, G97, N103, P20
"Wake, Awake, for Night Is Flying" (Rom, Matt)
  E61, EL436, G349, L31, P17, UM720 (PD), VU711, W371
    H-3   Chr-174, 203; Org-172
"Come, Thou Long-Expected Jesus" (Rom, Matt) (C)
  B77, C125, E66, EL254, F168, G82/83, L30, N122, P1/2,
  UM196 (PD), VU2, W364
    H-3   Hbl-46; Chr-26, 134; Desc-53; Org-56
    S-1   #168-71. Various treatments
    V-1 p. 5 or V-10 p. 11. Vocal solo

Additional Hymn Suggestions
"We've a Story to Tell to the Nations" (Isa)
  B586, C484, F659, UM569 (PD)
"O God of Every Nation" (Isa)
  C680, E607, EL713, G756, L416, P289, UM435, VU677
"Let There Be Light" (Isa)
  UM440, VU679, W653
"O Day of Peace That Dimly Shines" (Isa)
  C711, E597, EL711, G373, P450, UM729, VU682, W654
"O Day of God, Draw Nigh" (Isa)
  B623, C700, E601, N611, P452, UM730 (PD), VU688 and
  VU689 (Fr.)
"O Holy City, Seen of John" (Isa, Pss)
  E582/583, G374, N613, P453, UM726, VU709
"Lead Me, Guide Me" (Isa, Rom, Advent)
  C583, EL768, G740, S2214, SF2214
"Awake, My Soul, and with the Sun" (Isa, Rom)
  E11, EL557 (PD), G663, L269, P456
"Send Your Word" (Isa, Matt)
  N317, UM195
"All Who Love and Serve Your City" (Isa, Matt)
  C670, E570/E571, EL724, G351, L436, P413, UM433, W621
"Come, We That Love the Lord" (Isa, Matt)
  B525, E392, N379, UM732, VU715, W552
"Marching to Zion" (Isa, Matt)
  AH4153, B524, C707, EL625, F550, N382, UM733 (PD),
  VU714
"Welcome" ("Let Us Build a House") (Pss)
  EL641, G301, WS3152
"*Dona Nobis Pacem*" (Pss)
  C297, E712, EL753, G752, UM376 (PD)
"When Morning Gilds the Skies" (Rom)
  B221, C100, E427, EL853 (PD), F322, G667, L546, N86,
  P487, UM185, VU339 (Fr.), W675
"Awake, O Sleeper" (Rom)
  E547, EL452, UM551, VU566, W586
"People, Look East" (Rom, Matt)
  C142, EL248, G105, P12, UM202, VU9, W359
"My Lord, What a Morning" (Rom, Matt)
  C708, EL438 (PD), G352, P449, UM719, VU708
"O Come, O Come, Emmanuel" (Matt)
  B76, C119, E56, EL257, F169, G88, L34 (PD), N116, P9,
  UM211, VU1(Fr.), W357
"Savior of the Nations, Come" (Matt)
  E54, EL263, G102, P14 (PD), UM214, W372

"O Lord, How Shall I Meet You?" (Matt)
  EL241, G104, L23, N102, P11, VU31
"Soon and Very Soon" (Matt) (C)
  B192, EL439, G384, UM706
"Let All Mortal Flesh Keep Silence" (Advent, Comm.)
  B80, C124, E324, EL490, F166, G347, L198, N345, P5,
  UM626 (PD), VU473 (Fr.), W523

Additional Contemporary Suggestions
"How Great Is Our God" (Isa)
  M117, WS3003
"Marvelous Light" (Isa)
  M249
"Come Now, O Prince of Peace" (Isa, Matt)
  EL247, G103, S2232, SF2232
"We Are Marching" ("*Siyahamba*") (Isa, Matt)
  C442, EL866, G853, N526, S2235-ab, SF2235-ab, VU646
"Here I Am to Worship" (Isa, Matt, Advent)
  M116, WS3177
"I Will Enter His Gates" (Pss)
  S2270, SF2270, SP168
"In the Lord I'll Be Ever Thankful" (Pss)
  G654, S2195, SF2195
"Blessed Be Your Name" (Rom)
  M163, WS3002
"Salvation Is Here" (Rom)
  M242
"There's Something about That Name" (Matt)
  B177, C115, F227, SP89, UM171
"Wait for the Lord" (Matt, Advent)
  EL262, G90, VU22, WS3049
"Days of Elijah" (Matt, Thanks.)
  M139, WS3186

Vocal Solos
"Peace, Perfect Peace" (Isa, Pss)
  V-5 (1)   p. 69
"My Lord, What a Morning" (Rom, Matt, Advent)
  V-3 (1)   p. 39
  V-7   p. 68

Anthems
"Where the Promise Shines" (Isa, Pss)
Arr. Joel Raney; Hope C5613
Two-part mixed, piano, opt. handbells

"Processional on 'Let All Mortal Flesh Keep Silence'" (Advent)
Arr. Robert A. Hobby; MorningStar MSM-50-1950
SATB, brass, handbells, and organ

Other Suggestions
Visuals:
  O   Mountain/hills/nations, paths, scales/justice, light
  P   Ps 122:1, feet/gates, Jerusalem, worship, wall/tower
  E   Alarm clock, dawn, dark/light, armor, Rom 13:14
  G   Clock, angels, Christ, Noah/ark/flood, one in field,
Introit: C583, EL768, G740, S2214, SF2214. "Lead Me, Guide
  Me" (Matt, Advent)
Call to Worship: N823 (Advent)
Advent Candle Response: C128 or G85 (Advent)

2013

Isaiah 11:1-10

[1]A shoot will grow up from the stump of Jesse;
  a branch will sprout from his roots.
[2]The LORD's spirit will rest upon him,
  a spirit of wisdom and understanding,
  a spirit of planning and strength,
  a spirit of knowledge and fear of the LORD.
[3]He will delight in fearing the LORD.
He won't judge by appearances,
  nor decide by hearsay.
[4]He will judge the needy with righteousness,
  and decide with equity for those who suffer in the land.
He will strike the violent with the rod of his mouth;
  by the breath of his lips he will kill the wicked.
[5]Righteousness will be the belt around his hips,
  and faithfulness the belt around his waist.
[6]The wolf will live with the lamb,
  and the leopard will lie down with the young goat;
  the calf and the young lion will feed together,
  and a little child will lead them.
[7]The cow and the bear will graze.
  Their young will lie down together,
  and a lion will eat straw like an ox.
[8]A nursing child will play over the snake's hole;
  toddlers will reach right over the serpent's den.
[9]They won't harm or destroy anywhere on my holy mountain.
  The earth will surely be filled with the knowledge of the
     LORD,
  just as the water covers the sea.
[10]On that day, the root of Jesse will stand as a signal to the peoples. The nations will seek him out, and his dwelling will be glorious.

Psalm 72:1-7, 18-19 (G149, N667, P205, UM795)

[1]God, give your judgments to the king. / Give your righteousness to the king's son. / [2]Let him judge your people with righteousness / and your poor ones with justice. / [3]Let the mountains bring peace to the people; / let the hills bring righteousness. / [4]Let the king bring justice to people who are poor; / let him save the children of those who are needy, / but let him crush oppressors! / [5]Let the king live as long as the sun, / as long as the moon, / generation to generation. / [6]Let him fall like rain upon fresh-cut grass, / like showers that water the earth. / [7]Let the righteous flourish throughout their lives, / and let peace prosper until the moon is no more. . . .
[18]Bless the LORD God, the God of Israel— / the only one who does wondrous things! / [19]Bless God's glorious name forever; / let his glory fill all the earth! / Amen and Amen!

Romans 15:4-13

[4]Whatever was written in the past was written for our instruction so that we could have hope through endurance and through the encouragement of the scriptures. [5]May the God of endurance and encouragement give you the same attitude toward each other, similar to Christ Jesus' attitude. [6]That way you can glorify the God and Father of our Lord Jesus Christ together with one voice.
[7]So welcome each other, in the same way that Christ also welcomed you, for God's glory. [8]I'm saying that Christ became a servant of those who are circumcised for the sake of God's truth, in order to confirm the promises given to the ancestors, [9]and so that the Gentiles could glorify God for his mercy. As it is written,
  Because of this I will confess you among the Gentiles,
    and I will sing praises to your name.
[10]And again, it says,
  Rejoice, Gentiles, with his people.
[11]And again,
  Praise the Lord, all you Gentiles,
    and all the people should sing his praises.
[12]And again, Isaiah says,
  There will be a root of Jesse,
    who will also rise to rule the Gentiles.
    The Gentiles will place their hope in him.
[13]May the God of hope fill you with all joy and peace in faith so that you overflow with hope by the power of the Holy Spirit.

Matthew 3:1-12

[1]In those days John the Baptist appeared in the desert of Judea announcing, [2]"Change your hearts and lives! Here comes the kingdom of heaven!" [3]He was the one of whom Isaiah the prophet spoke when he said:
  The voice of one shouting in the wilderness,
    "Prepare the way for the Lord;
    make his paths straight."
[4]John wore clothes made of camel's hair, with a leather belt around his waist. He ate locusts and wild honey.
[5]People from Jerusalem, throughout Judea, and all around the Jordan River came to him. [6]As they confessed their sins, he baptized them in the Jordan River. [7]Many Pharisees and Sadducees came to be baptized by John. He said to them, "You children of snakes! Who warned you to escape from the angry judgment that is coming soon? [8]Produce fruit that shows you have changed your hearts and lives. [9]And don't even think about saying to yourselves, Abraham is our father. I tell you that God is able to raise up Abraham's children from these stones. [10]The ax is already at the root of the trees. Therefore, every tree that doesn't produce good fruit will be chopped down and tossed into the fire. [11]I baptize with water those of you who have changed your hearts and lives. The one who is coming after me is stronger than I am. I'm not worthy to carry his sandals. He will baptize you with the Holy Spirit and with fire. [12]The shovel he uses to sift the wheat from the husks is in his hands. He will clean out his threshing area and bring the wheat into his barn. But he will burn the husks with a fire that can't be put out."

Primary Hymns and Songs for the Day

"Hail to the Lord's Anointed" (Isa, Pss, Rom) (O)
C140, E616, EL311, G149, L87, N104, P205, UM203, VU30
H-3   Hbl-16, 22, 68; Chr-101; Desc-37
S-1   #114. Desc.
        #115. Harm.

"Lo, How a Rose E'er Blooming" (Isa)
B78, C160, E81, EL272, F174, G129, L58, N127, P48 (PD),
UM216, VU8, W374
H-3   Chr-129; Org-38
S-2   #56-57. Various treatments

"O Morning Star, How Fair and Bright" (Isa, Rom)
C105, E497, EL308, G827, L76, N158, P69, UM247, VU98
H-3   Chr-147; Desc-104; Org-183

"Wild and Lone the Prophet's Voice" (Matt)
G163, P409, S2089, SF2089

"O Come, O Come, Emmanuel" (Isa) (C)
B76, C119, E56, EL257, F169, G88, L34 (PD), N116, P9,
UM211, VU1 (Fr.), W357
H-3   Hbl-14, 79; Chr-141; Org-168
S-1   #342. Handbell accompaniment

Additional Hymn Suggestions

"Isaiah the Prophet Has Written of Old" (Isa)
G77, N108, P337, VU680

"Who Would Think That What Was Needed" (Isa)
G138, N153

"I Come with Joy" (Isa, Comm.)
B371, C420, E304, EL482, G515, N349, P507, UM617,
VU477, W726

"Soon and Very Soon" (Isa)
B192, EL439, G384, UM706, S-2 #187. Piano arr.

"O Day of Peace That Dimly Shines" (Isa)
C711, E597, EL711, G373, P450, UM729, VU682, W654

"O Day of God, Draw Nigh" (Isa)
B623, C700, E601, N611, P452, UM730 (PD), VU688 and
VU689 (Fr.)

"Come, Thou Almighty King" (Isa, Pss)
B247, C27, E365, EL408, F341, G2, L522, N275, P139, UM61
(PD), VU314, W487

"Come, Thou Long-Expected Jesus" (Isa, Rom, Matt)
B77, C125, E66, EL254, F168, G82/83, L30, N122, P1/2,
UM196 (PD), VU2, W364

"Savior of the Nations, Come" (Isa, Rom)
E54, EL263, G102, P14 (PD), UM214, W372

"Blessed Be the God of Israel" (Isa, Matt)
C135, E444, EL250/552, G109, P602, UM209, VU901

"*Toda la Tierra*" ("All Earth Is Waiting") (Isa, Matt)
C139, EL266, N121, UM210, VU5

"The Church of Christ, in Every Age" (Pss)
B402, C475, EL729, G320, L433, N306, P421, UM589,
VU601, W626

"Jesus Shall Reign" (Pss, Rom)
B587, C95, E544, EL434, F238, G265, L530, N157, P423,
UM157 (PD), VU330, W492

"O For a World" (Rom)
C683, G372, N575, P386, VU697

"I Greet Thee, Who My Sure Redeemer Art" (Rom)
G624, N251, P457, VU393

"Jesus, the Very Thought of Thee" (Rom)
C102, E642, EL754, G629, L316, N507, P310, UM175

"Hope of the World" (Rom)
C538, E472, G734, L493, N46, P360, UM178, VU215

"Help Us Accept Each Other" (Rom)
C487, G754, N388, P358, UM560, W656

"Lord of All Hopefulness" (Rom)
E482, EL765, G683, L469, S2197, SF2197, W568

"God Almighty, We Are Waiting" (Rom, Matt, Advent)
WS3047

"On Jordan's Bank the Baptist's Cry" (Matt)
E76, EL249, G96, L36, N115, P10, W356, VU20

"Come, Holy Ghost, Our Souls Inspire" (Matt)
E503/504, L472/473, N268, G278, P125, UM651, VU201

"There's a Voice in the Wilderness" (Matt)
E75, EL255, N120, VU18

Additional Contemporary Suggestions

"I've Got Peace Like a River" (Isa, Rom)
B418, C530, G623, N478, P368, S2145, VU577

"King of Kings" (Pss, Advent)
B234, S2075, SF2075, SP94, VU167

"The King of Glory Comes" (Pss, Advent)
B127, S2091, SF2091, W501

"Holy Spirit, Come to Us" (Pss, Matt)
EL406, G281, S2118, SF2118, W473

"Glorify Thy Name" (Rom)
B249, S2016, SF2016, SP19

"Song of Hope" ("*Canto de Esperanza*") (Rom)
G765, P432, S2186, VU424

"Grace Alone" (Rom)
M100, S2162, SF2162

"Spirit Song" (Rom, Matt)
C352, SP134, UM347

"Alleluia" (Matt)
B223, C106, F361, N765, SP108, UM186

"Refiner's Fire" (Matt)
M50

"Prepare Ye the Way" ("You Reign on High") (Matt)
M275

Vocal Solos

"In the First Light" (Isa, Rom, Advent)
V-5 (1)   p. 28

"Come, Thou Long-Expected Jesus" (Rom)
V-1   p. 5
V-10   p. 11

Anthems

"Lo, How a Rose E'er Blooming" (Isa)
Arr. Howard Helvey; Beckenhorst BP2048
SATB, piano

"Come, Thou Long-Expected Jesus" (SOCM8) (Isa, Rom, Matt)
Arr. Michael Cox; Augsburg 9781451499032
TTBB a cappella with bongos and conga drum

Other Suggestions

Visuals:
O   Stump/branch/roots, lamp, scales, belt, named
     animals, child, asp, adder's den, mountain/sea,
     nations
P   Crown, scales, mountains/hills, poor/needy, sun/
     moon, rain, lunar eclipse, Ps 72:18, 19
E   Bible/OT, circle, welcome, nations/Christ, stump/
     root
G   Baptism, ax/root/fire, sandals, fork/wheat/chaff/fire
Introit: C121, G95, UM207, W369. "Prepare the Way of the
Lord" (Matt)
Canticle: C126. "The Peaceful Realm" (Isa)

201³

Isaiah 35:1-10

¹The desert and the dry land will be glad;
    the wilderness will rejoice and blossom like the crocus.
²They will burst into bloom,
    and rejoice with joy and singing.
They will receive the glory of Lebanon,
    the splendor of Carmel and Sharon.
They will see the LORD's glory,
    the splendor of our God.
³Strengthen the weak hands,
    and support the unsteady knees.
⁴Say to those who are panicking:
    "Be strong! Don't fear!
    Here's your God,
        coming with vengeance;
        with divine retribution
    God will come to save you."
⁵Then the eyes of the blind will be opened,
    and the ears of the deaf will be cleared.
⁶Then the lame will leap like the deer,
    and the tongue of the speechless will sing.
Waters will spring up in the desert,
    and streams in the wilderness.
⁷The burning sand will become a pool,
    and the thirsty ground, fountains of water.
The jackals' habitat, a pasture;
    grass will become reeds and rushes.
⁸A highway will be there.
    It will be called The Holy Way.
The unclean won't travel on it,
    but it will be for those walking on that way.
Even fools won't get lost on it;
⁹   no lion will be there,
    and no predator will go up on it.
None of these will be there;
    only the redeemed will walk on it.
¹⁰The LORD's ransomed ones will return and enter Zion with
        singing,
    with everlasting joy upon their heads.
Happiness and joy will overwhelm them;
    grief and groaning will flee away.

Luke 1:46b-55

⁴⁶ᵇ "With all my heart I glorify the Lord!
⁴⁷In the depths of who I am I rejoice in God my savior.
⁴⁸He has looked with favor on the low status of his servant.
    Look! From now on, everyone will consider me highly
        favored
⁴⁹   because the mighty one has done great things for me.
    Holy is his name.
⁵⁰ He shows mercy to everyone,
        from one generation to the next,
        who honors him as God.
⁵¹ He has shown strength with his arm.
    He has scattered those with arrogant thoughts and proud
        inclinations.
⁵² He has pulled the powerful down from their thrones
        and lifted up the lowly.

⁵³ He has filled the hungry with good things
        and sent the rich away empty-handed.
⁵⁴ He has come to the aid of his servant Israel,
        remembering his mercy,
⁵⁵ just as he promised to our ancestors,
        to Abraham and to Abraham's descendants forever."

James 5:7-10

⁷Therefore, brothers and sisters, you must be patient as you wait for the coming of the Lord. Consider the farmer who waits patiently for the coming of rain in the fall and spring, looking forward to the precious fruit of the earth. ⁸You also must wait patiently, strengthening your resolve, because the coming of the Lord is near. ⁹Don't complain about each other, brothers and sisters, so that you won't be judged. Look! The judge is standing at the door! ¹⁰Brothers and sisters, take the prophets who spoke in the name of the Lord as an example of patient resolve and steadfastness.

Matthew 11:2-11

²Now when John heard in prison about the things Jesus was doing, he sent word by his disciples to Jesus, asking, ³"Are you the one who is to come, or should we look for another?" ⁴Jesus responded, "Go, report to John what you hear and see. ⁵*Those who were blind are able to see.* Those who were crippled are walking. People with skin diseases are cleansed. Those *who were deaf now hear. Those who were dead are raised up. The poor have good news proclaimed to them.* ⁶Happy are those who don't stumble and fall because of me."

⁷When John's disciples had gone, Jesus spoke to the crowds about John: "What did you go out to the wilderness to see? A stalk blowing in the wind? ⁸What did you go out to see? A man dressed up in refined clothes? Look, those who wear refined clothes are in royal palaces. ⁹What did you go out to see? A prophet? Yes, I tell you, and more than a prophet. ¹⁰He is the one of whom it is written: *Look, I'm sending my messenger before you, who will prepare your way before you.*

¹¹"I assure you that no one who has ever been born is greater than John the Baptist. Yet whoever is least in the kingdom of heaven is greater than he."

Primary Hymns and Songs for the Day

"Come, Thou Long-Expected Jesus" (Jas) (O)
  B77, C125, E66, EL254, F168, G82/83, L30, N122, P1/2,
  UM196 (PD), VU2, W364
    H-3   Hbl-46; Chr-26, 134; Desc-53; Org-56
    S-1   #168-71. Various treatments
"Word of God, Come Down on Earth" (Matt)
  E633, EL510, UM182, W513
"Prepare the Way of the Lord" (Matt)
  C121, G95, UM207, W369
"My Soul Gives Glory to My God" (Luke) (C)
  C130, EL251, G99, N119, P600, UM198, VU899
    H-3   Chr-139, 145; Desc-77
    S-1   #241-42. Orff arr. and desc.

Additional Hymn Suggestions

"Awake! Awake, and Greet the New Morn" (Isa)
  C138, EL242, G107, N107, W360
"Lift Up Your Heads, Ye Mighty Gates" (Isa)
  B128, C129, E436, F239, G93, N117, P8, UM213 (PD), W363
"Lo, How a Rose E'er Blooming" (Isa)
  B78, C160, E81, EL272, F174, G129, L58, N127, P48 (PD),
  UM216, VU8, W374
"I Want to Walk as a Child of the Light" (Isa, Jas)
  E490, EL815, G377, UM206, W510
"It Came upon the Midnight Clear" (Isa, Jas, Matt)
  B93, C153, E89, EL282, F197, G123, L54, N131, P38, UM218
  (PD), VU44, W400
"Jesus Shall Reign" (Isa, Luke, Matt)
  B587, C95, E544, EL434, F238, G265, L530, N157, P423,
  UM157 (PD), VU330, W492
"Hail to the Lord's Anointed" (Isa, Matt)
  C140, E616, EL311, G149, L87, N104, P205, UM203, VU30
"Good Christian Friends, Rejoice" (Isa, Matt)
  B96, C164, E107 (PD), EL288, F177, G132, L55, N129, P28,
  UM224, VU35, W391
"Thou Didst Leave Thy Throne" (Isa, Matt, Advent)
  B121, F170, S2100, SF2100
"Canticle of the Turning" (Luke)
  EL723, G100
"I'll Praise My Maker While I've Breath" (Luke)
  B35, C20, E429 (PD), G806, P253, UM60, VU867
"Tell Out, My Soul" (Luke)
  B81, E437/E438, UM200, W534
"To a Maid Engaged to Joseph" (Luke)
  G98, P19, UM215, VU14
"The Snow Lay on the Ground" (Luke)
  E110, G116, S2093, P57
"The Virgin Mary Had a Baby Boy" (Luke)
  AH4037, S2098, VU73
"Blessed Be the God of Israel" (Luke, Matt)
  C135, E444, EL250/552, G109, P602, UM209, VU901
"In the Cross of Christ I Glory" (Jas)
  B554, C207, E441, EL324, F251, G213, L104, N193, P84,
  UM295
"All Who Love and Serve Your City" (Jas)
  C670, E570/E571, EL724, G351, L436, P413, UM433, W621
"Be Still, My Soul" (Jas)
  C566, F77, G819, N488, UM534, VU652
"Watchman, Tell Us of the Night" (Jas)
  E640, G97, N103, P20
"Prepare the Way, O Zion" (Jas)
  EL264, G106, L26, P13, VU882
"Once in Royal David's City" (Matt)
  C165, EL269, G140, N45, P49, UM250 (PD), VU62, W402

"Wake, Awake, for Night Is Flying" (Matt)
  E61, EL436, G349, L31, P17, UM720 (PD), VU711, W371
"Wild and Lone the Prophet's Voice" (Matt, Advent)
  G163, P409, S2089, SF2089

Additional Contemporary Suggestions

"Trading My Sorrows" (Isa)
  M75, WS3108
"All Who Are Thirsty" (Isa, Advent)
  M159
"Give Thanks" (Isa, Luke)
  C528, G647, S2036, SF2036, SP170
"Awesome in This Place" (Isa, Luke)
  M36
"While We Are Waiting, Come" (Jas)
  G92, SP130
"Forever" (Jas, Luke)
  M68, WS3023
"Shout to the North" (Luke)
  G319, M99, WS3042
"Praise to the Lord" (Luke)
  EL844, S2029, SF2029, VU835
"Shout to the Lord" (Luke)
  EL821, M16, S2074, SF2074; V-3 (2) p. 32 Vocal solo
"Your Grace Is Enough (Luke)
  M191, WS3106
"You Are My All in All" (Luke, Matt)
  G519, SP220, WS3040
"Here I Am to Worship" (Matt)
  M116, WS3177
"Emmanuel, Emmanuel" (Matt)
  B82, C134, SP75, UM204
"Prepare Ye the Way" ("You Reign on High") (Matt)
  M275

Vocal Solos

"God Will Make a Way" (with "He Leadeth Me") (Isa)
  V-3 (2)   p. 9
"Prepare Thyself, Zion" (Isa, Advent)
  V-9   p. 2

Anthems

"There Is No Rose" (Luke)
Conner Koppin; MorningStar MSM-50-1121
SATB divisi, a cappella

"God's Mother Be" (Luke)
Matthew Culloton; MorningStar MSM-50-0075
SATB divisi, harp, piano, or guitar

Other Suggestions

Visuals:
  O   Blooms, healing, singing, river/stream, oasis, spring
  P   Mary, joy, arm/scatter, toppled throne, feeding, chest
  E   Second Coming, farmer/cross, gavel, scales, doors
  G   John, prison, Jesus with men, Matt 11:5 imagery
Introit: N142. "*Manglakat na Kita sa Belen*" ("Let Us Even Now
  Go to Bethlehem") (Luke, Advent)
Canticle: UM199. "Canticle of Mary" ("Magnificat") (Luke)
Movement or dance can enhance Luke 1 songs and readings.

2013

Isaiah 7:10-16

[10]Again the LORD spoke to Ahaz: [11]"Ask a sign from the LORD your God. Make it as deep as the grave or as high as heaven."

[12]But Ahaz said, "I won't ask; I won't test the LORD."

[13]Then Isaiah said, "Listen, house of David! Isn't it enough for you to be tiresome for people that you are also tiresome before my God? [14]Therefore, the Lord will give you a sign. The young woman is pregnant and is about to give birth to a son, and she will name him Immanuel. [15]He will eat butter and honey, and learn to reject evil and choose good. [16]Before the boy learns to reject evil and choose good, the land of the two kings you dread will be abandoned.

Psalm 80:1-7, 17-19 (G355, N672, P206, UM801)

[1]Shepherd of Israel, listen! / You, the one who leads Joseph as if he were a sheep. / You, who are enthroned upon the winged heavenly creatures. / Show yourself [2]before Ephraim, Benjamin, and Manasseh! / Wake up your power! / Come to save us! / [3]Restore us, God! / Make your face shine so that we can be saved!

[4]LORD God of heavenly forces, / how long will you fume against your people's prayer? / [5]You've fed them bread made of tears; / you've given them tears to drink three times over! / [6]You've put us at odds with our neighbors; / our enemies make fun of us. / [7]Restore us, God of heavenly forces! / Make your face shine so that we can be saved! . . .

[17]Let your hand be with the one on your right side— / with the one whom you secured as your own— / [18]then we will not turn away from you! / Revive us so that we can call on your name. / [19]Restore us, LORD God of heavenly forces! / Make your face shine so that we can be saved!

Romans 1:1-7

[1]From Paul, a slave of Christ Jesus, called to be an apostle and set apart for God's good news. [23]God promised this good news about his Son ahead of time through his prophets in the holy scriptures. His Son was descended from David. [4]He was publicly identified as God's Son with power through his resurrection from the dead, which was based on the Spirit of holiness. This Son is Jesus Christ our Lord. [5]Through him we have received God's grace and our appointment to be apostles. This was to bring all Gentiles to faithful obedience for his name's sake. [6]You who are called by Jesus Christ are also included among these Gentiles.

[7]To those in Rome who are dearly loved by God and called to be God's people.

Grace to you and peace from God our Father and the Lord Jesus Christ.

Matthew 1:18-25

[18]This is how the birth of Jesus Christ took place. When Mary his mother was engaged to Joseph, before they were married, she became pregnant by the Holy Spirit. [19]Joseph her husband was a righteous man. Because he didn't want to humiliate her, he decided to call off their engagement quietly. [20]As he was thinking about this, an angel from the Lord appeared to him in a dream and said, "Joseph son of David, don't be afraid to take Mary as your wife, because the child she carries was conceived by the Holy Spirit. [21]She will give birth to a son, and you will call him Jesus, because he will save his people from their sins." [22]Now all of this took place so that what the Lord had spoken through the prophet would be fulfilled:

[23]   *Look! A virgin will become pregnant and give birth to a son,*
     And they will call him, Emmanuel.

(Emmanuel means "God with us.")

[24]When Joseph woke up, he did just as an angel from God commanded and took Mary as his wife. [25]But he didn't have sexual relations with her until she gave birth to a son. Joseph called him Jesus.

Primary Hymns and Songs for the Day

"Emmanuel, Emmanuel" (Isa, Matt) (O)
B82, C134, SP75, UM204

"O Come, O Come, Emmanuel" (Isa, Matt) (O)
B76, C119, E56, EL257, F169, G88, L34 (PD), N116, P9,
UM211, VU1(Fr.), W357
H-3   Hbl-14, 79; Chr-141; Org-168
S-1   #342. Handbell accompaniment

"Once in Royal David's City" (Isa, Matt)
C165, EL269, G140, N45, P49, UM250 (PD), VU62, W402
H-3   Hbl-83; Chr-68, 156; Desc-57; Org-63
S-1   #182-84. Various treatments

"To a Maid Engaged to Joseph" (Isa, Matt)
G98, P19, UM215, VU14

"Joseph Dearest, Joseph Mine" (Matt)
N105, S2099, SF2099

"The King of Glory Comes" (Matt)
B127, S2091, SF2091, W501

"Hark! the Herald Angels Sing" (Matt) (C)
B88, C150, E87, EL270, F184, G119, L60, N144, P31, UM240
(PD), VU48, W387
H-3   Hbl-26, 67; Chr-91; Desc-75; Org-89
S-1   #234-36. Harms. and desc.
V-1   p. 13. Vocal solo

Additional Hymn Suggestions

"It Came upon the Midnight Clear" (Isa)
B93, C153, E89, EL282, F197, G123, L54, N131, P38, UM218
(PD), VU44, W400

"I Want to Walk as a Child of the Light" (Isa, Pss, Advent)
E490, EL815, G377, UM206, W510

"*Toda la Tierra*" ("All Earth Is Waiting") (Isa, Matt)
C139, EL266, N121, UM210, VU5

"Savior of the Nations, Come" (Isa, Matt)
E54, EL263, G102, P14 (PD), UM214, W372

"Lo, How a Rose E'er Blooming" (Isa, Matt)
B78, C160, E81, EL272, F174, G129, L58, N127, P48 (PD),
UM216, VU8, W374

"Lead Me, Guide Me" (Pss, Advent)
C583, EL768, G740, S2214, SF2214

"People, Look East" (Pss, Advent)
C142, EL248, G105, P12, UM202, VU9, W359

"Alleluia, Alleluia" (Rom)
B170, E178, G240, P106, UM162, VU179, W441

"Rise, Shine, You People" (Rom, Advent)
EL665, L393, UM187

"What Child Is This" (Rom)
B118, C162, E115, EL296, F180, G145, L40, N148, P53,
UM219 (PD), VU74, W411

"While Shepherds Watched Their Flocks" (Rom)
C154, E94/E95, F175, G117/118, P58, UM236, VU75, W382

"O Come, All Ye Faithful" (Rom, Matt)
B89, C148, E83, EL283, F193, G133, L45, N135, P41, UM234
(PD), VU60 (Fr.), W392

"Come, Thou Long-Expected Jesus" (Matt)
B77, C125, E66, EL254, F168, G82/83, L30, N122, P1/2,
UM196 (PD), VU2, W364

"Angels from the Realms of Glory" (Matt)
B94, C149, E93, EL275, F190, G143, L50, N126, P22, UM220
(PD), VU36, W377

"O Little Town of Bethlehem" (Matt)
B86, C144, E78/79, EL279, F178, G121, L41, N133, P43/44,
UM230, VU64, W386

"Go, Tell It on the Mountain" (Matt)
B95, C167, E99, EL290, F205, G136, L70, N154, P29, UM251,
VU43, W397

"Like a Child" (Matt)
C133, S2092, SF2092, VU366

"Rise Up, Shepherd, and Follow" (Matt)
G135, P50, S2096, SF2096, VU70

"O Holy Spirit, Root of Life" (Matt, Advent)
C251, EL399, N57, S2121, SF2121, VU379

Additional Contemporary Suggestions

"All Hail King Jesus" (Isa, Matt)
S2069, SF2069, SP63

"Jesus, Name above All Names" (Isa, Matt)
S2071, SF2071, SP76

"Glory in the Highest" (Isa, Matt)
M231

"Shine, Jesus, Shine" (Pss)
B579, EL671, G192, S2173, SF2173, SP142;
V-3 (2) p. 48 Vocal solo

"Refresh My Heart" (Rom, Advent)
M49

"Let the Peace of God Reign" (Rom)
M87

"There's Something about That Name" (Matt)
B177, C115, F227, SP89, UM171

"Jesus, the Light of the World" (Matt, Advent)
WS3056 (See also AH4038, G127, N160)

"Lord, I Lift Your Name on High" (Matt, Christmas)
AH4071, EL857, M2, S2088, SF2088

"Come and Behold Him" (Matt, Advent)
M18

"Jesus, We Crown You with Praise" (Matt)
M24

Vocal Solos

"Behold! A Virgin Shall Conceive" and
"O Thou That Tellest Good Tidings to Zion" (Isa, Matt)
V-2

"Glory Hallelujah to de New-Born King" (Isa, Matt)
V-7   p. 80

Anthems

"I Wonder as I Wander" (SOCM17) (Matt)
Arr. Kyle Haugen; Augsburg 9781451499032
TTBB, piano, opt. cello

"The Hands That First Held Mary's Child" (Matt)
Dan Forrest; Beckenhorst BP1928
SATB, piano

Other Suggestions

Visuals:
O   Test, pregnant woman, baby, Immanuel, curds/honey
P   Shepherd, seat, anger/ tears/laughter, returning
E   Letter, Bible, resurrection, Rom 1:7b
G   Pregnant Mary, Joseph, Spirit symbol, birth, angel
Emmanuel (God with us), "Jesus"

Introit: N137. "*Hitsuji wa nemureri*" ("Sheep Fast Asleep") (Isa)
Response: C158. "Her Baby, Newly Breathing" (Matt)
Advent Candle Response: C128 or G85(Advent)
Prayer: WSL11. "Radiant Morning Star" (Matt)

Isaiah 9:2-7

[2]The people walking in darkness have seen a great light.
　　On those living in a pitch-dark land, light has dawned.
[3]You have made the nation great;
　　you have increased its joy.
They rejoiced before you as with joy at the harvest,
　　as those who divide plunder rejoice.
[4]As on the day of Midian, you've shattered the yoke that
　　　　burdened them,
　　the staff on their shoulders,
　　and the rod of their oppressor.
[5]Because every boot of the thundering warriors,
　　and every garment rolled in blood
　　will be burned, fuel for the fire.
[6]A child is born to us, a son is given to us,
　　and authority will be on his shoulders.
　　He will be named
　　Wonderful Counselor, Mighty God,
　　Eternal Father, Prince of Peace.
[7]There will be vast authority and endless peace
　　for David's throne and for his kingdom,
　　establishing and sustaining it
　　with justice and righteousness
　　now and forever.
The zeal of the LORD of heavenly forces will do this.

Psalm 96 (G304, N684, P216/217, UM815)

[1]Sing to the LORD a new song! / Sing to the LORD, all the earth! / [2]Sing to the LORD! Bless his name! / Share the news of his saving work every single day! / [3]Declare God's glory among the nations; / declare his wondrous works among all people / [4]because the LORD is great and so worthy of praise. / He is awesome beyond all other gods / [5]because all the gods of the nations are just idols, / but it is the LORD who created heaven! / [6]Greatness and grandeur are in front of him; / strength and beauty are in his sanctuary.

[7]Give to the LORD, all families of the nations— / give to the LORD glory and power! / [8]Give to the LORD the glory due his name! / Bring gifts! / Enter his courtyards! / [9]Bow down to the LORD in his holy splendor! / Tremble before him, all the earth!

[10]Tell the nations, "The LORD rules! / Yes, he set the world firmly in place; / it won't be shaken. / He will judge all people fairly." / [11]Let heaven celebrate! Let the earth rejoice! / Let the sea and everything in it roar! / [12]Let the country-side and everything in it celebrate! / Then all the trees of the forest too / will shout out joyfully / [13]before the LORD because he is coming! / He is coming to establish justice on the earth! / He will establish justice in the world rightly. / He will establish justice among all people fairly.

Titus 2:11-14

[11]The grace of God has appeared, bringing salvation to all people. [12]It educates us so that we can live sensible, ethical, and godly lives right now by rejecting ungodly lives and the desires of this world. [13]At the same time we wait for the blessed hope and the glorious appearance of our great God and savior Jesus Christ. [14]He gave himself for us in order to rescue us from every kind of lawless behavior, and cleanse a special people for himself who are eager to do good actions.

Luke 2:1-20

[1]In those days Caesar Augustus declared that everyone throughout the empire should be enrolled in the tax lists. [2]This first enrollment occurred when Quirinius governed Syria. [3]Everyone went to their own cities to be enrolled. [4]Since Joseph belonged to David's house and family line, he went up from the city of Nazareth in Galilee to David's city, called Bethlehem, in Judea. [5]He went to be enrolled together with Mary, who was promised to him in marriage and who was pregnant. [6]While they were there, the time came for Mary to have her baby. [7]She gave birth to her firstborn child, a son, wrapped him snugly, and laid him in a manger, because there was no place for them in the guestroom.

[8]Nearby shepherds were living in the fields, guarding their sheep at night. [9]The Lord's angel stood before them, the Lord's glory shone around them, and they were terrified. [10]The angel said, "Don't be afraid! Look! I bring good news to you—wonderful, joyous news for all people. [11]Your savior is born today in David's city. He is Christ the Lord. [12]This is a sign for you: you will find a newborn baby wrapped snugly and lying in a manger." [13]Suddenly a great assembly of the heavenly forces was with the angel praising God. They said, [14]"Glory to God in heaven, and on earth peace among those whom he favors."

[15]When the angels returned to heaven, the shepherds said to each other, "Let's go right now to Bethlehem and see what's happened. Let's confirm what the Lord has revealed to us." [16]They went quickly and found Mary and Joseph, and the baby lying in the manger. [17]When they saw this, they reported what they had been told about this child. [18]Everyone who heard it was amazed at what the shepherds told them. [19]Mary committed these things to memory and considered them carefully. [20]The shepherds returned home, glorifying and praising God for all they had heard and seen. Everything happened just as they had been told.

Primary Hymns and Songs for the Day

"Angels We Have Heard on High" (Luke) (O)
   B100, C155, E96, EL289, F192, G113, L71, P23, N125,
   UM238, VU38 (Fr.), W376
       H-3   Hbl-47; Chr-31; Desc-43; Org-45
"On Christmas Night" (Isa, Titus, Luke)
   EL274, G112, N143, WS3064
"Silent Night, Holy Night" (Luke)
   B91, C145, E111, EL281, F195, G122, L65, N134, P60,
   UM239 (PD), VU67 (Fr.), W379
       H-3   Hbl-92; Chr-171; Desc-99; Org-159
       S-1   #322. Desc.
              #323. Guitar/autoharp chords
       S-2   #167. Handbell arr.
"Joy to the World" (Titus, Luke) (C)
   B87, C143, E100, EL267, F171, G134/266, L39, N132, P40,
   UM246 (PD), VU59, W399
       S-1   #19-20. Trumpet descs.
"Go, Tell It on the Mountain" (Luke) (C)
   B95, C167, E99, EL290, F205, G136, L70, N154, P29, UM251,
   VU43, W397
       H-3   Hbl-17; Chr-73; Desc-45; Org-46

Additional Hymn Suggestions

"Born in the Night, Mary's Child" (Isa)
   G158, N152, P30, VU95
"Break Forth, O Beauteous Heavenly Light" (Isa)
   B114 (PD), E91, F207, G130, N140, P26, UM223, VU83
"O Morning Star, How Fair and Bright" (Isa)
   C105, E497, EL308, G827, L76, N158, P69, UM247, VU98
"Come Now, O Prince of Peace" (Isa)
   EL247, G103, S2232, SF2232
"It Came upon the Midnight Clear" (Isa, Luke) (O)
   B93, C153, E89, EL282, F197, G123, L54, N131, P38, UM218
   (PD), VU44, W400
"Angels from the Realms of Glory" (Isa, Luke)
   B94, C149, E93, EL275, F190, G143, L50, N126, P22, UM220
   (PD), VU36, W377
"Hark! the Herald Angels Sing" (Isa, Luke) (O)
   B88, C150, E87, EL270, F184, G119, L60, N144, P31, UM240
   (PD), VU48, W387
"Love Has Come" (Isa, Titus, Luke, Christmas)
   EL292, G110, WS3059
"In the Bleak Midwinter" (Pss, Titus, Luke)
   E112, EL294, G144, N128, P36, UM221 (PD), VU55
"On This Day Earth Shall Ring" (Pss, Titus, Luke) (O)
   E92, G141, P46, UM248 (PD)
"We Sing of Your Glory" (Pss, Luke)
   EL849, S2011, SF2011
"Away in a Manger" (Luke)
   B103, C147, E101, EL277, F185/F187, G114/115, L67, N124,
   P24/P25, UM217, VU69, W378
"What Child Is This" (Luke)
   B118, C162, E115, EL296, F180, G145, L40, N148, P53,
   UM219 (PD), VU74, W411
"*Niño Lindo*" ("Child So Lovely") (Luke)
   UM222
"Infant Holy, Infant Lowly" (Luke)
   B106, C163, EL276, F194, G128, L44, P37, UM229, VU58,
   W393
"O Come, All Ye Faithful" (Luke)
   B89, C148, E83, EL283, F193, G133, L45, N135, P41, UM234
   (PD), VU60 (Fr.), W392

"'Twas in the Moon of Wintertime" (Luke)
   C166, E114, EL284, G142, L72, N151, P61, UM244, VU71,
   W380
"Once in Royal David's City" (Luke)
   C165, EL269, G140, N45, P49, UM250 (PD), VU62, W402
"Like a Child" (Luke)
   C133, S2092, SF2092, VU366
"Rise Up, Shepherd, and Follow" (Luke)
   G135, P50, S2096, SF2096, VU70
"One Holy Night in Bethlehem" (Luke)
   S2097, SF2097
"Glory to God in the Highest" (Luke)
   S2276, SF2276
"Still, Still, Still" (Luke)
   G124, P47, VU47, WS3066

Additional Contemporary Suggestions

"His Name Is Wonderful" (Isa)
   B203, F230, SP90, UM174
"How Majestic Is Your Name" (Isa)
   C63, G613, S2023, SF2023, SP14
"Jesus, Name above All Names" (Isa)
   S2071, SF2071, SP76
"King of Kings" (Isa)
   B234, S2075, SF2075, SP94, VU167
"How Great Is Our God" (Isa, Pss)
   M117, WS3003
"Jesus, Jesus, Oh, What a Wonderful Child" (Isa, Luke)
   EL297, G126, N136, WS3060
"Sing Alleluia to the Lord" (Titus)
   B214, C32, S2258, SF2258, SP93
"Lord, I Lift Your Name on High" (Luke)
   AH4071, EL857, M2, S2088, SF2088
"Bethlehem" (Luke)
   AH4033, WS3053

Vocal Solos

"O Holy Night" (Luke)
   V-8   p. 93
"Sing Noel!" (Luke)
   V-11   p. 13

Anthems

"In a Lowly Manger Born" (SOCM25) (Luke)
Arr. Christopher Aspaas; Augsburg 9781451499032
TTBB, piano, opt. percussion

"South African Gloria" (Luke)
William Bradley Roberts; MorningStar MSM-50-1215
SATB, percussion

Other Suggestions

Visuals:
   O   Darkness/light, joy, yoke, boots, fire, child, names
   P   New song, nations, glory, Ps. 96:10a, gavel, nature
            images
   E   Jesus, Second Coming, crucifix
   G   Tax register, manger scene, shepherds, angels, Luke
            2:14
Introit: C146. "From Heaven Above" (Luke)
Response: N758 or N756, UM72. "Gloria" (Luke)
Communion Hymn: EL487, WS3170. "What Feast of Love"
   (same tune as "What Child Is This")

Isaiah 52:7-10

[7]How beautiful upon the mountains
    are the feet of a messenger
    who proclaims peace,
    who brings good news,
    who proclaims salvation,
    who says to Zion, "Your God rules!"
[8]Listen! Your lookouts lift their voice;
    they sing out together!
    Right before their eyes they see the LORD returning to
        Zion.
[9]Break into song together, you ruins of Jerusalem!
The LORD has comforted his people and has redeemed
        Jerusalem.
[10]The LORD has bared his holy arm in view of all the nations;
    all the ends of the earth have seen our God's victory.

Psalm 98 (G276/371, N686, P218-219, UM818)

[1]Sing to the LORD a new song / because he has done wonderful things! / His own strong hand and his own holy arm / have won the victory! / [2]The LORD has made his salvation widely known; / he has revealed his righteousness / in the eyes of all the nations. / [3]God has remembered his loyal love / and faithfulness to the house of Israel; / every corner of the earth has seen our God's salvation. / [4]Shout triumphantly to the LORD, all the earth! / Be happy! / Rejoice out loud! / Sing your praises! / [5]Sing your praises to the LORD with the lyre— / with the lyre and the sound of music. / [6]With trumpets and a horn blast, / shout triumphantly before the LORD, the king! / [7]Let the sea and everything in it roar; / the world and all its inhabitants too. / [8]Let all the rivers clap their hands; / let the mountains rejoice out loud altogether [9]before the LORD / because he is coming to establish justice on the earth! / He will establish justice in the world rightly; / he will establish justice among all people fairly.

Hebrews 1:1-4, (5-12)

[1]In the past, God spoke through the prophets to our ancestors in many times and many ways. [2]In these final days, though, he spoke to us through a Son. God made his Son the heir of everything and created the world through him. [3]The Son is the light of God's glory and the imprint of God's being. He maintains everything with his powerful message. After he carried out the cleansing of people from their sins, he sat down at the right side of the highest majesty. [4]And the Son became so much greater than the other messengers, such as angels, that he received a more important title than theirs.

[5]After all, when did God ever say to any of the angels:
    You are my Son.
        Today I have become your Father?
  Or, even,
    I will be his Father,
        and he will be my Son?
[6]But then, when he brought his firstborn into the world, he
    said,
    All of God's angels must worship him.
[7]He talks about the angels:
    He's the one who uses the spirits for his messengers
        and who uses flames of fire as ministers.
[8]But he says to his Son,
    God, your throne is forever
        and your kingdom's scepter is a rod of justice.

[9]   *You loved righteousness and hated lawless behavior.*
        That is why God, your God,
        has anointed you with oil instead of your companions.
[10]And he says,
    You, Lord, laid the earth's foundations in the beginning,
        and the heavens are made by your hands.
[11]   *They will pass away,*
        but you remain.
    They will all wear out like old clothes.
[12]   *You will fold them up like a coat.*
    They will be changed like a person changes clothes,
        but you stay the same,
        and the years of your life won't come to an end.

John 1:1-14

[1]In the beginning was the Word
    and the Word was with God
    and the Word was God.
[2] The Word was with God in the beginning.
[3] Everything came into being through the Word,
    and without the Word
    nothing came into being.
  What came into being
[4]   through the Word was life,
    and the life was the light for all people.
[5] The light shines in the darkness,
    and the darkness doesn't extinguish the light.
[6]A man named John was sent from God. [7]He came as a witness to testify concerning the light, so that through him everyone would believe in the light. [8]He himself wasn't the light, but his mission was to testify concerning the light.
[9] The true light that shines on all people
    was coming into the world.
[10] The light was in the world,
    and the world came into being through the light,
        but the world didn't recognize the light.
[11] The light came to his own people,
    and his own people didn't welcome him.
[12] But those who did welcome him,
    those who believed in his name,
    he authorized to become God's children,
[13]   born not from blood
    nor from human desire or passion,
    but born from God.
[14] The Word became flesh
    and made his home among us.
  We have seen his glory,
    glory like that of a father's only son,
        full of grace and truth.

Primary Hymns and Songs for the Day

"Joy to the World" (Isa, Pss) (O)
    B87, C143, E100, EL267, F171, G134/266, L39, N132, P40, UM246 (PD), VU59, W399
        H-3   Hbl-8, 29; Chr-119; Desc-15; Org-6
        S-1   #19-20. Trumpet descs.

"O Come, All Ye Faithful" (John) (O)
    B89, C148, E83, EL283, F193, L45, N135, P41, UM234 (PD), VU60 (Fr.), W392
        H-3   Hbl-78; Desc-12; Org-2
        S-1   #7-13. Various treatments

"Good Christian Friends, Rejoice" (Isa)
    B96, C164, E107 (PD), EL288, F177, G132, L55, N129, P28, UM224, VU35, W391
        H-3   Hbl-19, 30; Chr-83; Desc-55; Org-62
        S-1   #180. Rhythm instr. acc.

"Go, Tell It on the Mountain" (Isa)
    B95, C167, E99, EL290, F205, G136, L70, N154, P29, UM251, VU43, W397
        H-3   Hbl-17, 28, 61; Chr-73; Desc-45; Org-46

"Love Came Down at Christmas" (John)
    B109, E84, N165, UM242

"Jesus, Name above All Names" (John)
    S2071, SF2071, SP76

"I Want to Walk as a Child of the Light" (John) (C)
    E490, EL815, G377, UM206, W510
        S-2   #91. Desc.

"Hark! the Herald Angels Sing" (Heb, John) (C)
    B88, C150, E87, EL270, F184, G119, L60, N144, P31, UM240 (PD), VU48, W387
        H-3   Hbl-26, 67; Chr-91; Desc-75; Org-89
        S-1   #234-36. Harm. and desc.

Additional Hymn Suggestions

"Wake, Awake, for Night Is Flying" (Isa)
    E61, EL436, G349, L31, P17, UM720 (PD), VU711, W371

"On This Day Earth Shall Ring" (Isa, John, Comm.)
    E92, G141, P46, UM248 (PD)

"It Came upon the Midnight Clear" (Heb)
    B93, C153, E89, EL282, F197, G123, L54, N131, P38, UM218 (PD), VU44, W400

"What Child Is This" (Heb)
    B118, C162, E115, EL296, F180, G145, L40, N148, P53, UM219 (PD), VU74, W411

"Angels from the Realms of Glory" (Heb)
    B94, C149, E93, EL275, F190, G143, L50, N126, P22, UM220 (PD), VU36, W377

"Infant Holy, Infant Lowly" (Heb)
    B106, C163, EL276, F194, G128, L44, P37, UM229, VU58, W393

"Angels We Have Heard on High" (Heb)
    B100, C155, E96, EL289, F192, G113, L71, P23, N125, UM238, VU38 (Fr.), W376

"The Snow Lay on the Ground" (Heb, Christmas)
    E110, G116, S2093, P57

"Of the Father's Love Begotten" (John)
    B251, C104, E82, EL295, F172 (PD), G108, L42, N118, P309, UM184, VU61, W398

"Womb of Life" (John)
    C14, G3, N274, S2046, SF2046

"Mothering God, You Gave Me Birth" (John)
    C83, EL735, G7, N467, S2050, SF2050, VU320

"O Holy Spirit, Root of Life" (John)
    C251, EL399, N57, S2121, SF2121, VU379

"Love Has Come" (John, Christmas)
    EL292, G110, WS3059

"Thou Didst Leave Thy Throne" (John, Christmas)
    B121, F170, S2100, SF2100

"In the Bleak Midwinter" (Christmas)
    E112, EL294, G144, N128, P36, UM221 (PD), VU55

"'Twas in the Moon of Wintertime" (Christmas)
    C166, E114, EL284, G142, L72, N151, P61, UM244, VU71, W380

"Deck Thyself, My Soul, With Gladness" (Christmas, Comm.)
    E339, EL488/EL489, G514, P506, UM612 (PD), VU463

Additional Contemporary Suggestions

"Welcome to Our World" (Isa, Heb, John, Christmas)
    WS3067, V-5 (1) p. 34 Vocal solo

"Our God Reigns" (Isa)
    SP64

"Shout to the Lord" (Pss)
    EL821, M16, S2074, SF2074; V-3 (2) p. 32 Vocal solo

"Sing unto the Lord a New Song" (Pss)
    SP23

"Jesus, the Light of the World" (Heb, John)
    WS3056 (See also AH4038, G127, N160)

"Jesus, Jesus, Oh, What a Wonderful Child" (Heb, Christmas)
    EL297, G126, N136, WS3060

"Shine, Jesus, Shine" (John)
    B579, EL671, G192, S2173, SF2173, SP142;
    V-3 (2) p. 48 Vocal solo

"In Christ Alone" ("My Hope Is Found") (John)
    M138, WS3105

"Here I Am to Worship" (John) (O)
    M116, WS3177

"Shine on Us" (John)
    M19

"Forevermore" (John)
    M229

"Glory in the Highest" (John, Christmas)
    M231

Vocal Solos

"Love Came Down at Christmas" (John)
    V-8   p. 90

"This Christmas Morning" (Christmas)
    V-5 (1)   p. 41

Anthems

"Jesus, What a Wonderful Child" (Heb, Christmas)
Arr. Rollo Dilworth; Daybreak Music 08745948
SATB, piano

"Hark! the Herald Angels Sing" (Heb, John)
Arr. Dan Forrest; Beckenhorst BP-2051
SATB, piano (4-hands) or organ, opt. handbells

Other Suggestions

Visuals:
    O   Mountains, feet, sheet music, singing, ruins, nations
    P   Singing, hand, creation, musical instruments, Ps 98:11, 14
    E   Angels, scepter/crown/royal cloak, oil, flames
    G   Light/darkness, Christ candle, John 1:1, 5, 14
Introit: G158, N152, P30, VU95, st. 1–2. "Born in the Night, Mary's Child" (John, Christmas)

Ecclesiastes 3:1-13

[1]There's a season for everything
and a time for every matter under the heavens:
[2] a time for giving birth and a time for dying,
a time for planting and a time for uprooting what was planted,
[3] a time for killing and a time for healing,
a time for tearing down and a time for building up,
[4] a time for crying and a time for laughing,
a time for mourning and a time for dancing,
[5] a time for throwing stones and a time for gathering stones,
a time for embracing and a time for avoiding embraces,
[6] a time for searching and a time for losing,
a time for keeping and a time for throwing away,
[7] a time for tearing and a time for repairing,
a time for keeping silent and a time for speaking,
[8] a time for loving and a time for hating,
a time for war and a time for peace.

[9]What do workers gain from all their hard work? [10]I have observed the task that God has given human beings. [11]God has made everything fitting in its time, but has also placed eternity in their hearts, without enabling them to discover what God has done from beginning to end.

[12]I know that there's nothing better for them but to enjoy themselves and do what's good while they live. [13]Moreover, this is the gift of God: that all people should eat, drink, and enjoy the results of their hard work.

Psalm 8 (G25, N624, P162/163, UM743)

[1]LORD, our Lord, how majestic / is your name throughout the earth! / You made your glory higher than heaven! / [2]From the mouths of nursing babies / you have laid a strong foundation / because of your foes, / in order to stop vengeful enemies. / [3]When I look up at your skies, / at what your fingers made— / the moon and the stars / that you set firmly in place— / [4]what are human beings / that you think about them; / what are human beings / that you pay attention to them? / [5]You've made them only slightly less than divine, / crowning them with glory and grandeur. / [6]You've let them rule over your handiwork, / putting everything under their feet— / [7]all sheep and all cattle, / the wild animals too, / [8]the birds in the sky, / the fish of the ocean, / everything that travels the pathways of the sea. / [9]LORD, our Lord, how majestic is your name throughout the earth!

Revelation 21:1-6a

[1]Then I saw a new heaven and a new earth, for the former heaven and the former earth had passed away, and the sea was no more. [2]I saw the holy city, New Jerusalem, coming down out of heaven from God, made ready as a bride beautifully dressed for her husband. [3]I heard a loud voice from the throne say, "Look! God's dwelling is here with humankind. He will dwell with them, and they will be his peoples. God himself will be with them as their God. [4]He will wipe away every tear from their eyes. Death will be no more. There will be no mourning, crying, or pain anymore, for the former things have passed away." [5]Then the one seated on the throne said, "Look! I'm making all things new." He also said, "Write this down, for these words are trustworthy and true."

[6a]Then he said to me, "All is done. I am the Alpha and the Omega, the beginning and the end."

Matthew 25:31-46

[31]"Now when the Human One comes in his majesty and all his angels are with him, he will sit on his majestic throne. [32]All the nations will be gathered in front of him. He will separate them from each other, just as a shepherd separates the sheep from the goats. [33]He will put the sheep on his right side. But the goats he will put on his left.

[34]"Then the king will say to those on his right, 'Come, you who will receive good things from my Father. Inherit the kingdom that was prepared for you before the world began. [35]I was hungry and you gave me food to eat. I was thirsty and you gave me a drink. I was a stranger and you welcomed me. [36]I was naked and you gave me clothes to wear. I was sick and you took care of me. I was in prison and you visited me.'

[37]"Then those who are righteous will reply to him, 'Lord, when did we see you hungry and feed you, or thirsty and give you a drink? [38]When did we see you as a stranger and welcome you, or naked and give you clothes to wear? [39]When did we see you sick or in prison and visit you?'

[40]"Then the king will reply to them, 'I assure you that when you have done it for one of the least of these brothers and sisters of mine, you have done it for me.'

[41]"Then he will say to those on his left, 'Get away from me, you who will receive terrible things. Go into the unending fire that has been prepared for the devil and his angels. [42]I was hungry and you didn't give me food to eat. I was thirsty and you didn't give me anything to drink. [43]I was a stranger and you didn't welcome me. I was naked and you didn't give me clothes to wear. I was sick and in prison, and you didn't visit me.'

[44]"Then they will reply, 'Lord, when did we see you hungry or thirsty or a stranger or naked or sick or in prison and didn't do anything to help you?' [45]Then he will answer, 'I assure you that when you haven't done it for one of the least of these, you haven't done it for me.' [46]And they will go away into eternal punishment. But the righteous ones will go into eternal life."

Primary Hymns and Songs for the Day

"O God, Our Help in Ages Past" (Eccl) (O)
B74, C67, E680, EL632, F370, G687, L320, N25, P210,
UM117 (PD), VU806, W579
> H-3   Hbl-33, 80; Chr-60, 143; Desc-93; Org-132
> S-1   #293-96. Various treatments

"Hymn of Promise" (Eccl)
C638, G250. N433, UM707, VU703

"In His Time" (Eccl)
B53, S2203, SF2203, SP39

"How Great Thou Art" (Pss)
AH4015, B10, C33, EL856, F2, G625, L532, N35, P467,
UM77, VU238 (Fr.)

"O Holy City, Seen of John" (Rev)
E582/583, G374, N613, P453, UM726, VU709
> H-3   Chr-139, 145; Desc-77
> S-1   #241-42. Orff arr. and desc.

"Cuando el Pobre" ("When the Poor Ones") (Matt)
C662, EL725, G762, P407, UM434, VU702

"Here Am I" (Matt) (C)
C654, S2178, SF2178

Additional Hymn Suggestions

"Great Is Thy Faithfulness" (Eccl)
B54, C86, EL733, F98, G39, N423, P276, UM140, VU288

"O God, in a Mysterious Way" (Eccl)
B73, E677, F603, G30, L483, N412, P270

"For the Beauty of the Earth" (Eccl)
B44, C56, E416, EL879, F1, G14, L561, P473, N28, UM92
(PD), VU226, W557

"Sing Praise to God Who Reigns Above" (Eccl)
B20, C6, E408, EL871, F343, G645, N6, P483, UM126 (PD),
VU216, W528

"By Gracious Powers" (Eccl)
E695/696, EL626, G818, N413, P342, UM517, W577

"For the Fruits of This Creation" (Pss) (O) *(Alternate Tune #688)*
B643, C714, E424, EL679, G36, L563, N425, P553, UM97,
VU227, W562

"Glorious Things of Thee Are Spoken" (Pss)
B398, C709, E522 (or 523), EL647, F376, G81, L358, N307,
P446, UM731 (PD)

"Rejoice! Rejoice, Believers" (Rev)
E68, EL244, G362, L25, P15

"This Is a Day of New Beginnings" (Rev)
B370, C518, N417, UM383, W661

"For the Healing of the Nations" (Rev)
C668, G346, N576, UM428, VU678, W643

"This Is the Feast of Victory" (Rev, Comm.)
E417/418, EL165/EL166/EL167, G513, P594, UM638,
VU904, W458

"Come, Ye Disconsolate" (Rev, Matt)
B67, C502, EL607, SF2132, UM510 (PD)

"All Who Hunger" (Rev, Matt)
C419, EL461, G509, S2126, SF2126, VU460

"Like a Mother Who Has Borne Us" (Matt)
G44, N583

"We Praise You, O God, Our Redeemer" (Matt)
B19, F334, EL870, G612, L241, N420, VU218

"Where Cross the Crowded Ways of Life" (Matt)
C665, E609, EL719, F665, G343, L429, N543, P408, UM427
(PD), VU681

"All Who Love and Serve Your City" (Matt)
C670, E570/E571, EL724, G351, L436, P413, UM433, W621

"Lord God, Your Love Has Called Us Here" (Matt)
EL358, P353, UM579

"Lord, Whose Love Through Humble Service" (Matt)
C461, E610, EL712, L423, P427, UM581, W630

"I Come with Joy" (Matt, New Year, Comm.)
B371, C420, E304, EL482, G515, N349, P507, UM617,
VU477, W726

"Together We Serve" (Matt)
G767, S2175, SF2175

"We Are Called" (Matt, Epiphany)
EL720, G749, S2172, SF2172

"Now It Is Evening" (Matt)
C471, EL572, S2187, SF2187

"In Remembrance of Me" (Matt, Comm.)
B365, C403, G521, S2254

Additional Contemporary Suggestions

"Be Glorified" (Eccl)
M152

"How Majestic Is Your Name" (Pss)
C63, G613, S2023, SF2023, SP14

"How Great Is Our God" (Pss)
M117, WS3003

"Hallelujah" ("Your Love Is Amazing") (Pss)
M118, WS3027

"God of Wonders" (Pss)
M80, WS3034

"God with Us" (Pss)
M252

"There's Something about That Name" (Rev)
B177, C115, F227, SP89, UM171

"Spirit Song" (Rev)
C352, SP134, UM347

"Soon and Very Soon" (Rev)
B192, EL439, G384, UM706, S-2 #187. Piano arr.

"We Will Glorify" (Rev)
B213, S2087, SF2087, SP68

Vocal Solos

"Come to the Water" (Rev, Matt)
WS3114

"Reach Out to Your Neighbor" (Matt)
V-8   p. 372

Anthems

"Come, Ye Disconsolate" (SOCM10) (Rev, Matt)
Arr. Christopher Aspaas; Augsburg 9781451499032
TTBB, piano

"To Everything a Season" (Eccles)
Taylor Davis; Choristers Guild CGA-1347
SATB, piano, opt. oboe

Other Suggestions

Visuals:
> **O**   Clock, birth/death, plant/pluck up, etc.
> **P**   Glory, newborns, fingers, moon/stars, humanity, earth,
> **E**   Earth/space, heaven, bride, throne, wipe tears, Rev 21:5a
> **G**   Second Coming, nations, goats/sheep, feeding, etc.

These lections and ideas may be used on January 1.
Canticle: UM734. "Canticle of Hope" (Rev)
Offertory Prayer: WSL98 (Matt) or WSL105 (Rev)
Litany: C157. "For All Who Give You a Face" (Matt)

Isaiah 63:7-9

[7]I will recount the LORD's faithful acts;
    I will sing the LORD's praises,
    because of all the Lord did for us,
    for God's great favor toward the house of Israel.
    God treated them compassionately
    and with deep affection.
[8]God said, "Truly, they are my people,
    children who won't do what is wrong."
    God became their savior.
[9]During all their distress, God also was distressed,
    so a messenger who served him saved them.
In love and mercy God redeemed them,
    lifting and carrying them throughout earlier times.

Psalm 148 (G16/17, N721, P256, UM861)

[1]Praise the LORD! / Praise the LORD from heaven! / Praise God on the heights! / [2]Praise God, all of you who are his messengers! / Praise God, all of you who comprise his heavenly forces! / [3]Sun and moon, praise God! / All of you bright stars, praise God! / [4]You highest heaven, praise God! / Do the same, you waters that are above the sky! / [5]Let all of these praise the LORD's name / because God gave the command and they were created! / [6]God set them in place always and forever. / God made a law that will not be broken. / [7]Praise the LORD from the earth, / you sea monsters and all you ocean depths! / [8]Do the same, fire and hail, snow and smoke, / stormy wind that does what God says! / [9]Do the same, you mountains, every single hill, / fruit trees, and every single cedar! / [10]Do the same, you animals—wild or tame— / you creatures that creep along and you birds that fly! / [11]Do the same, you kings of the earth and every single person, / you princes and every single ruler on earth! / [12]Do the same, you young men—young women too!— / you who are old together with you who are young! / [13]Let all of these praise the LORD's name / because only God's name is high over all. / Only God's majesty is over earth and heaven. / [14]God raised the strength of his people, / the praise of all his faithful ones— / that's the Israelites, / the people who are close to him. / Praise the LORD!

Hebrews 2:10-18

[10]It was appropriate for God, for whom and through whom everything exists, to use experiences of suffering to make perfect the pioneer of salvation. This salvation belongs to many sons and daughters whom he's leading to glory. [11]This is because the one who makes people holy and the people who are being made holy all come from one source. That is why Jesus isn't ashamed to call them brothers and sisters when he says,
[12]*I will publicly announce your name to my brothers and sisters.*
    I will praise you in the middle of the assembly.
    [13]He also says,
I will rely on him.
    And also,
Here I am with the children whom God has given to me.
    [14]Therefore, since the children share in flesh and blood, he also shared the same things in the same way. He did this to destroy the one who holds the power over death—the devil—by dying. [15]He set free those who were held in slavery their entire lives by their fear of death. [16]Of course, he isn't trying to help angels, but rather he's helping Abraham's descendants. [17]Therefore, he had to be made like his brothers and sisters in every way. This was so that he could become a merciful and faithful high priest in things relating to God, in order to wipe away the sins of the people. [18]He's able to help those who are being tempted, since he himself experienced suffering when he was tempted.

Matthew 2:13-23

[13]When the magi had departed, an angel from the Lord appeared to Joseph in a dream and said, "Get up. Take the child and his mother and escape to Egypt. Stay there until I tell you, for Herod will soon search for the child in order to kill him." [14]Joseph got up and, during the night, took the child and his mother to Egypt. [15]He stayed there until Herod died. This fulfilled what the Lord had spoken through the prophet: *I have called my son out of Egypt.*

[16]When Herod knew the magi had fooled him, he grew very angry. He sent soldiers to kill all the children in Bethlehem and in all the surrounding territory who were two years old and younger, according to the time that he had learned from the magi. [17]This fulfilled the word spoken through Jeremiah the prophet:
[18]   *A voice was heard in Ramah,*
        weeping and much grieving.
        Rachel weeping for her children,
        and she did not want to be comforted,
        because they were no more.

[19]After King Herod died, an angel from the Lord appeared in a dream to Joseph in Egypt. [20]"Get up," the angel said, "and take the child and his mother and go to the land of Israel. Those who were trying to kill the child are dead." [21]Joseph got up, took the child and his mother, and went to the land of Israel. [22]But when he heard that Archelaus ruled over Judea in place of his father Herod, Joseph was afraid to go there. Having been warned in a dream, he went to the area of Galilee. [23]He settled in a city called Nazareth so that what was spoken through the prophets might be fulfilled: He will be called a Nazarene.

Primary Hymns and Songs for the Day

"Hark! the Herald Angels Sing" (Isa, Matt) (O)
B88, C150, E87, EL270, F184, G119, L60, N144, P31, UM240
(PD), VU48, W387
H-3   Hbl-26, 67; Chr-91; Desc-75; Org-89
S-1   #234-36. Harms. and desc.

"O Sing a Song of Bethlehem" (Isa, Heb, Matt)
B120, F208, G159, N51, P308, UM179 (PD)
H-3   Hbl-15, 20, 34, 84; Chr-150; Org-67
S-2   #100-103. Various treatments

"Jesus, the Light of the World" (Isa, Matt, Epiphany)
WS3056 (See also AH4038, G127, N160)

"All Creatures of Our God and King" (Pss) (O)
B27, C22, E400, EL835, F347, G15, L527, N17, P455, UM62,
VU217 (Fr.), W520
H-3   Hbl-44; Chr-21; Desc-66; Org-73
S-1   #198-204. Various treatments

"What Child Is This" (Matt, Christmas, Epiphany) (C)
B118, C162, E115, EL296, F180, G145, L40, N148, P53,
UM219 (PD), VU74, W411
H-3   Hbl-102; Chr-210; Desc-46; Org-47
S-1   #150. Guitar chords

"Joy to the World" (Matt, Christmas, Epiphany) (C)
B87, C143, E100, EL267, F171, G134/266, L39, N132, P40,
UM246 (PD), VU59, W399

Additional Hymn Suggestions

"Great Is Thy Faithfulness" (Isa)
B54, C86, EL733, F98, G39, N423, P276, UM140, VU288

"Children of the Heavenly Father" (Isa)
B55, EL781, F89, L474, N487, UM141

"We Sing of Your Glory" (Isa, Christmas)
EL849, S2011, SF2011

"On Christmas Night" (Isa, Pss, Christmas)
EL274, G112, N143, WS3064

"Love Came Down at Christmas" (Isa, Matt) (C)
B109, E84, N165, UM242

"From All That Dwell below the Skies" (Pss)
B13, C49, E380, G327, L550, N27, P229, UM101 (PD)

"Good Christian Friends, Rejoice" (Pss, Heb, Matt)
B96, C164, E107 (PD), EL288, F177, G132, L55, N129, P28,
UM224, VU35, W391

"O God, We Bear the Imprint of Your Face" (Heb)
C681, G759, N585, P385

"Jesus Entered Egypt" (Heb)
G154

"Holy God, We Praise Thy Name" (Heb) (O)
E366, F385, EL414 (PD), G4, L535, N276, P460, UM79,
VU894 (Fr.), W524

"To God Be the Glory" (Heb)
B4, C72, F363, G634, P485, UM98 (PD)

"At the Name of Jesus" (Heb)
B198, E435, EL416, F351, G264, L179, P148, UM168, VU335,
W499

"Break Forth, O Beauteous Heavenly Light" (Heb, Matt)
B114 (PD), E91, F207, G130, N140, P26, UM223, VU83

"Infant Holy, Infant Lowly" (Heb, Matt)
B106, C163, EL276, F194, G128, L44, P37, UM229, VU58,
W393

"Once in Royal David's City" (Heb, Matt) (O)
C165, EL269, G140, N45, P49, UM250 (PD), VU62, W402

"In Bethlehem a Newborn Boy" (Matt)
E246, G153, P35 (PD), VU77

"Star-Child" (Matt)
S2095, SF2095

"Joseph Dearest, Joseph Mine" (Matt)
N105, S2099, SF2099

"Bethlehem" (Matt, Christmas)
AH4033, WS3053

"Bread of the World" (Comm.)
C387, E301, G499, N346, P502, UM624, VU461

Additional Contemporary Suggestions

"Great Is the Lord" (Isa)
B12, G614, S2022, SF2022, SP30

"The Steadfast Love of the Lord" (Isa)
SP185

"Glory to God" ("Gloria a Dios") (Pss, Christmas)
EL164, G585, S2033, SF2033

"Glory to God in the Highest" (Pss, Christmas)
S2276, SF2276

"We Will Glorify" (Pss)
B213, S2087, SF2087, SP68

"God of Wonders" (Pss)
M80, WS3034

"Let Everything That Has Breath" (Pss)
M59

"Glory in the Highest" (Pss, Christmas)
M231

"You Are My All in All" (Heb)
G519, SP220, WS3040

"You Are My King" ("Amazing Love") (Heb)
M82, WS3102

"The Virgin Mary Had a Baby Boy" (Matt, Christmas)
AH4037, S2098, VU73

"In Christ Alone" (Christmas)
M138, WS3105

Vocal Solos

"Jesus, What a Wonderful Child" (Matt, Christmas)
V-5 (1)   p. 48

"Mary Had a Baby" (Matt, Christmas)
V-7   p. 46

"Sing Noel!" (Christmas)
V-11   p. 13

Anthems

"Good Christian Friends, Rejoice" (Pss, Heb, Matt)
Arr. Trevor Manor; Choristers Guild CGA-1353
Unison/two-part, piano, opt. handbells

"Love Came Down at Christmas" (Matt)
Arr. Matthew Oldman; Hinshaw Music HMC2381
SATB divisi, a cappella

Other Suggestions

Visuals:
O   Salvation history, people, children, Christ
P   Ps. 148;1a, angels, sun/moon/stars, nature imagery
E   Pioneer, crucifix, brothers/sisters, Jesus, manacles
G   Angel/Joseph, escape, Herod/Wise Men, suffering
       children, return, Nazareth

*Today may also be celebrated as Epiphany Sunday using the suggestions
for Jan. 6. If celebrating the New Year, use lections and suggestions
for Dec. 31/Jan. 1.*

Prayer: WSL11. "Radiant Morning Star" (Matt)

Isaiah 60:1-6

¹Arise! Shine! Your light has come;
the Lord's glory has shone upon you.
²Though darkness covers the earth
and gloom the nations,
the Lord will shine upon you;
God's glory will appear over you.
³Nations will come to your light
and kings to your dawning radiance.
⁴Lift up your eyes and look all around:
they are all gathered; they have come to you.
Your sons will come from far away,
and your daughters on caregivers' hips.
⁵Then you will see and be radiant;
your heart will tremble and open wide,
because the sea's abundance will be turned over to you;
the nations' wealth will come to you.
⁶Countless camels will cover your land,
young camels from Midian and Ephah.
They will all come from Sheba,
carrying gold and incense,
proclaiming the Lord's praises.

Psalm 72:1-7, 10-14 (G149, N667, P205, UM795)

¹God, give your judgments to the king. / Give your righteousness to the king's son. / ²Let him judge your people with righteousness / and your poor ones with justice. / ³Let the mountains bring peace to the people; / let the hills bring righteousness. / ⁴Let the king bring justice to people who are poor; / let him save the children of those who are needy, / but let him crush oppressors! / ⁵Let the king live as long as the sun, / as long as the moon, / generation to generation. / ⁶Let him fall like rain upon fresh-cut grass, / like showers that water the earth. / ⁷Let the righteous flourish throughout their lives, / and let peace prosper until the moon is no more. . . .
¹⁰Let the kings of Tarshish and the islands bring tribute; / let the kings of Sheba and Seba present gifts. / ¹¹Let all the kings bow down before him; / let all the nations serve him. / ¹²Let it be so, because he delivers the needy who cry out, / the poor, and those who have no helper. / ¹³He has compassion on the weak and the needy; / he saves the lives of those who are in need. / ¹⁴He redeems their lives from oppression and violence; / their blood is precious in his eyes.

Ephesians 3:1-12

¹This is why I, Paul, am a prisoner of Christ for you Gentiles. ²You've heard, of course, about the responsibility to distribute God's grace, which God gave to me for you, right? ³God showed me his secret plan in a revelation, as I mentioned briefly before (⁴when you read this, you'll understand my insight into the secret plan about Christ). ⁵Earlier generations didn't know this hidden plan that God has now revealed to his holy apostles and prophets through the Spirit. ⁶This plan is that the Gentiles would be coheirs and parts of the same body, and that they would share with the Jews in the promises of God in Christ Jesus through the gospel. ⁷I became a servant of the gospel because of the grace that God showed me through the exercise of his power.
⁸God gave his grace to me, the least of all God's people, to preach the good news about the immeasurable riches of Christ to the Gentiles. ⁹God sent me to reveal the secret plan that had been hidden since the beginning of time by God, who created everything. ¹⁰God's purpose is now to show the rulers and powers in the heavens the many different varieties of his wisdom through the church. ¹¹This was consistent with the plan he had from the beginning of time that he accomplished through Christ Jesus our Lord. ¹²In Christ we have bold and confident access to God through faith in him.

Matthew 2:1-12

¹After Jesus was born in Bethlehem in the territory of Judea during the rule of King Herod, magi came from the east to Jerusalem. ²They asked, "Where is the newborn king of the Jews? We've seen his star in the east, and we've come to honor him."
³When King Herod heard this, he was troubled, and everyone in Jerusalem was troubled with him. ⁴He gathered all the chief priests and the legal experts and asked them where the Christ was to be born. ⁵They said, "In Bethlehem of Judea, for this is what the prophet wrote:
⁶ *You, Bethlehem, land of Judah,*
by no means are you least among the rulers of Judah,
because from you will come one who governs,
who will shepherd my people Israel."
⁷Then Herod secretly called for the magi and found out from them the time when the star had first appeared. ⁸He sent them to Bethlehem, saying, "Go and search carefully for the child. When you've found him, report to me so that I too may go and honor him." ⁹When they heard the king, they went; and look, the star they had seen in the east went ahead of them until it stood over the place where the child was. ¹⁰When they saw the star, they were filled with joy. ¹¹They entered the house and saw the child with Mary his mother. Falling to their knees, they honored him. Then they opened their treasure chests and presented him with gifts of gold, frankincense, and myrrh. ¹²Because they were warned in a dream not to return to Herod, they went back to their own country by another route.

Primary Hymns and Songs for the Day

"Hail to the Lord's Anointed" (Pss) (O)
   C140, E616, EL311, G149, L87, N104, P205, UM203, VU30
"We Three Kings" (Matt, Pss) (O)
   B113, C172, E128, F206, G151, P66, UM254 (PD), W406
      H-3   Chr-208; Org-65
      S-2   #97-98. Various treatments
"O Morning Star, How Fair and Bright" (Isa, Pss, Eph, Matt)
   C105, E497, EL308, G827, L76, N158, P69, UM247, VU98
"Star-Child" (Matt)
   S2095, SF2095
"A Star Shone Bright" (Matt)
   WS3051
"Jesus Shall Reign" (Isa, Pss, Eph) (C)
   B587, C95, E544, EL434, F238, G265, L530, N157, P423,
   UM157 (PD), VU330, W492
"Go, Tell It on the Mountain" (Eph, Christmas) (C)
   B95, C167, E99, EL290, F205, G136, L70, N154, P29, UM251,
   VU43, W397
      H-3   Hbl-17, 28, 61; Chr-73; Desc-45; Org-46

Additional Hymn Suggestions

"Arise, Your Light Is Come" (Isa)
   B83, EL314, G744, N164, P411, VU79
"Awake! Awake, and Greet the New Morn" (Isa)
   C138, EL242, G107, N107, W360
"Break Forth, O Beauteous Heavenly Light" (Isa)
   B114 (PD), E91, F207, G130, N140, P26, UM223, VU83
"Rise, Shine, You People" (Isa)
   EL665, L393, UM187
"Blessed Be the God of Israel" (Isa, Christmas)
   C135, E444, EL250/552, G109, P602, UM209, VU901
"This Little Light of Mine" (Isa)
   N525, UM585 (See also AH4150, EL677, N524)
"We Are Called" (Isa, Pss)
   EL720, G749, S2172, SF2172
"From All That Dwell below the Skies" (Pss)
   B13, C49, E380, G327, L550, N27, P229, UM101 (PD)
"Christ, Whose Glory Fills the Skies" (Eph)
   EL553, F293, G662, L265, P462/463, UM173 (PD), VU336
"Ye Servants of God" (Eph)
   B589, C110, E535, EL825 (PD), F360, G299, N305, P477,
   UM181 (PD), VU342
"Blessed Jesus, at Thy Word" (Eph)
   E440, EL520, G395, N74, P454, UM596 (PD), VU500
"I'm Gonna Live So God Can Use Me" (Eph)
   C614, G700, P369, S2153, VU575
"Joy to the World" (Eph, Matt)
   B87, C143, E100, EL267, F171, G134/266, L39, N132, P40,
   UM246 (PD), VU59, W399
"What Star Is This, with Beams so Bright" (Matt)
   E124, G152, P68, W407
"What Child Is This" (Matt)
   B118, C162, E115, EL296, F180, G145, L40, N148, P53,
   UM219 (PD), VU74, W411
"The First Noel" (Matt)
   B85, C151, E109, EL300, F179, G147, L56, N139, P56,
   UM245 (PD), VU90 (Fr.) and VU91, W408
"Rise Up, Shepherd, and Follow" (Matt)
   G135, P50, S2096, SF2096, VU70
"Love Has Come" (Matt, Epiphany)
   EL292, G110, WS3059
"Angels from the Realms of Glory" (Matt)
   B94, C149, E93, EL275, F190, G143, L50, N126, P22, UM220
   (PD), VU36, W377

"In the Bleak Midwinter" (Matt)
   E112, EL294, G144, N128, P36, UM221 (PD), VU55
"Silent Night, Holy Night" (Matt)
   B91, C145, E111, EL281, F195, G122, L65, N134, P60,
   UM239 (PD), VU67 (Fr.), W379
"Love Came Down at Christmas" (Matt)
   B109, E84, N165, UM242
"On This Day Earth Shall Ring" (Matt)
   E92, G141, P46, UM248 (PD)
"Carol of the Epiphany" (Matt)
   S2094, SF2094
"The Virgin Mary Had a Baby Boy" (Matt)
   AH4037, S2098, VU73
"We Are Marching" (Matt, Epiphany) (C)
   C442, EL866, G853, N526, S2235-ab, SF2235-ab, VU646

Additional Contemporary Suggestions

"Shine, Jesus, Shine" (Isa, Epiphany)
   B579, EL671, G192, S2173, SF2173, SP142;
   V-3 (2) p. 48 Vocal solo
"Mighty to Save" (Isa)
   M246, WS3038
"Shine on Us" (Isa, Epiphany)
   M19
"Holy Spirit, Come to Us" (Pss)
   EL406, G281, S2118, SF2118, W473
"Grace Alone" (Eph)
   M100, S2162, SF2162
"Alleluia" (Matt)
   B223, C106, F361, N765, SP108, UM186
"All Hail King Jesus" (Matt, Epiphany)
   S2069, SF2069, SP63
"Here I Am to Worship" (Matt, Epiphany)
   M116, WS3177
"Come and Behold Him" (Matt, Epiphany)
   M18

Vocal Solos

"The Kings" (Matt, Epiphany)
   V-9   p. 13
"Fit for a King" (Matt, Epiphany)
   V-10   p. 32

Anthems

"In the Bleak Midwinter" (SOCM38) (Matt)
Christopher Aspaas; Augsburg 9781451499032
TTBB, piano

"Silent Night, Holy Night" (Matt)
Arr.Mark Patterson; Choristers Guild CGA-1315
Unison/two-part, piano

Other Suggestions

Visuals:
   O   Light, glory, darkness, daughters/nurses, sea, camels
   P   Scales of justice, Christ, mountains/hills, poor/needy
   E   Manacles, letter, Christ, all nations
   G   Herod, Wise Men, star, Bethlehem, Mary/baby, gifts
These scriptures and ideas can be used on January 1.
Introit: F181, WS3065. "Some Children See Him" (Matt)
Response: C175. "Lovely Star in the Sky" (Matt)
Sung Benediction: WS3062. "Spirit-Child Jesus" (Matt)

Isaiah 42:1-9

[1]But here is my servant, the one I uphold;
    my chosen, who brings me delight.
I've put my spirit upon him;
    he will bring justice to the nations.
[2]He won't cry out or shout aloud
    or make his voice heard in public.
[3]He won't break a bruised reed;
    he won't extinguish a faint wick,
    but he will surely bring justice.
[4]He won't be extinguished or broken
    until he has established justice in the land.
The coastlands await his teaching.
[5]God the LORD says—
    the one who created the heavens,
    the one who stretched them out,
    the one who spread out the earth and its offspring,
    the one who gave breath to its people
    and life to those who walk on it—
[6]I, the LORD, have called you for a good reason.
    I will grasp your hand and guard you,
    and give you as a covenant to the people,
    as a light to the nations,
[7]   to open blind eyes, to lead the prisoners from prison,
    and those who sit in darkness from the dungeon.
[8]I am the LORD;
    that is my name;
    I don't hand out my glory to others
        or my praise to idols.
[9]The things announced in the past—look—they've already
        happened,
    but I'm declaring new things.
    Before they even appear,
    I tell you about them.

Psalm 29 (G10, N638, P180, UM761)

[1]You, divine beings! Give to the LORD— / give to the LORD glory and power! / [2]Give to the LORD the glory due his name! / Bow down to the LORD in holy splendor!

[3]The LORD's voice is over the waters; / the glorious God thunders; / the LORD is over the mighty waters. / [4]The LORD's voice is strong; / the LORD's voice is majestic. / [5]The LORD's voice breaks cedar trees— / yes, the LORD shatters the cedars of Lebanon. / [6]He makes Lebanon jump around like a young bull, / makes Sirion jump around like a young wild ox. / [7]The LORD's voice unleashes fiery flames; / [8]the LORD's voice shakes the wilderness— / yes, the LORD shakes the wilderness of Kadesh. / [9]The LORD's voice convulses the oaks, / strips the forests bare, / but in his temple everyone shouts, "Glory!" / [10]The LORD sits enthroned over the floodwaters; / the LORD sits enthroned—king forever!

[11]Let the LORD give strength to his people! / Let the LORD bless his people with peace!

Acts 10:34-43

[34]Peter said, "I really am learning that God doesn't show partiality to one group of people over another. [35]Rather, in every nation, whoever worships him and does what is right is acceptable to him. [36]This is the message of peace he sent to the Israelites by proclaiming the good news through Jesus Christ: He is Lord of all! [37]You know what happened throughout Judea, beginning in Galilee after the baptism John preached. [38]You know about Jesus of Nazareth, whom God anointed with the Holy Spirit and endowed with power. Jesus traveled around doing good and healing everyone oppressed by the devil because God was with him. [39]We are witnesses of everything he did, both in Judea and in Jerusalem. They killed him by hanging him on a tree, [40]but God raised him up on the third day and allowed him to be seen, [41]not by everyone but by us. We are witnesses whom God chose beforehand, who ate and drank with him after God raised him from the dead. [42]He commanded us to preach to the people and to testify that he is the one whom God appointed as judge of the living and the dead. [43]All the prophets testify about him that everyone who believes in him receives forgiveness of sins through his name."

Matthew 3:13-17

[13]At that time Jesus came from Galilee to the Jordan River so that John would baptize him. [14]John tried to stop him and said, "I need to be baptized by you, yet you come to me?"

[15]Jesus answered, "Allow me to be baptized now. This is necessary to fulfill all righteousness."

So John agreed to baptize Jesus. [16]When Jesus was baptized, he immediately came up out of the water. Heaven was opened to him, and he saw the Spirit of God coming down like a dove and resting on him. [17]A voice from heaven said, "This is my Son whom I dearly love; I find happiness in him."

Primary Hymns and Songs for the Day

"Fairest Lord Jesus" (Isa, Matt) (O)
   B176, C97, E383, EL838, F240, G630, L518, N44, P306,
   UM189 (PD), VU341
         H-3   Hbl-57; Chr-63; Desc-25, 94; Org-22,135
         S-1   #301. Desc.
         S-2   #158. Choral harm.
"When Jesus Came to Jordan" (Isa, Matt)
   P72, EL305, UM252, W697
         H-3   Chr-211
"Wash, O God, Our Sons and Daughters" (Matt)
   C365, EL445, G490, UM605, VU442
         H-3   Hbl-14, 64; Chr-132, 203
         S-2   #22. Desc.
"Spirit of God, Descend upon My Heart" (Matt)
   B245, C265, EL800, F147, G688, L486, N290, P326, UM500
   (PD), VU378
"Take Me to the Water" (Matt, Baptism)
   AH4045, C367, G480, N322, WS3165
"Song of Hope" ("Canto de Esperanza") (Isa) (C)
   G765, P432, S2186, VU424

Additional Hymn Suggestions

"Today We All Are Called to Be Disciples" (Isa)
   G757, P434, VU507
"Jesus Shall Reign" (Isa)
   B587, C95, E544, EL434, F238, G265, L530, N157, P423,
   UM157 (PD), VU330, W492
"Jesus, the Very Thought of Thee" (Isa)
   C102, E642, EL754, G629, L316, N507, P310, UM175
"Breathe on Me, Breath of God" (Isa)
   B241, C254, E508, F161, G286, L488, N292, P316, UM420
   (PD), VU382 (Fr.), W725
"The Church of Christ, in Every Age" (Isa) (C)
   B402, C475, EL729, G320, L433, N306, P421, UM589,
   VU601, W626
"Gather Us In" (Isa)
   C284, EL532, G401, S2236, SF2236, W665
"For the Healing of the Nations" (Isa, Acts)
   C668, G346, N576, UM428, VU678, W643
"O For a Thousand Tongues to Sing" (Isa, Pss) (O)
   B216, C5, E493, EL886, F349, G610, L559, N42, P466, UM57
   (PD), VU326 (See also WS3001)
"I'll Praise My Maker While I've Breath" (Pss) (O)
   B35, C20, E429 (PD), G806, P253, UM60, VU867
"We Meet You, O Christ" (Acts)
   C183, P311, UM257, VU183
"The Strife Is O'er, the Battle Done" (Acts)
   B171, C221, E208, EL366, G236, L135, N242, P119, UM306,
   VU159, W451
"Come, Ye Faithful, Raise the Strain" (Acts)
   C215, E199, EL363, G234, L132, N230, P115, UM315 (PD),
   VU165, W456
"This Is My Song" (Acts)
   C722, EL887, G340, N591, UM437
"Filled with the Spirit's Power" (Acts)
   L160, N266, UM537, VU194
"I Come with Joy" (Acts, Comm.)
   B371, C420, E304, EL482, G515, N349, P507, UM617,
   VU477, W726
"In Christ There Is No East or West" (Acts, Matt)
   B385, C687, E529, EL650 (PD), F685, G317/318, L359,
   N394/N395, P439/P440, UM548, VU606, W659
"On Jordan's Bank the Baptist's Cry" (Acts, Matt)
   E76, EL249, G96, L36, N115, P10, W356, VU20

"Wild and Lone the Prophet's Voice" (Acts, Matt)
   G163, P409, S2089, SF2089
"O Breath of Life" (Acts, Matt)
   C250, UM543, VU202, WS3146
"Sweet, Sweet Spirit" (Matt)
   B243, C261, F159, G408, N293, P398, SP136, UM334
"I Was There to Hear Your Borning Cry" (Matt)
   C75, EL732, G488, N351, S2051, SF2051, VU644
"The Lone, Wild Bird" (Matt)
   P320, S2052, SF2052, VU384
"Loving Spirit" (Matt, Baptism)
   C244, EL397, G293, P323, S2123, VU387
"Wonder of Wonders" (Matt, Baptism)
   C378, G489, N328, P499, S2247
"Baptized in Water" (Matt, Baptism)
   B362, E294, EL456, P492, S2248, W720
"Water, River, Spirit, Grace" (Matt, Baptism)
   C366, N169, S2253, SF2253
"This Is the Spirit's Entry Now" (Matt, Baptism)
   EL448, L195, UM608, VU451, W722

Additional Contemporary Suggestions

"I'm Goin' a Sing When the Spirit Says Sing" (Isa, Matt)
   AH4073, UM333
"Days of Elijah" (Isa)
   M139, WS3186
"Holy" ("Santo") (Isa)
   EL762, G594, S2019, SF2019
"We Are Marching" (Isa)
   C442, EL866, G853, N526, S2235-ab, SF2235-ab, VU646
"Awesome God" (Pss)
   G616, S2040, SF2040, SP11
"Surely the Presence of the Lord" (Matt)
   C263, SP243, UM328; S-2 #200. Stanzas for soloist
"Wade in the Water" (Matt, Baptism)
   AH4046, C371, EL459 (PD), S2107, SF2107

Vocal Solos

"Wash, O God, Our Sons and Daughters" (Matt, Baptism)
   V-5 (1)   p. 64
"This Is De Healin' Water" (Matt, Baptism)
   V-7   p. 52

Anthems

"Wade in the Water" (Matt, Baptism)
Aaron David Miller; Morningstar MSM-50-2613
SATB a cappella

"Take Me to the Water" (Matt, Baptism)
Arr. Rollo Dilworth; Hal Leonard 08745366
SATB, piano

Other Suggestions

Visuals:
   O   Christ, dove, scales, bent reed, lighted wick, earth
   P   Ps 29:1-2, worship, sea, storm, cedars, calf, ox, flames
   E   Jesus/baptism/dove, healing, risen Christ, witness
   G   John baptizing Jesus, dove, Matt 3:17
Call to Worship: WS3044. "Make Way" (Isa)
Baptism Readings: C370, C372, C377, UM253

Isaiah 49:1-7

[1]Listen to me, coastlands;
    pay attention, peoples far away.
The Lord called me before my birth,
    called my name when I was in my mother's womb.
[2]He made my mouth like a sharp sword,
    and hid me in the shadow of God's own hand.
He made me a sharpened arrow,
        and concealed me in God's quiver,
[3]   saying to me, "You are my servant,
        Israel, in whom I show my glory."
[4]But I said, "I have wearied myself in vain.
    I have used up my strength for nothing."
Nevertheless, the Lord will grant me justice;
    my reward is with my God.
[5]And now the Lord has decided—
    the one who formed me from the womb as his servant—
    to restore Jacob to God,
    so that Israel might return to him.
    Moreover, I'm honored in the Lord's eyes;
    my God has become my strength.
[6]He said: It is not enough, since you are my servant,
    to raise up the tribes of Jacob
    and to bring back the survivors of Israel.
    Hence, I will also appoint you as light to the nations
    so that my salvation may reach to the end of the earth.
[7]The Lord, redeemer of Israel and its holy one,
    says to one despised,
    rejected by nations,
    to the slave of rulers:
    Kings will see and stand up;
    commanders will bow down
    on account of the Lord, who is faithful,
    the holy one of Israel,
    who has chosen you.

Psalm 40:1-11 (G651, N647, UM774)

[1]I put all my hope in the Lord. / He leaned down to me; / he listened to my cry for help. / [2]He lifted me out of the pit of death, / out of the mud and filth, / and set my feet on solid rock. / He steadied my legs. / [3]He put a new song in my mouth, / a song of praise for our God. / Many people will learn of this and be amazed; / they will trust the Lord. / [4]Those who put their trust in the Lord, / who pay no attention to the proud / or to those who follow lies, / are truly happy! / [5]You, Lord my God! / You've done so many things— / your wonderful deeds and your plans for us— / no one can compare with you! / If I were to proclaim and talk about all of them, / they would be too numerous to count! / [6]You don't relish sacrifices or offerings; / you don't require entirely burned offerings or compensation offerings— / but you have given me ears! / [7]So I said, "Here I come! / I'm inscribed in the written scroll. / [8]I want to do your will, my God. / Your Instruction is deep within me." / [9]I've told the good news of your righteousness / in the great assembly. / I didn't hold anything back— / as you well know, Lord! / [10]I didn't keep your righteousness only to myself. / I declared your faithfulness and your salvation. / I didn't hide your loyal love and trustworthiness / from the great assembly. / [11]So now you, Lord— / don't hold back any of your compassion from me. / Let your loyal love and faithfulness always protect me, /

1 Corinthians 1:1-9

[1]From Paul, called by God's will to be an apostle of Jesus Christ, and from Sosthenes our brother.
[2]To God's church that is in Corinth:
To those who have been made holy to God in Christ Jesus, who are called to be God's people.
Together with all those who call upon the name of our Lord Jesus Christ in every place—he's their Lord and ours!
[3]Grace to you and peace from God our Father and the Lord Jesus Christ.
[4]I thank my God always for you, because of God's grace that was given to you in Christ Jesus. [5]That is, you were made rich through him in everything: in all your communication and every kind of knowledge, [6]in the same way that the testimony about Christ was confirmed with you. [7]The result is that you aren't missing any spiritual gift while you wait for our Lord Jesus Christ to be revealed. [8]He will also confirm your testimony about Christ until the end so that you will be blameless on the day of our Lord Jesus Christ. [9]God is faithful, and you were called by him to partnership with his Son, Jesus Christ our Lord.

John 1:29-42

[29]The next day John saw Jesus coming toward him and said, "Look! The Lamb of God who takes away the sin of the world! [30]This is the one about whom I said, 'He who comes after me is really greater than me because he existed before me.' [31]Even I didn't recognize him, but I came baptizing with water so that he might be made known to Israel." [32]John testified, "I saw the Spirit coming down from heaven like a dove, and it rested on him. [33]Even I didn't recognize him, but the one who sent me to baptize with water said to me, 'The one on whom you see the Spirit coming down and resting is the one who baptizes with the Holy Spirit.' [34]I have seen and testified that this one is God's Son."

[35]The next day John was standing again with two of his disciples. [36]When he saw Jesus walking along he said, "Look! The Lamb of God!" [37]The two disciples heard what he said, and they followed Jesus.

[38]When Jesus turned and saw them following, he asked, "What are you looking for?"

They said, "Rabbi (which is translated *Teacher*), where are you staying?"

[39]He replied, "Come and see." So they went and saw where he was staying, and they remained with him that day. It was about four o'clock in the afternoon.

[40]One of the two disciples who heard what John said and followed Jesus was Andrew, the brother of Simon Peter. [41]He first found his own brother Simon and said to him, "We have found the Messiah" (which is translated *Christ*). [42]He led him to Jesus.

Primary Hymns and Songs for the Day
"We Are Called" (Isa, Epiphany, MLK, Jr. Day) (O)
  EL720, G749, S2172, SF2172
"Great Is Thy Faithfulness" (Isa, 1 Cor)
  B54, C86, EL733, F98, G39, N423, P276, UM140, VU288
      H-3   Chr-87; Desc-39; Org-39
      S-2   #59. Piano arr.
"O Jesus, I Have Promised" (1 Cor)
  B276, C612, E655, EL810, F402, G724/725, L503, N493,
  P388/389, UM396 (PD), VU120
"The Summons" ("Will You Come and Follow Me") (John)
  EL798, G726, S2130, SF2130, VU567
"We Are Marching" (Isa, MLK, Jr. Day) (C)
  C442, EL866, G853, N526, S2235-ab, SF2235-ab, VU646

Additional Hymn Suggestions
"Holy God, We Praise Thy Name" (Isa) (O)
  E366, F385, EL414 (PD), G4, L535, N276, P460, UM79,
  VU894 (Fr.), W524
"Immortal, Invisible, God Only Wise" (Isa) (C)
  B6, C66, E423, EL834, F319, G12, L526, N1, P263, UM103
  (PD), VU264, W512
"Womb of Life" (Isa)
  C14, G3, N274, S2046, SF2046
"I Was There to Hear Your Borning Cry" (Isa)
  C75, EL732, G488, N351, S2051, SF2051, VU644
"Mothering God, You Gave Me Birth" (Isa, Comm.)
  C83, EL735, G7, N467, S2050, SF2050, VU320
"What Does the Lord Require?" (Pss)
  C659, E605, P405, UM441, W624
"What Does the Lord Require of You?" (Pss)
  C661, G70, S2174, SF2174, VU701
"Jesus, Thou Joy of Loving Hearts" (1 Cor)
  C101, E649, F451, G494, L356, N329, P510, VU472, W605
"How Great Thou Art" (1 Cor)
  AH4015, B10, C33, EL856, F2, G625, L532, N35, P467,
  UM77, VU238 (Fr.)
"Leaning on the Everlasting Arms" (1 Cor)
  AH4100, B333, C560, EL774 (PD), G837, N471, UM133
"Amazing Grace" (1 Cor)
  AH4091, B330, C546, E671, EL779, F107, G649, L448, N547
  and N548, P280, UM378 (PD), VU266 (Fr.), W583
"Lord God, Your Love Has Called Us Here" (1 Cor, John)
  EL358, P353, UM579
"I Love to Tell the Story" (John)
  B572, C480, EL661, G462, L390, N522, UM156, VU343
"Tú Has Venido a la Orilla" ("Lord, You Have Come to the
  Lakeshore") (John)
  C342, EL817, G721, N173, P377, UM344, VU563
"Just as I Am" (John)
  B303/307, C339, E693, EL592, F417, G442, L296, N207,
  P370, UM357 (PD), VU508
"Jesus, Priceless Treasure" (John)
  E701, EL775, F277, G830, L457, N480 P365, UM532 (PD),
  VU667 and VU668 (Fr.)
"Lead On, O King Eternal" (John)
  B621, C632, E555, EL805, F595, G269, L495, N573, P447/
  P448, UM580
"Take, O Take Me As I Am" (John)
  EL814, G698, WS3119

Additional Contemporary Suggestions
"Lord, Be Glorified" (Isa)
  B457, EL744, G468, S2150, SF2150, SP196

"Be Glorified" (Isa)
  M13
"Be Glorified" (Isa)
  M152
"Shout to the North" (Isa)
  G319, M99, WS3042
"You Are My All in All" (Isa, John)
  G519, SP220, WS3040
"You Are Mine" (Isa, John)
  EL581, G177, S2218, SF2218
"Shout to the Lord" (Pss)
  EL821, M16, S2074, SF2074; V-3 (2) p. 32 Vocal solo
"You Are Good" (Pss)
  AH4018, M124, WS3014
"Hallelujah" ("Your Love Is Amazing") (Pss)
  M118, WS3027
"You Are My Hiding Place" (Pss)
  C554, S2055, SF2055
"Amazing Grace" ("My Chains Are Gone") (1 Cor)
  M205, WS3104
"Grace Like Rain" (1 Cor)
  M251
"Spirit Song" (John)
  C352, SP134, UM347
"Jesus, Name above All Names" (John)
  S2071, SF2071, SP76
"Cry of My Heart" (John)
  M39, S2165, SF2165
"Step by Step" (John)
  G743, M51, WS3004
"You Are My All in All" (John)
  G519, SP220, WS3040
"Now Behold the Lamb" (John)
  EL341, WS3081
"Agnus Dei" (John)
  M15

Vocal Solos
"Ye Servants of God" (Isa, John)
  V-1   p. 41
"Lamb of God" (John)
  V-5 (2)   p. 5

Anthems
"I Waited for the Lord" (Pss)
F. Mendelssohn; Carl Fischer CM 6250
SATB, piano

"Leaning on the Everlasting Arms" (1 Cor)
Arr. Eric Nelson; MorningStar MSM-50-8970
SATB, piano, flute, and cello

Other Suggestions
Visuals:
  O   Coast, pregnancy, hand, arrow, light, earth, Christ
  P   Clasped hands, pit, bog, feet/rock, sing, preach
  E   People, speak, learning, Bible, gifts, Second Coming
  G   Jesus, Lamb, baptism, Spirit, John, witnessing
Response: N192, UM300. "O the Lamb" (John)
Medley: "Take This Moment, Sign, and Space" (WS3118) and
  "Take, O Take Me As I Am" (EL814, G698, WS3119) (John)

Isaiah 9:1-4

[1]Nonetheless, those who were in distress won't be exhausted. At an earlier time, God cursed the land of Zebulun and the land of Naphtali, but later he glorified the way of the sea, the far side of the Jordan, and the Galilee of the nations.

[2] The people walking in darkness have seen a great light.
  On those living in a pitch-dark land, light has dawned.

[3] You have made the nation great;
  you have increased its joy.
  They rejoiced before you as with joy at the harvest,
  as those who divide plunder rejoice.

[4] As on the day of Midian, you've shattered the yoke that
      burdened them,
  the staff on their shoulders,
  and the rod of their oppressor.

Psalm 27:1, 4-9 (G90/841/842, N637, P179, UM758)

[1]The Lord is my light and my salvation. / Should I fear anyone? / The Lord is a fortress protecting my life. / Should I be frightened of anything? . . .

[4]I have asked one thing from the Lord— / it's all I seek— / to live in the Lord's house all the days of my life, / seeing the Lord's beauty / and constantly adoring his temple. / [5]Because he will shelter me in his own dwelling / during troubling times; / he will hide me in a secret place in his own tent; / he will set me up high, safe on a rock.

[6]Now my head is higher than the enemies surrounding me, / and I will offer sacrifices in God's tent— / sacrifices with shouts of joy! / I will sing and praise the Lord.

[7]Lord, listen to my voice when I cry out— / have mercy on me and answer me! / [8]Come, my heart says, seek God's face. / Lord, I do seek your face! / [9]Please don't hide it from me! / Don't push your servant aside angrily— / you have been my help! / God who saves me, / don't neglect me! / Don't leave me all alone! /

---

1 Corinthians 1:10-18

[10]Now I encourage you, brothers and sisters, in the name of our Lord Jesus Christ: Agree with each other and don't be divided into rival groups. Instead, be restored with the same mind and the same purpose. [11]My brothers and sisters, Chloe's people gave me some information about you, that you're fighting with each other. [12]What I mean is this: that each one of you says, "I belong to Paul," "I belong to Apollos," "I belong to Cephas," "I belong to Christ." [13]Has Christ been divided? Was Paul crucified for you, or were you baptized in Paul's name? [14]Thank God that I didn't baptize any of you, except Crispus and Gaius, [15]so that nobody can say that you were baptized in my name! [16]Oh, I baptized the house of Stephanas too. Otherwise, I don't know if I baptized anyone else. [17]Christ didn't send me to baptize but to preach the good news. And Christ didn't send me to preach the good news with clever words so that Christ's cross won't be emptied of its meaning.

[18]The message of the cross is foolishness to those who are being destroyed. But it is the power of God for those of us who are being saved.

Matthew 4:12-23

[12]Now when Jesus heard that John was arrested, he went to Galilee. [13]He left Nazareth and settled in Capernaum, which lies alongside the sea in the area of Zebulun and Naphtali. [14]This fulfilled what Isaiah the prophet said:

[15] *Land of Zebulun and land of Naphtali,*
  alongside the sea, across the Jordan, Galilee of the Gentiles,
[16] *the people who lived in the dark have seen a great light,*
  and a light has come upon those who lived in the region and in
    shadow of death.

[17]From that time Jesus began to announce, "Change your hearts and lives! Here comes the kingdom of heaven!"

[18]As Jesus walked alongside the Galilee Sea, he saw two brothers, Simon, who is called Peter, and Andrew, throwing fishing nets into the sea, because they were fishermen. [19]"Come, follow me," he said, "and I'll show you how to fish for people." [20]Right away, they left their nets and followed him. [21]Continuing on, he saw another set of brothers, James the son of Zebedee and his brother John. They were in a boat with Zebedee their father repairing their nets. Jesus called them and [22]immediately they left the boat and their father and followed him.

[23]Jesus traveled throughout Galilee, teaching in their synagogues. He announced the good news of the kingdom and healed every disease and sickness among the people.

Primary Hymns and Songs for the Day

"The Church's One Foundation" (1 Cor) (O)
B350, C272, E525, EL654, F547, G321, L369, N386, P442, UM545/546, VU332 (Fr.)
      H-3   Hbl-94; Chr-180; Desc-16; Org-9
      S-1   #25-26. Desc. and harm.

"*Tú Has Venido a la Orilla*" ("Lord, You Have Come to the Lakeshore") (Matt)
C342, EL817, G721, N173, P377, UM344, VU563
      H-3   Chr-133; Org-114

"Jesus Calls Us" (Matt)
B293, C337, E549/551, EL696, G720, L494, N171/172, UM398, VU562
      H-3   Chr-115
      S-2   #65. Harm.

"Two Fishermen" (Matt)
S2101, SF2101, W633

"I Have Decided to Follow Jesus" (Matt) (C)
B305, C344, S2129, SF2129

Additional Hymn Suggestions

"Break Forth, O Beauteous Heavenly Light" (Isa)
B114 (PD), E91, F207, G130, N140, P26, UM223, VU83

"How Firm a Foundation" (Isa)
B338, C618, E636/637, EL796, F32, G463, L507, N407, P361, UM529 (PD), VU660, W585

"Christ, Whose Glory Fills the Skies" (Isa, Matt)
EL553, F293, G662, L265, P462/463, UM173 (PD), VU336

"Dear Lord and Father of Mankind" (Isa, Matt)
B267, C594, E652/563, F422, G169, L506, N502, P345, UM358 (PD), VU608

"I Want to Walk as a Child of the Light" (Isa, Matt)
E490, EL815, G377, UM206, W510

"O Morning Star, How Fair and Bright" (Isa, Matt)
C105, E497, EL308, G827, L76, N158, P69, UM247, VU98

"Gather Us In" (Isa, Matt)
C284, EL532, G401, S2236, SF2236, W665

"Praise, My Soul, the King of Heaven" (Pss)
B32, C23, E410, EL864/865, F339, G619/620, L549, P478/479, UM66 (PD), VU240, W530

"Immortal, Invisible, God Only Wise" (Pss)
B6, C66, E423, EL834, F319, G12, L526, N1, P263, UM103 (PD), VU264, W512

"Where Charity and Love Prevail" (1 Cor)
E581, EL359, G316, L126, N396, UM549

"In the Cross of Christ I Glory" (1 Cor)
B554, C207, E441, EL324, F251, G213, L104, N193, P84, UM295

"We Are One in Christ Jesus" (1 Cor)
C493, EL643, G322, S2229, SF2229

"Fight the Good Fight" (1 Cor)
E552, F613, G846, L461, P307 (PD), VU674

"All My Hope Is Firmly Grounded" (1 Cor)
C88, E665, EL757, N408, UM132, VU654/655

"Blest Be the Tie That Binds" (1 Cor) (C)
B387, C433, EL656, F560, G306, L370, N393, P438, UM557 (PD), VU602

"Help Us Accept Each Other" (1 Cor)
C487, G754, N388, P358, UM560, W656

"Tell Me the Stories of Jesus" (Matt)
B129, C190, F212, UM277 (PD), VU357

"Softly and Tenderly Jesus Is Calling" (Matt)
B312, C340, EL608 (PD), F432, G418, N449, UM348

"The Summons" ("Will You Come and Follow Me") (Matt)
EL798, G726, S2130, SF2130, VU567

"Somebody's Knockin' at Your Door" (Matt)
G728, P382, W415, WS3095

"O Jesus, I Have Promised" (Matt)
B276, C612, E655, EL810, F402, G724/725, L503, N493, P388/389, UM396 (PD), VU120

"Where Cross the Crowded Ways of Life" (Matt)
C665, E609, EL719, F665, G343, L429, N543, P408, UM427 (PD), VU681

"O Master, Let Me Walk with Thee" (Matt) (C)
B279, C602, E659/E660, EL818, F442, G738, L492, N503, P357, UM430 (PD), VU560

Additional Contemporary Suggestions

"How Great Is Our God" (Isa, Pss, Matt)
M117, WS3003

"Here I Am to Worship" (Isa, Pss, Matt, Epiphany)
M116, WS3177

"Shine, Jesus, Shine" (Isa, Pss, Matt, Epiphany)
B579, EL671, G192, S2173, SF2173, SP142; V-3 (2) p. 48 Vocal solo

"Shine on Us" (Isa, Pss, Matt, Epiphany)
M19

"Marvelous Light" (Pss, Matt, Epiphany)
M249

"I Will Call upon the Lord" (Pss)
G621, S2002, SF2002, SP224

"Shout to the Lord" (Pss)
EL821, M16, S2074, SF2074; V-3 (2) p. 32 Vocal Solo

"The Lord Is My Light" (Pss)
SP209

"Step by Step" (Pss, Matt)
G743, M51, WS3004

"We Are Singing" ("*Siyahamba*") (Pss, Matt)
C442, EL866, G853, N526, S2235-ab, SF2235-ab, VU646

"Cry of My Heart" (Matt)
M39, S2165, SF2165

Vocal Solos

"The Lord Is My Light" (Pss)
    V-8   p. 57

"Softly and Tenderly" (Matt)
    V-5 (3)   p. 52

Anthems

"Christ, Whose Glory Fills the Skies" (Isa, Matt)
Gilbert Martin; Lorenz 10/3727L
SATB, piano

"Who at My Door Is Standing?" (Matt)
Arr. K. Lee Scott; Hinshaw HMC728
Two-part mixed, keyboard

Other Suggestions

Visuals:
    O   Light/darkness, sea/land, joy, harvest, yoke, rod
    P   Light, church, seekers, tent/rock, joy, singing
    E   Walls torn down, baptism, crucifix, stone
    G   John, sea, light/darkness, dawn, fishnet, net with people, mending nets, boat, Jesus teaching
Introit: WS3137. "Lord Jesus Christ, Your Light" (Isa, Pss)
Canticle: UM205. "Canticle of Light and Darkness" (Isa)
Litany: N880 or F380 or C664 (Isa, Matt)

Micah 6:1-8

[1]Hear what the LORD is saying:
Arise, lay out the lawsuit before the mountains;
   let the hills hear your voice!
[2]Hear, mountains, the lawsuit of the LORD!
   Hear, eternal foundations of the earth!
The LORD has a lawsuit against his people;
   with Israel he will argue.
[3]"My people, what did I ever do to you?
   How have I wearied you? Answer me!
[4]I brought you up out of the land of Egypt;
   I redeemed you from the house of slavery.
   I sent Moses, Aaron, and Miriam before you.
[5]My people, remember what Moab's King Balak had planned,
   and how Balaam, Beor's son, answered him!
   Remember everything from Shittim to Gilgal,
   that you might learn to recognize the righteous acts of
     the LORD!"
[6]With what should I approach the LORD
   and bow down before God on high?
Should I come before him with entirely burned offerings,
   with year-old calves?
[7]Will the LORD be pleased with thousands of rams,
   with many torrents of oil?
Should I give my oldest child for my crime;
   the fruit of my body for the sin of my spirit?
[8]He has told you, human one, what is good and
   what the LORD requires from you:
      to do justice, embrace faithful love, and walk humbly
       with your God.

Psalm 15 (G419, N627, P164, UM747)

[1]Who can live in your tent, LORD? / Who can dwell on your holy mountain? / [2]The person who / lives free of blame, / does what is right, / and speaks the truth sincerely; / [3]who does no damage with their talk, / does no harm to a friend, / doesn't insult a neighbor; / [4]someone who despises / those who act wickedly, / but who honors those / who honor the LORD; / someone who keeps their promise even when it hurts; / [5]someone who doesn't lend money with interest, / who won't accept a bribe against any innocent person. / Whoever does these things will never stumble.

1 Corinthians 1:18-31

[18]The message of the cross is foolishness to those who are being destroyed. But it is the power of God for those of us who are being saved. [19]It is written in scripture: *I will destroy the wisdom of the wise, and I will reject the intelligence of the intelligent.* [20]Where are the wise? Where are the legal experts? Where are today's debaters? Hasn't God made the wisdom of the world foolish? [21]In God's wisdom, he determined that the world wouldn't come to know him through its wisdom. Instead, God was pleased to save those who believe through the foolishness of preaching. [22]Jews ask for signs, and Greeks look for wisdom, [23]but we preach Christ crucified, which is a scandal to Jews and foolishness to Gentiles. [24]But to those who are called—both Jews and Greeks—Christ is God's power and God's wisdom. [25]This is because the foolishness of God is wiser than human wisdom, and the weakness of God is stronger than human strength.

[26]Look at your situation when you were called, brothers and sisters! By ordinary human standards not many were wise, not many were powerful, not many were from the upper class. [27]But God chose what the world considers foolish to shame the wise. God chose what the world considers weak to shame the strong. [28]And God chose what the world considers low-class and low-life—what is considered to be nothing—to reduce what is considered to be something to nothing. [29]So no human being can brag in God's presence. [30]It is because of God that you are in Christ Jesus. He became wisdom from God for us. This means that he made us righteous and holy, and he delivered us. [31]This is consistent with what was written: *The one who brags should brag in the Lord!*

Matthew 5:1-12

[1]Now when Jesus saw the crowds, he went up a mountain. He sat down and his disciples came to him. [2]He taught them, saying:

[3]"Happy are people who are hopeless, because the kingdom of heaven is theirs.

[4]"Happy are people who grieve, because they will be made glad.

[5]"Happy are people who are humble, because they will inherit the earth.

[6]"Happy are people who are hungry and thirsty for righteousness, because they will be fed until they are full.

[7]"Happy are people who show mercy, because they will receive mercy.

[8]"Happy are people who have pure hearts, because they will see God.

[9]"Happy are people who make peace, because they will be called God's children.

[10]"Happy are people whose lives are harassed because they are righteous, because the kingdom of heaven is theirs.

[11]"Happy are you when people insult you and harass you and speak all kinds of bad and false things about you, all because of me. [12]Be full of joy and be glad, because you have a great reward in heaven. In the same way, people harassed the prophets who came before you."

Primary Hymns and Songs for the Day

"Rejoice in God's Saints" (Matt) (O)
    C476, EL418, G732, UM708
        H-3   Hbl-90, 105; Chr-221; Desc-49; Org-51
        S-2   #71-74. Intro. and harms.
"We Are Called" (Mic) (O)
    EL720, G749, S2172, SF2172
"What Does the Lord Require of You?" (Mic)
    C661, G70, S2174, SF2174, VU701
"What Does the Lord Require?" (Mic)
    C659, E605, P405, UM441, W624
"Be Thou My Vision" (1 Cor, Matt)
    B60, C595, E488, EL793, G450, N451, P339, UM451, VU642
        H-3   Hbl-15, 48; Chr-36; Org-153
        S-1   #319. Arr. for organ and voices in canon
"Blest Are They" (Matt)
    EL728, G172, S2155, SF2155, VU896
"Lord, You Give the Great Commission" (Mic, Pss) (C)
    C459, E528, EL579, G298, P429, UM584, VU512, W470
        H-3   Hbl-61; Chr-132; Org-2
        S-1   #4-5. Instrumental and vocal desc.
"Sent Out in Jesus' Name" ("*Enviado Soy de Dios*") (Mic) (C)
    EL538, G747, S2184, SF2184

Additional Hymn Suggestions

"O for a Closer Walk with God" (Mic)
    E684, G739, N450, P396
"Softly and Tenderly Jesus Is Calling" (Mic)
    B312, C340, EL608 (PD), F432, G418, N449, UM348
"I'm Gonna Live so God Can Use Me" (Mic)
    C614, G700, P369, S2153, VU575
"Healer of Our Every Ill" (Mic)
    C506, EL612, G795, S2213, SF2213, VU619
"All Who Love and Serve Your City" (Mic, Matt)
    C670, E570/E571, EL724, G351, L436, P413, UM433, W621
"*Cuando el Pobre*" ("When the Poor Ones") (Mic, Matt)
    C662, EL725, G762, P407, UM434, VU702
"Lift Up Your Heads, Ye Mighty Gates" (Pss, Matt)
    B128, C129, E436, F239, G93, N117, P8, UM213 (PD), W363
"Fairest Lord Jesus" (1 Cor)
    B176, C97, E383, EL838, F240, G630, L518, N44, P306,
    UM189 (PD), VU341
"In the Cross of Christ I Glory" (1 Cor)
    B554, C207, E441, EL324, G213, L104, N193, P84, UM295
"When I Survey the Wondrous Cross" (1 Cor)
    B144, C195, EL803, F258, G223, N224, P101, UM298
    E474, L482, G224, P100, UM299 (PD), VU149 (Fr.)
"Help Us Accept Each Other" (1 Cor)
    C487, G754, N388, P358, UM560, W656
"O for a World" (1 Cor)
    C683, G372, N575, P386, VU697
"All My Hope Is Firmly Grounded" (1 Cor)
    C88, E665, EL757, N408, UM132, VU654/655
"Ask Ye What Great Thing I Know" (1 Cor)
    B538, N49, UM163 (PD), VU338
"My Faith Looks Up to Thee" (1 Cor, Matt)
    B416, C576, E691, EL759, G829, L479, P383, UM452, VU663
"Holy Spirit, Truth Divine" (1 Cor, Matt)
    C241, EL398, L257, N63, P321, UM465 (PD), VU368
"O Love That Wilt Not Let Me Go" (1 Cor, Matt)
    B292, C540, G833, L324, N485, P384, UM480 (PD), VU658
"Lord, I Want to Be a Christian" (Matt)
    B489, C589, F421, G729, N454, P372 (PD), UM402
"Near to the Heart of God" (Matt)
    B295, C581, F35, G824, P527, UM472 (PD)

"For All the Saints" (Matt)
    B355, C637, E287, EL422, F614, G326, L174, N299, P526,
    UM711 (PD), VU705, W705
"I Sing a Song of the Saints of God" (Matt)
    E293, G730, N295, P364, UM712 (PD)
"All Who Hunger" (Matt)
    C419, EL461, G509, S2126, SF2126, VU460
"Since Jesus Came into My Heart" (Matt)
    B441, F639, S2140, SF2140

Additional Contemporary Suggestions

"Live in Charity" ("*Ubi Caritas*") (Mic)
    C523, EL642, G205, S2179, SF2179, W604
"Rule of Life" (Mic, Matt)
    AH4056, WS3117
"You Are My All in All" (1 Cor)
    G519, SP220, WS3040
"Shout to the North" (1 Cor)
    G319, M99, WS3042
"Let It Be Said of Us" (1 Cor)
    M53
"The Wonderful Cross" (1 Cor)
    M76
"I Will Boast" (1 Cor)
    M227
"Here Is Bread, Here Is Wine" (1 Cor, Comm.)
    EL483, S2266, SF2266
"Give Thanks" (1 Cor, Matt)
    C528, G647, S2036, SF2036, SP170
"Open Our Eyes, Lord" (Matt)
    B499, S2086, SF2086, SP199
"Open the Eyes of My Heart" (Matt)
    G452, M57, WS3008

Vocal Solos

"Fit for a King" (Mic)
    V-10   p. 32
"Maybe the Rain" (Matt)
    V-5 (2)   p. 27

Anthems

"When I Survey the Wondrous Cross" (1 Cor)
Arr. Fettke/Grassi; Lorenz 10/4628L
SATB, piano

"Blessed" (Matt)
Bern H. Herbolsheimer; G. Schirmer 50486220
SA, piano

Other Suggestions

Visuals:
    O   Briefcase, Exodus, prayer, scales of justice, ministry
    P   Tent, hill, walking, speaking, destructive behavior,
           ministry, justice, money
    E   Empty cross, clown, debate, crucifix, block, Christ,
           world upside down
    G   Jesus teaching, examples of ministry described
Canticle: C185. "The Beatitudes" (Matt)
Dance Solo: N180. "Blessed Are the Poor in Spirit" (Matt)

Isaiah 58:1-9a (9b -12)

[1]Shout loudly; don't hold back;
    raise your voice like a trumpet!
Announce to my people their crime,
    to the house of Jacob their sins.
[2]They seek me day after day,
    desiring knowledge of my ways
    like a nation that acted righteously,
    that didn't abandon their God.
They ask me for righteous judgments,
    wanting to be close to God.
[3]"Why do we fast and you don't see;
    why afflict ourselves and you don't notice?"
Yet on your fast day you do whatever you want,
    and oppress all your workers.
[4]You quarrel and brawl, and then you fast;
    you hit each other violently with your fists.
You shouldn't fast as you are doing today
    if you want to make your voice heard on high.
[5]Is this the kind of fast I choose,
    a day of self-affliction,
    of bending one's head like a reed
    and of lying down in mourning clothing and ashes?
    Is this what you call a fast,
    a day acceptable to the LORD?
[6]Isn't this the fast I choose:
    releasing wicked restraints, untying the ropes of a yoke,
    setting free the mistreated,
    and breaking every yoke?
[7]Isn't it sharing your bread with the hungry
    and bringing the homeless poor into your house,
    covering the naked when you see them,
    and not hiding from your own family?
[8]Then your light will break out like the dawn,
    and you will be healed quickly.
Your own righteousness will walk before you,
    and the LORD's glory will be your rear guard.
[9]Then you will call, and the LORD will answer;
    you will cry for help, and God will say, "I'm here."
If you remove the yoke from among you,
    the finger-pointing, the wicked speech;
[10]   if you open your heart to the hungry,
    and provide abundantly for those who are afflicted,
    your light will shine in the darkness,
    and your gloom will be like the noon.
[11]The LORD will guide you continually
    and provide for you, even in parched places.
    He will rescue your bones.
You will be like a watered garden,
    like a spring of water that won't run dry.
[12]They will rebuild ancient ruins on your account;
    the foundations of generations past you will restore.
You will be called Mender of Broken Walls,
    Restorer of Livable Streets.

Psalm 112:1-9 (10) (G755, N697, UM833)

[1]Praise the LORD! / Those who honor the LORD, / who adore God's commandments, are truly happy! / [2]Their descendants will be strong throughout the land. / The offspring of those who do right will be blessed; / [3]wealth and riches will be in their houses. / Their righteousness stands forever. / [4]They shine in the dark for others who do right. / They are merciful, compassionate, and righteous. / [5]Those who lend generously are good people— / as are those who conduct their affairs with justice. / [6]Yes, these sorts of people will never be shaken; / the righteous will be remembered forever! / [7]They won't be frightened at bad news. / Their hearts are steady, trusting in the LORD. / [8]Their hearts are firm; they aren't afraid. / In the end, they will witness their enemies' defeat. / [9]They give freely to those in need. / Their righteousness stands forever. / Their strength increases gloriously. / [10]The wicked see all this and fume; / they grind their teeth, but disappear to nothing. / What the wicked want to see happen comes to nothing!

1 Corinthians 2:1-12 (13-16)

[1]When I came to you, brothers and sisters, I didn't come preaching God's secrets to you like I was an expert in speech or wisdom. [2]I had made up my mind not to think about anything while I was with you except Jesus Christ, and to preach him as crucified. [3]I stood in front of you with weakness, fear, and a lot of shaking. [4]My message and my preaching weren't presented with convincing wise words but with a demonstration of the Spirit and of power. [5]I did this so that your faith might not depend on the wisdom of people but on the power of God.

[6]What we say is wisdom to people who are mature. It isn't a wisdom that comes from the present day or from today's leaders who are being reduced to nothing. [7]We talk about God's wisdom, which has been hidden as a secret. God determined this wisdom in advance, before time began, for our glory. [8]It is a wisdom that none of the present-day rulers have understood, because if they did understand it, they would never have crucified the Lord of glory! [9]But this is precisely what is written: *God has prepared things for those who love him that no eye has seen, or ear has heard, or that haven't crossed the mind of any human being.* [10]God has revealed these things to us through the Spirit. The Spirit searches everything, including the depths of God. [11]Who knows a person's depths except their own spirit that lives in them? In the same way, no one has known the depths of God except God's Spirit. [12]We haven't received the world's spirit but God's Spirit so that we can know the things given to us by God. [13]These are the things we are talking about—not with words taught by human wisdom but with words taught by the Spirit—we are interpreting spiritual things to spiritual people. [14]But people who are unspiritual don't accept the things from God's Spirit. They are foolishness to them and can't be understood, because they can only be comprehended in a spiritual way. [15]Spiritual people comprehend everything, but they themselves aren't understood by anyone. [16]*Who has known the mind of the Lord, who will advise him?* But we have the mind of Christ.

Matthew 5:13-20

[13]"You are the salt of the earth. But if salt loses its saltiness, how will it become salty again? It's good for nothing except to be thrown away and trampled under people's feet. [14]You are the light of the world. A city on top of a hill can't be hidden. [15]Neither do people light a lamp and put it under a basket. Instead, they put it on top of a lampstand, and it shines on all who are in the house. [16]In the same way, let your light shine before people, so they can see the good things you do and praise your Father who is in heaven.

[17]"Don't even begin to think that I have come to do away with the Law and the Prophets. I haven't come to do away with them but to fulfill them. [18]I say to you very seriously that as long as heaven and earth exist, neither the smallest letter nor even the smallest stroke of a pen will be erased from the Law until everything there becomes a reality. [19]Therefore, whoever ignores one of the least of these commands and teaches others to do the same will be called the lowest in the kingdom of heaven. But whoever keeps these commands and teaches people to keep them will be called great in the kingdom of heaven. [20]I say to you that unless your righteousness is greater than the righteousness of the legal experts and the Pharisees, you will never enter the kingdom of heaven."

Primary Hymns and Songs for the Day

"For the Healing of the Nations" (Isa) (O)
  C668, G346, N576, UM428, VU678, W643
"Gather Us In" (Isa, Matt, Comm.) (O)
  C284, EL532, G401, S2236, SF2236, W665
"All Who Love and Serve Your City" (Isa)
  C670, E570/E571, EL724, G351, L436, P413, UM433, W621
      H-3   Chr-26, 65; Org-19
      S-1   #62. Desc.
"I Want to Walk as a Child of the Light" (Matt)
  E490, EL815, G377, UM206, W510
      S-2   #91. Desc.
"Bring Forth the Kingdom" (Matt)
  S2190, SF2190
"*Sois la Semilla*" ("You Are the Seed") (Matt) (C)
  C478, N528, UM583
"This Little Light of Mine" (Matt, Black History) (C)
  N525, UM585 (See also AH4150, EL677, N524)

Additional Hymn Suggestions

"Guide Me, O Thou Great Jehovah" (Isa)
  B56, C622, E690, EL618, F608, G65, L343, N18/19, P281,
  UM127 (PD), VU651 (Fr.)
"God Is So Good" (Isa)
  B23, G658, S2056, SF2056
"What Does the Lord Require of You?" (Isa)
  C661, G70, S2174, SF2174, VU701
"O For a Thousand Tongues to Sing" (Isa)
  B216, C5, E493, EL886, F349, G610, L559, N42, P466,
  UM57/58 (PD), VU326 (See also WS3001)
"I'll Praise My Maker While I've Breath" (Isa)
  B35, C20, E429 (PD), G806, P253, UM60, VU867
"*Cuando el Pobre*" ("When the Poor Ones") (Isa)
  C662, EL725, G762, P407, UM434, VU702
"What Does the Lord Require?" (Isa)
  C659, E605, P405, UM441, W624
"Here I Am, Lord" (Isa)
  C452, EL574, G69, P525, UM593, VU509
"Draw Us in the Spirit's Tether" (Isa, Comm.)
  C392, EL470, G529, N337, P504, UM632, VU479, W731
"The Battle Hymn of the Republic" (Isa)
  B633, C705, EL890, F692, G354, L332, N610, UM717 (PD)
"When Morning Gilds the Skies" (Pss)
  B221, C100, E427, EL853 (PD), F322, G667, L546, N86,
  P487, UM185, VU339 (Fr.), W675
"All Praise to Thee, for Thou, O King Divine" (Pss, 1 Cor)
  B229, E477, UM166, VU327
"Lord, Speak to Me" (Pss, 1 Cor)
  B568, EL676, F625, G722, L403, N531, P426, UM463 (PD),
  VU589
"Jesus, the Very Thought of Thee" (1 Cor)
  C102, E642, EL754, G629, L316, N507, P310, UM175
"Ask Ye What Great Thing I Know" (1 Cor)
  B538, N49, UM163 (PD), VU338
"Forth in Thy Name, O Lord" (1 Cor)
  L505, UM438 (PD), VU416
"Be Thou My Vision" (1 Cor)
  B60, C595, E488, EL793, G450, N451, P339, UM451, VU642
"Woke Up This Morning" (1 Cor)
  C623, N85, S2082, SF2082
"Blessed Jesus, At Thy Word" (Matt)
  E440, EL520, G395, N74, P454, UM596 (PD), VU500
"I'm Gonna Live so God Can Use Me" (Matt)
  C614, G700, P369, S2153, VU575

"We All Are One in Mission" (Matt)
  EL576, G733, P435, S2243, SF2243
"Today We All Are Called to Be Disciples" (Matt)
  G757, P434, VU507
"Together We Serve" (Matt)
  G767, S2175, SF2175
"Lead Me, Guide Me" (Matt)
  C583, EL768, G740, S2214, SF2214
"You Are Mine" (Matt)
  EL581, G177, S2218, SF2218
"As a Fire Is Meant for Burning" (Matt)
  S2237, SF2237, VU578
"Life-Giving Bread" (Matt, Comm.)
  S2261, SF2261
"In the Desert, on God's Mountain" (Matt)
  WS3029

Additional Contemporary Suggestions

"Shout to the Lord" (Isa)
  EL821, M16, S2074, SF2074; V-3 (2) p. 32 Vocal Solo
"Knowing You" ("All I Once Held Dear") (1 Cor)
  M30
"Take My Life" (1 Cor)
  M91
"I Have a Hope" (1 Cor)
  M265
"In Christ Alone" (1 Cor, Matt)
  M138, WS3105
"Shine, Jesus, Shine" (Matt)
  B579, EL671, G192, S2173, SF2173, SP142
"We Are Marching" ("*Siyahamba*") (Matt)
  C442, EL866, G853, N526, S2235-ab, SF2235-ab, VU646
"Mighty to Save" (Matt)
  M246, WS3038
"May We Be a Shining Light to the Nations" (Matt)
  SP144

Vocal Solos

"A Song of Joy" (Isa)
  V-11   p. 2
"Here I Am" (1 Cor)
  V-11   p. 19

Anthems

"We All Are One in Mission" (Matt)
Kevin Riehle; Oxford 9780193863668
SATB

"This Little Light of Mine" (Matt)
David Bone; Hinshaw Music HMC-1966
SATB divisi, a cappella

Other Suggestions

Visuals:
  O   Trumpet, fist, open shackles, yoke, bread, light, water
  P   Bible, light/dark, justice, heart, ministry to poor,
          anger
  E   Bible, heart, emotion, praise, walking
  G   Salt/light, globe, city, lamp/basket/lampstand, Bible,
          teaching
Prayer: UM456. For Courage to Do Justice (Isa)
Blessing: WSL59. "You are the salt" (Matt)
Boy Scout Sunday may be observed today or any Sunday in February.

Deuteronomy 30:15-20

[15]Look here! Today I've set before you life and what's good versus death and what's wrong. [16]If you obey the LORD your God's commandments that I'm commanding you right now by loving the LORD your God, by walking in his ways, and by keeping his commandments, his regulations, and his case laws, then you will live and thrive, and the LORD your God will bless you in the land you are entering to possess. [17]But if your heart turns away and you refuse to listen, and so are misled, worshipping other gods and serving them, [18]I'm telling you right now that you will definitely die. You will not prolong your life on the fertile land that you are crossing the Jordan River to enter and possess. [19]I call heaven and earth as my witnesses against you right now: I have set life and death, blessing and curse before you. Now choose life—so that you and your descendants will live— [20]by loving the LORD your God, by obeying his voice, and by clinging to him. That's how you will survive and live long on the fertile land the LORD swore to give to your ancestors: to Abraham, Isaac, and Jacob.

Psalm 119:1-8 (G64, N701, UM840)

[1]Those whose way is blameless— / who walk in the LORD's Instruction—are truly happy! / [2]Those who guard God's laws are truly happy! / They seek God with all their hearts. / [3]They don't even do anything wrong! / They walk in God's ways. / [4]God, you have ordered that your decrees / should be kept most carefully. / [5]How I wish my ways were strong / when it comes to keeping your statutes! / [6]Then I wouldn't be ashamed / when I examine all your commandments. / [7]I will give thanks to you with a heart that does right / as I learn your righteous rules. / [8]I will keep your statutes. / Please don't leave me all alone!

1 Corinthians 3:1-9

[1]Brothers and sisters, I couldn't talk to you like spiritual people but like unspiritual people, like babies in Christ. [2]I gave you milk to drink instead of solid food, because you weren't up to it yet. [3]Now you are still not up to it because you are still unspiritual. When jealousy and fighting exist between you, aren't you unspiritual and living by human standards? [4]When someone says, "I belong to Paul," and someone else says, "I belong to Apollos," aren't you acting like people without the Spirit? [5]After all, what is Apollos? What is Paul? They are servants who helped you to believe. Each one had a role given to them by the Lord: [6]I planted, Apollos watered, but God made it grow. [7]Because of this, neither the one who plants nor the one who waters is anything, but the only one who is anything is God who makes it grow. [8]The one who plants and the one who waters work together, but each one will receive their own reward for their own labor. [9]We are God's coworkers, and you are God's field, God's building.

Matthew 5:21-37

[21]"You have heard that it was said to those who lived long ago, *Don't commit murder,* and all who commit murder will be in danger of judgment. [22]But I say to you that everyone who is angry with their brother or sister will be in danger of judgment. If they say to their brother or sister, 'You idiot,' they will be in danger of being condemned by the governing council. And if they say, 'You fool,' they will be in danger of fiery hell. [23]Therefore, if you bring your gift to the altar and there remember that your brother or sister has something against you, [24]leave your gift at the altar and go. First make things right with your brother or sister and then come back and offer your gift. [25]Be sure to make friends quickly with your opponents while you are with them on the way to court. Otherwise, they will haul you before the judge, the judge will turn you over to the officer of the court, and you will be thrown into prison. [26]I say to you in all seriousness that you won't get out of there until you've paid the very last penny.

[27]"You have heard that it was said, *Don't commit adultery.* [28]But I say to you that every man who looks at a woman lustfully has already committed adultery in his heart. [29]And if your right eye causes you to fall into sin, tear it out and throw it away. It's better that you lose a part of your body than that your whole body be thrown into hell. [30]And if your right hand causes you to fall into sin, chop it off and throw it away. It's better that you lose a part of your body than that your whole body go into hell.

[31]"It was said, 'Whoever divorces his wife must *give her a divorce certificate.*' [32]But I say to you that whoever divorces his wife except for sexual unfaithfulness forces her to commit adultery. And whoever marries a divorced woman commits adultery.

[33]"Again you have heard that it was said to those who lived long ago: *Don't make a false solemn pledge, but you should follow through on what you have pledged to the Lord.* [34]But I say to you that you must not pledge at all. You must not pledge by heaven, because it's God's throne. [35]You must not pledge by the earth, because it's God's footstool. You must not pledge by Jerusalem, because it's the city of the great king. [36]And you must not pledge by your head, because you can't turn one hair white or black. [37]Let your *yes* mean yes, and your *no* mean no. Anything more than this comes from the evil one."

Primary Hymns and Songs for the Day

"The Church's One Foundation" (1 Cor) (O)
B350, C272, E525, EL654, F547, G321, L369, N386, P442, UM545/546, VU332 (Fr.)
  H-3 Hbl-94; Chr-180; Desc-16; Org-9
  S-1 #25-26. Desc. and harm.

"God, How Can We Forgive" (Matt)
G445, S2169, SF2169
  H-3 Hbl-62, 95; Chr-59; Org-77
  S-1 #211. Harm.

"Spirit of God, Descend upon My Heart" (Deut) (C)
B245, C265, EL800, F147, G688, L486, N290, P326, UM500 (PD), VU378
  H-3 Chr-175; Desc-77; Org-94
  S-2 #125-28. Various treatments

Additional Hymn Suggestions

"Love the Lord Your God" (Deut)
G62, S2168, SF2168

"As We Gather at Your Table" (Deut, Comm.)
EL522, N332, S2268, SF2268, VU457

"O Master, Let Me Walk with Thee" (Deut, Pss)
B279, C602, E659/E660, EL818, F442, G738, L492, N503, P357, UM430 (PD), VU560

"Dear Lord, Lead Me Day by Day" (Deut, Pss, Matt)
B459, UM411, VU568

"Walk with Me" (Pss, 1 Cor)
S2242, SF2242, VU649

"Like the Murmur of the Dove's Song" (1 Cor)
C245, E513, EL403, G285, N270, P314, UM544, VU205

"In Christ There Is No East or West" (1 Cor)
B385, C687, E529, EL650 (PD), F685, G317/318, L359, N394/N395, P439/P440, UM548, VU606, W659

"Lord, Whose Love Through Humble Service" (1 Cor)
C461, E610, EL712, L423, P427, UM581, W630

"Sois la Semilla" ("You Are the Seed") (1 Cor)
C478, N528, UM583

"Together We Serve" (1 Cor)
G767, S2175, SF2175

"We Need a Faith" (1 Cor)
S2181, SF2181

"They'll Know We Are Christians" (1 Cor)
AH4074, C494, G300, S2223, SF2223

"One God and Father of Us All" (1 Cor)
S2240, SF2240

"We All Are One in Mission" (1 Cor)
EL576, G733, P435, S2243, SF2243

"When Cain Killed Abel" (1 Cor, Matt)
S2135, SF2135

"God Made from One Blood" (1 Cor, Matt)
C500, N427, S2170, SF2170, VU554

"Come, Share the Lord" (1 Cor, Matt, Comm.)
C408, G510, S2269, SF2269, VU469

"Christ for the World We Sing" (1 Cor)
E537, F686, UM568 (PD)

"Forward Through the Ages" (1 Cor)
N355, UM555 (PD)

"Forgive Our Sins as We Forgive" (Matt)
E674, EL605, G444, L307, P347, UM390, VU364

"Sunday's Palms Are Wednesday's Ashes" (Matt)
S2138, SF2138, VU107

"The Lord's Prayer" (Matt)
B462, C307-C310, F440, G464, P589, S2278, SF2278. UM271, WS3068-WS3071

"The Gift of Love" (Matt)
B423, C526, G693, P335, UM408, VU372

"Breathe on Me, Breath of God" (Matt)
B241, C254, E508, F161, G286, L488, N292, P316, UM420 (PD), VU382 (Fr.), W725

"Blest Be the Tie That Binds" (Matt)
B387, C433, EL656, F560, G306, L370, N393, P438, UM557 (PD), VU602

"Help Us Accept Each Other" (Matt)
C487, G754, N388, P358, UM560, W656

Additional Contemporary Suggestions

"The Family Prayer Song" ("As for Me and My House") (Deut)
M54, S2188, SF2188

"Love the Lord" (Deut)
M270, WS3116

"Cry of My Heart" (Deut, Pss)
M39, S2165, SF2165

"Step by Step" (Deut, Pss)
G743, M51, WS3004

"Take This Life" (Deut, Pss)
M98

"Let It Be Said of Us" (Deut, 1 Cor)
M53

"Thy Word Is a Lamp" (Pss)
C326, G458, SP183, UM601

"Ancient Words" (Pss)
M149

"Seek Ye First" (Matt)
B478, C354, E711, G175, P333, UM405, SP182, VU356

"Give Me a Clean Heart" (Matt)
AH4125, C515, N188, S2133, SF2133

"Make Me a Channel of Your Peace" (Matt)
G753, S2171, SF2171, VU684

Vocal Solos

"Turn My Heart to You" (Deut)
  V-5 (2) p. 14

"This Is My Commandment" (Matt)
  V-8 p. 284

Anthems

"Spirit of God, Descend upon My Heart" (Deut, Matt)
Arr. Joan Pinkston; Soundforth Music / Lorenz 10/5016SF
SATB, piano

"Ubi Caritas" (1 Cor, Matt)
Ola Gjeilo; Walton Music WW1386
SATB a cappella

Other Suggestions

Visuals:
 O Ten Commandments, heart, river, "choose life"
 P Bible, heart, devotion, praise, walking
 E Infants, milk, quarrel, plant/water/growth, work, field, building
 G Anger, fire, gift/altar, reconcile, jail, eye, hand, divorce certificate, stool

Sung Prayer: B462, C307-310, F440, G464, P589, S2278, SF2278, UM270-271, WS3068-3071. "Lord's Prayer" (Matt)

Response: EL814, G698, WS3119. "Take, O Take Me As I Am" (Deut)

Leviticus 19:1-2, 9-18

[1]The LORD said to Moses, [2]Say to the whole community of the Israelites: You must be holy, because I, the LORD your God, am holy. . . .

[9]When you harvest your land's produce, you must not harvest all the way to the edge of your field; and don't gather up every remaining bit of your harvest. [10]Also do not pick your vineyard clean or gather up all the grapes that have fallen there. Leave these items for the poor and the immigrant; I am the LORD your God.

[11]You must not steal nor deceive nor lie to each other. [12]You must not swear falsely by my name, desecrating your God's name in doing so; I am the LORD. [13]You must not oppress your neighbors or rob them. Do not withhold a hired laborer's pay overnight. [14]You must not insult a deaf person or put some obstacle in front of a blind person that would cause them to trip. Instead, fear your God; I am the LORD.

[15]You must not act unjustly in a legal case. Do not show favoritism to the poor or deference to the great; you must judge your fellow Israelites fairly. [16]Do not go around slandering your people. Do not stand by while your neighbor's blood is shed;I am the LORD. [17]You must not hate your fellow Israelite in your heart. Rebuke your fellow Israelite strongly, so you don't become responsible for his sin. [18]You must not take revenge nor hold a grudge against any of your people; instead, you must love your neighbor as yourself; I am the LORD.

Psalm 119:33-40 (G64, N701, UM840)

[33]LORD, teach me what your statutes are about, / and I will guard every part of them. / [34]Help me understand so I can guard your Instruction / and keep it with all my heart. / [35]Lead me on the trail of your commandments / because that is what I want. / [36]Turn my heart to your laws, / not to greedy gain. / [37]Turn my eyes away from looking at worthless things. / Make me live by your way. / [38]Confirm your promise to your servant— / the promise that is for all those who honor you. / [39]Remove the insults that I dread / because your rules are good. / [40]Look how I desire your precepts! / Make me live by your righteousness.

1 Corinthians 3:10-11, 16-23

[10]I laid a foundation like a wise master builder according to God's grace that was given to me, but someone else is building on top of it. Each person needs to pay attention to the way they build on it. [11]No one can lay any other foundation besides the one that is already laid, which is Jesus Christ. . . .

[16]Don't you know that you are God's temple and God's Spirit lives in you? [17]If someone destroys God's temple, God will destroy that person, because God's temple is holy, which is what you are.

[18]Don't fool yourself. If some of you think they are worldly-wise, then they should become foolish so that they can become wise. [19]This world's wisdom is foolishness to God. As it's written, *He catches the wise in their cleverness.* [20]And also, *The Lord knows that the thoughts of the wise are silly.* [21]So then, no one should brag about human beings. Everything belongs to you— [22]Paul, Apollos, Cephas, the world, life, death, things in the present, things in the future—everything belongs to you, [23]but you belong to Christ, and Christ belongs to God.

Matthew 5:38-48

[38]"You have heard that it was said, *An eye for an eye and a tooth for a tooth.* [39]But I say to you that you must not oppose those who want to hurt you. If people slap you on your right cheek, you must turn the left cheek to them as well. [40]When they wish to haul you to court and take your shirt, let them have your coat too. [41]When they force you to go one mile, go with them two. [42]Give to those who ask, and don't refuse those who wish to borrow from you.

[43]"You have heard that it was said, *You must love your neighbor* and hate your enemy. [44]But I say to you, love your enemies and pray for those who harass you [45]so that you will be acting as children of your Father who is in heaven. He makes the sun rise on both the evil and the good and sends rain on both the righteous and the unrighteous. [46]If you love only those who love you, what reward do you have? Don't even the tax collectors do the same? [47]And if you greet only your brothers and sisters, what more are you doing? Don't even the Gentiles do the same? [48]Therefore, just as your heavenly Father is complete in showing love to everyone, so also you must be complete."

Primary Hymns and Songs for the Day
"Take Time to Be Holy" (Lev, Matt) (O)
   B446, C572, F457, UM395 (PD), VU672
         H-3   Chr-178
         S-1   #159. Harm.
"Live in Charity" ("*Ubi Caritas*") (Lev, Matt)
   C523, EL642, G205, S2179, SF2179, W604
"Lord I Want to Be a Christian" (Lev, Matt)
   B489, C589, F421, G729, N454, P372 (PD), UM402
         H-3   Chr-130
"How Firm a Foundation" (Lev)
   B338, C618, E636/637, EL796, F32, G463, L507, N407, P361,
   UM529 (PD), VU660, W585
"The Church's One Foundation" (1 Cor)
   B350, C272, E525, EL654, F547, G321, L369, N386, P442,
   UM545/546, VU332 (Fr.)
"Sacred the Body" (1 Cor)
   G27, S2228, SF2228
"Forgive Our Sins as We Forgive" (Matt)
   E674, EL605, G444, L307, P347, UM390, VU364
         H-3   Chr-68; Desc-28; Org-27
         S-1   #85. Choral harm.
"Christ Is Made the Sure Foundation" (1 Cor) (C)
   B356 (PD), C275, E518, EL645, F557, G394, N400,
   P416/417, UM559 (PD), VU325, W617
         H-3   Chr-49; Desc-103; Org-180
         S-1   #346. Desc.

Additional Hymn Suggestions
"I Want to Walk as a Child of the Light" (Lev) (C)
   E490, EL815, G377, UM206, W510
"Take My Life, and Let It Be" (Lev) (C)
   B277/B283, C609, E707, EL583/EL685, G697, L406, P391,
   N448, UM399 (PD), VU506
"Lord, Make Us More Holy" (Lev)
   G313, N75 (PD), P536
"Every Time I Feel the Spirit" (Lev)
   C592, G66, N282, P315, UM404
"For the Healing of the Nations" (Lev) (O)
   C668, G346, N576, UM428, VU678, W643
"*Jesu, Jesu*" (Lev, Matt)
   B501, C600, E602, EL708, G203, N498, P367, UM432,
   VU593, W431, S-1 #63. Vocal part
"*Cuando el Pobre*" ("When the Poor Ones") (Lev, Matt)
   C662, EL725, G762, P407, UM434, VU702
"Love the Lord Your God" (Lev, Matt)
   G62, S2168, SF2168
"Make Me a Channel of Your Peace" (Lev, Matt)
   G753, S2171, SF2171, VU684
"Lord, Speak to Me" (Pss)
   B568, EL676, F625, G722, L403, N531, P426, UM463 (PD),
   VU589
"Precious Lord, Take My Hand" (Pss, Black History)
   B456, C628, EL773, G834, N472, P404, UM474, VU670
"Thy Word Is a Lamp" (Pss)
   C326, G458, SP183, UM601
"Be Thou My Vision" (Pss, 1 Cor)
   B60, C595, E488, EL793, G450, N451, P339, UM451, VU642
"Open My Eyes, That I May See" (Pss, 1 Cor)
   B502, C586, F486, G451, P324, UM454, VU371
"Open Now Thy Gates of Beauty" (1 Cor)
   EL533 (PD), G403, L250, N67, P489
"We All Are One in Mission" (1 Cor)
   EL576, G733, P435, S2243, SF2243

"God, How Can We Forgive" (Matt)
   G445, S2169, SF2169
"The Gift of Love" (Matt)
   B423, C526, G693, P335, UM408, VU372
"Our Parent, By Whose Name" (Matt)
   E587, EL640, L357, UM447, VU555, W570
"Where Charity and Love Prevail" (Matt)
   E581, EL359, G316, L126, N396, UM549
"Awake, O Sleeper" (Matt)
   E547, EL452, UM551, VU566, W586
"Help Us Accept Each Other" (Matt)
   C487, G754, N388, P358, UM560, W656
"Come, Share the Lord" (Matt, Comm.)
   C408, G510, S2269, SF2269, VU469

Additional Contemporary Suggestions
"Love the Lord" (Lev, Matt)
   M270, WS3116
"Seek Ye First" (Lev, Pss)
   B478, C354, E711, G175, P333, UM405, SP182, VU356
"Turn Your Eyes Upon Jesus" (Pss)
   B320, F621, SP218, UM349
"As the Deer" (Pss)
   G626, S2025, SF2025, SP200, VU766 (*See also* G778)
"Cry of My Heart" (Pss)
   M39, S2165, SF2165
"Open the Eyes of My Heart" (Pss)
   G452, M57, WS3008
"Knowing You" (Pss, 1 Cor)
   M30
"Grace Alone" (1 Cor)
   M100, S2162, SF2162
"Sanctuary" (1 Cor)
   G701, M52, S2164, SF2164
"Holy, Holy" (Matt)
   B254, F149, P140, S2039, SP141

Vocal Solos
"Here I Am" (Lev)
   V-11   p. 19
"The Gift of Love" (Matt)
   V-8   p. 120

Anthems
"How Firm a Foundation" (Lev)
Arr. Dan Forrest; Hinshaw HMC2217
SATB, piano

"The Best of Rooms" (1 Cor)
Z. Randall Stroope; Morningstar 50-5808
SATB, organ

Other Suggestions
Visuals:
   O   Ten Commandments, wheat/grapes, block, scales
   P   Bible, heart, path, eyes, turning
   E   Builder, foundation, Christ, temple, people
   G   Eye, tooth, cheeks, coat/cloak, second mile,
           heart, prayer, sun/rain
Sung Confession: E148, UM450. "Creator of the Earth and
   Skies" (Lev, Pss)
Response: G274, SF2102, VU210. WS3043, st. 1 and 3. "You,
   Lord Are Both Lamb and Shepherd" (Matt)

Exodus 24:12-18

[12]The LORD said to Moses, "Come up to me on the mountain and wait there. I'll give you the stone tablets with the instructions and the commandments that I've written in order to teach them."

[13]So Moses and his assistant Joshua got up, and Moses went up God's mountain. [14]Moses had said to the elders, "Wait for us here until we come back to you. Aaron and Hur will be here with you. Whoever has a legal dispute may go to them."

[15]Then Moses went up the mountain, and the cloud covered the mountain. [16]The LORD's glorious presence settled on Mount Sinai, and the cloud covered it for six days. On the seventh day the LORD called to Moses from the cloud. [17]To the Israelites, the LORD's glorious presence looked like a blazing fire on top of the mountain. [18]Moses entered the cloud and went up the mountain. Moses stayed on the mountain for forty days and forty nights.

Psalm 99 (G57, N687, UM819)

[1]The LORD rules— / the nations shake! / He sits enthroned on the winged heavenly creatures— / the earth quakes! / [2]The LORD is great in Zion; / he is exalted over all the nations. / [3]Let them thank your great and awesome name. / He is holy! / [4]Strong king who loves justice, / you are the one who established what is fair. / You worked justice and righteousness in Jacob. / [5]Magnify the LORD, our God! / Bow low at his footstool! / He is holy! / [6]Moses and Aaron were among his priests, / Samuel too among those who called on his name. / They cried out to the LORD, and he himself answered them— / [7]he spoke to them from a pillar of cloud. / They kept the laws and the rules God gave to them. / [8]LORD our God, you answered them. / To them you were a God who forgives / but also the one who avenged their wrong deeds. / [9]Magnify the LORD our God! / Bow low at his holy mountain / because the LORD our God is holy!

2 Peter 1:16-21

[16]We didn't repeat crafty myths when we told you about the powerful coming of our Lord Jesus Christ. Quite the contrary, we witnessed his majesty with our own eyes. [17]He received honor and glory from God the Father when a voice came to him from the magnificent glory, saying, "This is my dearly loved Son, with whom I am well-pleased." [18]We ourselves heard this voice from heaven while we were with him on the holy mountain. [19]In addition, we have a most reliable prophetic word, and you would do well to pay attention to it, just as you would to a lamp shining in a dark place, until the day dawns and the morning star rises in your hearts. [20]Most important, you must know that no prophecy of scripture represents the prophet's own understanding of things, [21]because no prophecy ever came by human will. Instead, men and women led by the Holy Spirit spoke from God.

Matthew 17:1-9

[1]Six days later Jesus took Peter, James, and John his brother, and brought them to the top of a very high mountain. [2]He was transformed in front of them. His face shone like the sun, and his clothes became as white as light. [3]Moses and Elijah appeared to them, talking with Jesus. [4]Peter reacted to all of this by saying to Jesus, "Lord, it's good that we're here. If you want, I'll make three shrines: one for you, one for Moses, and one for Elijah."

[5]While he was still speaking, look, a bright cloud overshadowed them. A voice from the cloud said, "This is my Son whom I dearly love. I am very pleased with him. Listen to him!" [6]Hearing this, the disciples fell on their faces, filled with awe.

[7]But Jesus came and touched them. "Get up," he said. "Don't be afraid." [8]When they looked up, they saw no one except Jesus.

[9]As they were coming down the mountain, Jesus commanded them, "Don't tell anybody about the vision until the Human One is raised from the dead."

Primary Hymns and Songs for the Day

"Christ, Whose Glory Fills the Skies" (2 Pet, Matt) (O)
    EL553, F293, G662, L265, P462/463, UM173 (PD), VU336
        H-3   Hbl-51; Chr-206; Desc-89; Org-120
        S-1   #278-79. Harms.
"O Wondrous Sight! O Vision Fair" (2 Pet, Matt)
    E137, UM258 (PD)
        H-3   Hbl-93; Chr-84; Desc-102; Org-175
        S-2   #191. Harm.
    E136, EL316 (PD), G189, L80, N184, P75
"Swiftly Pass the Clouds of Glory" (Matt)
    G190, P73, S2102
        H-3   Chr-98; Org-43
"Holy Ground" (Matt)
    B224, C112, G406, S2272, SF2272, SP86
"You, Lord, Are Both Lamb and Shepherd" (Matt)
    G274, SF2102, VU210. WS3043
"Immortal, Invisible, God Only Wise" (Exod) (C)
    B6, C66, E423, EL834, F319, G12, L526, N1, P263, UM103
    (PD), VU264, W512
        H-3   Hbl-15, 71; Chr-65; Desc-93; Org-135
        S-1   #300. Harm.

Additional Hymn Suggestions

"O Worship the King" (Exod)
    B16, C17, E388, EL842, F336, G41, L548, N26, P476, UM73
    (PD), VU235
"Source and Sovereign, Rock and Cloud" (Exod)
    C12, G11, UM113
"Guide Me, O Thou Great Jehovah" (Exod)
    B56, C622, E690, EL618, F608, G65, L343, N18/19, P281,
    UM127 (PD), VU651 (Fr.)
"Glorious Things of Thee Are Spoken" (Exod)
    B398, C709, E522 (or 523), EL647, F376, G81, L358, N307,
    P446, UM731 (PD)
"You Alone Are Holy" (Exod, Transfig.)
    S2077, SF2077
"Spirit, Spirit of Gentleness" (Exod)
    C249, EL396, G291, N286, P319, S2120, VU375 (Fr.)
"Praise God for This Holy Ground" (Exod, Matt)
    G405, WS3009
"The God of Abraham Praise" (Exod, Matt)
    B34, C24, E401, EL831, F332, G49, L544, N24, P488, UM116
    (PD), VU255, W537
"Every Time I Feel the Spirit" (Exod, Matt)
    C592, G66, N282, P315, UM404
"Be Thou My Vision" (Exod, Matt, Transfig.)
    B60, C595, E488, EL793, G450, N451, P339, UM451, VU642
"A Hymn of Glory Let Us Sing" (2 Pet)
    E218, G258, L157, N259, P141, W469
"Lord of All Hopefulness" (2 Pet)
    E482, EL765, G683, L469, S2197, SF2197, W568
"Deep in the Shadows of the Past" (2 Pet)
    G50, N320, P330, S2246
"Wellspring of Wisdom" (2 Pet)
    C596, UM506, VU287
"O Morning Star, How Fair and Bright" (2 Pet, Matt)
    C105, E497, EL308, G827, L76, N158, P69, UM247, VU98
"Christ, upon the Mountain Peak" (2 Pet, Matt)
    E129/E130, EL317, P74, UM260, VU102, W701
"Jesus, Take Us to the Mountain" (Matt)
    N183, G193
"I Stand Amazed in the Presence" (Matt)
    B547, F223, UM371 (PD)

"Here, O My Lord, I See Thee" (Matt, Comm.)
    C416, E318, G517, L211, N336, P520, UM623, VU459
"Let Us with a Joyful Mind" (Matt)
    E389, G31, L521. N16, P244, S2012, SF2012, VU234
"We Have Come at Christ's Own Bidding" (Matt)
    G191, N182, S2103, SF2103, VU104

Additional Contemporary Suggestions

"Awesome God" (Exod, Pss)
    G616, S2040, SF2040, SP11
"Majesty, Worship His Majesty" (Pss)
    B215, SP73, UM176
"Ancient Words" (2 Pet)
    M149
"Open the Eyes of My Heart" (2 Pet)
    G452, M57, WS3008
"All Hail King Jesus" (Matt, Transfig.)
    S2069, SF2069, SP63
"He Is Exalted" (Matt, Transfig.)
    S2070, SF2070, SP66
"Shine, Jesus, Shine" (Matt, Transfig.)
    B579, EL671, G192, S2173, SF2173, SP142
"Turn Your Eyes upon Jesus" (Matt)
    B320, F621, SP218, UM349
"We Fall Down" (Matt, Transfig.)
    G368, M66, WS3187
"Awesome in This Place" (Matt, Transfig.)
    M36
"We Declare Your Majesty" (Matt, Transfig.)
    M43
"When I Look into Your Holiness" (Matt, Transfig.)
    SP171
"Great and Mighty Is He" (Transfig.)
    SP4, M11
"Hosanna" (Transfig.)
    M268, WS3188

Vocal Solos

"Be Thou My Vision" (Exod, Matt, Transfig.)
    V-6   p. 13
"Ev'ry Time I Feel De Spirit" (Exod, Matt)
    V-7   p. 78

Anthems

"*Verbum Caro Factum Est*" (Matt)
Dan Forrest; Hinshaw Music HMC2404
SATB divisi, piano

"Christ upon the Mountain Peak" (Matt)
John Eggert; Concordia 98-4108
SATB, organ, opt. trumpet

Other Suggestions

Visuals:
    O   Exod 24:12b, mountain, tablets, cloud, glory, volcano
    P   Throne, quake, Ps 99:3, scales, footstool, cloud, tablet
    E   Majesty, 2 Pet 1:17b, mountain, lamp, dawn, star
    G   Mountain, three figures/booths, cloud, Matt 17:5b
Sung Prayer: EL529, G392, S2273. "Jesus, We Are Here" (Matt)
Prayer: F503, F508, N831, N872, UM259, WSL13 (Exod, Matt)
Alternate Lesson: Ps 2

Joel 2:1-2, 12-17

[1]Blow the horn in Zion;
    give a shout on my holy mountain!
Let all the people of the land tremble,
    for the day of the Lord is coming.
It is near—
    [2]a day of darkness and no light,
    a day of clouds and thick darkness!
Like blackness spread out upon the mountains,
    a great and powerful army comes,
        unlike any that has ever come before them,
        or will come after them in centuries ahead.
……………………..…………………..

[12]Yet even now, says the Lord,
    return to me with all your hearts,
        with fasting, with weeping, and with sorrow;
[13]tear your hearts
    and not your clothing.
Return to the Lord your God,
    for he is merciful and compassionate,
    very patient, full of faithful love,
        and ready to forgive.
[14]Who knows whether he will have a change of heart
    and leave a blessing behind him,
    a grain offering and a drink offering
        for the Lord your God?
[15]Blow the horn in Zion;
    demand a fast;
    request a special assembly.
[16]Gather the people;
    prepare a holy meeting;
    assemble the elders;
    gather the children,
        even nursing infants.
Let the groom leave his room
    and the bride her chamber.
[17]Between the porch and the altar
    let the priests, the Lord's ministers, weep.
    Let them say, "Have mercy, Lord, on your people,
        and don't make your inheritance a disgrace,
        an example of failure among the nations.
    Why should they say among the peoples,
        'Where is their God?'"

Psalm 51:1-17 (G421/422/423, N657, P195/196, UM785)

[1]Have mercy on me, God, according to your faithful love! / Wipe away my wrongdoings according to your great compassion! / [2]Wash me completely clean of my guilt; / purify me from my sin! / [3]Because I know my wrongdoings, / my sin is always right in front of me. / [4]I've sinned against you—you alone. / I've committed evil in your sight. / That's why you are justified when you render your verdict, / completely correct when you issue your judgment. / [5]Yes, I was born in guilt, in sin, / from the moment my mother conceived me. / [6]And yes, you want truth in the most hidden places; / you teach me wisdom in the most secret space.

[7]Purify me with hyssop and I will be clean; / wash me and I will be whiter than snow. / [8]Let me hear joy and celebration again; / let the bones you crushed rejoice once more. / [9]Hide your face from my sins; / wipe away all my guilty deeds! / [10]Create a clean heart for me, God; / put a new, faithful spirit deep inside me! / [11]Please don't throw me out of your presence; / please don't take your holy spirit away from me. / [12]Return the joy of your salvation to me / and sustain me with a willing spirit. / [13]Then I will teach wrongdoers your ways, / and sinners will come back to you.

[14]Deliver me from violence, God, God of my salvation, / so that my tongue can sing of your righteousness. / [15]Lord, open my lips, / and my mouth will proclaim your praise. / [16]You don't want sacrifices. / If I gave an entirely burned offering, / you wouldn't be pleased. / [17]A broken spirit is my sacrifice, God. / You won't despise a heart, God, that is broken and crushed.

2 Corinthians 5:20b–6:10

[20]So we are ambassadors who represent Christ. God is negotiating with you through us. We beg you as Christ's representatives, "Be reconciled to God!" [21]God caused the one who didn't know sin to be sin for our sake so that through him we could become the righteousness of God.

6 Since we work together with him, we are also begging you not to receive the grace of God in vain. [2]He says, *I listened to you at the right time, and I helped you on the day of salvation.* Look, now is the right time! Look, now is the day of salvation!

[3]We don't give anyone any reason to be offended about anything so that our ministry won't be criticized. [4]Instead, we commend ourselves as ministers of God in every way. We did this with our great endurance through problems, disasters, and stressful situations. [5]We went through beatings, imprisonments, and riots. We experienced hard work, sleepless nights, and hunger. [6]We displayed purity, knowledge, patience, and generosity. We served with the Holy Spirit, genuine love, [7]telling the truth, and God's power. We carried the weapons of righteousness in our right hand and our left hand. [8]We were treated with honor and dishonor and with verbal abuse and good evaluation. We were seen as both fake and real, [9]as unknown and well known, as dying—and look, we are alive! We were seen as punished but not killed, [10]as going through pain but always happy, as poor but making many rich, and as having nothing but owning everything.

Matthew 6:1-6, 16-21

[1]"Be careful that you don't practice your religion in front of people to draw their attention. If you do, you will have no reward from your Father who is in heaven.

[2]"Whenever you give to the poor, don't blow your trumpet as the hypocrites do in the synagogues and in the streets so that they may get praise from people. I assure you, that's the only reward they'll get. [3]But when you give to the poor, don't let your left hand know what your right hand is doing [4]so that you may give to the poor in secret. Your Father who sees what you do in secret will reward you.

[5]"When you pray, don't be like hypocrites. They love to pray standing in the synagogues and on the street corners so that people will see them. I assure you, that's the only reward they'll get. [6]But when you pray, go to your room, shut the door, and pray to your Father who is present in that secret place. Your Father who sees what you do in secret will reward you. . . .

[16]"And when you fast, don't put on a sad face like the hypocrites. They distort their faces so people will know they are fasting. I assure you that they have their reward. [17]When you fast, brush your hair and wash your face. [18]Then you won't look like you are fasting to people, but only to your Father who is present in that secret place. Your Father who sees in secret will reward you.

[19]"Stop collecting treasures for your own benefit on earth, where moth and rust eat them and where thieves break in and steal them. [20]Instead, collect treasures for yourselves in heaven, where moth and rust don't eat them and where thieves don't break in and steal them. [21]Where your treasure is, there your heart will be also."

Primary Hymns and Songs for the Day

"Take Time to Be Holy" (Matt) (O)
    B446, C572, F457, UM395 (PD), VU672
        H-3   Chr-178
        S-1   #159. Harm.
"Give Me a Clean Heart" (Pss, Ash Wed.)
    AH4125, C515, N188, S2133, SF2133
"Sunday's Palms Are Wednesday's Ashes" (Pss, Ash Wed.)
    S2138, SF2138, VU107
        H-3   Hbl-14, 64; Chr-132, 203
        S-2   #22. Desc.
"Dust and Ashes" (Ash Wednesday)
    N186, VU105, WS3098
"Lord, I Want to Be a Christian" (Joel, Matt) (C)
    B489, C589, F421, G729, N454, P372 (PD), UM402
        H-3   Chr-130

Additional Hymn Suggestions

"There's a Wideness in God's Mercy" (Joel)
    B25, C73, E470, EL587/88F115, F115, G435, L290, N23,
    P298, UM121, VU271, W595
"Come Back Quickly to the Lord" (Joel)
    G416, P381, UM343
"O Master, Let Me Walk with Thee" (Joel)
    B279, C602, E659/E660, EL818, F442, G738, L492, N503,
    P357, UM430 (PD), VU560
"Today We All Are Called to Be Disciples" (Joel)
    G757, P434, VU507
"Gather Us In" (Joel, Comm.)
    C284, EL532, G401, S2236, SF2236, W665
"O for a Closer Walk with God" (Pss)
    E684, G739, N450, P396
"Jesus, the Very Thought of Thee" (2 Cor)
    C102, E642, EL754, G629, L316, N507, P310, UM175
"What Wondrous Love Is This" (2 Cor)
    B143 (PD), C200, E439, EL666, F283, G215, L385, N223,
    P85, UM292, VU147 (Fr.), W600
"Alas! And Did My Savior Bleed" (2 Cor, Lent)
    AH4067, B139/145, C204, EL337, F274, G212, L98, N199/
    N200, P78, UM294/UM359
"Lord, Speak to Me" (2 Cor)
    B568, EL676, F625, G722, L403, N531, P426, UM463 (PD),
    VU589
"We Walk by Faith" (2 Cor, Matt)
    E209, EL635, G817, N256, P399, S2196, SF2196, W572
"In the Singing" (2 Cor, Comm.)
    EL466, G533, S2255, SF2255
"Amazing Grace" (Matt)
    AH4091, B330, C546, E671, EL779, F107, G649, L448, N547
    and N548, P280, UM378 (PD), VU266 (Fr.), W583
"Be Thou My Vision" (Matt)
    B60, C595, E488, EL793, G450, N451, P339, UM451, VU642
"Lord of All Hopefulness" (Matt)
    E482, EL765, G683, L469, S2197, SF2197, W568
"The Glory of These Forty Days" (Matt)
    E143, EL320, G165, P87, W422
"Forty Days and Forty Nights" (Matt)
    C179, E150, G167, N205, P77, VU114, W419
"Near to the Heart of God" (Matt)
    B295, C581, F35, G824, P527, UM472 (PD)
"More Love to Thee, O Christ" (Matt)
    B473, C527, F476, G828, N456, P359, UM453 (PD)
"Sweet Hour of Prayer" (Matt)
    B445, C570, F439, N505, UM496 (PD)

"Come and Find the Quiet Center" (Matt, Ash Wed.)
    C575, S2128, SF2128, VU374
"The Lord's Prayer" (Matt, Lent)
    B462, C307-C310, F440, G464, P589, S2278, SF2278, UM271,
    WS3068-WS3071
"Lord, Who Throughout These Forty Days" (Matt, Lent) (C)
    C180, E142, EL319, G166, N211, P81, UM269, W417 (PD)

Additional Contemporary Suggestions

"You Are My Hiding Place" (Pss)
    C554, S2055, SF2055
"Open Our Eyes, Lord" (Pss)
    B499, S2086, SF2086, SP199
"Change My Heart, O God" (Pss)
    EL801, G695, S2152, SF2152, SP195,
"Open the Eyes of My Heart" (Pss)
    G452, M57, WS3008
"Purify My Heart" (Pss)
    M90
"Give Us Clean Hands" (Pss)
    M153
"Because of Your Love" (Pss)
    M224
"Amazing Grace" ("My Chains Are Gone") (Matt)
    M205, WS3104
"Grace Like Rain" (Matt)
    M251
"You Are My All in All" (Matt, Lent)
    G519, SP220, WS3040

Vocal Solos

"Give Me a Clean Heart" (Pss, Ash Wednesday)
    V-5 (2)   p. 52
"How Quiet Is the Night" (Matt, Ash Wednesday)
    V-8   p. 158

Anthems

"We Walk by Faith" (2 Cor, Matt)
Kenneth Kosche; MorningStar MSM-50-6031
SATB a cappella

"Create in Me a Clean Heart" (Pss)
Mark Burrows; Abingdon Press 0687491649
SATB, piano

Other Suggestions

Visuals:
    O   Black cloth, grain, trumpet, empty plate, weeping
    P   Water, snow, rejoicing, Ps 51:10, 15, 17, heart
    E   Clock, calendar with today's date, black/gold
    G   Praying hands, oil/water, closed door, empty plate,
            rusty items, Matt 6:21, ashes of last year's palms, oil
    Ash Wednesday: Ashes, rough fabrics
Isaiah 58:1-12 gives another interpretation of fasting.
Call to Prayer: EL538, G466, S2157, SF2157, W561. "Come and
    Fill Our Hearts" (Pss)
Call to Confession: N833 or WSL93 (Pss, Healing)
Prayer: N846, UM353, WSL15 (Pss, Matt, Ash Wednesday)
Meditative Songs in Taizé Style: S2057, S2058, S2118, S2133,
    S2156, S2157, S2159, S2200, S2275

Genesis 2:15-17; 3:1-7   *2014*

¹⁵The LORD God took the human and settled him in the garden of Eden to farm it and to take care of it. ¹⁶The LORD God commanded the human, "Eat your fill from all of the garden's trees; ¹⁷but don't eat from the tree of the knowledge of good and evil, because on the day you eat from it, you will die!" . . .

3The snake was the most intelligent of all the wild animals that the LORD God had made. He said to the woman, "Did God really say that you shouldn't eat from any tree in the garden?"

²The woman said to the snake, "We may eat the fruit of the garden's trees ³but not the fruit of the tree in the middle of the garden. God said, 'Don't eat from it, and don't touch it, or you will die.'"

⁴The snake said to the woman, "You won't die! ⁵God knows that on the day you eat from it, you will see clearly and you will be like God, knowing good and evil." ⁶The woman saw that the tree was beautiful with delicious food and that the tree would provide wisdom, so she took some of its fruit and ate it, and also gave some to her husband, who was with her, and he ate it. ⁷Then they both saw clearly and knew that they were naked. So they sewed fig leaves together and made garments for themselves.

Psalm 32 (G446, N642, P184, UM766)

¹The one whose wrongdoing is forgiven, / whose sin is covered over, is truly happy! / ²The one the LORD doesn't consider guilty— / in whose spirit there is no dishonesty— / that one is truly happy!

³When I kept quiet, my bones wore out; / I was groaning all day long— / every day, every night!— / ⁴because your hand was heavy upon me. / My energy was sapped as if in a summer drought. *[Selah]* ⁵So I admitted my sin to you; / I didn't conceal my guilt. / "I'll confess my sins to the LORD," is what I said. / Then you removed the guilt of my sin. *[Selah]*

⁶That's why all the faithful should pray to you during troubled times, / so that a great flood of water won't reach them. / ⁷You are my secret hideout! / You protect me from trouble. / You surround me with songs of rescue! *[Selah]*

⁸I will instruct you and teach you / about the direction you should go. / I'll advise you and keep my eye on you. / ⁹Don't be like some senseless horse or mule, / whose movement must be controlled / with a bit and a bridle. / Don't be anything like that! / ¹⁰The pain of the wicked is severe, / but faithful love surrounds the one who trusts the LORD. / ¹¹You who are righteous, rejoice in the LORD and be glad! / All you whose hearts are right, sing out in joy!

Romans 5:12-19

¹²So, in the same way that sin entered the world through one person, and death came through sin, so death spread to all human beings with the result that all sinned. ¹³Although sin was in the world, since there was no Law, it wasn't taken into account until the Law came. ¹⁴But death ruled from Adam until Moses, even over those who didn't sin in the same way Adam did—Adam was a type of the one who was coming.

¹⁵But the free gift of Christ isn't like Adam's failure. If many people died through what one person did wrong, God's grace is multiplied even more for many people with the gift—of the one person Jesus Christ—that comes through grace. ¹⁶The gift isn't like the consequences of one person's sin. The judgment that came from one person's sin led to punishment, but the free gift that came out of many failures led to the verdict of acquittal. ¹⁷If death ruled because of one person's failure, those who receive the multiplied grace and the gift of righteousness will even more certainly rule in life through the one person Jesus Christ.

¹⁸So now the righteous requirements necessary for life are met for everyone through the righteous act of one person, just as judgment fell on everyone through the failure of one person. ¹⁹Many people were made righteous through the obedience of one person, just as many people were made sinners through the disobedience of one person.

Matthew 4:1-11

¹Then the Spirit led Jesus up into the wilderness so that the devil might tempt him. ²After Jesus had fasted for forty days and forty nights, he was starving. ³The tempter came to him and said, "Since you are God's Son, command these stones to become bread."

⁴Jesus replied, "It's written, *People won't live only by bread, but by every word spoken by God.*"

⁵After that the devil brought him into the holy city and stood him at the highest point of the temple. He said to him, ⁶"Since you are God's Son, throw yourself down; for it is written, *I will command my angels concerning you, and they will take you up in their hands so that you won't hit your foot on a stone.*"

⁷Jesus replied, "Again it's written, *Don't test the Lord your God.*"

⁸Then the devil brought him to a very high mountain and showed him all the kingdoms of the world and their glory. ⁹He said, "I'll give you all these if you bow down and worship me."

¹⁰Jesus responded, "Go away, Satan, because it's written, *You will worship the Lord your God and serve only him.*" ¹¹The devil left him, and angels came and took care of him.

temptation
identity
hunger

Primary Hymns and Songs for the Day

"Lord, Who Throughout These Forty Days" (Matt) (O)
  C180, E142, G166, N211, P81, W417 (PD)
    H-3   Chr-132; Desc-94; Org-137
  UM269
    H-3   Chr-106; Desc-65; Org-72
    S-2   #105. Flute/violin desc.
           #106. Harm.
  EL319, L99
"Jesus, Tempted in the Desert" (Matt)
  S2105, SF2105, VU115
    H-3   Chr-53; Org-33
    S-1   #109-10. Desc. and harm.
"Jesus Walked This Lonesome Valley" (Matt)
  C211, F217, P80, S2112, W427
"Amazing Grace" (Pss, Rom) (C)
  AH4091, B330, C546, E671, EL779, F107, G649, L448, N547
  and N548, P280, UM378 (PD), VU266 (Fr.), W583
    H-3   Hbl-14, 46; Chr-27; Desc-14; Org-4
    S-2   #5-7. Various treatments

Additional Hymn Suggestions

"All My Hope Is Firmly Grounded" (Gen)
  C88, E665, EL757, N408, UM132, VU654/655
"God Who Stretched the Spangled Heavens" (Gen)
  C651, E580, EL771, G24, L463, N556, P268, UM150
"Creator of the Stars of Night" (Gen)
  C127, E60, EL245, G84, L323, N111, P4, UM692 (PD)
"God Made from One Blood" (Gen)
  C500, N427, S2170, SF2170, VU554
"O Worship the King" (Gen, Rom)
  B16, C17, E388, EL842, F336, G41, L548, N26, P476, UM73
  (PD), VU235
"Taste and See" (Pss, Comm.)
  EL493, G520, S2267, SF2267
"Alas! and Did My Savior Bleed" (Rom)
  AH4067, B139/145, C204, EL337, F274, G212, L98, N199/
  N200, P78, UM294/UM359
"When I Survey the Wondrous Cross" (Rom) (C)
  B144, C195, EL803, F258, G223, N224, P101, UM298
  E474, L482, G224, P100, UM299 (PD), VU149 (Fr.)
"*Cristo Vive*" ("Christ Is Risen") (Rom)
  B167, N235, P109, UM313
"Because He Lives" (Rom,)
  B407, C562, F292, UM364
"Lord, Dismiss Us With Thy Blessing" (Rom) (C)
  C439, E344, EL545, F520, G546, L259, N77, P538, UM671
  (PD), VU425
"In the Singing" (Rom, Comm.)
  EL466, G533, S2255, SF2255
"Bread of the World" (Rom, Matt, Comm.)
  C387, E301, G499, N346, P502, UM624, VU461
"O Love, How Deep" (Matt)
  E448/449, EL322, G618, L88, N209, P83, UM267, VU348
"It Is Well with My Soul" (Matt)
  B410, C561, EL785, F495, G840, L346, N438, UM377
"Be Still, My Soul" (Matt)
  C566, F77, G819, N488, UM534, VU652
"I Was There to Hear Your Borning Cry" (Matt)
  C75, EL732, G488, N351, S2051, SF2051, VU644
"The Glory of These Forty Days" (Matt)
  E143, EL320, G165, P87, W422
"Forty Days and Forty Nights" (Matt)
  C179, E150, G167, N205, P77, VU114, W419

"My Song Is Love Unknown" (Matt, Lent)
  E458, EL343, G209, L94, N222, P76, S2083, SF2083, VU143,
  W439
"Praise God for This Holy Ground" (Matt, Lent)
  G405, WS3009
"Dust and Ashes" (Matt, Lent)
  N186, VU105, WS3098
"Wild and Lone the Prophet's Voice" (Lent)
  G163, P409, S2089, SF2089

Additional Contemporary Suggestions

"You Are My Hiding Place" (Pss)
  C554, S2055, SF2055
"My Redeemer Lives" (Pss, Lent)
  M73
"Hallelujah" ("Your Love Is Amazing") (Pss, Lent)
  M118, WS3027
"Amazing Grace" ("My Chains Are Gone") (Pss, Rom)
  M205, WS3104
"Grace Like Rain" (Pss, Rom)
  M251
"We Fall Down" (Rom)
  G368, M66, WS3187
"O Lord, You're Beautiful" (Rom)
  S2064, SF2064
"Sing Alleluia to the Lord" (Rom)
  B214, C32, S2258, SF2258, SP93
"Glorious Day" (Rom)
  M279
"Lamb of God" (Matt, Lent)
  EL336, G518, S2113, SF2113
"Lord, I Lift Your Name on High" (Matt, Lent)
  AH4071, EL857, M2, S2088, SF2088

Vocal Solos

"And Can It Be That I Should Gain" (Rom)
  V-1   p. 29
"Grace Greater Than Our Sin" (Rom)
  V-8   p. 180
"Holy Is the Lamb" (Matt)
  V-5 (1)   p. 5

Anthems

"Pater Noster" ("Our Father") (Matt)
Alejandro Consolacion II; Hinshaw Music HMC2398
SATB divisi, a cappella

"O Lord Throughout These Forty Days" (Matt)
Walter Pelz; Augsburg 0800637534
SAB, organ

Other Suggestions

Visuals:
  O   Garden, fruit tree, serpent, fig leaves/loin cloth
  P   Hand, dry/heat, praying hands, waterfall, hiding
       place, teaching, bit/bridle, joy, Ps 32:11
  E   Target/arrows (sin), gift, Christ, crucifix
  G   Dove/flames, 40/40, stones/bread, Bible, pinnacle,
       angels ministering, Matt 4:7, mountain, vista
Introit: G274, SF2102, VU210. WS3043, st. 3. "You, Lord, Are
  Both Lamb and Shepherd" (Matt, Lent)

Genesis 12:1-4a

2014

[1]The Lord said to Abram, "Leave your land, your family, and your father's household for the land that I will show you. [2]I will make of you a great nation and will bless you. I will make your name respected, and you will be a blessing.
[3] I will bless those who bless you,
        those who curse you I will curse;
            all the families of earth
                will be blessed because of you."
[4]Abram left just as the Lord told him, and Lot went with him. Now Abram was 75 years old when he left Haran.

Psalm 121 (P45/845, N704, P234, UM844)

[1]I raise my eyes toward the mountains. / Where will my help come from? / [2]My help comes from the Lord, / the maker of heaven and earth. / [3]God won't let your foot slip. / Your protector won't fall asleep on the job. / [4]No! Israel's protector / never sleeps or rests! / [5]The Lord is your protector; / the Lord is your shade right beside you. / [6]The sun won't strike you during the day; / neither will the moon at night. / [7]The Lord will protect you from all evil; / God will protect your very life. / [8]The Lord will protect you on your journeys— / whether going or coming— / from now until forever from now.

Romans 4:1-5, 13-17

[1]So what are we going to say? Are we going to find that Abraham is our ancestor on the basis of genealogy? [2]Because if Abraham was made righteous because of his actions, he would have had a reason to brag, but not in front of God. [3]What does the scripture say? *Abraham had faith in God, and it was credited to him as righteousness.* [4]Workers' salaries aren't credited to them on the basis of an employer's grace but rather on the basis of what they deserve. [5]But faith is credited as righteousness to those who don't work, because they have faith in God who makes the ungodly righteous. . . .

[13]The promise to Abraham and to his descendants, that he would inherit the world, didn't come through the Law but through the righteousness that comes from faith. [14]If they inherit because of the Law, then faith has no effect and the promise has been canceled. [15]The Law brings about wrath. But when there isn't any law, there isn't any violation of the law. [16]That's why the inheritance comes through faith, so that it will be on the basis of God's grace. In that way, the promise is secure for all of Abraham's descendants, not just for those who are related by Law but also for those who are related by the faith of Abraham, who is the father of all of us. [17]As it is written: *I have appointed you to be the father of many nations.* So Abraham is our father in the eyes of God in whom he had faith, the God who gives life to the dead and calls things that don't exist into existence.

John 3:1-17

[1]There was a Pharisee named Nicodemus, a Jewish leader. [2]He came to Jesus at night and said to him, "Rabbi, we know that you are a teacher who has come from God, for no one could do these miraculous signs that you do unless God is with him."

[3]Jesus answered, "I assure you, unless someone is born anew, it's not possible to see God's kingdom."

[4]Nicodemus asked, "How is it possible for an adult to be born? It's impossible to enter the mother's womb for a second time and be born, isn't it?"

[5]Jesus answered, "I assure you, unless someone is born of water and the Spirit, it's not possible to enter God's kingdom. [6]Whatever is born of the flesh is flesh, and whatever is born of the Spirit is spirit. [7]Don't be surprised that I said to you, 'You must be born anew.' [8]God's Spirit blows wherever it wishes. You hear its sound, but you don't know where it comes from or where it is going. It's the same with everyone who is born of the Spirit."

[9]Nicodemus said, "How are these things possible?"

[10]"Jesus answered, "You are a teacher of Israel and you don't know these things? [11]I assure you that we speak about what we know and testify about what we have seen, but you don't receive our testimony. [12]If I have told you about earthly things and you don't believe, how will you believe if I tell you about heavenly things? [13]No one has gone up to heaven except the one who came down from heaven, the Human One. [14]Just as Moses lifted up the snake in the wilderness, so must the Human Onebe lifted up [15]so that everyone who believes in him will have eternal life. [16]God so loved the world that he gave his only Son, so that everyone who believes in him won't perish but will have eternal life. [17]God didn't send his Son into the world to judge the world, but that the world might be saved through him."

To condemn
  or
To save

Primary Hymns and Songs for the Day
"The God of Abraham Praise" (Gen) (O)
B34, C24, E401, EL831, F332, G49, L544, N24, P488, UM116 (PD), VU255, W537
    H-3   Hbl-62, 95; Chr-59; Org-77
    S-1   #211. Harm.
"To God Be the Glory" (John)
B4, C72, F363, G634, P485, UM98 (PD)
    H-3   Chr-201
    S-2   #176. Piano arr.
"Lift High the Cross" (John) (C)
B594, C108, E473, EL660, G826, L377, N198, P371, UM159, VU151, W704
    H-3   Hbl-75; Chr-128; Desc-25; Org-21
    S-1   #71-75. Various treatments

Additional Hymn Suggestions
"Let All Things Now Living" (Gen)
B640, C717, EL881, F389, G37, L557, P554, S2008, VU242
"Deep in the Shadows of the Past" (Gen)
G50, N320, P330, S2246
"O God, Our Help in Ages Past" (Gen, Pss)
B74, C67, E680, EL632, F370, G687, L320, N25, P210, UM117 (PD), VU806, W579
"If Thou But Suffer God to Guide Thee" (Gen, Pss)
B57, C565, E635, EL769, G816, L453, N410, P282, UM142 (PD), VU285 (Fr.) and VU286
"Immortal, Invisible, God Only Wise" (Pss, Rom)
B6, C66, E423, EL834, F319, G12, L526, N1, P263, UM103 (PD), VU264, W512
"Sing Praise to God Who Reigns Above" (Pss)
B20, C6, E408, EL871, F343, G645, N6, P483, UM126 (PD), VU216, W528
"Jesus, Lover of My Soul" (Pss, Rom)
B180 (PD), C542, E699, G440, N546, P303, UM479, VU669
"My Faith Looks Up to Thee" (Rom)
B416, C576, E691, EL759, G829, L479, P383, UM452, VU663
"Faith of Our Fathers" (Rom)
B352, C635, EL812/813, F526, L500, N381, UM710 (PD), VU580, W571
"We Walk by Faith" (Rom)
E209, EL635, G817, N256, P399, S2196, SF2196, W572
"Dearest Jesus, We Are Here" (John)
EL443, G483, L187, P493
"Of the Father's Love Begotten" (John)
B251, C104, E82, EL295, F172 (PD), G108, L42, N118, P309, UM184, VU61, W398
"Because He Lives" (John)
B407, C562, F292, UM364
"Blessed Assurance" (John)
B334, C543, EL638, F67, G839, N473, P341, UM369 (PD), VU337
"Gather Us In" (John)
C284, EL532, G401, S2236, SF2236, W665
"How Blest Are They Who Trust in Christ" (John)
C646, N365, UM654
"Like a Child" (John)
C133, S2092, SF2092, VU366
"O Holy Spirit, Root of Life" (John)
C251, EL399, N57, S2121, SF2121, VU379
"Wash, O God, Our Sons and Daughters" (John, Baptism)
C365, EL445, G490, UM605, VU442
"We Know That Christ Is Raised" (John, Baptism)
E296, EL449, G485, L189, P495, UM610, VU448, W721

"Womb of Life" (John, Comm.)
C14, G3, N274, S2046, SF2046
"Mothering God, You Gave Me Birth" (John, Comm.)
C83, EL735, G7, N467, S2050, SF2050, VU320

Additional Contemporary Suggestions
"Shout to the Lord" (Pss)
EL821, M16, S2074, SF2074; V-3 (2) p. 32 Vocal solo
"Holy Spirit, Come to Us" (Pss)
EL406, G281, S2118, SF2118, W473
"Sing Alleluia to the Lord" (Rom)
B214, C32, S2258, SF2258, SP93
"Here Is Bread, Here Is Wine" (Rom, Comm.)
EL483, S2266, SF2266
"O How He Loves You and Me!" (John)
B146, F622, S2108, SF2108, SP113
"He Came Down" (John)
EL253, G137, S2085, SF2085
"Lord, I Lift Your Name on High" (John, Lent)
AH4071, EL857, M2, S2088, SF2088
"There Is a Redeemer" (John)
G443, SP111
"In Christ Alone" (John)
M138, WS3105
"You Are My All in All" (John)
G519, SP220, WS3040
"No Greater Love" (John, Lent)
M25
"God Is Good All the Time" (John)
AH4010, M45, WS3026
"Above All" (John)
M77; V-3 (2) p. 17 Vocal solo
"You Are My King" ("Amazing Love") (John)
M82, WS3102

Vocal Solos
"Oh, What Love!" (Rom, John)
V-8   p. 144
"The Gospel of Grace" (Rom, John)
V-3 (1)   p. 44

Anthems
"Psalm 121" (Pss)
Gordon Ramsay; Fred Bock Music 08739825
SATB a cappella, violin

"For God So Loved the World" (John)
Allen Pote; Hope C5386
SATB, piano

Other Suggestions
Visuals:
  O   Luggage, multitude, farewell, walking
  P   Hills, foot, sleep, sun/moon, evils, open door
  E   Abraham, paycheck, will, trust
  G   Cloak/night, newborn, water/Spirit, wind, serpent lifted, crucifix, John 3:16, Ascension, world
The scripture from John can lead into a baptism ritual.
Call to Prayer: G782, WS3131, st. 1. "Hear My Prayer, O God" (Pss)

2014

Exodus 17:1-7

[1]The whole Israelite community broke camp and set out from the Sin desert to continue their journey, as the LORD commanded. They set up their camp at Rephidim, but there was no water for the people to drink. [2]The people argued with Moses and said, "Give us water to drink."

Moses said to them, "Why are you arguing with me? Why are you testing the LORD?"

[3]But the people were very thirsty for water there, and they complained to Moses, "Why did you bring us out of Egypt to kill us, our children, and our livestock with thirst?"

[4]So Moses cried out to the LORD, "What should I do with this people? They are getting ready to stone me."

[5]The LORD said to Moses, "Go on ahead of the people, and take some of Israel's elders with you. Take in your hand the shepherd's rod that you used to strike the Nile River, and go. [6]I'll be standing there in front of you on the rock at Horeb. Hit the rock. Water will come out of it, and the people will be able to drink." Moses did so while Israel's elders watched. [7]He called the place Massah and Meribah, because the Israelites argued with and tested the LORD, asking, "Is the LORD really with us or not?"

Psalm 95 (G386/638, N683, P214/215, UM814)

[1]Come, let's sing out loud to the LORD! / Let's raise a joyful shout to the rock of our salvation! / [2]Let's come before him with thanks! / Let's shout songs of joy to him! / [3]The LORD is a great God, / the great king over all other gods. / [4]The earth's depths are in his hands; / the mountain heights belong to him; / [5]the sea, which he made, is his / along with the dry ground, / which his own hands formed. / [6]Come, let's worship and bow down! / Let's kneel before the LORD, our maker! / [7]He is our God, / and we are the people of his pasture, / the sheep in his hands. / If only you would listen to his voice right now! / [8]"Don't harden your hearts / like you did at Meribah, / like you did when you were at Massah, / in the wilderness, / [9]when your ancestors tested me / and scrutinized me, / even though they had already seen my acts. / [10]For forty years I despised that generation, / and I said, 'These people have twisted hearts. / They don't know my ways.' / [11]So in anger I swore: / 'They will never enter my place of rest!'"

Romans 5:1-11

[1]Therefore, since we have been made righteous through his faithfulness combined with our faith, we have peace with God through our Lord Jesus Christ. [2]We have access by faith into this grace in which we stand through him, and we boast in the hope of God's glory. [3]But not only that! We even take pride in our problems, because we know that trouble produces endurance, [4]endurance produces character, and character produces hope. [5]This hope doesn't put us to shame, because the love of God has been poured out in our hearts through the Holy Spirit, who has been given to us.

[6]While we were still weak, at the right moment, Christ died for ungodly people. [7]It isn't often that someone will die for a righteous person, though maybe someone might dare to die for a good person. [8]But God shows his love for us, because while we were still sinners Christ died for us. [9]So, now that we have been made righteous by his blood, we can be even more certain that we will be saved from God's wrath through him. [10]If we were reconciled to God through the death of his Son while we were still enemies, now that we have been reconciled, how much more certain is it that we will be saved by his life? [11]And not only that: we even take pride in God through our Lord Jesus Christ, the one through whom we now have a restored relationship with God.

John 4:5-42

[5]He came to a Samaritan city called Sychar, which was near the land Jacob had given to his son Joseph. [6]Jacob's well was there. Jesus was tired from his journey, so he sat down at the well. It was about noon.

[7]A Samaritan woman came to the well to draw water. Jesus said to her, "Give me some water to drink." [8]His disciples had gone into the city to buy him some food.

[9]The Samaritan woman asked, "Why do you, a Jewish man, ask for something to drink from me, a Samaritan woman?" (Jews and Samaritans didn't associate with each other.)

[10]Jesus responded, "If you recognized God's gift and who is saying to you, 'Give me some water to drink,' you would be asking him and he would give you living water."

[11]The woman said to him, "Sir, you don't have a bucket and the well is deep. Where would you get this living water? [12]You aren't greater than our father Jacob, are you? He gave this well to us, and he drank from it himself, as did his sons and his livestock."

[13]Jesus answered, "Everyone who drinks this water will be thirsty again, [14]but whoever drinks from the water that I will give will never be thirsty again. The water that I give will become in those who drink it a spring of water that bubbles up into eternal life."

[15]The woman said to him, "Sir, give me this water, so that I will never be thirsty and will never need to come here to draw water!"

[16]Jesus said to her, "Go, get your husband, and come back here."

[17]The woman replied, "I don't have a husband."

"You are right to say, 'I don't have a husband,'" Jesus answered. [18]"You've had five husbands, and the man you are with now isn't your husband. You've spoken the truth."

[19]The woman said, "Sir, I see that you are a prophet. [20]Our ancestors worshipped on this mountain, but you and your people say that it is necessary to worship in Jerusalem."

[21]Jesus said to her, "Believe me, woman, the time is coming when you and your people will worship the Father neither on this mountain nor in Jerusalem. [22]You and your people worship what you don't know; we worship what we know because salvation is from the Jews. [23]But the time is coming—and is here!—when true worshippers will worship in spirit and truth. The Father looks for those who worship him this way. [24]God is spirit, and it is necessary to worship God in spirit and truth."

[25]The woman said, "I know that the Messiah is coming, the one who is called the Christ. When he comes, he will teach everything to us."

[26]Jesus said to her, "I Am—the one who speaks with you."

[27]Just then, Jesus' disciples arrived and were shocked that he was talking with a woman. But no one asked, "What do you want?" or "Why are you talking with her?"[28]The woman put down her water jar and went into the city. She said to the people, [29]"Come and see a man who has told me everything I've done! Could this man be the Christ?" [30]They left the city and were on their way to see Jesus.

[31]In the meantime the disciples spoke to Jesus, saying, "Rabbi, eat."

[32]Jesus said to them, "I have food to eat that you don't know about."

[33]The disciples asked each other, "Has someone brought him food?"

[34]Jesus said to them, "I am fed by doing the will of the one who sent me and by completing his work. [35]Don't you have a saying, 'Four more months and then it's time for harvest'? Look, I tell you: open your eyes and notice that the fields are already ripe for the harvest. [36]Those who harvest are receiving their pay and gathering fruit for eternal life so that those who sow and those who harvest can celebrate together. [37]This is a true saying, that one sows and another harvests. [38]I have sent you to harvest what you didn't work hard for; others worked hard, and you will share in their hard work."

[39]Many Samaritans in that city believed in Jesus because of the woman's word when she testified, "He told me everything I've ever done." [40]So when the Samaritans came to Jesus, they asked him to stay with them, and he stayed there two days. [41]Many more believed because of his word, [42]and they said to the woman, "We no longer believe because of what you said, for we have heard for ourselves and know that this one is truly the savior of the world."

Outsider / Insider

Primary Hymns and Songs for the Day

"Guide Me, O Thou Great Jehovah" (Exod, John) (O)
  B56, C622, E690, EL618, F608, G65, L343, N18/19, P281,
  UM127 (PD), VU651 (Fr.)
      H-3   Hbl-25, 51, 58; Chr-89; Desc-26; Org-23
      S-1   #76-77. Desc. and harm.
"You Who Are Thirsty" (Exod, John)
  S2132, SP219
"O How He Loves You and Me!" (Rom)
  B146, F622, S2108, SF2108, SP113
"When I Survey the Wondrous Cross" (Rom) (C)
  B144, C195, EL803, F258, G223, N224, P101, UM298
      H-3   Hbl-6, 102; Chr-213; Desc-49; Org-49
      S-1   #155. Desc.
  E474, L482, G224, P100, UM299 (PD), VU149 (Fr.)
      H-3   Hbl-47; Chr-214; Desc-90; Org-127
      S-1   #288. Transposition to E-flat major

Additional Hymn Suggestions

"All My Hope Is Firmly Grounded" (Exod)
  C88, E665, EL757, N408, UM132, VU654/655
"Rock of Ages" (Exod)
  B342, C214, E685, EL623, F108, G438, L327, N596, UM361
"Jesus, Thou Joy of Loving Hearts" (Exod, John)
  C101, E649, F451, G494, L356, N329, P510, VU472, W605
"Glorious Things of Thee Are Spoken" (Exod, John)
  B398, C709, E522 (or 523), EL647, F376, G81, L358, N307,
  P446, UM731 (PD)
"Joyful, Joyful, We Adore Thee" (Pss, John)
  B7, C2, E376, EL836, F377, G611, L551, N4, P464, UM89
  (PD), VU232, W525
"We Walk by Faith" (Pss, Rom)
  E209, EL635, G817, N256, P399, S2196, SF2196, W572
"O Love That Wilt Not Let Me Go" (Rom)
  B292, C540, G833, L324, N485, P384, UM480 (PD), VU658
"Spirit of God, Descend upon My Heart" (Rom)
  B245, C265, EL800, F147, G688, L486, N290, P326, UM500
  (PD), VU378
"In the Singing" (Rom, Comm.)
  EL466, G533, S2255, SF2255
"You, Lord, Are Both Lamb and Shepherd" (Rom, Lent)
  G274, SF2102, VU210. WS3043
"Healer of Our Every Ill" (Rom, John)
  C506, EL612, G795, S2213, SF2213, VU619
"Source and Sovereign, Rock and Cloud" (John)
  C12, G11, UM113
"The King of Love, My Shepherd Is" (John)
  E645, EL502, G802, L456, P171, UM138 (PD), VU273, W609
"Jesus, Lover of My Soul" (John)
  B180 (PD), C542, E699, G440, N546, P303, UM479, VU669
"O Splendor of God's Glory Bright" (John)
  E5, G666, N87, P474, UM679, VU413
"Come, Labor On" (John)
  E541, G719, N532, P415
"Gather Us In" (John)
  C284, EL532, G401, S2236, SF2236, W665
"Dust and Ashes" (John, Lent)
  N186, VU105, WS3098
"All Who Hunger" (John, Comm.)
  C419, EL461, G509, S2126, SF2126, VU460
"Come to the Table" (John, Comm.)
  EL481, S2264, SF2264
"Feed Us, Lord" (John, Comm.)
  G501, WS3167
"You Satisfy the Hungry Heart" (John, Comm.)
  C429, EL484, G523, P521, UM629, VU478, W736

Additional Contemporary Suggestions

"Forever" (Exod, Pss)
  M68, WS3023
"God of Wonders" (Exod, Pss)
  M80, WS3034
"Great Is the Lord" (Pss)
  B12, G614, S2022, SF2022, SP30
"Come, All You People" ("Uyai Mose") (Pss)
  EL819, G388, S2274, SF2274
"Sing Alleluia to the Lord" (Rom)
  B214, C32, S2258, SF2258, SP93
"You Are My King" ("Amazing Love") (Rom)
  M82, WS3102
"Here Is Bread, Here Is Wine" (Rom, John, Comm.)
  EL483, S2266, SF2266
"Jesus, Name above All Names" (John)
  S2071, SF2071, SP76
"Fill My Cup, Lord" (John, Comm.)
  C351, F481, UM641 (refrain only), WS3093
"Falling on My Knees" ("Hungry") (John)
  M155, WS3099
"Come, Now Is the Time to Worship" (John)
  M56, WS3176
"Who Can Satisfy My Soul Like You?" (John)
  M28
"Come Just as You Are" (John)
  M47
"All Who Are Thirsty" (John)
  M159
"Just to Be with You" (John)
  M255

Vocal Solos

"Leanin' on Dat Lamb" (Exod, Lent)
  V-7   p. 42
"Maybe the Rain" (John)
  V-5 (2)   p. 27

Anthems

"Uyai Mose" (Pss)
Arr. Kevin Holland; Choristers Guild CGA-1373
SATB, opt. percussion

"Just as I Am" (John)
Bob Chilcott; Oxford 9780193511491
SATB, organ

Other Suggestions

Visuals:
  O   Wilderness, quarrel, stones, staff, rock, water, Exod
           17:7c
  P   Singing, rock, instruments, mountain, sea, dry land
  E   Christ, glory/suffering, hearts/Spirit, crucifix
  G   Well, noon, water jar, living water, clock
Introit: WS3113, st. 1. "A Wilderness Wandering People" (Exod,
  Lent)
Call to Confession: N833 (Lent)
Words of Assurance: Rom 5:8

2014

1 Samuel 16:1-13

¹The Lord said to Samuel, "How long are you going to grieve over Saul? I have rejected him as king over Israel. Fill your horn with oil and get going. I'm sending you to Jesse of Bethlehem because I have found my next king among his sons."

²"How can I do that?" Samuel asked. "When Saul hears of it he'll kill me!"

"Take a heifer with you," the Lord replied, "and say, 'I have come to make a sacrifice to the Lord.' ³Invite Jesse to the sacrifice, and I will make clear to you what you should do. You will anoint for me the person I point out to you."

⁴Samuel did what the Lord instructed. When he came to Bethlehem, the city elders came to meet him. They were shaking with fear. "Do you come in peace?" they asked.

⁵"Yes," Samuel answered. "I've come to make a sacrifice to the Lord. Now make yourselves holy, then come with me to the sacrifice." Samuel made Jesse and his sons holy and invited them to the sacrifice as well.

⁶When they arrived, Samuel looked at Eliab and thought, That must be the Lord's anointed right in front.

⁷But the Lord said to Samuel, "Have no regard for his appearance or stature, because I haven't selected him. God doesn't look at things like humans do. Humans see only what is visible to the eyes, but the Lord sees into the heart."

⁸Next Jesse called for Abinadab, who presented himself to Samuel, but he said, "The Lord hasn't chosen this one either." ⁹So Jesse presented Shammah, but Samuel said, "No, the Lord hasn't chosen this one." ¹⁰Jesse presented seven of his sons to Samuel, but Samuel said to Jesse, "The Lord hasn't picked any of these." ¹¹Then Samuel asked Jesse, "Is that all of your boys?"

"There is still the youngest one," Jesse answered, "but he's out keeping the sheep."

"Send for him," Samuel told Jesse, "because we can't proceed until he gets here."

¹²So Jesse sent and brought him in. He was reddish brown, had beautiful eyes, and was good-looking. The Lord said, "That's the one. Go anoint him." ¹³So Samuel took the horn of oil and anointed him right there in front of his brothers. The Lord's spirit came over David from that point forward.

Then Samuel left and went to Ramah.

Psalm 23 (UM134/754)

¹The Lord is my shepherd. / I lack nothing. / ²He lets me rest in grassy meadows; / he leads me to restful waters; / ³he keeps me alive. / He guides me in proper paths / for the sake of his good name.

⁴Even when I walk / through the darkest valley, / I fear no danger because you are with me. / Your rod and your staff— / they protect me.

⁵You set a table for me / right in front of my enemies. / You bathe my head in oil; / my cup is so full it spills over! / ⁶Yes, goodness and faithful love / will pursue me all the days of my life, / and I will live in the Lord's house / as long as I live.

Ephesians 5:8-14

⁸You were once darkness, but now you are light in the Lord, so live your life as children of light. ⁹Light produces fruit that consists of every sort of goodness, justice, and truth. ¹⁰Therefore, test everything to see what's pleasing to the Lord, ¹¹and don't participate in the unfruitful actions of darkness. Instead, you should reveal the truth about them. ¹²It's embarrassing to even talk about what certain persons do in secret. ¹³But everything exposed to the light is revealed by the light. ¹⁴Everything that is revealed by the light is light. Therefore, it says, *Wake up, sleeper! Get up from the dead, and Christ will shine on you.*

John 9:1-41

¹As Jesus walked along, he saw a man who was blind from birth. ²Jesus' disciples asked, "Rabbi, who sinned so that he was born blind, this man or his parents?"

³Jesus answered, "Neither he nor his parents. This happened so that God's mighty works might be displayed in him. ⁴While it's

daytime, we must do the works of him who sent me. Night is coming when no one can work. ⁵While I am in the world, I am the light of the world." ⁶After he said this, he spit on the ground, made mud with the saliva, and smeared the mud on the man's eyes. ⁷Jesus said to him, "Go, wash in the pool of Siloam" (this word means *sent*). So the man went away and washed. When he returned, he could see.

⁸The man's neighbors and those who used to see him when he was a beggar said, "Isn't this the man who used to sit and beg?"

⁹Some said, "It is," and others said, "No, it's someone who looks like him."

But the man said, "Yes, it's me!"

¹⁰So they asked him, "How are you now able to see?"

¹¹He answered, "The man they call Jesus made mud, smeared it on my eyes, and said, 'Go to the Pool of Siloam and wash.' So I went and washed, and then I could see."

¹²They asked, "Where is this man?"

He replied, "I don't know."

¹³Then they led the man who had been born blind to the Pharisees. ¹⁴Now Jesus made the mud and smeared it on the man's eyes on a Sabbath day. ¹⁵So Pharisees also asked him how he was able to see.

The man told them, "He put mud on my eyes, I washed, and now I see."

¹⁶Some Pharisees said, "This man isn't from God, because he breaks the Sabbath law." Others said, "How can a sinner do miraculous signs like these?" So they were divided. ¹⁷Some of the Pharisees questioned the man who had been born blind again: "What do you have to say about him, since he healed your eyes?"

He replied, "He's a prophet."

¹⁸The Jewish leaders didn't believe the man had been blind and received his sight until they called for his parents. ¹⁹The Jewish leaders asked them, "Is this your son? Are you saying he was born blind? How can he now see?"

²⁰His parents answered, "We know he is our son. We know he was born blind. ²¹But we don't know how he now sees, and we don't know who healed his eyes. Ask him. He's old enough to speak for himself." ²²His parents said this because they feared the Jewish authorities. This is because the Jewish authorities had already decided that whoever confessed Jesus to be the Christ would be expelled from the synagogue. ²³That's why his parents said, "He's old enough. Ask him."

²⁴Therefore, they called a second time for the man who had been born blind and said to him, "Give glory to God. We know this man is a sinner."

²⁵The man answered, "I don't know whether he's a sinner. Here's what I do know: I was blind and now I see."

²⁶They questioned him: "What did he do to you? How did he heal your eyes?"

²⁷He replied, "I already told you, and you didn't listen. Why do you want to hear it again? Do you want to become his disciples too?"

²⁸They insulted him: "You are his disciple, but we are Moses' disciples. ²⁹We know that God spoke to Moses, but we don't know where this man is from."

³⁰The man answered, "This is incredible! You don't know where he is from, yet he healed my eyes! ³¹We know that God doesn't listen to sinners. God listens to anyone who is devout and does God's will. ³²No one has ever heard of a healing of the eyes of someone born blind. ³³If this man wasn't from God, he couldn't do this."

³⁴They responded, "You were born completely in sin! How is it that you dare to teach us?" Then they expelled him.

³⁵Jesus heard they had expelled the man born blind. Finding him, Jesus said, "Do you believe in the Human One?"

³⁶He answered, "Who is he, sir? I want to believe in him."

³⁷Jesus said, "You have seen him. In fact, he is the one speaking with you."

³⁸The man said, "Lord, I believe." And he worshipped Jesus.

³⁹Jesus said, "I have come into the world to exercise judgment so that those who don't see can see and those who see will become blind."

⁴⁰Some Pharisees who were with him heard what he said and asked, "Surely we aren't blind, are we?"

⁴¹Jesus said to them, "If you were blind, you wouldn't have any sin, but now that you say, 'We see,' your sin remains."

sin light sight blame

Primary Hymns and Songs for the Day

"Savior, Like a Shepherd Lead Us" (Pss) (O)
  B61, C558, E708, EL789, F601, G187, L481, N252, P387,
  UM381 (PD)
    H-3   Chr-167; Org-15
    S-2   #29. Harm.
"Open My Eyes, That I May See" (John) (O)
  B502, C586, F486, G451, P324, UM454, VU371
    H-3   Chr-157; Org-108
"Shepherd Me, O God" (Pss)
  EL780, G473, S2058, SF2058
"Open Our Eyes, Lord" (John)
  B499, S2086, SF2086, SP199
"I Want to Walk as a Child of the Light" (Eph, John)
  E490, EL815, G377, UM206, W510
    S-2   #91. Desc.
"He Leadeth Me: O Blessed Thought" (1 Sam, Pss) (C)
  B52, C545, F606, L501, UM128 (PD), VU657

Additional Hymn Suggestions

"O God, in a Mysterious Way" (1 Sam)
  B73, E677, F603, G30, L483, N412, P270
"Awake, My Soul, and with the Sun" (1 Sam)
  E11, EL557 (PD), G663, L269, P456
"Great Is Thy Faithfulness" (1 Sam)
  B54, C86, EL733, F98, G39, N423, P276, UM140, VU288
"I Sing the Almighty Power of God" (1 Sam)
  B42, C64, E398, G32, N12, P288, UM152, VU231, W502
"Spirit of the Living God" (1 Sam)
  B244, C259, G288, N283, P322, SP131, UM393, VU376
"Precious Lord, Take My Hand" (1 Sam, Pss)
  B456, C628, EL773, G834, N472, P404, UM474, VU670
"The Lord's My Shepherd" (Pss)
  C78/79, EL778, F40/42, G801, L451, N479, P170, UM136,
  VU747/748
"The King of Love My Shepherd Is" (Pss)
  E645, EL502, G802, L456, P171, UM138 (PD), VU273, W609
"Lead Me, Guide Me" (Pss, Eph)
  C583, EL768, G740, S2214, SF2214
"O For a Closer Walk with God" (Eph)
  E684, G739, N450, P396
"We Are Called" (Eph)
  EL720, G749, S2172, SF2172
"You Are Mine" (Eph, John)
  EL581, G177, S2218, SF2218
"Gather Us In" (Eph, Comm.)
  C284, EL532, G401, S2236, SF2236, W665
"O For a Thousand Tongues to Sing" (John)
  B216, C5, E493, EL886, F349, G610, L559, N42, P466, UM57
  (PD), VU326 (See also WS3001)
"I'll Praise My Maker While I've Breath" (John)
  B35, C20, E429 (PD), G806, P253, UM60, VU867
"O Christ, the Healer" (John)
  C503. EL610, G793, L360, N175, P380, UM265, W747
"All Who Love and Serve Your City" (John)
  C670, E570/E571, EL724, G351, L436, P413, UM433, W621
"Be Thou My Vision" (John)
  B60, C595, E488, EL793, G450, N451, P339, UM451, VU642
"Lord, Whose Love Through Humble Service" (John)
  C461, E610, EL712, L423, P427, UM581, W630
"Wash, O God, Our Sons and Daughters" (John)
  C365, EL445, G490, UM605, VU442
"Come, Labor On" (John)
  E541, G719, N532, P415

"In Remembrance of Me" (John, Comm.)
  B365, C403, G521, S2254

Additional Contemporary Suggestions

"Nothing Can Trouble" ("*Nada Te Turbe*") (Pss)
  G820, S2054, SF2054, VU290
"Lamb of God" (Pss, Lent)
  EL336, G518, S2113, SF2113
"God Is Good All the Time" (Pss)
  AH4010, M45, WS3026
"Your Grace Is Enough" (Pss, Lent)
  M191, WS3106
"You Never Let Go" (Pss, Eph, John)
  M258
"I Have a Hope" (Pss, Eph, John)
  M265
"Shine on Us" (Eph)
  M19
"Everyday" (Eph)
  M150
"We Are Marching" ("*Siyahamba*") (Eph)
  C442, EL866, G853, N526, S2235-ab, SF2235-ab, VU646
"Shine, Jesus, Shine" (Eph, John)
  B579, EL671, G192, S2173, SF2173, SP142
"In Christ Alone" (Eph, John)
  M138, WS3105
"Turn Your Eyes upon Jesus" (John)
  B320, F621, SP218, UM349
"Water, River, Spirit, Grace" (John, Baptism)
  C366, N169, S2253, SF2253
"Open the Eyes of My Heart" (John)
  G452, M57, WS3008
"Above All" (John)
  M77; V-3 (2) p. 17 Vocal solo
"There Is a Redeemer" (John, Comm.)
  G443, SP111

Vocal Solos

"The Lord Is My Shepherd" (Pss)
  V-5 (3)   p. 30
"My Shepherd Will Supply My Need" (Pss)
  V-10   p. 4

Anthems

"The King of Love My Shepherd Is" (SOCB72) (Pss)
Arr. Christopher Aspaas; Augsburg 9781451499032
TTBB, piano

"I Believe" (John)
Mark Miller; Choristers Guild CGA-1310
SATB, piano

Other Suggestions

Visuals:
  O   Oil/horn, crown, heifer, washing hands, seven sons
  P   Shepherd/sheep, pasture, water, path, dark valley,
          rod/ staff, banquet, oil, overflowing cup, house of
          God
  E   Dark/light, children, ministry, waking, Christ
  G   Mud, dark glasses, day/night, light/dark, water
Introit: C593, N774, UM473 (PD), VU662. "Lead Me, Lord"
  (Pss)

Ezekiel 37:1-14

2014

[1] The LORD's power overcame me, and while I was in the LORD's spirit, he led me out and set me down in the middle of a certain valley. It was full of bones. [2] He led me through them all around, and I saw that there were a great many of them on the valley floor, and they were very dry.

[3] He asked me, "Human one, can these bones live again?"

I said, "LORD God, only you know."

[4] He said to me, "Prophesy over these bones, and say to them, Dry bones, hear the LORD's word! [5] The LORD God proclaims to these bones: I am about to put breath in you, and you will live again. [6] I will put sinews on you, place flesh on you, and cover you with skin. When I put breath in you, and you come to life, you will know that I am the LORD."

[7] I prophesied just as I was commanded. There was a great noise as I was prophesying, then a great quaking, and the bones came together, bone by bone. [8] When I looked, suddenly there were sinews on them. The flesh appeared, and then they were covered over with skin. But there was still no breath in them.

[9] He said to me, "Prophesy to the breath; prophesy, human one! Say to the breath, The LORD God proclaims: Come from the four winds, breath! Breathe into these dead bodies and let them live."

[10] I prophesied just as he commanded me. When the breath entered them, they came to life and stood on their feet, an extraordinarily large company.

[11] He said to me, "Human one, these bones are the entire house of Israel. They say, 'Our bones are dried up, and our hope has perished. We are completely finished.' [12] So now, prophesy and say to them, The LORD God proclaims: I'm opening your graves! I will raise you up from your graves, my people, and I will bring you to Israel's fertile land. [13] You will know that I am the LORD, when I open your graves and raise you up from your graves, my people. [14] I will put my breath in you, and you will live. I will plant you on your fertile land, and you will know that I am the LORD. I've spoken, and I will do it. This is what the LORD says."

Psalm 130 (G424/791, N709, P240, UM848)

[1] I cry out to you from the depths, LORD— / [2] my Lord, listen to my voice! / Let your ears pay close attention to my request for mercy! / [3] If you kept track of sins, LORD— / my Lord, who would stand a chance? / [4] But forgiveness is with you— / that's why you are honored. / [5] I hope, LORD. / My whole being hopes, / and I wait for God's promise. / [6] My whole being waits for my Lord— / more than the night watch waits for morning; / yes, more than the night watch waits for morning! / [7] Israel, wait for the LORD! / Because faithful love is with the LORD; / because great redemption is with our God! / [8] He is the one who will redeem Israel / from all its sin.

Romans 8:6-11

[6] The attitude that comes from selfishness leads to death, but the attitude that comes from the Spirit leads to life and peace. [7] So the attitude that comes from selfishness is hostile to God. It doesn't submit to God's Law, because it can't. [8] People who are self-centered aren't able to please God.

[9] But you aren't self-centered. Instead you are in the Spirit, if in fact God's Spirit lives in you. If anyone doesn't have the Spirit of Christ, they don't belong to him. [10] If Christ is in you, the Spirit is your life because of God's righteousness, but the body is dead because of sin. [11] If the Spirit of the one who raised Jesus from the dead lives in you, the one who raised Christ from the dead will give life to your human bodies also, through his Spirit that lives in you.

John 11:1-45

[1] A certain man, Lazarus, was ill. He was from Bethany, the village of Mary and her sister Martha. ([2] This was the Mary who anointed the Lord with fragrant oil and wiped his feet with her hair. Her brother Lazarus was ill.) [3] So the sisters sent word to Jesus, saying, "Lord, the one whom you love is ill."

[4] When he heard this, Jesus said, "This illness isn't fatal. It's for the glory of God so that God's Son can be glorified through it." [5] Jesus loved Martha, her sister, and Lazarus. [6] When he heard that Lazarus was ill, he stayed where he was. After two days, [7] he said to his disciples, "Let's return to Judea again."

[8] The disciples replied, "Rabbi, the Jewish opposition wants to stone you, but you want to go back?"

[9] Jesus answered, "Aren't there twelve hours in the day? Whoever walks in the day doesn't stumble because they see the light of the world. [10] But whoever walks in the night does stumble because the light isn't in them."

[11] He continued, "Our friend Lazarus is sleeping, but I am going in order to wake him up."

[12] The disciples said, "Lord, if he's sleeping, he will get well." [13] They thought Jesus meant that Lazarus was in a deep sleep, but Jesus had spoken about Lazarus' death.

[14] Jesus told them plainly, "Lazarus has died. [15] For your sakes, I'm glad I wasn't there so that you can believe. Let's go to him." [16] Then Thomas (the one called Didymus) said to the other disciples, "Let us go too so that we may die with Jesus."

[17] When Jesus arrived, he found that Lazarus had already been in the tomb for four days. [18] Bethany was a little less than two miles from Jerusalem. [19] Many Jews had come to comfort Martha and Mary after their brother's death. [20] When Martha heard that Jesus was coming, she went to meet him, while Mary remained in the house. [21] Martha said to Jesus, "Lord, if you had been here, my brother wouldn't have died. [22] Even now I know that whatever you ask God, God will give you."

[23] Jesus told her, "Your brother will rise again."

[24] Martha replied, "I know that he will rise in the resurrection on the last day."

[25] Jesus said to her, "I am the resurrection and the life. Whoever believes in me will live, even though they die. [26] Everyone who lives and believes in me will never die. Do you believe this?"

[27] She replied, "Yes, Lord, I believe that you are the Christ, God's Son, the one who is coming into the world."

[28] After she said this, she went and spoke privately to her sister Mary, "The teacher is here and he's calling for you." [29] When Mary heard this, she got up quickly and went to Jesus. [30] He hadn't entered the village but was still in the place where Martha had met him. [31] When the Jews who were comforting Mary in the house saw her get up quickly and leave, they followed her. They assumed she was going to mourn at the tomb.

[32] When Mary arrived where Jesus was and saw him, she fell at his feet and said, "Lord, if you had been here, my brother wouldn't have died."

[33] When Jesus saw her crying and the Jews who had come with her crying also, he was deeply disturbed and troubled. [34] He asked, "Where have you laid him?"

They replied, "Lord, come and see."

[35] Jesus began to cry. [36] The Jews said, "See how much he loved him!" [37] But some of them said, "He healed the eyes of the man born blind. Couldn't he have kept Lazarus from dying?"

[38] Jesus was deeply disturbed again when he came to the tomb. It was a cave, and a stone covered the entrance. [39] Jesus said, "Remove the stone."

Martha, the sister of the dead man, said, "Lord, the smell will be awful! He's been dead four days."

[40] Jesus replied, "Didn't I tell you that if you believe, you will see God's glory?" [41] So they removed the stone. Jesus looked up and said, "Father, thank you for hearing me. [42] I know you always hear me. I say this for the benefit of the crowd standing here so that they will believe that you sent me." [43] Having said this, Jesus shouted with a loud voice, "Lazarus, come out!" [44] The dead man came out, his feet bound and his hands tied, and his face covered with a cloth. Jesus said to them, "Untie him and let him go."

[45] Therefore, many of the Jews who came with Mary and saw what Jesus did believed in him.

what's our response, what do we say

Primary Hymns and Songs for the Day
"Lord of the Dance" (John, Lent) (O)
  G157, P302, UM261, VU352, W636
"Now the Green Blade Riseth" (Ezek, John)
  C230, E204, EL379, G247, L148, N238, UM311, VU186
"This Is a Day of New Beginnings" (Ezek, John, Comm.)
  B370, C518, N417, UM383, W661
    H-3   Chr-196
"Spirit of the Living God" (Rom, Comm.)
  SP131;
    S-1#212 Vocal desc. idea
  B244, C259, G288, N283, P322, SP131, UM393, VU376
"Why Has God Forsaken Me?" (Pss, John)
  G809, P406, S2110, VU154
    H-3   Chr-220
"Breathe on Me, Breath of God" (Ezek) (C)
  B241, C254, E508, F161, G286, L488, N292, P316, UM420
  (PD), VU382 (Fr.), W725
    H-3   Hbl-49; Chr-45; Desc-101; Org-166

Additional Hymn Suggestions
"Let It Breathe on Me" (Ezek)
  C260, N288, UM503
"Hope of the World" (Ezek, John)
  C538, E472, G734, L493, N46, P360, UM178, VU215
"The Day of Resurrection" (Ezek, John)
  B164, C228, E210, EL361, G233, L141, N245, P118, UM303
  (PD), VU164
"*Camina, Pueblo de Dios*" ("Walk On, O People of God") (Ezek, John)
  N614, P296, UM305
"Come, Ye Faithful, Raise the Strain" (Ezek, John)
  C215, E199, EL363, G234, L132, N230, P115, UM315 (PD), VU165, W456
"Out of the Depths I Cry to You" (Pss)
  EL600, G424, L295, N483, P240, UM515
"Out of the Depths" (Pss)
  C510, N554, S2136, SF2136, VU611
"I Love the Lord" (Pss)
  G799, P362, N511, VU617, WS3142
"To God Be the Glory" (Rom)
  B4, C72, F363, G634, P485, UM98 (PD)
"Alas! And Did My Savior Bleed" (Rom)
  AH4067, B139/145, C204, EL337, F274, G212, L98, N199/N200, P78, UM294/UM359
"Every Time I Feel the Spirit" (Rom)
  C592, G66, N282, P315, UM404
"Spirit Divine, Attend Our Prayers" (Rom)
  E509, G407, P325, VU385, W476
"Holy Spirit, Truth Divine" (Rom)
  C241, EL398, L257, N63, P321, UM465 (PD), VU368
"Trust and Obey" (Rom, John)
  B447, C556, F454, UM467 (PD)
"Spirit of God, Descend upon My Heart" (Rom, John)
  B245, C265, EL800, F147, G688, L486, N290, P326, UM500
  (PD), VU378
"Hymn of Promise" (John)
  C638, G250. N433, UM707, VU703
"O Christ, the Healer" (John)
  C503, EL610, G793, L360, N175, P380, UM265, W747
"Somebody's Knockin' at Your Door" (John)
  G728, P382, W415, WS3095
"Christ Jesus Lay in Death's Strong Bonds" (John)
  E186, EL370, G237, L134, P110, UM319 (PD)

"When Jesus Wept" (John)
  C199, E715, G194, P312, S2106, SF2106, VU146
"We Are Called" (John)
  EL720, G749, S2172, SF2172
"Just a Closer Walk with Thee" (John, Lent)
  B448, C557, EL697, F591, G835, S2158, SF2158
"Lead Me, Guide Me" (John, Lent)
  C583, EL768, G740, S2214, SF2214
"Womb of Life" (John, Comm.)
  C14, G3, N274, S2046, SF2046

Additional Contemporary Suggestions
"Holy Spirit, Come to Us" (Ezek)
  EL406, G281, S2118, SF2118, W473
"Days of Elijah" (Ezek)
  M139, WS3186
"Oh, I Know the Lord's Laid His Hands on Me" (Ezek, John)
  S2139, SF2139
"Lord, I Lift Your Name on High" (Ezek, Rom, John, Lent)
  AH4071, EL857, M2, S2088, SF2088
"Let Your Spirit Rise" (Ezek, Rom, John)
  SP235
"Lord, Be Glorified" (Rom, John)
  B457, EL744, G468, S2150, SF2150, SP196
"Cares Chorus" (John)
  S2215, SF2215, SP221
"Halle, Halle, Halleluja" (John)
  C41, EL172, G591, N236, S2026, SF2026, VU958
"Light of the World" (John)
  S2204, SF2204
"We Are Marching" ("*Siyahamba*") (John)
  C442, EL866, G853, N526, S2235-ab, SF2235-ab, VU646
"I Believe in Jesus" (John)
  M7
"Everyday" (John)
  M150

Vocal Solos
"Like a Child" (Pss)
  V-8   p. 356
"Just a Closer Walk with Thee" (John, Lent)
  V-5 (2)   p. 31
  V-8   p. 323

Anthems
"Somebody's Knockin'" (John)
Ken Berg; Choristers Guild CGA-1303
Unison/two-part, piano

"When Jesus Wept" (John)
Arr. Peter Paul Olejar; MorningStar MSM-50-3220
SA(T)B, keyboard

Other Suggestions
Visuals:
  O   Valley/bones, wilderness, multitude, open graves
  P   Listening, praying hands/waiting, rescue
  E   Coffin, Spirit symbols, Christ, open tomb
  G   Jar/woman, hair/feet, message, night/stumbling block, woman/Jesus/kneeling, tears, tomb, strips of cloth
Introit: N231, st. 1. "Because You Live" (Ezek, John)
Prayers: N831, UM461 (John) or WSL52 (Ezek, Rom)
Sung Confession: WS3111. "Redemption" (Rom, Lent)

PALM READINGS
Matthew 21:1-11

[1]When they approached Jerusalem and came to Bethphage on the Mount of Olives, Jesus gave two disciples a task. [2]He said to them, "Go into the village over there. As soon as you enter, you will find a donkey tied up and a colt with it. Untie them and bring them to me. [3]If anybody says anything to you, say that the Lord needs it." He sent them off right away. [4]Now this happened to fulfill what the prophet said, [5]*Say to Daughter Zion, "Look, your king is coming to you, humble and riding on a donkey, and on a colt the donkey's offspring."* [6]The disciples went and did just as Jesus had ordered them. [7]They brought the donkey and the colt and laid their clothes on them. Then he sat on them.

[8]Now a large crowd spread their clothes on the road. Others cut palm branches off the trees and spread them on the road. [9]The crowds in front of him and behind him shouted, "*Hosanna to the Son of David! Blessings on the one who comes in the name of the Lord! Hosanna in the highest!*" [10]And when Jesus entered Jerusalem, the whole city was stirred up. "Who is this?" they asked. [11]The crowds answered, "It's the prophet Jesus from Nazareth in Galilee."

Psalm 118:1-2, 19-29 (G391/6681, N700, P232, UM839)

[1]Give thanks to the LORD because he is good, / because his faithful love lasts forever. / [2]Let Israel say it: / "God's faithful love lasts forever!" . . . .

[19]Open the gates of righteousness for me / so I can come in and give thanks to the LORD! / [20]This is the LORD's gate; / those who are righteous enter through it.

[21]I thank you because you answered me, / because you were my saving help. / [22]The stone rejected by the builders / is now the main foundation stone! / [23]This has happened because of the LORD; / it is astounding in our sight! / [24]This is the day the LORD acted; / we will rejoice and celebrate in it!

[25]LORD, please save us! / LORD, please let us succeed!

[26]The one who enters in the LORD's name is blessed; / we bless all of you from the LORD's house. / [27]The LORD is God! / He has shined a light on us! / So lead the festival offering with ropes / all the way to the horns of the altar. / [28]You are my God—I will give thanks to you! / You are my God—I will lift you up high! / [29]Give thanks to the LORD because he is good, / because his faithful love lasts forever.

PASSION READINGS
Isaiah 50:4-9a

2014

[4]The LORD God
 gave me an educated tongue
 to know how to respond to the weary
 with a word that will awaken them
  in the morning.
 God awakens my ear
  in the morning to listen,
 as educated people do.
[5]The LORD God opened my ear;
 I didn't rebel; I didn't turn my back.
[6]Instead, I gave my body to attackers,
 and my cheeks to beard pluckers.
I didn't hide my face
 from insults and spitting.
[7]The LORD God will help me;
 therefore, I haven't been insulted.

Therefore, I set my face like flint,
 and knew I wouldn't be ashamed.
[8]The one who will declare me innocent
 is near.
 Who will argue with me?
Let's stand up together.
 Who will bring judgment against me?
 Let him approach me.
[9a]Look! the LORD God will help me.
 Who will condemn me?

Psalm 31:9-16 (G214/814, N641, P182, UM764)

[9]Have mercy on me, LORD, because I'm depressed. / My vision fails because of my grief, / as do my spirit and my body. / [10]My life is consumed with sadness; / my years are consumed with groaning. / Strength fails me because of my suffering; / my bones dry up. / [11]I'm a joke to all my enemies, / still worse to my neighbors. / I scare my friends, / and whoever sees me in the street, runs away! / [12]I am forgotten, like I'm dead, / completely out of mind; / I am like a piece of pottery, destroyed. / [13]Yes, I've heard all the gossiping, / terror all around; / so many gang up together against me, / they plan to take my life!

[14]But me? I trust you, LORD! / I affirm, "You are my God." / [15]My future is in your hands. / Don't hand me over to my enemies, / to all who are out to get me! / [16]Shine your face on your servant; / save me by your faithful love!

Philippians 2:5-11

[5]Adopt the attitude that was in Christ Jesus:
[6] Though he was in the form of God,
  he did not consider being equal with God something to exploit.
[7] But he emptied himself
  by taking the form of a slave
  and by becoming like human beings.
 When he found himself in the form of a human,
[8] he humbled himself by becoming obedient to the point of death,
  even death on a cross.
[9] Therefore, God highly honored him
  and gave him a name above all names,
[10] so that at the name of Jesus everyone
  in heaven, on earth, and under the earth might bow
[11] and every tongue confess that
  Jesus Christ is Lord, to the glory of God the Father.

Matthew 26:14–27:66 (27:11-54)

[14]Then one of the Twelve, who was called Judas Iscariot, went to the chief priests [15]and said, "What will you give me if I turn Jesus over to you?" They paid him thirty pieces of silver. [16]From that time on he was looking for an opportunity to turn him in.

[17]On the first day of the Festival of Unleavened Bread, the disciples came to Jesus and said, "Where do you want us to prepare for you to eat the Passover meal?"

[18]He replied, "Go into the city, to a certain man, and say, 'The teacher says, "My time is near. I'm going to celebrate the Passover with my disciples at your house."'" [19]The disciples did just as Jesus instructed them. They prepared the Passover.

20That evening he took his place at the table with the twelve disciples. 21As they were eating he said, "I assure you that one of you will betray me."

22Deeply saddened, each one said to him, "I'm not the one, am I, Lord?"

23He replied, "The one who will betray me is the one who dips his hand with me into this bowl. 24The Human One goes to his death just as it is written about him. But how terrible it is for that person who betrays the Human One! It would have been better for him if he had never been born."

25Now Judas, who would betray him, replied, "It's not me, is it, Rabbi?"

Jesus answered, "You said it."

26While they were eating, Jesus took bread, blessed it, broke it, and gave it to the disciples and said, "Take and eat. This is my body." 27He took a cup, gave thanks, and gave it to them, saying, "Drink from this, all of you. 28This is my blood of the covenant, which is poured out for many so that their sins may be forgiven. 29I tell you, I won't drink wine again until that day when I drink it in a new way with you in my Father's kingdom." 30Then, after singing songs of praise, they went to the Mount of Olives.

31Then Jesus said to his disciples, "Tonight you will all fall away because of me. This is because it is written, *I will hit the shepherd, and the sheep of the flock will go off in all directions.* 32But after I'm raised up, I'll go before you to Galilee."

33Peter replied, "If everyone else stumbles because of you, I'll never stumble."

34Jesus said to him, "I assure you that, before the rooster crows tonight, you will deny me three times."

35Peter said, "Even if I must die alongside you, I won't deny you." All the disciples said the same thing.

36Then Jesus went with his disciples to a place called Gethsemane. He said to the disciples, "Stay here while I go and pray over there." 37When he took Peter and Zebedee's two sons, he began to feel sad and anxious. 38Then he said to them, "I'm very sad. It's as if I'm dying. Stay here and keep alert with me." 39Then he went a short distance farther and fell on his face and prayed, "My Father, if it's possible, take this cup of suffering away from me. However—not what I want but what you want."

40He came back to the disciples and found them sleeping. He said to Peter, "Couldn't you stay alert one hour with me? 41Stay alert and pray so that you won't give in to temptation. The spirit is eager, but the flesh is weak." 42A second time he went away and prayed, "My Father, if it's not possible that this cup be taken away unless I drink it, then let it be what you want."

43Again he came and found them sleeping. Their eyes were heavy with sleep. 44But he left them and again went and prayed the same words for the third time. 45Then he came to his disciples and said to them, "Will you sleep and rest all night? Look, the time has come for the Human One to be betrayed into the hands of sinners. 46Get up. Let's go. Look, here comes my betrayer."

47While Jesus was still speaking, Judas, one of the Twelve, came. With him was a large crowd carrying swords and clubs. They had been sent by the chief priests and elders of the people. 48His betrayer had given them a sign: "Arrest the man I kiss." 49Just then he came to Jesus and said, "Hello, Rabbi." Then he kissed him.

50But Jesus said to him, "Friend, do what you came to do." Then they came and grabbed Jesus and arrested him.

51One of those with Jesus reached for his sword. Striking the high priest's slave, he cut off his ear. 52Then Jesus said to him, "Put the sword back into its place. All those who use the sword will die by the sword. 53Or do you think that I'm not able to ask my Father and he will send to me more than twelve battle groups of angels right away? 54But if I did that, how would the scriptures be fulfilled that say this must happen?" 55Then Jesus said to the crowds, "Have you come with swords and clubs to arrest me, like a thief? Day after day, I sat in the temple teaching, but you didn't arrest me. 56But all this has happened so that what the prophets said in the scriptures might be fulfilled." Then all the disciples left Jesus and ran away.

57Those who arrested Jesus led him to Caiaphas the high priest. The legal experts and the elders had gathered there. 58Peter followed him from a distance until he came to the high priest's courtyard. He entered that area and sat outside with the officers to see how it would turn out.

59The chief priests and the whole council were looking for false testimony against Jesus so that they could put him to death. 60They didn't find anything they could use from the many false witnesses who were willing to come forward. But finally they found two 61who said, "This man said, 'I can destroy God's temple and rebuild it in three days.'"

62Then the high priest stood and said to Jesus, "Aren't you going to respond to the testimony these people have brought against you?"

63But Jesus was silent.

The high priest said, "By the living God, I demand that you tell us whether you are the Christ, God's Son."

64"You said it," Jesus replied. "But I say to you that from now on you'll see the Human One sitting on the right side of the Almighty and coming on the heavenly clouds."

65Then the high priest tore his clothes and said, "He's insulting God! Why do we need any more witnesses? Look, you've heard his insult against God. 66What do you think?"

And they answered, "He deserves to die!" 67Then they spit in his face and beat him. They hit him 68and said, "Prophesy for us, Christ! Who hit you?"

69Meanwhile, Peter was sitting outside in the courtyard. A servant woman came and said to him, "You were also with Jesus the Galilean."

70But he denied it in front of all of them, saying, "I don't know what you are talking about."

71When he went over to the gate, another woman saw him and said to those who were there, "This man was with Jesus, the man from Nazareth."

72With a solemn pledge, he denied it again, saying, "I don't know the man."

73A short time later those standing there came and said to Peter, "You must be one of them. The way you talk gives you away."

74Then he cursed and swore, "I don't know the man!" At that very moment the rooster crowed. 75Peter remembered Jesus' words, "Before the rooster crows you will deny me three times." And Peter went out and cried uncontrollably.

27Early in the morning all the chief priests and the elders of the people reached the decision to have Jesus put to death. 2They bound him, led him away, and turned him over to Pilate the governor.

[3]When Judas, who betrayed Jesus, saw that Jesus was condemned to die, he felt deep regret. He returned the thirty pieces of silver to the chief priests and elders, and[4]said, "I did wrong because I betrayed an innocent man."

But they said, "What is that to us? That's your problem." [5]Judas threw the silver pieces into the temple and left. Then he went and hanged himself.

[6]The chief priests picked up the silver pieces and said, "According to the Law it's not right to put this money in the treasury. Since it was used to pay for someone's life, it's unclean." [7]So they decided to use it to buy the potter's field where strangers could be buried. [8]That's why that field is called "Field of Blood" to this very day. [9]This fulfilled the words of Jeremiah the prophet: *And I took the thirty pieces of silver, the price for the one whose price had been set by some of the Israelites,* [10]*and I gave them for the potter's field, as the Lord commanded me.*

[11]Jesus was brought before the governor. The governor said, "Are you the king of the Jews?"

Jesus replied, "That's what you say." [12]But he didn't answer when the chief priests and elders accused him.

[13]Then Pilate said, "Don't you hear the testimony they bring against you?" [14]But he didn't answer, not even a single word. So the governor was greatly amazed.

[15]It was customary during the festival for the governor to release to the crowd one prisoner, whomever they might choose. [16]At that time there was a well-known prisoner named Jesus Barabbas. [17]When the crowd had come together, Pilate asked them, "Whom would you like me to release to you, Jesus Barabbas or Jesus who is called Christ?" [18]He knew that the leaders of the people had handed him over because of jealousy.

[19]While he was serving as judge, his wife sent this message to him, "Leave that righteous man alone. I've suffered much today in a dream because of him."

[20]But the chief priests and the elders persuaded the crowds to ask for Barabbas and kill Jesus. [21]The governor said, "Which of the two do you want me to release to you?"

"Barabbas," they replied.

[22]Pilate said, "Then what should I do with Jesus who is called Christ?"

They all said, "Crucify him!"

[23]But he said, "Why? What wrong has he done?"

They shouted even louder, "Crucify him!"

[24]Pilate saw that he was getting nowhere and that a riot was starting. So he took water and washed his hands in front of the crowd. "I'm innocent of this man's blood," he said. "It's your problem."

[25]All the people replied, "Let his blood be on us and on our children." [26]Then he released Barabbas to them. He had Jesus whipped, then handed him over to be crucified.

[27]The governor's soldiers took Jesus into the governor's house, and they gathered the whole company of soldiers around him. [28]They stripped him and put a red military coat on him. [29]They twisted together a crown of thorns and put it on his head. They put a stick in his right hand. Then they bowed down in front of him and mocked him, saying, "Hey! King of the Jews!" [30]After they spit on him, they took the stick and struck his head again and again. [31]When they finished mocking him, they stripped him of the military coat and put his own clothes back on him. They led him away to crucify him.

[32]As they were going out, they found Simon, a man from Cyrene. They forced him to carry his cross. [33]When they came to a place called Golgotha, which means Skull Place, [34]they gave Jesus wine mixed with vinegar to drink. But after tasting it, he didn't want to drink it. [35]After they crucified him, they divided up his clothes among them by drawing lots. [36]They sat there, guarding him. [37]They placed above his head the charge against him. It read, "This is Jesus, the king of the Jews." [38]They crucified with him two outlaws, one on his right side and one on his left.

[39]Those who were walking by insulted Jesus, shaking their heads [40]and saying, "So you were going to destroy the temple and rebuild it in three days, were you? Save yourself! If you are God's Son, come down from the cross."

[41]In the same way, the chief priests, along with the legal experts and the elders, were making fun of him, saying, [42]"He saved others, but he can't save himself. He's the king of Israel, so let him come down from the cross now. Then we'll believe in him. [43]He trusts in God, so let God deliver him now if he wants to. He said, 'I'm God's Son.'" [44]The outlaws who were crucified with him insulted him in the same way.

[45]From noon until three in the afternoon the whole earth was dark. [46]At about three Jesus cried out with a loud shout, *"Eli, Eli, lama sabachthani,"* which means, "My God, my God, why have you left me?"

[47]After hearing him, some standing there said, "He's calling Elijah." [48]One of them ran over, took a sponge full of vinegar, and put it on a pole. He offered it to Jesus to drink. [49]But the rest of them said, "Let's see if Elijah will come and save him."

[50]Again Jesus cried out with a loud shout. Then he died. [51]Look, the curtain of the sanctuary was torn in two from top to bottom. The earth shook, the rocks split, [52]and the bodies of many holy people who had died were raised. [53]After Jesus' resurrection they came out of their graves and went into the holy city where they appeared to many people. [54]When the centurion and those with him who were guarding Jesus saw the earthquake and what had just happened, they were filled with awe and said, "This was certainly God's Son."

[55]Many women were watching from a distance. They had followed Jesus from Galilee to serve him. [56]Among them were Mary Magdalene, Mary the mother of James and Joseph, and the mother of Zebedee's sons.

[57]That evening a man named Joseph came. He was a rich man from Arimathea who had become a disciple of Jesus. [58]He came to Pilate and asked for Jesus' body. Pilate gave him permission to take it. [59]Joseph took the body, wrapped it in a clean linen cloth, [60]and laid it in his own new tomb, which he had carved out of the rock. After he rolled a large stone at the door of the tomb, he went away. [61]Mary Magdalene and the other Mary were there, sitting in front of the tomb.

[62]The next day, which was the day after Preparation Day, the chief priests and the Pharisees gathered before Pilate. [63]They said, "Sir, we remember that while that deceiver was still alive he said, 'After three days I will arise.' [64]Therefore, order the grave to be sealed until the third day. Otherwise, his disciples may come and steal the body and tell the people, 'He's been raised from the dead.' This last deception will be worse than the first."

[65]Pilate replied, "You have soldiers for guard duty. Go and make it as secure as you know how." [66]Then they went and secured the tomb by sealing the stone and posting the guard.

Primary Hymns and Songs for the Day

"All Glory, Laud, and Honor" (Palms Gospel) (O)
    B126, C192, E154/ E155, EL344, F249, G196, L108, N216/
    N217, P88, UM280 (PD), VU122, W428
"Tell Me the Stories of Jesus" (Palms Gospel)
    B129, C190, F212, UM277 (PD), VU357
"*Mantos y Palmas*" ("Filled with Excitement") (Palms Gospel)
    G199, N214, UM279
        S-2   #90. Performance note
                #89. Harm.
"Lamb of God" (Passion Gospel)
    EL336, G518, S2113, SF2113
"O Sacred Head, Now Wounded" (Passion)
    B137, C202, E168/169, EL351/352, F284, G221, L116/117,
    N226, P98, UM286, VU145 (Fr.), W434
        H-3   Hbl-82; Chr-148; Desc-86; Org-111
"Lord Whose Love Through Humble Service" (C) (Passion)
    C461, E610, EL712, L423, P427, UM581, W630

Additional Hymn Suggestions

"Hosanna, Loud Hosanna" (Palms Gospel)
    B130, F248, G197, N213, P89, UM278 (PD), VU123
"Ride On! Ride On in Majesty!" (Palms Gospel)
    C191, EL346, G198, N215, P90/91, VU127
"Holy" ("*Santo*") (Palms Gospel)
    EL762, G594, S2019, SF2019
"Bring Many Names" (Palms)
    C10, G760, N11, S2047, SF2047, VU268
"My Song Is Love Unknown" (Palms/Passion)
    E458, EL343, G209, L94, N222, P76, S2083, SF2083, VU143,
    W439
"He Never Said a Mumbalin' Word" (Isa, Passion)
    C208, EL350, G219, P95 (PD), UM291, VU141
"All Praise to Thee, for Thou, O King Divine" (Phil)
    B229, E477, UM166, VU327
"At the Name of Jesus" (Phil)
    B198, E435, EL416, F351, G264, L179, P148, UM168, VU335,
    W499
"Thou Didst Leave Thy Throne" (Phil, Passion)
    B121, F170, S2100, SF2100
"Ah, Holy Jesus" (Passion Gospel)
    C210, E158, EL349, G218, N218, P93, UM289, VU138
"Sing, My Tongue, the Glorious Battle" (Passion)
    E165/166, EL355/356, G225, L118, N220, UM296, W437
"The Bread of Life for All Is Broken" (Passion, Comm.)
    E342, N333, UM633
"Depth of Mercy" (Passion, Holy Week)
    B306, UM355, WS3097
"An Upper Room Did Our Lord Prepare" (Passion Gospel)
    C385, G202, P94, VU130
"An Outcast among Outcasts" (Passion Gospel)
    N201, S2104, SF2104
"Why Has God Forsaken Me?" (Passion Gospel)
    G809, P406, S2110, VU154
"Would I Have Answered When You Called" (Passion Gospel)
    S2137, SF2137
"Sunday's Palms Are Wednesday's Ashes" (Passion)
    S2138, SF2138, VU107
"How Long, O Lord" (Passion Gospel)
    G777, S2209, SF2209
"Life-Giving Bread" (Passion Gospel, Comm.)
    S2261, SF2261
"You, Lord, Are Both Lamb and Shepherd" (Passion)
    G274, SF2102, VU210. WS3043

Additional Contemporary Suggestions

"All Hail King Jesus" (Palms Gospel)
    S2069, SF2069, SP63
"King of Kings" (Palms Gospel)
    B234, S2075, SF2075, SP94, VU167
"The King of Glory Comes" (Palms Gospel)
    B127, S2091, SF2091, W501
"Holy Is the Lord" (Palms Gospel)
    WS3028, M131
"Hosanna" (Palms Gospel)
    M268, WS3188
"Alleluia" (Ps 118)
    EL174, G587, S2043, SF2043
"I Will Enter His Gates" (Ps 118)
    S2270, SF2270, SP168
"Shout to the North" (Phil)
    G319, M99, WS3042
"He Is Lord" (Phil)
    B178, C117, F234, SP122, UM177
"How Majestic Is Your Name" (Phil)
    C63, G613, S2023, SF2023, SP14
"I Exalt You" (Phil)
    SP18
"Stay with Me" ("*Nohu pū*") (Passion Gospel)
    EL348, G204, S2198, SF2198
"Jesus, We Crown You with Praise" (Passion Gospel)
    M24
"Above All" (Passion Gospel)
    M77; V-3 (2) p. 17 Vocal solo
"Once Again" (Passion Gospel)
    M78

Vocal Solos

"Ride On, Ride On in Majesty!" (Palm Sunday)
    V-5 (2)   p. 57
"Ride On, Jesus" (Palm Sunday)
    V-7   p. 8

Anthems

"Sing Hosanna! Blessed Is He!" (Palms Liturgy)
Arr. Fettke/Grassi; Shawnee Press 35029828
SATB, keyboard, opt. children's choir

"*Kyrie*" (Passion Liturgy)
Dvořák/Arr. Jay Rouse; Lorenz 10/4500L
SATB, piano, English horn or C instrument

Other Suggestions

Visuals:

Palms	Donkey, colt/cloaks/crowd/branches
Ps 188	Gate, cornerstone, branches, joy
O	Jesus teaching, morning, Christ, passion, flint
Ps 31	Tears, praying/comforting hands, broken pottery
E	Manacles, wood cross, crucifix, resurrection,
Passion	Thirty coins, praying hands, sword, robe, crucifix, crown of thorns, INRI, dice/robe, tombstone

For additional Passion ideas, consult Good Friday suggestions.
Introit: WS3078. "Hosanna" (Palms Gospel, Ps 118)

Exodus 12:1-4 (5-10) 11-14

¹The LORD said to Moses and Aaron in the land of Egypt, ²"This month will be the first month; it will be the first month of the year for you. ³Tell the whole Israelite community: On the tenth day of this month they must take a lamb for each household, a lamb per house. ⁴If a household is too small for a lamb, it should share one with a neighbor nearby. You should divide the lamb in proportion to the number of people who will be eating it. ⁵Your lamb should be a flawless year-old male. You may take it from the sheep or from the goats. ⁶You should keep close watch over it until the fourteenth day of this month. At twilight on that day, the whole assembled Israelite community should slaughter their lambs. ⁷They should take some of the blood and smear it on the two doorposts and on the beam over the door of the houses in which they are eating. ⁸That same night they should eat the meat roasted over the fire. They should eat it along with unleavened bread and bitter herbs. ⁹Don't eat any of it raw or boiled in water, but roasted over fire with its head, legs, and internal organs. ¹⁰Don't let any of it remain until morning, and burn any of it left over in the morning. ¹¹This is how you should eat it. You should be dressed, with your sandals on your feet and your walking stick in your hand. You should eat the meal in a hurry. It is the Passover of the LORD. ¹²I'll pass through the land of Egypt that night, and I'll strike down every oldest child in the land of Egypt, both humans and animals. I'll impose judgments on all the gods of Egypt. I am the LORD. ¹³The blood will be your sign on the houses where you live. Whenever I see the blood, I'll pass over you. No plague will destroy you when I strike the land of Egypt.

¹⁴"This day will be a day of remembering for you. You will observe it as a festival to the LORD. You will observe it in every generation as a regulation for all time.

Psalm 116:1-4, 12-19 (G655, N699, P228, UM837)

¹I love the LORD because he hears / my requests for mercy. / ²I'll call out to him as long as I live / because he listens closely to me. / ³Death's ropes bound me; / the distress of the grave found me— / I came face-to-face / with trouble and grief. / ⁴So I called on the LORD's name: / "LORD, please save me!" . . . .

¹²What can I give back to the LORD / for all the good things he has done for me? / ¹³I'll lift up the cup of salvation. / I'll call on the LORD's name. / ¹⁴I'll keep the promises I made to the LORD / in the presence of all God's people. / ¹⁵The death of the LORD's faithful / is a costly loss in his eyes.

¹⁶Oh yes, LORD, I am definitely your servant! / I am your servant and the son of your female servant— / you've freed me from my chains. / ¹⁷So I'll offer a sacrifice of thanksgiving to you, / and I'll call on the LORD's name. / ¹⁸I'll keep the promises I made to the LORD / in the presence of all God's people, / ¹⁹in the courtyards of the LORD's house, / which is in the center of Jerusalem. / Praise the LORD!

1 Corinthians 11:23-26

²³I received a tradition from the Lord, which I also handed on to you: on the night on which he was betrayed, the Lord Jesus took bread. ²⁴After giving thanks, he broke it and said, "This is my body, which is for you; do this to remember me." ²⁵He did the same thing with the cup, after they had eaten, saying, "This cup is the new covenant in my blood. Every time you drink it, do this to remember me." ²⁶Every time you eat this bread and drink this cup, you broadcast the death of the Lord until he comes.

John 13:1-17, 31b -35

¹Before the Festival of Passover, Jesus knew that his time had come to leave this world and go to the Father. Having loved his own who were in the world, he loved them fully. ²Jesus and his disciples were sharing the evening meal. The devil had already provoked Judas, Simon Iscariot's son, to betray Jesus. ³Jesus knew the Father had given everything into his hands and that he had come from God and was returning to God. ⁴So he got up from the table and took off his robes. Picking up a linen towel, he tied it around his waist. ⁵Then he poured water into a washbasin and began to wash the disciples' feet, drying them with the towel he was wearing. ⁶When Jesus came to Simon Peter, Peter said to him, "Lord, are you going to wash my feet?"

⁷Jesus replied, "You don't understand what I'm doing now, but you will understand later."

⁸"No!" Peter said. "You will never wash my feet!"

Jesus replied, "Unless I wash you, you won't have a place with me."

⁹Simon Peter said, "Lord, not only my feet but also my hands and my head!"

¹⁰Jesus responded, "Those who have bathed need only to have their feet washed, because they are completely clean. You disciples are clean, but not every one of you." ¹¹He knew who would betray him. That's why he said, "Not every one of you is clean."

¹²After he washed the disciples' feet, he put on his robes and returned to his place at the table. He said to them, "Do you know what I've done for you? ¹³You call me 'Teacher' and 'Lord,' and you speak correctly, because I am. ¹⁴If I, your Lord and teacher, have washed your feet, you too must wash each other's feet. ¹⁵I have given you an example: just as I have done, you also must do. ¹⁶I assure you, servants aren't greater than their master, nor are those who are sent greater than the one who sent them. ¹⁷Since you know these things, you will be happy if you do them. . . .

³¹ᵇJesus said, "Now the Human One has been glorified, and God has been glorified in him. ³²If God has been glorified in him, God will also glorify the Human One in himself and will glorify him immediately. ³³Little children, I'm with you for a little while longer. You will look for me—but, just as I told the Jewish leaders, I also tell you now—'Where I'm going, you can't come.'

³⁴"I give you a new commandment: Love each other. Just as I have loved you, so you also must love each other. ³⁵This is how everyone will know that you are my disciples, when you love each other."

Primary Hymns and Songs for the Day

"What Wondrous Love Is This" (Pss, John) (O)
  B143 (PD), C200, E439, EL666, F283, G215, L385, N223,
  P85, UM292, VU147 (Fr.), W600
          H-3   Hbl-102; Chr-212; Org-185
          S-1   #347. Harm.
"In Remembrance of Me" (Pss, 1 Cor, Comm.)
  B365, C403, G521, S2254
"*Jesu, Jesu*" (John, Footwashing) (C)
  B501, C600, E602, EL708, G203, N498, P367, UM432,
  VU593, W431, S-1 #63. Vocal part

Additional Hymn Suggestions

"O God, Our Help in Ages Past" (Exod)
  B74, C67, E680, EL632, F370, G687, L320, N25, P210,
  UM117 (PD), VU806, W579
"Deep in the Shadows of the Past" (Exod)
  G50, N320, P330, S2246
"*Saranam, Saranam*" ("Refuge") (Exod, Pss)
  G789, UM523
"Out of the Depths I Cry to You" (Pss)
  EL600, G424, L295, N483, P240, UM515
"Fill My Cup, Lord" (Pss, Comm.)
  C351, F481, UM641 (refrain only), WS3093
"I Love the Lord" (Pss)
  G799, P362, N511, VU617, WS3142
"For the Bread Which You Have Broken (1 Cor, Comm.)
  C411, E340/E341, EL494, G516, L200, P508/P509, UM614/
  UM615, VU470
"Now The Silence" (Comm.)
  C415, E333, EL460, G534, L205, UM619, VU475, W668
"*Una Espiga*" ("Sheaves of Summer") (1 Cor, Comm.)
  C396, G532, N338, UM637
"Mothering God, You Gave Me Birth" (1 Cor, Comm.)
  C83, EL735, G7, N467, S2050, SF2050, VU320
"Come, Share the Lord" (1 Cor, Comm.)
  C408, G510, S2269, SF2269, VU469
"Ah, Holy Jesus" (John)
  C210, E158, EL349, G218, N218, P93, UM289, VU138
"O Master, Let Me Walk with Thee" (John)
  B279, C602, E659/E660, EL818, F442, G738, L492, N503,
  P357, UM430 (PD), VU560
"Lord God, Your Love Has Called Us Here" (John)
  EL358, P353, UM579
"Together We Serve" (John)
  G767, S2175, SF2175
"Wounded World That Cries for Healing" (John)
  S2177, SF2177
"Healer of Our Every Ill" (John)
  C506, EL612, G795, S2213, SF2213, VU619
"Jesus Is a Rock in a Weary Land" (John, Holy Week)
  EL333, WS3074 (PD)
"We Sang Our Glad Hosannas" (John, Holy Week)
  S2111, SF2111
"What Wondrous Love Is This" (John, Holy Week)
  B143 (PD), C200, E439, EL666, F283, G215, L385, N223,
  P85, UM292, VU147 (Fr.), W600
"As We Gather at Your Table" (John, Comm.)
  EL522, N332, S2268, SF2268, VU457
"Draw Us in the Spirit's Tether" (John, Comm.)
  C392, EL470, G529, N337, P504, UM632, VU479, W731

Additional Contemporary Suggestions

"I Will Call upon the Lord" (Pss)
  G621, S2002, SF2002, SP224

"We Bring the Sacrifice of Praise" (Pss)
  S2031, SF2031, SP1
"I Love You, Lord" (Pss)
  B212, G627, S2068, SF2068, SP72
"I Stand Amazed" (Pss, Lent)
  M79
"Beautiful Savior" (Pss, Holy Week)
  M243
"God with Us" (Pss, Holy Week)
  M252
"Eat This Bread" (1 Cor, Comm.)
  C414, EL472, G527, N788, UM628, VU466, W734
"Here Is Bread, Here Is Wine" (1 Cor, Comm.)
  EL483, S2266, SF2266
"Father, I Adore You" (John)
  B256, F414, S2038, SF2038, SP194
"Make Me a Servant" (John)
  S2176, SF2176, SP193
"Live in Charity" ("*Ubi Caritas*") (John)
  C523, EL642, G205, S2179, SF2179, W604
"The Servant Song" (John)
  C490, EL659, G727, N539, S2222, SF2222, VU595
"They'll Know We Are Christians" (John)
  AH4074, C494, G300, S2223, SF2223
"Make Us One" (John)
  AH4142, S2224, SF2224, SP137
"Bind Us Together" (John)
  S2226, SF2226, SP140
"The Jesus in Me" (John)
  AH4109, WS3151

Vocal Solos

"In Remembrance" (John, Comm.)
  V-5 (2)   p. 7
"He Breaks the Bread, He Pours the Wine" (John)
  V-10   p. 43

Anthems

"Lamb of God" (SOCM49) (Good Friday)
Arr. Christopher Aspaas; Augsburg 9781451499032
TTBB a cappella

"O Master, Let Me Walk with Thee" (John)
Hal H. Hopson; MorningStar MSM-50-9212
SATB, keyboard, opt. violin, viola, or cello

Other Suggestions

Visuals:
  O   Goat/lamb, blood/doorposts, unleavened bread,
            sandals, staff, Exod 12:11b, 14a
  P   Praying hands, lifted cup, death, open manacles
  E   Broken loaf, cup, Last Supper
  G   Robe/towel/water/basin, John 13:12b or 13:34ab,
            Last Supper, Jesus speaking, acts of love
*For a quiet service of acoustic or a cappella music, consider: UM292,
  UM432, UM618, UM620, UM625, S2157, S2179, S2258,
  S2260, S2261, S2264, S2267, WS3168*
Reading: C388. Remember Me (1 Cor)
Invitation to Communion: WS3152. "Welcome" (John)
Sung Communion: WS3171. "Communion Setting" (1 Cor)

Isaiah 52:13–53:12

¹³Look, my servant will succeed.
    He will be exalted and lifted very high.
¹⁴Just as many were appalled by you,
    he too appeared disfigured, inhuman,
    his appearance unlike that of mortals.
¹⁵But he will astonish many nations.
    Kings will be silenced because of him,
    because they will see what they haven't seen before;
    what they haven't heard before, they will ponder.
53Who can believe what we have heard,
    and for whose sake has the LORD's arm been revealed?
²He grew up like a young plant before us,
    like a root from dry ground.
He possessed no splendid form for us to see,
    no desirable appearance.
³He was despised and avoided by others;
    a man who suffered, who knew sickness well.
Like someone from whom people hid their faces,
    he was despised, and we didn't think about him.

⁴It was certainly our sickness that he carried,
    and our sufferings that he bore,
    but we thought him afflicted,
    struck down by God and tormented.
⁵He was pierced because of our rebellions
    and crushed because of our crimes.
    He bore the punishment that made us whole;
    by his wounds we are healed.
⁶Like sheep we had all wandered away,
    each going its own way,
    but the LORD let fall on him all our crimes.
⁷He was oppressed and tormented,
    but didn't open his mouth.
Like a lamb being brought to slaughter,
    like a ewe silent before her shearers,
    he didn't open his mouth.

⁸Due to an unjust ruling he was taken away,
    and his fate—who will think about it?
He was eliminated from the land of the living,
    struck dead   because of my people's rebellion.
⁹His grave was among the wicked,
    his tomb with evildoers,
    though he had done no violence,
    and had spoken nothing false.

¹⁰But the LORD wanted to crush him
    and to make him suffer.
If his life is offered as restitution,
    he will see his offspring; he will enjoy long life.
    The LORD's plans will come to fruition through him.
¹¹After his deep anguish he will see light, and he will be
        satisfied.
Through his knowledge, the righteous one, my servant,
    will make many righteous,
    and will bear their guilt.
¹²Therefore, I will give him a share with the great,
    and he will divide the spoil with the strong,
    in return for exposing his life to death
    and being numbered with rebels,
    though he carried the sin of many
    and pleaded on behalf of those who rebelled.

Psalm 22 (G210/631, N632, UM752)

¹My God! My God, / why have you left me all alone? / Why are you so far from saving me— / so far from my anguished groans? / ²My God, I cry out during the day, / but you don't answer; / even at nighttime I don't stop. / ³You are the holy one, enthroned. / You are Israel's praise. / ⁴Our ancestors trusted you— / they trusted you and you rescued them; / ⁵they cried out to you and they were saved; / they trusted you and they weren't ashamed.

⁶But I'm just a worm, less than human; / insulted by one person, / despised by another. / ⁷All who see me make fun of me— / they gape, shaking their heads: / ⁸"He committed himself to the LORD, / so let God rescue him; / let God deliver him / because God likes him so much." / ⁹But you are the one who pulled me from the womb, / placing me safely at my mother's breasts. / ¹⁰I was thrown on you from birth; / you've been my God / since I was in my mother's womb. / ¹¹Please don't be far from me / because trouble is near / and there's no one to help.

¹²Many bulls surround me; / mighty bulls from Bashan encircle me. / ¹³They open their mouths at me / like a lion ripping and roaring! / ¹⁴I'm poured out like water. / All my bones have fallen apart. / My heart is like wax; / it melts inside me. / ¹⁵My strength is dried up / like a piece of broken pottery. / My tongue sticks to the roof of my mouth; / you've set me down in the dirt of death. / ¹⁶Dogs surround me; / a pack of evil people circle me like a lion— / oh, my poor hands and feet! / ¹⁷I can count all my bones! / Meanwhile, they just stare at me, watching me. / ¹⁸They divvy up my garments among themselves; / they cast lots for my clothes.

¹⁹But you, LORD! Don't be far away! / You are my strength! / Come quick and help me! / ²⁰Deliver me from the sword. / Deliver my life from the power of the dog. / ²¹Save me from the mouth of the lion. / From the horns of the wild oxen / you have answered me!

²²I will declare your name to my brothers and sisters; / I will praise you in the very center of the congregation! / ²³All of you who revere the LORD—praise him! / All of you who are Jacob's descendants—honor him! / All of you who are all Israel's offspring— / stand in awe of him! / ²⁴Because he didn't despise or detest / the suffering of the one who suffered— / he didn't hide his face from me. / No, he listened when I cried out to him for help.

²⁵I offer praise in the great congregation / because of you; / I will fulfill my promises / in the presence of those who honor God. / ²⁶Let all those who are suffering eat and be full! / Let all who seek the LORD praise him! / I pray your hearts live forever! / ²⁷Every part of the earth / will remember and come back to the LORD; / every family among all the nations will worship you. / ²⁸Because the right to rule belongs to the LORD, / he rules all nations. / ²⁹Indeed, all the earth's powerful / will worship him; / all who are descending to the dust / will kneel before him; / my being also lives for him. / ³⁰Future descendants will serve him; / generations to come will be told about my Lord. / ³¹They will proclaim God's righteousness / to those not yet born, / telling them what God has done.

Hebrews 10:16-25

[16] *This is the covenant that I will make with them.*
  After these days, says the Lord,
    I will place my laws in their hearts
    and write them on their minds.
[17] *And I won't remember their sins*
    and their lawless behavior anymore.

[18]When there is forgiveness for these things, there is no longer an offering for sin.

[19]Brothers and sisters, we have confidence that we can enter the holy of holies by means of Jesus' blood, [20]through a new and living way that he opened up for us through the curtain, which is his body, [21]and we have a great high priest over God's house.

[22]Therefore, let's draw near with a genuine heart with the certainty that our faith gives us, since our hearts are sprinkled clean from an evil conscience and our bodies are washed with pure water.

[23]Let's hold on to the confession of our hope without wavering, because the one who made the promises is reliable.

[24]Let's also think about how to motivate each other to show love and to do good works. [25]Don't stop meeting together with other believers, which some people have gotten into the habit of doing. Instead, encourage each other, especially as you see the day drawing near.

John 18:1–19:42

[1]After he said these things, Jesus went out with his disciples and crossed over to the other side of the Kidron Valley. He and his disciples entered a garden there. [2]Judas, his betrayer, also knew the place because Jesus often gathered there with his disciples. [3]Judas brought a company of soldiers and some guards from the chief priests and Pharisees. They came there carrying lanterns, torches, and weapons. [4]Jesus knew everything that was to happen to him, so he went out and asked, "Who are you looking for?"

[5]They answered, "Jesus the Nazarene."

He said to them, "I Am." (Judas, his betrayer, was standing with them.) [6]When he said, "I Am," they shrank back and fell to the ground. [7]He asked them again, "Who are you looking for?"

They said, "Jesus the Nazarene."

[8]Jesus answered, "I told you, 'I Am.' If you are looking for me, then let these people go." [9]This was so that the word he had spoken might be fulfilled: "I didn't lose anyone of those whom you gave me."

[10]Then Simon Peter, who had a sword, drew it and struck the high priest's servant, cutting off his right ear. (The servant's name was Malchus.) [11]Jesus told Peter, "Put your sword away! Am I not to drink the cup the Father has given me?" [12]Then the company of soldiers, the commander, and the guards from the Jewish leaders took Jesus into custody. They bound him [13]and led him first to Annas. He was the father-in-law of Caiaphas, the high priest that year. [14](Caiaphas was the one who had advised the Jewish leaders that it was better for one person to die for the people.)

[15]Simon Peter and another disciple followed Jesus. Because this other disciple was known to the high priest, he went with Jesus into the high priest's courtyard. [16]However, Peter stood outside near the gate. Then the other disciple (the one known to the high priest) came out and spoke to the woman stationed at the gate, and she brought Peter in. [17]The servant woman stationed at the gate asked Peter, "Aren't you one of this man's disciples?"

"I'm not," he replied. [18]The servants and the guards had made a fire because it was cold. They were standing around it, warming themselves. Peter joined them there, standing by the fire and warming himself.

[19]Meanwhile, the chief priest questioned Jesus about his disciples and his teaching. [20]Jesus answered, "I've spoken openly to the world. I've always taught in synagogues and in the temple, where all the Jews gather. I've said nothing in private. [21]Why ask me? Ask those who heard what I told them. They know what I said."

[22]After Jesus spoke, one of the guards standing there slapped Jesus in the face. "Is that how you would answer the high priest?" he asked.

[23]Jesus replied, "If I speak wrongly, testify about what was wrong. But if I speak correctly, why do you strike me?" [24]Then Annas sent him bound to Caiaphas the high priest.

[25]Meanwhile, Simon Peter was still standing with the guards, warming himself. They asked, "Aren't you one of his disciples?"

Peter denied it, saying, "I'm not."

[26]A servant of the high priest, a relative of the one whose ear Peter had cut off, said to him, "Didn't I see you in the garden with him?" [27]Peter denied it again, and immediately a rooster crowed.

[28]The Jewish leaders led Jesus from Caiaphas to the Roman governor's palace. It was early in the morning. So that they could eat the Passover, the Jewish leaders wouldn't enter the palace; entering the palace would have made them ritually impure.

[29]So Pilate went out to them and asked, "What charge do you bring against this man?"

[30]They answered, "If he had done nothing wrong, we wouldn't have handed him over to you."

[31]Pilate responded, "Take him yourselves and judge him according to your Law."

The Jewish leaders replied, "The Law doesn't allow us to kill anyone." ([32]This was so that Jesus' word might be fulfilled when he indicated how he was going to die.)

[33]Pilate went back into the palace. He summoned Jesus and asked, "Are you the king of the Jews?"

[34]Jesus answered, "Do you say this on your own or have others spoken to you about me?"

[35]Pilate responded, "I'm not a Jew, am I? Your nation and its chief priests handed you over to me. What have you done?"

[36]Jesus replied, "My kingdom doesn't originate from this world. If it did, my guards would fight so that I wouldn't have been arrested by the Jewish leaders. My kingdom isn't from here."

[37]"So you are a king?" Pilate said.

Jesus answered, "You say that I am a king. I was born and came into the world for this reason: to testify to the truth. Whoever accepts the truth listens to my voice."

[38]"What is truth?" Pilate asked.

After Pilate said this, he returned to the Jewish leaders and said, "I find no grounds for any charge against him. [39]You have a custom that I release one prisoner for you at Passover. Do you want me to release for you the king of the Jews?"

[40]They shouted, "Not this man! Give us Barabbas!" (Barabbas was an outlaw.)

19Then Pilate had Jesus taken and whipped. ²The soldiers twisted together a crown of thorns and put it on his head, and dressed him in a purple robe. ³Over and over they went up to him and said, "Greetings, king of the Jews!" And they slapped him in the face.

⁴Pilate came out of the palace again and said to the Jewish leaders, "Look! I'm bringing him out to you to let you know that I find no grounds for a charge against him." ⁵When Jesus came out, wearing the crown of thorns and the purple robe, Pilate said to them, "Here's the man."

⁶When the chief priests and their deputies saw him, they shouted out, "Crucify, crucify!"

Pilate told them, "You take him and crucify him. I don't find any grounds for a charge against him."

⁷The Jewish leaders replied, "We have a Law, and according to this Law he ought to die because he made himself out to be God's Son."

⁸When Pilate heard this word, he was even more afraid. ⁹He went back into the residence and spoke to Jesus, "Where are you from?" Jesus didn't answer. ¹⁰So Pilate said, "You won't speak to me? Don't you know that I have authority to release you and also to crucify you?"

¹¹Jesus replied, "You would have no authority over me if it had not been given to you from above. That's why the one who handed me over to you has the greater sin." ¹²From that moment on, Pilate wanted to release Jesus.

However, the Jewish leaders cried out, saying, "If you release this man, you aren't a friend of the emperor! Anyone who makes himself out to be a king opposes the emperor!"

¹³When Pilate heard these words, he led Jesus out and seated him on the judge's bench at the place called Stone Pavement (in Aramaic, *Gabbatha*). ¹⁴It was about noon on the Preparation Day for the Passover. Pilate said to the Jewish leaders, "Here's your king."

¹⁵The Jewish leaders cried out, "Take him away! Take him away! Crucify him!"

Pilate responded, "What? Do you want me to crucify your king?"

"We have no king except the emperor," the chief priests answered. ¹⁶Then Pilate handed Jesus over to be crucified.

The soldiers took Jesus prisoner. ¹⁷Carrying his cross by himself, he went out to a place called Skull Place (in Aramaic, *Golgotha*). ¹⁸That's where they crucified him—and two others with him, one on each side and Jesus in the middle. ¹⁹Pilate had a public notice written and posted on the cross. It read "Jesus the Nazarene, the king of the Jews." ²⁰Many of the Jews read this sign, for the place where Jesus was crucified was near the city and it was written in Aramaic, Latin, and Greek. ²¹Therefore, the Jewish chief priests complained to Pilate, "Don't write, 'The king of the Jews' but 'This man said, "I am the king of the Jews."'"

²²Pilate answered, "What I've written, I've written."

²³When the soldiers crucified Jesus, they took his clothes and his sandals, and divided them into four shares, one for each soldier. His shirt was seamless, woven as one piece from the top to the bottom. ²⁴They said to each other, "Let's not tear it. Let's cast lots to see who will get it." This was to fulfill the scripture,

They divided my clothes among themselves,
and they cast lots for my clothing.
That's what the soldiers did.

²⁵Jesus' mother and his mother's sister, Mary the wife of Clopas, and Mary Magdalene stood near the cross. ²⁶When Jesus saw his mother and the disciple whom he loved standing nearby, he said to his mother, "Woman, here is your son." ²⁷Then he said to the disciple, "Here is your mother." And from that time on, this disciple took her into his home.

²⁸After this, knowing that everything was already completed, in order to fulfill the scripture, Jesus said, "I am thirsty." ²⁹A jar full of sour wine was nearby, so the soldiers soaked a sponge in it, placed it on a hyssop branch, and held it up to his lips. ³⁰When he had received the sour wine, Jesus said, "It is completed." Bowing his head, he gave up his life.

³¹It was the Preparation Day and the Jewish leaders didn't want the bodies to remain on the cross on the Sabbath, especially since that Sabbath was an important day. So they asked Pilate to have the legs of those crucified broken and the bodies taken down. ³²Therefore, the soldiers came and broke the legs of the two men who were crucified with Jesus. ³³When they came to Jesus, they saw that he was already dead so they didn't break his legs. ³⁴However, one of the soldiers pierced his side with a spear, and immediately blood and water came out. ³⁵The one who saw this has testified, and his testimony is true. He knows that he speaks the truth, and he has testified so that you also can believe. ³⁶These things happened to fulfill the scripture, *They won't break any of his bones.* ³⁷And another scripture says, *They will look at him whom they have pierced.*

³⁸After this Joseph of Arimathea asked Pilate if he could take away the body of Jesus. Joseph was a disciple of Jesus, but a secret one because he feared the Jewish authorities. Pilate gave him permission, so he came and took the body away. ³⁹Nicodemus, the one who at first had come to Jesus at night, was there too. He brought a mixture of myrrh and aloe, nearly seventy-five pounds in all. ⁴⁰Following Jewish burial customs, they took Jesus' body and wrapped it, with the spices, in linen cloths. ⁴¹There was a garden in the place where Jesus was crucified, and in the garden was a new tomb in which no one had ever been laid. ⁴²Because it was the Jewish Preparation Day and the tomb was nearby, they laid Jesus in it.

Primary Hymns and Songs for the Day

"Were You There" (John) (O)
B156, C198, E172, EL353, F287, G228, L92, N230, P102, UM288, VU144, W436
- H-3   Hbl-101; Chr-209
- S-2   #195-96. Desc. and harm.
- V-7   p. 60 Vocal solo

"O Sacred Head, Now Wounded" (John)
B137, C202, E168/169, EL351/352, F284, G221, L116/117, N226, P98, UM286, VU145 (Fr.), W434
- H-3   Hbl-82; Chr-148; Desc-86; Org-111

"When I Survey the Wondrous Cross" (John) (C)
B144, C195, EL803, F258, G223, N224, P101, UM298
- H-3   Hbl-6, 102; Chr-213; Desc-49; Org-49
- S-1   #155. Desc.

"When I Survey the Wondrous Cross" (John) (C)
E474, L482, G224, P100, UM299 (PD), VU149 (Fr.)
- H-3   Hbl-47; Chr-214; Desc-90; Org-127
- S-1   #288. Transposition to E-flat major

Additional Hymn Suggestions

"He Never Said a Mumbalin' Word" (Isa, John)
C208, EL350, G219, P95 (PD), UM291, VU141

"Alas! And Did My Savior Bleed" (Isa, John)
AH4067, B139/145, C204, EL337, F274, G212, L98, N199/N200, P78, UM294/UM359

"You, Lord, Are Both Lamb and Shepherd" (Isa, John)
G274, SF2102, VU210. WS3043

"Out of the Depths I Cry to You" (Pss)
EL600, G424, L295, N483, P240, UM515

"Why Stand so Far Away, My God?" (Pss, John)
C671, G786, S2180, SF2180

"I Am Thine, O Lord" (Heb)
AH4087, B290, C601, F455, N455, UM419 (PD)

"Near to the Heart of God" (Heb)
B295, C581, F35, G824, P527, UM472 (PD)

"Since Jesus Came into My Heart" (Heb)
B441, F639, S2140, SF2140

"Victim Divine" (Heb, Comm.)
L202, S2259, SF2259

"Living for Jesus" (Heb, John, Good Friday)
B282, C610, F462, S2149, SF2149

"Ah, Holy Jesus" (John)
C210, E158, EL349, G218, N218, P93, UM289, VU138

"Go to Dark Gethsemane" (John)
C196, E171, EL347, F281, G220, L109, N219, P97, UM290 (PD), VU133

"Must Jesus Bear the Cross Alone" (John)
B475, F504, SF2112, UM424 (PD)

"The Bread of Life for All Is Broken" (John)
E342, N333, UM633

"Thou Didst Leave Thy Throne" (John)
B121, F170, S2100, SF2100

"When Jesus Wept" (John)
C199, E715, G194, P312, S2106, SF2106, VU146

"Why Has God Forsaken Me?" (John)
G809, P406, S2110, VU154

"Jesus Walked This Lonesome Valley" (John)
C211, F217, P80, S2112, W427

"My Song Is Love Unknown" (Good Friday)
E458, EL343, G209, L94, N222, P76, S2083, SF2083, VU143, W439

Additional Contemporary Suggestions

"Our God Reigns" (Isa)
SP64

"Wholly Yours" (Isa)
M239

"O How He Loves You and Me!" (Isa, John)
B146, F622, S2108, SF2108, SP113

"There Is a Redeemer" (Isa, John)
G443, SP111

"You Are My King" ("Amazing Love") (Heb)
M82, WS3102

"Because of Your Love" (Heb, Good Friday)
M224

"I Come to the Cross" (Heb, Good Friday)
M106

"Jesus, Remember Me" (John)
C569, EL616, G227, P599, UM488, VU148, W423

"Stay with Me" ("Nohu pû") (John, Good Friday)
EL348, G204, S2198, SF2198

"Lamb of God" (John, Good Friday)
EL336, G518, S2113, SF2113

"The Power of the Cross" (John, Good Friday)
M222, WS3085

"In Christ Alone" (John, Good Friday)
M138, WS3105

"The Wonderful Cross" (John, Good Friday)
M76

"Above All" (John, Good Friday)
M77; V-3 (2) p. 17 Vocal solo

"Revelation Song" (Good Friday)
M274

Vocal Solos

"He Was Cut off Out of the Land of the Living" (recitative) and "But Thou Didst Not Leave His Soul in Hell" (aria) (John)
V-2

"Sing of Mary, Pure and Lowly" (John, Good Friday)
V-5 (1)   p. 21

"He Carried My Cross" (John, Good Friday)
V-8   p. 213

Anthems

"Were You There" (SOCB87) (John)
Arr. Robert Scholz; Augsburg 9781451499032
TTBB a cappella

"O Sacred Head" (John)
Arr. Craig Courtney; Lorenz 10/4329L
SATB or SAB, piano

Other Suggestions

Visuals:
- O   Plant, root, suffering, crucifix, lamb/shears
- P   Crucifix, Exodus, nursing, water, bones, sword, dog/lion/ox, feeding the poor
- E   Heb 10:16b, eraser, crucifix, curtain, worship
- G   Sword, fire, cock, whip, robe, rugged cross, crucifix nails, crown (thorns), ladder, sponge, spear, shroud

Good Friday: Black-draped cross, altar stripped
For additional ideas, consult Palm/Passion Sunday suggestions.
Prayers: F286, F566, N833, N880, and UM284 (John)
Litany: C201 or C209 (John)
Reading: C205 or F257 or UM293 (John, Good Friday)

Acts 10:34-43

³⁴Peter said, "I really am learning that God doesn't show partiality to one group of people over another. ³⁵Rather, in every nation, whoever worships him and does what is right is acceptable to him. ³⁶This is the message of peace he sent to the Israelites by proclaiming the good news through Jesus Christ: He is Lord of all! ³⁷You know what happened throughout Judea, beginning in Galilee after the baptism John preached. ³⁸You know about Jesus of Nazareth, whom God anointed with the Holy Spirit and endowed with power. Jesus traveled around doing good and healing everyone oppressed by the devil because God was with him. ³⁹We are witnesses of everything he did, both in Judea and in Jerusalem. They killed him by hanging him on a tree, ⁴⁰but God raised him up on the third day and allowed him to be seen, ⁴¹not by everyone but by us. We are witnesses whom God chose beforehand, who ate and drank with him after God raised him from the dead. ⁴²He commanded us to preach to the people and to testify that he is the one whom God appointed as judge of the living and the dead. ⁴³All the prophets testify about him that everyone who believes in him receives forgiveness of sins through his name."

Psalm 118:1-2, 14-24 (G391/681, N700, P230/232, UM839)

¹Give thanks to the LORD because he is good, / because his faithful love lasts forever. / ²Let Israel say it: / "God's faithful love lasts forever!" . . . .

¹⁴The LORD was my strength and protection; / he was my saving help! / ¹⁵The sounds of joyful songs and deliverance / are heard in the tents of the righteous: / "The LORD's strong hand is victorious! / ¹⁶The LORD's strong hand is ready to strike! / The LORD's strong hand is victorious!"

¹⁷I won't die—no, I will live / and declare what the LORD has done. / ¹⁸Yes, the LORD definitely disciplined me, / but he didn't hand me over to death.

¹⁹Open the gates of righteousness for me / so I can come in and give thanks to the LORD! / ²⁰This is the LORD's gate; / those who are righteous enter through it.

²¹I thank you because you answered me, / because you were my saving help. / ²²The stone rejected by the builders / is now the main foundation stone! / ²³This has happened because of the LORD; / it is astounding in our sight! / ²⁴This is the day the LORD acted; / we will rejoice and celebrate in it!

Colossians 3:1-4

¹Therefore if you were raised with Christ, look for the things that are above where Christ is sitting at God's right side. ²Think about the things above and not things on earth. ³You died, and your life is hidden with Christ in God. ⁴When Christ, who is your life, is revealed, then you also will be revealed with him in glory.

John 20:1-18

¹Early in the morning of the first day of the week, while it was still dark, Mary Magdalene came to the tomb and saw that the stone had been taken away from the tomb. ²She ran to Simon Peter and the other disciple, the one whom Jesus loved, and said, "They have taken the Lord from the tomb, and we don't know where they've put him." ³Peter and the other disciple left to go to the tomb. ⁴They were running together, but the other disciple ran faster than Peter and was the first to arrive at the tomb. ⁵Bending down to take a look, he saw the linen cloths lying there, but he didn't go in. ⁶Following him, Simon Peter entered the tomb and saw the linen cloths lying there. ⁷He also saw the face cloth that had been on Jesus' head. It wasn't with the other clothes but was folded up in its own place. ⁸Then the other disciple, the one who arrived at the tomb first, also went inside. He saw and believed. ⁹They didn't yet understand the scripture that Jesus must rise from the dead. ¹⁰Then the disciples returned to the place where they were staying.

¹¹Mary stood outside near the tomb, crying. As she cried, she bent down to look into the tomb. ¹²She saw two angels dressed in white, seated where the body of Jesus had been, one at the head and one at the foot. ¹³The angels asked her, "Woman, why are you crying?"

She replied, "They have taken away my Lord, and I don't know where they've put him." ¹⁴As soon as she had said this, she turned around and saw Jesus standing there, but she didn't know it was Jesus.

¹⁵Jesus said to her, "Woman, why are you crying? Who are you looking for?"

Thinking he was the gardener, she replied, "Sir, if you have carried him away, tell me where you have put him and I will get him."

¹⁶Jesus said to her, "Mary."

She turned and said to him in Aramaic, "Rabbouni" (which means *Teacher*).

¹⁷Jesus said to her, "Don't hold on to me, for I haven't yet gone up to my Father. Go to my brothers and sisters and tell them, 'I'm going up to my Father and your Father, to my God and your God.'"

¹⁸Mary Magdalene left and announced to the disciples, "I've seen the Lord." Then she told them what he said to her.

Primary Hymns and Songs for the Day

"Christ the Lord Is Risen Today" (John, Matt) (O)
B159, C216, F289, N233, UM302 (PD), VU155 and VU157
    H-3   Hbl-8, 51; Chr-49; Desc-31; Org-32
    S-1   #104-108. Various treatments
G245, P113, W463
    H-3   Hbl-72; Chr-50; Desc-69; Org-78
    S-1   #213. Desc.
EL373, L130

"Christ Has Risen" (John, Matt)
S2115, SF2115
    H-3   Chr-80; Desc-52
    S-1   #160-62. Various treatments
    S-2   #87-88. Brass/timpani intro. and arr.

"Crown Him with Many Crowns" (John) (C)
B161, C234, E494, EL855, F345, G268, L170, N301, P151, UM327 (PD), VU211
    H-3   Hbl-55; Chr-60; Desc-30; Org-27
    S-1   #86-88. Various treatments

Additional Hymn Suggestions

"At the Font We Start Our Journey" (Acts, Baptism)
N308, S2114, SF2114

"Ask Ye What Great Thing I Know" (Acts, Easter)
B538, N49, UM163 (PD), VU338

"We Meet You, O Christ" (Acts)
C183, P311, UM257, VU183

"Lord of the Dance" (Acts)
G157, P302, UM261, VU352, W636

"The Strife Is O'er, the Battle Done" (Acts)
B171, C221, E208, EL366, G236, L135, N242, P119, UM306, VU159, W451

"This Is the Day" (Pss)
AH4149, B359, C286, N84, SP236, UM657, VU412

"This Is the Day the Lord Hath Made" (Pss)
B358, G681, P230, UM658

"Taste and See" (Pss, Comm.)
EL493, G520, S2267, SF2267

"O Sons and Daughters, Let Us Sing" (Pss, John)
C220, E203, EL386/E387, G235/255, L139, N244, P116 (PD), UM317, VU170, W447

"All Praise to Thee, for Thou, O King Divine" (Col)
B229, E477, UM166, VU327

"Woke Up This Morning" (Col)
C623, N85, S2082, SF2082

"The Day of Resurrection" (John, Matt)
B164, C228, E210, EL361, G233, L141, N245, P118, UM303 (PD), VU164

"Thine Be the Glory" (John, Matt)
B163, C218, EL376, F291, G238, L145, N253, P122, UM308, VU173 (Fr.)

"He Lives" (John, Matt)
B533, C226, F299, UM310

"Cristo Vive" ("Christ Is Risen") (John, Matt)
B167, N235, P109, UM313

"In the Garden" (John)
B187, C227, F588, N237, UM314

"Come, Ye Faithful, Raise the Strain" (John, Matt)
C215, E199, EL363, G234, L132, N230, P115, UM315 (PD), VU165, W456

"He Rose" (John, Matt)
N239, UM316

"Christ Is Alive" (John, Matt)
B173, E182, EL389, G246, L363, P108, UM318, VU158

"Up from the Grave He Arose" (John, Matt)
B160, C224, UM322 (PD)

Additional Contemporary Suggestions

"Halle, Halle, Halleluja" (Easter, Opening)
C41, EL172, G591, N236, S2026, SF2026, VU958

"You Are Good" (Pss)
AH4018, M124, WS3014

"You Are My All in All" (Pss)
G519, SP220, WS3040

"Forever" (Pss)
M68, WS3023

"Hallelujah" ("Your Love Is Amazing") (Pss)
M118, WS3027

"Lord, I Lift Your Name on High" (Col, Easter)
AH4071, EL857, M2, S2088, SF2088

"Alleluia" (John, Matt, Easter)
B223, C106, F361, N765, SP108, UM186

"Jesus Is Alive" (John, Matt, Easter)
M20

"See What a Morning" ("Resurrection Hymn") (John)
M259

"My Redeemer Lives" (Easter)
M73

"Alive Forever, Amen" (Easter)
M201

"Holy, Holy" (Easter)
B254, F149, P140, S2039, SP141

"Alleluia" (Easter)
EL174, G587, S2043, SF2043

"Sing Alleluia to the Lord" (Easter, Comm.)
B214, C32, S2258, SF2258, SP93

"Amen, Amen" (Easter, Closing)
N161, P299, S2072

"In Christ Alone" (Easter)
M138, WS3105

Vocal Solos

"Jesus Christ Is Risen Today" (John, Matt, Easter)
    V-1   p. 50

"I Know That My Redeemer Lives" (Easter)
    V-5 (2)   p. 22

Anthems

"Christ the Lord Is Risen Today" (John, Matt)
Arr. Todd Kendall; Lorenz 10/2011L
SATB, piano and organ duet

"That Easter Day with Joy Was Bright" (John, Matt, Easter)
Arr. Hal Hopson; MorningStar MSM-50-4125
SATB, organ, opt. brass quartet

Other Suggestions

Visuals:
    O   Crucifix, resurrection, Acts 10:39*a*
    P   Ps 118:29, singing, tents, gates, cornerstone
    E   Butterfly, empty cross, open tomb, Christ returning
    G   Basket/spices, open tomb, grave clothes, napkin, runners, tears, risen Christ, "I have seen . . ."
Introit: WS3044. "Make Way" (Pss, Easter)
Litany: C217. Easter Affirmations
Benediction: N872 (John)

Acts 2:14a, 22-32

[14]Peter stood with the other eleven apostles. He raised his voice and declared, "Judeans and everyone living in Jerusalem! Know this! Listen carefully to my words! . . .

[22]"Fellow Israelites, listen to these words! Jesus the Nazarene was a man whose credentials God proved to you through miracles, wonders, and signs, which God performed through him among you. You yourselves know this. [23]In accordance with God's established plan and foreknowledge, he was betrayed. You, with the help of wicked men, had Jesus killed by nailing him to a cross. [24]God raised him up! God freed him from death's dreadful grip, since it was impossible for death to hang on to him. [25]David says about him,

> *I foresaw that the Lord was always with me;*
> *because he is at my right hand I won't be shaken.*
> [26] *Therefore, my heart was glad*
> *and my tongue rejoiced.*
> *Moreover, my body will live in hope,*
> [27] *because you won't abandon me to the grave,*
> *nor permit your holy one to experience decay.*
> [28] *You have shown me the paths of life;*
> *your presence will fill me with happiness.*

[29]"Brothers and sisters, I can speak confidently about the patriarch David. He died and was buried, and his tomb is with us to this very day. [30]Because he was a prophet, he knew that God promised him with a solemn pledge to seat one of his descendants on his throne. [31]Having seen this beforehand, David spoke about the resurrection of Christ, that *he wasn't abandoned to the grave, nor did his body experience decay.* [32]This Jesus, God raised up. We are all witnesses to that fact."

Psalm 16 (G810, N628, P165, UM748)

[1]Protect me, God, because I take refuge in you. / [2]I say to the LORD, "You are my Lord. / Apart from you, I have nothing good." / [3]Now as for the "holy ones" in the land, / the "magnificent ones" that I was so happy about; / [4]let their suffering increase because / they hurried after a different god. / I won't participate in their blood offerings; / I won't let their names cross my lips. / [5]You, LORD, are my portion, my cup; / you control my destiny. / [6]The property lines have fallen beautifully for me; / yes, I have a lovely home. / [7]I will bless the LORD who advises me; / even at night I am instructed / in the depths of my mind. / [8]I always put the LORD in front of me; / I will not stumble because he is on my right side. / [9]That's why my heart celebrates and my mood is joyous; / yes, my whole body will rest in safety / [10]because you won't abandon my life to the grave; / you won't let your faithful follower see the pit. / [11]You teach me the way of life. / In your presence is total celebration. / Beautiful things are always in your right hand.

1 Peter 1:3-9

[3]May the God and Father of our Lord Jesus Christ be blessed! On account of his vast mercy, he has given us new birth. You have been born anew into a living hope through the resurrection of Jesus Christ from the dead. [4]You have a pure and enduring inheritance that cannot perish—an inheritance that is presently kept safe in heaven for you. [5]Through his faithfulness, you are guarded by God's power so that you can receive the salvation he is ready to reveal in the last time.

[6]You now rejoice in this hope, even if it's necessary for you to be distressed for a short time by various trials. [7]This is necessary so that your faith may be found genuine. (Your faith is more valuable than gold, which will be destroyed even though it is itself tested by fire.) Your genuine faith will result in praise, glory, and honor for you when Jesus Christ is revealed. [8]Although you've never seen him, you love him. Even though you don't see him now, you trust him and so rejoice with a glorious joy that is too much for words. [9]You are receiving the goal of your faith: your salvation.

John 20:19-31

[19]It was still the first day of the week. That evening, while the disciples were behind closed doors because they were afraid of the Jewish authorities, Jesus came and stood among them. He said, "Peace be with you." [20]After he said this, he showed them his hands and his side. When the disciples saw the Lord, they were filled with joy. [21]Jesus said to them again, "Peace be with you. As the Father sent me, so I am sending you." [22]Then he breathed on them and said, "Receive the Holy Spirit. [23]If you forgive anyone's sins, they are forgiven; if you don't forgive them, they aren't forgiven."

[24]Thomas, the one called Didymus, one of the Twelve, wasn't with the disciples when Jesus came. [25]The other disciples told him, "We've seen the Lord!"

But he replied, "Unless I see the nail marks in his hands, put my finger in the wounds left by the nails, and put my hand into his side, I won't believe."

[26]After eight days his disciples were again in a house and Thomas was with them. Even though the doors were locked, Jesus entered and stood among them. He said, "Peace be with you." [27]Then he said to Thomas, "Put your finger here. Look at my hands. Put your hand into my side. No more disbelief. Believe!"

[28]Thomas responded to Jesus, "My Lord and my God!"

[29]Jesus replied, "Do you believe because you see me? Happy are those who don't see and yet believe."

[30]Then Jesus did many other miraculous signs in his disciples' presence, signs that aren't recorded in this scroll. [31]But these things are written so that you will believe that Jesus is the Christ, God's Son, and that believing, you will have life in his name.

Primary Hymns and Songs for the Day

"This Joyful Eastertide" (Acts) (O)
  E192, EL391, G244, L149, N232, VU177, W449
"Hail the Day That Sees Him Rise" (Acts) (O)
  B165, E214, N260, UM312, VU189, W471 (PD)
"Alleluia, Alleluia" (Acts)
  B170, E178, G240, P106, UM162, VU179, W441
      H-3   Hbl-46; Chr-26
      S-1   #14. Desc.
"We Walk by Faith" (1 Pet, John)
  E209, EL635, G817, L256, P399, S2196, SF2196, W572
"Thine Be the Glory" (Acts, John) (C)
  B163, C218, EL376, F291, G238, L145, N253, P122, UM308,
  VU173 (Fr.)
      H-3   Hbl-98; Chr-195; Desc-59
      S-1   #190. Arr.
      S-2   #95. Various treatments

Additional Hymn Suggestions

"How Firm a Foundation" (Acts, 1 Pet)
  B338, C618, E636/637, EL796, F32, G463, L507, N407, P361,
  UM529 (PD), VU660, W585
"Praise God for This Holy Ground" (Acts, John)
  G405, WS3009
"To God Be the Glory" (1 Pet)
  B4, C72, F363, G634, P485, UM98 (PD)
"Jesus, the Very Thought of Thee" (1 Pet)
  C102, E642, EL754, G629, L316, N507, P310, UM175
"Hope of the World" (1 Pet)
  C538, E472, G734, L493, N46, P360, UM178, VU215
"Mothering God, You Gave Me Birth" (1 Pet, Comm.)
  C83, EL735, G7, N467, S2050, SF2050, VU320
"There Are Some Things I May Not Know" (1 Pet)
  N405, S2147, SF2147
"The Day of Resurrection" (1 Pet, John, Easter)
  B164, C228, E210, EL361, G233, L141, N245, P118, UM303
  (PD), VU164
"O Sons and Daughters, Let Us Sing" (John)
  C220, E203, EL386/E387, G235/255, L139, N244, P116
  (PD), UM317, VU170, W447
"Christ Jesus Lay in Death's Strong Band" (John)
  E186, EL370, G237, L134, P110, UM319 (PD)
"Holy Spirit, Come, Confirm Us" (John)
  N264, UM331
"Dona Nobis Pacem" (John)
  C297, E712, EL753, G752, UM376 (PD)
"Breathe on Me, Breath of God" (John)
  B241, C254, E508, F161, G286, L488, N292, P316, UM420
  (PD), VU382 (Fr.), W725
"Holy Spirit, Truth Divine" (John)
  C241, EL398, L257, N63, P321, UM465 (PD), VU368
"Come Down, O Love Divine" (John)
  C582, E516, EL804, G282, L508, N289, P313, UM475,
  VU367, W472
"O Breath of Life" (John)
  C250, UM543, VU202, WS3146
"Praise the Source of Faith and Learning" (John)
  N411, S2004, SF2004
"Come, Share the Lord" (John, Comm.)
  C408, G510, S2269, SF2269, VU469
"Love Divine, All Loves Excelling" (John, Comm.)
  B208, C517, E657, EL631, F21, G366, N43, P376, UM384
  (PD), VU333, W588
"That Easter Day with Joy Was Bright" (John, Easter)
  C229, E193, EL384 (PD), G254, L154, P121, W457

Additional Contemporary Suggestions

"Surely the Presence of the Lord" (Acts, John)
  C263, SP243, UM328; S-2 #200. Stanzas for soloist
"Holy Ground" (Acts, John)
  B224, C112, G406, S2272, SF2272, SP86
"More Precious than Silver" (Pss, 1 Pet)
  S2065, SF2065, SP99
"Trading My Sorrows" (Pss, John)
  M75, WS3108
"In Christ Alone" (1 Pet)
  M138, WS3105
"My Tribute" ("To God Be the Glory") (1 Pet)
  B153, C39, F365, N14, SP118, UM99; V-8 p. 5 Vocal Solo
"Please Enter My Heart, Hosanna" (1 Pet, John)
  S2154, SF2154
"I'm So Glad Jesus Lifted Me" (1 Pet, John)
  C529, EL860 (PD), N474, S2151, SF2151
"God Is Good All the Time" (1 Pet, John)
  AH4010, M45, WS3026
"Blessing, Honour and Glory" (1 Pet, John, Easter)
  M21
"There Is a Redeemer" (1 Pet, John)
  G443, SP111
"Open Our Eyes, Lord" (John)
  B499, S2086, SF2086, SP199
"Open the Eyes of My Heart" (John)
  G452, M57, WS3008
"The Power of Your Love" (John)
  M26
"Where the Spirit of the Lord Is" (John, Comm.)
  C264, S2119, SF2119
"Here Is Bread, Here Is Wine" (John, Comm.)
  EL483, S2266, SF2266

Vocal Solos

"Crown Him, the Risen King" (Acts, 1 Peter, Easter)
  V-10   p. 55
"The First Day of My Life" (John, Easter)
  V-11   p. 22

Anthems

"This Joyful Eastertide" (SOCB78) (Acts)
Arr. John Ferguson; Augsburg 9781451499032
TTBB, organ

"A Better Resurrection" (1 Pet, John)
Craig Courtney; Beckenhorst CU-1000
SATB divisi, a cappella

Other Suggestions

Visuals:
  O   Eleven men, preaching, crucifix, open tomb, heart,
       joy
  P   Cup, boundary line, prayer, joy, rest, path, hand
  E   Newborn, butterfly/chrysalis, gold/fire, joy
  G   Locked door, Jesus, "Peace . . .," wind, wounds, John
       20:29b
Call to Prayer: M88. "Holy Spirit, Rain Down" (John)
Prayers: N827 and N847 (John)
Readings: F300 (Acts, Easter), F593 (John), and F90 (1 Pet)

Acts 2:14a, 36-41

[14]Peter stood with the other eleven apostles. He raised his voice and declared, ...

[36]"Therefore, let all Israel know beyond question that God has made this Jesus, whom you crucified, both Lord and Christ."

[37]When the crowd heard this, they were deeply troubled. They said to Peter and the other apostles, "Brothers, what should we do?"

[38]Peter replied, "Change your hearts and lives. Each of you must be baptized in the name of Jesus Christ for the forgiveness of your sins. Then you will receive the gift of the Holy Spirit. [39]This promise is for you, your children, and for all who are far away—as many as the Lord our God invites." [40]With many other words he testified to them and encouraged them, saying, "Be saved from this perverse generation." [41]Those who accepted Peter's message were baptized. God brought about three thousand people into the community on that day.

Psalm 116:1-4, 12-19 (G655, N699, P228, UM837)

[1]I love the LORD because he hears / my requests for mercy. / [2]I'll call out to him as long as I live / because he listens closely to me. / [3]Death's ropes bound me; / the distress of the grave found me— / I came face-to-face / with trouble and grief. / [4]So I called on the LORD's name: / "LORD, please save me!" . . . .

[12]What can I give back to the LORD / for all the good things he has done for me? / [13]I'll lift up the cup of salvation. / I'll call on the LORD's name. / [14]I'll keep the promises I made to the LORD / in the presence of all God's people. / [15]The death of the LORD's faithful / is a costly loss in his eyes.

[16]Oh yes, LORD, I am definitely your servant! / I am your servant and the son of your female servant— / you've freed me from my chains. / [17]So I'll offer a sacrifice of thanksgiving to you, / and I'll call on the LORD's name. / [18]I'll keep the promises I made to the LORD / in the presence of all God's people, / [19]in the courtyards of the LORD's house, / which is in the center of Jerusalem. / Praise the LORD!

1 Peter 1:17-23

[17]Since you call upon a Father who judges all people according to their actions without favoritism, you should conduct yourselves with reverence during the time of your dwelling in a strange land. [18]Live in this way, knowing that you were not liberated by perishable things like silver or gold from the empty lifestyle you inherited from your ancestors. [19]Instead, you were liberated by the precious blood of Christ, like that of a flawless, spotless lamb. [20]Christ was chosen before the creation of the world, but was only revealed at the end of time. This was done for you, [21]who through Christ are faithful to the God who raised him from the dead and gave him glory. So now, your faith and hope should rest in God.

[22]As you set yourselves apart by your obedience to the truth so that you might have genuine affection for your fellow believers, love each other deeply and earnestly. [23]Do this because you have been given new birth—not from the type of seed that decays but from seed that doesn't. This seed is God's life-giving and enduring word.

Luke 24:13-35

[13]On that same day, two disciples were traveling to a village called Emmaus, about seven miles from Jerusalem. [14]They were talking to each other about everything that had happened. [15]While they were discussing these things, Jesus himself arrived and joined them on their journey. [16]They were prevented from recognizing him.

[17]He said to them, "What are you talking about as you walk along?" They stopped, their faces downcast.

[18]The one named Cleopas replied, "Are you the only visitor to Jerusalem who is unaware of the things that have taken place there over the last few days?"

[19]He said to them, "What things?"

They said to him, "The things about Jesus of Nazareth. Because of his powerful deeds and words, he was recognized by God and all the people as a prophet. [20]But our chief priests and our leaders handed him over to be sentenced to death, and they crucified him. [21]We had hoped he was the one who would redeem Israel. All these things happened three days ago. [22]But there's more: Some women from our group have left us stunned. They went to the tomb early this morning [23]and didn't find his body. They came to us saying that they had even seen a vision of angels who told them he is alive. [24]Some of those who were with us went to the tomb and found things just as the women said. They didn't see him."

[25]Then Jesus said to them, "You foolish people! Your dull minds keep you from believing all that the prophets talked about. [26]Wasn't it necessary for the Christ to suffer these things and then enter into his glory?" [27]Then he interpreted for them the things written about himself in all the scriptures, starting with Moses and going through all the Prophets.

[28]When they came to Emmaus, he acted as if he was going on ahead. [29]But they urged him, saying, "Stay with us. It's nearly evening, and the day is almost over." So he went in to stay with them. [30]After he took his seat at the table with them, he took the bread, blessed and broke it, and gave it to them. [31]Their eyes were opened and they recognized him, but he disappeared from their sight. [32]They said to each other, "Weren't our hearts on fire when he spoke to us along the road and when he explained the scriptures for us?"

[33]They got up right then and returned to Jerusalem. They found the eleven and their companions gathered together. [34]They were saying to each other, "The Lord really has risen! He appeared to Simon!" [35]Then the two disciples described what had happened along the road and how Jesus was made known to them as he broke the bread.

Primary Hymns and Songs for the Day

"We Know That Christ Is Raised" (Acts) (O)
E296, EL449, G485, L189, P495, UM610, VU448, W721
- H-3 Hbl-100; Chr-214; Desc- ; Org-37
- S-1 #118-27. Various treatments

"Christ Is Alive" (Luke)
B173, E182, EL389, G246, L363, P108, UM318, VU158
- H-3 Hbl-91; Chr-129, 176; Desc-101; Org-167
- S-1 #334-35. Desc. and harm.

"Day of Arising" (Luke, Comm.)
G252, EL374, WS3086
- H-3 Hbl-77; Chr-136; Desc-21; Org-16
- S-1 #50-51. Flute and vocal descs.
- S-2 #55. Trumpet desc.

"Open My Eyes, That I May See" (Luke)
B502, C586, F486, G451, P324, UM454, VU371
- H-3 Chr-157; Org-108

"Lord, I Want to Be a Christian" (1 Pet) (C)
B489, C589, F421, G729, N454, P372 (PD), UM402

Additional Hymn Suggestions

"What Is This Place" (Acts)
C289, EL524, G404, W709

"Let Us Talents and Tongues Employ" (Acts)
C422, EL674, G526, N347, P514, VU468

"Let Us Break Bread Together" (Acts, Comm.)
B366, C425, EL471 (PD), F564, G525, L212, N330, P513,
UM618, VU480, W727

"Wonder of Wonders" (Acts, Baptism)
C378, G489, N328, P499, S2247

"Jesus, the Very Thought of Thee" (1 Pet)
C102, E642, EL754, G629, L316, N507, P310, UM175

"Just as I Am, Without One Plea" (1 Pet)
B303/307, C339, E693, EL592, F417, G442, L296, N207,
P370, UM357 (PD), VU508

"Blessed Assurance" (1 Pet)
B334, C543, EL638, F67, G839, N473, P341, UM369 (PD),
VU337

"It Is Well with My Soul" (1 Pet)
B410, C561, EL785, F495, G840, L346, N438, UM377

"Amazing Grace" (1 Pet)
AH4091, B330, C546, E671, EL779, F107, G649, L448, N547
and N548, P280, UM378 (PD), VU266 (Fr.), W583

"My Faith Looks up to Thee" (1 Pet)
B416, C576, E691, EL759, G829, L479, P383, UM452, VU663

"Jesus, Priceless Treasure" (1 Pet)
E701, EL775, F277, G830, L457, N480 P365, UM532 (PD),
VU667 and VU668 (Fr.)

"The Church's One Foundation" (1 Pet)
B350, C272, E525, EL654, F547, G321, L369, N386, P442,
UM545/546, VU332 (Fr.)

"Baptized in Water" (1 Pet, Baptism)
B362, EL456, G482, P492, S2248, W720

"Leaning on the Everlasting Arms" (Luke)
AH4100, B333, C560, EL774 (PD), G837, N471, UM133

"*Cuando el Pobre*" ("When the Poor Ones") (Luke)
C662, EL725, G762, P407, UM434, VU702

"By Gracious Powers" (Luke)
E695/696, EL626, G818, N413, P342, UM517, W577

"Abide with Me" (Luke)
B63, C636, E662, EL629, F500, G836, L272, N99, P543,
UM700 (PD), VU436

"Just a Closer Walk with Thee" (Luke)
B448, C557, EL697, F591, G835, S2158, SF2158

"We Walk by Faith" (Luke)
E209, EL635, G817, N256, P399, S2196, SF2196, W572

"Come, Share the Lord" (Luke, Comm.)
C408, G510, S2269, SF2269, VU469

"Feed Us, Lord" (Luke, Comm.)
G501, WS3167

"Be Known to Us in Breaking Bread" (Luke)
C398, G500, N342, P505

Additional Contemporary Suggestions

"I Will Call upon the Lord" (Pss)
G621, S2002, SF2002, SP224

"I Love You, Lord" (Pss)
B212, G627, S2068, SF2068, SP72

"Amazing Grace" ("My Chains Are Gone") (1 Pet)
M205, WS3104

"Take, O Take Me As I Am" (1 Pet)
EL814, G698, WS3119

"More Precious than Silver" (1 Pet)
S2065, SF2065, SP99

"Live in Charity" ("*Ubi Caritas*") (1 Pet)
C523, EL642, G205, S2179, SF2179, W604

"They'll Know We Are Christians" (1 Pet)
AH4074, C494, G300, S2223, SF2223

"Bind Us Together" (1 Pet)
S2226, SF2226, SP140

"*Agnus Dei*" (1 Pet, Easter)
M15

"Turn Your Eyes upon Jesus" (Luke)
B320, F621, SP218, UM349

"Open Our Eyes, Lord" (Luke)
B499, S2086, SF2086, SP199

"Open the Eyes of My Heart" (Luke)
G452, M57, WS3008

Vocal Solos

"Wash, O God, Our Sons and Daughters" (Acts, Baptism)
- V-5 (1)   p. 64

"Just a Closer Walk With Thee" (Luke)
- V-5 (2)   p. 31
- V-8   p. 323

Anthems

"Nothing but the Blood of Jesus" (1 Pet)
Arr. Craig Courtney; Beckenhorst BP2044
SATB, piano

"Blessed Assurance" (1 Pet)
Arr. Keith Hampton; Choristers Guild CGA-1238
SATB, piano, opt. solo

Other Suggestions

Visuals:
- **O** Christus Rex, repent, baptism, gift, Spirit, 3000
- **P** Ear, snare, anguish, prayer, cup, shackles, gifts
- **E** Silver/gold, blood, lamb, Jesus, baptism, Bible
- **G** Jesus, three men walking, Bible, broken bread, burning heart, blindness/vision

Introit: C231. "Sing of One Who Walks Beside Us" (Luke)
Opening Prayer: N831 or WSL66 (Luke)

Acts 2:42-47

⁴²The believers devoted themselves to the apostles' teaching, to the community, to their shared meals, and to their prayers. ⁴³A sense of awe came over everyone. God performed many wonders and signs through the apostles. ⁴⁴All the believers were united and shared everything. ⁴⁵They would sell pieces of property and possessions and distribute the proceeds to everyone who needed them. ⁴⁶Every day, they met together in the temple and ate in their homes. They shared food with gladness and simplicity. ⁴⁷They praised God and demonstrated God's goodness to everyone. The Lord added daily to the community those who were being saved.

Psalm 23 (G473/801–803, N633, P170–175, UM134/754)

¹The Lord is my shepherd. / I lack nothing. / ²He lets me rest in grassy meadows; / he leads me to restful waters; / ³he keeps me alive. / He guides me in proper paths / for the sake of his good name.

⁴Even when I walk / through the darkest valley, / I fear no danger because you are with me. / Your rod and your staff— / they protect me.

⁵You set a table for me / right in front of my enemies. / You bathe my head in oil; / my cup is so full it spills over! / ⁶Yes, goodness and faithful love / will pursue me all the days of my life, / and I will live in the Lord's house / as long as I live.

1 Peter 2:19-25

¹⁹Now, it is commendable if, because of one's understanding of God, someone should endure pain through suffering unjustly. ²⁰But what praise comes from enduring patiently when you have sinned and are beaten for it? But if you endure steadfastly when you've done good and suffer for it, this is commendable before God.

²¹You were called to this kind of endurance, because Christ suffered on your behalf. He left you an example so that you might follow in his footsteps. ²²He committed no sin, nor did he ever speak in ways meant to deceive. ²³When he was insulted, he did not reply with insults. When he suffered, he did not threaten revenge. Instead, he entrusted himself to the one who judges justly. ²⁴He carried in his own body on the cross the sins we committed. He did this so that we might live in righteousness, having nothing to do with sin. By his wounds you were healed. ²⁵Though you were like straying sheep, you have now returned to the shepherd and guardian of your lives.

John 10:1-10

¹I assure you that whoever doesn't enter into the sheep pen through the gate but climbs over the wall is a thief and an outlaw. ²The one who enters through the gate is the shepherd of the sheep. ³The guard at the gate opens the gate for him, and the sheep listen to his voice. He calls his own sheep by name and leads them out. ⁴Whenever he has gathered all of his sheep, he goes before them and they follow him, because they know his voice. ⁵They won't follow a stranger but will run away because they don't know the stranger's voice." ⁶Those who heard Jesus use this analogy didn't understand what he was saying.

⁷So Jesus spoke again, "I assure you that I am the gate of the sheep. ⁸All who came before me were thieves and outlaws, but the sheep didn't listen to them. ⁹I am the gate. Whoever enters through me will be saved. They will come in and go out and find pasture. ¹⁰The thief enters only to steal, kill, and destroy. I came so that they could have life—indeed, so that they could live life to the fullest."

Primary Hymns and Songs for the Day

"The Lord's My Shepherd, I'll Not Want" (Pss, John) (O)
C78/79, EL778, F40/42, G801, L451, N479, P170, UM136, VU747/748

"Where Charity and Love Prevail" (Acts)
E581, EL359, G316, L126, N396, UM549
       H-3   Hbl-71, 104; Chr-111; Desc-95; Org-143
       S-2   #162. Harm.

"The King of Love My Shepherd Is" (Pss, 1 Pet)
E645, EL502, G802, L456, P171, UM138 (PD), VU273, W609
       S-1   #298-99. Harms.

"Shepherd Me, O God" (Pss, John)
EL780, G473, S2058, SF2058

"They'll Know We Are Christians" (Acts) (C)
AH4074, C494, G300, S2223, SF2223

Additional Hymn Suggestions

"Let Us Talents and Tongues Employ" (Acts)
C422, EL674, G526, N347, P514, VU468

"O For a World" (Acts)
C683, G372, N575, P386, VU697

"Great Is Thy Faithfulness" (Acts)
B54, C86, EL733, F98, G39, N423, P276, UM140, VU288

"Sweet, Sweet Spirit" (Acts, 1 Pet)
B243, C261, F159, G408, N293, P398, SP136, UM334

"Filled with the Spirit's Power" (Acts)
L160, N266, UM537, VU194

"Blest Be the Tie That Binds" (Acts)
B387, C433, EL656, F560, G306, L370, N393, P438, UM557 (PD), VU602

"Out of the Depths" (Acts)
C510, N554, S2136, SF2136, VU611

"Together We Serve" (Acts)
G767, S2175, SF2175

"In the Midst of New Dimensions" (Acts)
G315, N391, S2238, SF2238

"We All Are One in Mission" (Acts)
EL576, G733, P435, S2243, SF2243

"I Come with Joy" (Acts, Comm.)
B371, C420, E304, EL482, G515, N349, P507, UM617, VU477, W726

"Let Us Break Bread Together" (Acts, Comm.)
B366, C425, EL471 (PD), F564, G525, L212, N330, P513, UM618, VU480, W727

"Come, Share the Lord" (Acts, Comm.)
C408, G510, S2269, SF2269, VU469

"Precious Lord, Take My Hand" (Pss)
B456, C628, EL773, G834, N472, P404, UM474, VU670

"Savior, Like a Shepherd Lead Us" (Pss, John) (C)
B61, C558, E708, EL789, F601, G187, L481, N252, P387, UM381 (PD)

"Lead Me, Guide Me" (Pss, John)
C583, EL768, G740, S2214, SF2214

"Christ Is Alive" (1 Pet)
B173, E182, EL389, G246, L363, P108, UM318, VU158

"O Jesus, I Have Promised" (1 Pet)
B276, C612, E655, EL810, F402, G724/725, L503, N493, P388/389, UM396 (PD), VU120

"Take Up Thy Cross" (1 Pet)
B494, E675, EL667, G718, L398, N204, P393, UM415, VU561, W634

"How Like a Gentle Spirit" (John)
C69, N443, UM115

"Lord of the Dance" (John, Easter)
G157, P302, UM261, VU352, W636

"You Satisfy the Hungry Heart" (John, Comm.)
C429, EL484, G523, P521, UM629, VU478, W736

"God Be With You till We Meet Again" (John) (C)
C434, EL536, F523, G541/542, N81, P540, UM672/673, VU422/423

Additional Contemporary Suggestions

"One Bread, One Body" (Acts, Comm.)
C393, EL496, G530, UM620, VU467

"Make Us One" (Acts)
AH4142, S2224, SF2224, SP137

"Nothing Can Trouble" ("Nada Te Turbe") (Pss)
G820, S2054, SF2054, VU290

"Lamb of God" (Pss)
EL336, G518, S2113, SF2113

"God Is Good All the Time" (Pss)
AH4010, M45, WS3026

"Your Grace Is Enough" (Pss)
M191, WS3106

"Lead Me, Lord" (Pss, 1 Pet)
M108

"His Name Is Wonderful" (Pss, John)
B203, F230, SP90, UM174

"Jesus, Name above All Names" (1 Pet)
S2071, SF2071, SP76

"Amen, Amen" (1 Pet)
N161, P299, S2072

"The Power of the Cross" (1 Pet, Easter)
M222, WS3085

"People Need the Lord" (John)
B557, S2244, SF2244

Vocal Solos

"The Lord Is My Shepherd" (Pss, John)
    V-5 (3)   p. 30

"In the Image of God" (1 Pet)
    V-8   p. 362

Anthems

"The King of Love My Shepherd Is" (Pss)
Philip W. J. Stopford; MorningStar 50-6218
SATB divisi, a cappella

"My Shepherd Will Supply My Need" (Pss)
Matthew Culloton; MorningStar MSM-50-3072
SATB, piano or harp with flute

Other Suggestions

Visuals:
   O   Teaching, fellowship, broken bread, prayer, meal
   P   Shepherd/sheep, pasture, lake, path, valley, rod, staff, banquet table, cup, sanctuary
   E   Whip/club, Passion, crucifix, healing, sheep
   G   Sheepfold, gate, robber's mask, sheep/shepherd

Reading: F25. God, Thou Art Love (Pss) or F41 Psalm 23
Canticle: UM137. Psalm 23 (Pss, John)
Additional prayers, calls to worship, and benedictions are available in
The Abingdon Worship Annual 2017.

Acts 7:55-60

[55]But Stephen, enabled by the Holy Spirit, stared into heaven and saw God's majesty and Jesus standing at God's right side. [56]He exclaimed, "Look! I can see heaven on display and the Human One standing at God's right side!" [57]At this, they shrieked and covered their ears. Together, they charged at him, [58]threw him out of the city, and began to stone him. The witnesses placed their coats in the care of a young man named Saul. [59]As they battered him with stones, Stephen prayed, "Lord Jesus, accept my life!" [60]Falling to his knees, he shouted, "Lord, don't hold this sin against them!" Then he died.

Psalm 31:1-5, 15-16 (G214/811, N640/641, P182/183, UM764)

[1]I take refuge in you, LORD. / Please never let me be put to shame. / Rescue me by your righteousness! / [2]Listen closely to me! / Deliver me quickly; / be a rock that protects me; / be a strong fortress that saves me! / [3]You are definitely my rock and my fortress. / Guide me and lead me for the sake of your good name! / [4]Get me out of this net that's been set for me / because you are my protective fortress. / [5]I entrust my spirit into your hands; / you, LORD, God of faithfulness— / you have saved me. . . .

[15]My future is in your hands. / Don't hand me over to my enemies, / to all who are out to get me! / [16]Shine your face on your servant; / save me by your faithful love!

1 Peter 2:2-10

[2]Instead, like a newborn baby, desire the pure milk of the word. Nourished by it, you will grow into salvation, [3]since you have tasted that the Lord is good.

[4]Now you are coming to him as to a living stone. Even though this stone was rejected by humans, from God's perspective it is chosen, valuable. [5]You yourselves are being built like living stones into a spiritual temple. You are being made into a holy priesthood to offer up spiritual sacrifices that are acceptable to God through Jesus Christ. [6]Thus it is written in scripture, *Look! I am laying a cornerstone in Zion, chosen, valuable. The person who believes in him will never be shamed.* [7]So God honors you who believe. For those who refuse to believe, though, the stone the builders tossed aside has become the capstone. [8]This is a stone that makes people stumble and a rock that makes them fall. Because they refuse to believe in the word, they stumble. Indeed, this is the end to which they were appointed. [9]But you are a chosen race, a royal priesthood, a holy nation, a people who are God's own possession. You have become this people so that you may speak of the wonderful acts of the one who called you out of darkness into his amazing light. [10]Once you weren't a people, but now you are God's people. Once you hadn't received mercy, but now you have received mercy.

John 14:1-14

"Don't be troubled. Trust in God. Trust also in me. [2]My Father's house has room to spare. If that weren't the case, would I have told you that I'm going to prepare a place for you? [3]When I go to prepare a place for you, I will return and take you to be with me so that where I am you will be too. [4]You know the way to the place I'm going."

[5]Thomas asked, "Lord, we don't know where you are going. How can we know the way?"

[6]Jesus answered, "I am the way, the truth, and the life. No one comes to the Father except through me. [7]If you have really known me, you will also know the Father. From now on you know him and have seen him."

[8]Philip said, "Lord, show us the Father; that will be enough for us."

[9]Jesus replied, "Don't you know me, Philip, even after I have been with you all this time? Whoever has seen me has seen the Father. How can you say, 'Show us the Father'? [10]Don't you believe that I am in the Father and the Father is in me? The words I have spoken to you I don't speak on my own. The Father who dwells in me does his works. [11]Trust me when I say that I am in the Father and the Father is in me, or at least believe on account of the works themselves. [12]I assure you that whoever believes in me will do the works that I do. They will do even greater works than these because I am going to the Father. [13]I will do whatever you ask for in my name, so that the Father can be glorified in the Son. [14]When you ask me for anything in my name, I will do it."

Primary Hymns and Songs for the Day

"The Church's One Foundation" (1 Pet, John) (O)
  B350, C272, E525, EL654, F547, G321, L369, N386, P442,
  UM545/546, VU332 (Fr.)
      H-3   Hbl-94; Chr-180; Desc-16; Org-9
      S-1   #25-26. Desc. and harm.
"Be Still, My Soul" (Acts, Pss)
  C566, F77, G819, N488, UM534, VU652
      H-3   Chr-36
"His Eye Is on the Sparrow" (John)
  C82, G661, N475, S2146, SF2146
"Christ Is Made the Sure Foundation" (1 Pet) (C)
  B356 (PD), C275, E518, EL645, F557, G394, L367, N400,
  P416/417, UM559 (PD), VU325, W617
      H-3   Chr-49; Desc-103; Org-180
      S-1   #346. Desc.

Additional Hymn Suggestions

"I'll Praise My Maker While I've Breath" (Acts)
  B35, C20, E429 (PD), G806, P253, UM60, VU867
"God of Grace and God of Glory" (Acts)
  B395, C464, E594/595, EL705, F528, G307, L415, N436,
  P420, UM577, VU686
"Dear Lord and Father of Mankind" (Acts)
  B267, C594, E652/563, F422, G169, L506, N502, P345,
  UM358 (PD), VU608
"God of Our Life" (Acts)
  C713, G686, N366, P275
"Deep in the Shadows of the Past" (Acts)
  G50, N320, P330, S2246
"Guide My Feet" (Acts, Pss)
  G741, N497, P354, S2208
"Lead Me, Guide Me" (Acts, Pss)
  C583, EL768, G740, S2214, SF2214
"Saranam, Saranam" ("Refuge") (Acts, Pss)
  G789, UM523
"How Firm a Foundation" (Acts, 1 Pet)
  B338, C618, E636/637, EL796, F32, G463, L507, N407, P361,
  UM529 (PD), VU660, W585
"Send Me, Lord" (Pss)
  C447, EL809, G746, N360, UM497, VU572
"From All That Dwell below the Skies" (1 Pet)
  B13, C49, E380, G327, L550, N27, P229, UM101 (PD)
"Sing Praise to God Who Reigns Above" (1 Pet)
  B20, C6, E408, EL871, F343, G645, N6, P483, UM126 (PD),
  VU216, W528
"God Is Here" (1 Pet)
  C280, EL526, G409, N70, P461, UM660, VU389, W667
"Christ, the Great Foundation" (1 Pet)
  G361, P443, W618
"Source and Sovereign, Rock and Cloud" (John)
  C12, G11, UM113
"Come, My Way, My Truth, My Life" (John)
  E487, EL816, L513, N331, UM164 (PD), VU628, W569
"Prayer Is the Soul's Sincere Desire" (John)
  F446 (PD), N508, UM492
"Here, O Lord, Your Servants Gather" (John)
  B179, C278, EL530, G311, N72, P465, UM552, VU362
"Nothing Can Trouble" ("Nada Te Turbe") (John)
  G820, S2054, SF2054, VU290
"Healer of Our Every Ill" (John)
  C506, EL612, G795, S2213, SF2213, VU619
"In Remembrance of Me" (John, Comm.)
  B365, C403, G521, S2254
"I'll Fly Away" (John)
  N595, S2282, SF2282

Additional Contemporary Suggestions

"Holy Ground" (Acts)
  B224, C112, G406, S2272, SF2272, SP86
"Guide My Feet" (Acts, Pss)
  G741, N497, P354, S2208
"I Will Call upon the Lord" (Pss)
  G621, S2002, SF2002, SP224
"Praise the Name of Jesus" (Pss)
  S2066, SF2066, SP87
"More Precious than Silver" (1 Pet)
  S2065, SF2065, SP99
"Grace Alone" (1 Pet)
  M100, S2162, SF2162
"Cornerstone" (1 Pet)
  SP177
"In Christ Alone" (1 Pet)
  M138, WS3105
"Be Glorified" (John)
  M13
"Be Glorified" (2 Thess)
  M152
"People Need the Lord" (John)
  B557, S2244, SF2244
"Halle, Halle, Halleluja" (John, Easter)
  C41, EL172, G591, N236, S2026, SF2026, VU958
"That's Why We Praise Him" (John, Easter)
  M94
"For All You've Done" (John, Easter)
  M233
"My Savior Lives" (John, Easter)
  M233

Vocal Solos

"How Firm a Foundation" (1 Pet)
  V-6   p. 31
"Because He Lives" (1 Pet, Easter)
  V-8   p. 24
"In Bright Mansions Above" (John)
  V-4   p. 39

Anthems

"Hiding in Thee" (Acts, Pss)
Arr. Cindy Berry; Alfred 32375
SATB, keyboard

"Nada Te Turbe" (John)
Joan Szymko, Santa Barbara Music SBMP399
SATB, cello

Other Suggestions

Visuals:
  O   Spirit/flames/dove, Christ, heavens opened, stones,
       coats, Acts 7:59b, 60b, life/death
  P   Rock, Ps 31:3a, fortress, net, hands, Ps 31:16ab
  E   Newborn, milk, stone(s), cornerstone, stumbling
       blocks, 1 Pet 2:9a, crowd, nations, dark/light
  G   Hearts, mourning, dwellings, Christ, works, John
       14:13, 14
Prayer: N856. Eternal Life (John)
See additional ideas in The Abingdon Worship Annual 2017.

Acts 17:22-31

[22]Paul stood up in the middle of the council on Mars Hill and said, "People of Athens, I see that you are very religious in every way. [23]As I was walking through town and carefully observing your objects of worship, I even found an altar with this inscription: 'To an unknown God.' What you worship as unknown, I now proclaim to you. [24]God, who made the world and everything in it, is Lord of heaven and earth. He doesn't live in temples made with human hands. [25]Nor is God served by human hands, as though he needed something, since he is the one who gives life, breath, and everything else. [26]From one person God created every human nation to live on the whole earth, having determined their appointed times and the boundaries of their lands. [27]God made the nations so they would seek him, perhaps even reach out to him and find him. In fact, God isn't far away from any of us. [28]In God we live, move, and exist. As some of your own poets said, 'We are his offspring.'

[29]"Therefore, as God's offspring, we have no need to imagine that the divine being is like a gold, silver, or stone image made by human skill and thought. [30]God overlooks ignorance of these things in times past, but now directs everyone everywhere to change their hearts and lives. [31]This is because God has set a day when he intends to judge the world justly by a man he has appointed. God has given proof of this to everyone by raising him from the dead."

Psalm 66:8-20 (G54, N662, UM790)

[8]All you nations, bless our God! / Let the sound of his praise be heard! / [9]God preserved us among the living; / he didn't let our feet slip a bit. / [10]But you, God, have tested us— / you've refined us like silver, / [11]trapped us in a net, / laid burdens on our backs, / [12]let other people run right over our heads— / we've been through fire and water. / But you brought us out to freedom! / [13]So I'll enter your house / with entirely burned offerings. / I'll keep the promises I made to you, / [14]the ones my lips uttered, / the ones my mouth spoke when I was in deep trouble. / [15]I will offer the best burned offerings to you / along with the smoke of sacrificed rams. / I will offer both bulls and goats. *[Selah]* / [16]Come close and listen, / all you who honor God; / I will tell you what God has done for me: / [17]My mouth cried out to him / with praise on my tongue. / [18]If I had cherished evil in my heart, / my Lord would not have listened. / [19]But God definitely listened. / He heard the sound of my prayer. / [20]Bless God! He didn't reject my prayer; / he didn't withhold his faithful love from me.

1 Peter 3:13-22

[13]Who will harm you if you are zealous for good? [14]But happy are you, even if you suffer because of righteousness! Don't be terrified or upset by them. [15]Instead, regard Christ as holy in your hearts. Whenever anyone asks you to speak of your hope, be ready to defend it. [16]Yet do this with respectful humility, maintaining a good conscience. Act in this way so that those who malign your good lifestyle in Christ may be ashamed when they slander you. [17]It is better to suffer for doing good (if this could possibly be God's will) than for doing evil.

[18]Christ himself suffered on account of sins, once for all, the righteous one on behalf of the unrighteous. He did this in order to bring you into the presence of God. Christ was put to death as a human, but made alive by the Spirit. [19]And it was by the Spirit that he went to preach to the spirits in prison. [20]In the past, these spirits were disobedient—when God patiently waited during the time of Noah. Noah built an ark in which a few (that is, eight) lives were rescued through water. [21]Baptism is like that. It saves you now—not because it removes dirt from your body but because it is the mark of a good conscience toward God. Your salvation comes through the resurrection of Jesus Christ, [22]who is at God's right side. Now that he has gone into heaven, he rules over all angels, authorities, and powers.

John 14:15-21

[15]"If you love me, you will keep my commandments. [16]I will ask the Father, and he will send another Companion, who will be with you forever. [17]This Companion is the Spirit of Truth, whom the world can't receive because it neither sees him nor recognizes him. You know him, because he lives with you and will be with you.

[18]"I won't leave you as orphans. I will come to you. [19]Soon the world will no longer see me, but you will see me. Because I live, you will live too. [20]On that day you will know that I am in my Father, you are in me, and I am in you. [21]Whoever has my commandments and keeps them loves me. Whoever loves me will be loved by my Father, and I will love them and reveal myself to them."

Primary Hymns and Songs for the Day

"I Sing the Almighty Power of God" (Acts, John) (O)
    C64, G32, N12, P288 (PD)
        H-3   Hbl-16, 22, 68; Chr-101; Desc-37
        S-1   #115. Harm.
    B42, E398, UM152 (PD)
        H-3   Hbl-44; Chr-21; Desc-40; Org-40
        S-1   #131-32. Intro. and desc.
    VU231 (PD), W502 (PD)
        H-3   Hbl-44; Chr-21; Desc-40; Org-40
        S-1   #131-132. Intro. and desc.
"Spirit of the Living God" (Acts, John)
    SP131
        S-1   #212. Vocal desc. idea
    B244, C259, G288, N283, P322, SP131, UM393, VU376
"Love Divine, All Loves Excelling" (John) (C)
    B208, C517, E657, EL631, F21, G366, N43, P376, UM384
    (PD), VU333, W588
        H-3   Chr-134; Desc-18; Org-13
        S-1   #41-42. Desc. and harm.

Additional Hymn Suggestions

"All Creatures of Our God and King" (Acts)
    B27, C22, E400, EL835, F347, G15, L527, N17, P455, UM62,
    VU217 (Fr.), W520
"For the Beauty of the Earth" (Acts, Comm.)
    B44, C56, E416, EL879, F1, G14, L561, P473, N28, UM92
    (PD), VU226, W557
"From All That Dwell below the Skies" (Acts)
    B13, C49, E380, G327, L550, N27, P229, UM101 (PD)
"Blessed Assurance" (Acts)
    B334, C543, EL638, F67, G839, N473, P341, UM369 (PD),
    VU337
"Draw Us in the Spirit's Tether" (Acts, Comm.)
    C392, EL470, G529, N337, P504, UM632, VU479, W731
"God Is Here" (Acts)
    C280, EL526, G409, N70, P461, UM660, VU389, W667
"God Made from One Blood" (Acts)
    C500, N427, S2170, SF2170, VU554
"If Thou But Suffer God to Guide Thee" (1 Pet)
    B57, C565, E635, EL769, G816, L453, N410, P282, UM142
    (PD), VU285 (Fr.) and VU286
"Wash, O God, Our Sons and Daughters" (1 Pet, Baptism)
    C365, EL445, G490, UM605, VU442
"We Know That Christ Is Raised" (1 Pet, Baptism)
    E296, EL449, G485, L189, P495, UM610, VU448, W721
"Wonder of Wonders" (1 Pet, Baptism)
    C378, G489, N328, P499, S2247
"Baptized in Water" (1 Pet, Baptism)
    B362, EL456, G482, P492, S2248, W720
"Joyful, Joyful, We Adore Thee" (John)
    B7, C2, E376, EL836, F377, G611, L551, N4, P464, UM89
    (PD), VU232, W525
"Source and Sovereign, Rock and Cloud" (John)
    C12, G11, UM113
"*Pues Si Vivimos*" ("When We Are Living") (John)
    C536, EL639, G822, N499, P400, UM356, VU581
"Lord, I Want to Be a Christian" (John)
    B489, C589, F421, G729, N454, P372 (PD), UM402
"Holy Spirit, Truth Divine" (John)
    C241, EL398, L257, N63, P321, UM465 (PD), VU368
"O Spirit of the Living God" (John)
    N263, UM539
"Abide with Me" (John)
    B63, C636, E662, EL629, F500, G836, L272, N99, P543,

    UM700 (PD), VU436
"Love the Lord Your God" (John)
    G62, S2168, SF2168
"Healer of Our Every Ill" (John)
    C506, EL612, G795, S2213, SF2213, VU619
"Hail the Day That Sees Him Rise" (John, Easter)
    B165, E214, N260, UM312, VU189, W471 (PD)
"Blessed Quietness" (John, Comm.)
    F145, C267, N284, S2142, SF2142

Additional Contemporary Suggestions

"Surely the Presence of the Lord" (Acts, John) (O)
    C263, SP243, UM328; S-2 #200. Stanzas for soloist
"More Precious than Silver" (Acts)
    S2065, SF2065, SP99
"We Bring the Sacrifice of Praise" (Pss)
    S2031, SF2031, SP1
"Blessed Be Your Name" (Pss)
    M163, WS3002
"All Heaven Declares" (Pss, Easter)
    M58
"God Claims You" (1 Pet, Baptism)
    S2249, SF2249
"Holy Spirit, Come to Us" (John)
    EL406, G281, S2118, SF2118, W473
"Where the Spirit of the Lord Is" (John)
    C264, S2119, SF2119
"Live in Charity" ("*Ubi Caritas*") (John)
    C523, EL642, G205, S2179, SF2179, W604
"Love the Lord" (John)
    M270, WS3116
"Behold, What Manner of Love" (John)
    SP48
"The Power of Your Love" (John)
    M26
"Dwell" (John)
    M154

Vocal Solos

"Wash, O God, Our Sons and Daughters" (1 Pet, Baptism)
    V-5 (1)   p. 64
"Gentle Like Jesus" (John, Easter)
    V-8   p. 42

Anthems

"Blessed Be Your Name" (Pss)
Arr. Joel Raney; Alfred 42955
SATB, piano

"For the Beauty of the Earth" (Acts, Comm.)
Arr. Phillip Keveren; Jubilate Music 44265
SATB, piano

Other Suggestions

Visuals:
    O   Preaching, globe, Acts 17:28a, risen Christ
    P   Feet, refine silver, fire/water, offering, prayer
    E   Hearts, readiness, briefcase, accounting, Christ,
            crucifix, prisoners, resurrection
    G   Advocate (briefcase), Spirit, open Bible, child
Litany: C189. Love One Another (John)
Sung Benediction: N249. "Peace I Leave with You" (John)

Acts 1:1-11

[1]Theophilus, the first scroll I wrote concerned everything Jesus did and taught from the beginning, [2]right up to the day when he was taken up into heaven. Before he was taken up, working in the power of the Holy Spirit, Jesus instructed the apostles he had chosen. [3]After his suffering, he showed them that he was alive with many convincing proofs. He appeared to them over a period of forty days, speaking to them about God's kingdom. [4]While they were eating together, he ordered them not to leave Jerusalem but to wait for what the Father had promised. He said, "This is what you heard from me: [5]John baptized with water, but in only a few days you will be baptized with the Holy Spirit."

[6]As a result, those who had gathered together asked Jesus, "Lord, are you going to restore the kingdom to Israel now?"

[7]Jesus replied, "It isn't for you to know the times or seasons that the Father has set by his own authority. [8]Rather, you will receive power when the Holy Spirit has come upon you, and you will be my witnesses in Jerusalem, in all Judea and Samaria, and to the end of the earth."

[9]After Jesus said these things, as they were watching, he was lifted up and a cloud took him out of their sight. [10]While he was going away and as they were staring toward heaven, suddenly two men in white robes stood next to them. [11]They said, "Galileans, why are you standing here, looking toward heaven? This Jesus, who was taken up from you into heaven, will come in the same way that you saw him go into heaven."

Psalm 47 (G261, N653, P194, UM781)

[1]Clap your hands, all you people! / Shout joyfully to God with a joyous shout! / [2]Because the LORD Most High is awesome, / he is the great king of the whole world. / [3]He subdues the nations under us, / subdues all people beneath our feet. / [4]He chooses our inheritance for us: / the heights of Jacob, which he loves. *[Selah]* / [5]God has gone up with a joyous shout— / the LORD with the blast of the ram's horn. / [6]Sing praises to God! Sing praises! / Sing praises to our king! Sing praises / [7]because God is king of the whole world! / Sing praises with a song of instruction! / [8]God is king over the nations. / God sits on his holy throne. / [9]The leaders of all people are gathered / with the people of Abraham's God / because the earth's guardians belong to God; / God is exalted beyond all.

Ephesians 1:15-23

[15]Since I heard about your faith in the Lord Jesus and your love for all God's people, this is the reason that [16]I don't stop giving thanks to God for you when I remember you in my prayers. [17]I pray that the God of our Lord Jesus Christ, the Father of glory, will give you a spirit of wisdom and revelation that makes God known to you. [18]I pray that the eyes of your heart will have enough light to see what is the hope of God's call, what is the richness of God's glorious inheritance among believers, [19]and what is the overwhelming greatness of God's power that is working among us believers. This power is conferred by the energy of God's powerful strength. [20]God's power was at work in Christ when God raised him from the dead and sat him at God's right side in the heavens, [21]far above every ruler and authority and power and angelic power, any power that might be named not only now but in the future. [22]God put everything under Christ's feet and made him head of everything in the church, [23]which is his body. His body, the church, is the fullness of Christ, who fills everything in every way.

Luke 24:44-53

[44]Jesus said to them, "These are my words that I spoke to you while I was still with you—that everything written about me in the Law of Moses, the Prophets, and the Psalms must be fulfilled." [45]Then he opened their minds to understand the scriptures. [46]He said to them, "This is what is written: the Christ will suffer and rise from the dead on the third day, [47]and a change of heart and life for the forgiveness of sins must be preached in his name to all nations, beginning from Jerusalem. [48]You are witnesses of these things. [49]Look, I'm sending to you what my Father promised, but you are to stay in the city until you have been furnished with heavenly power."

[50]He led them out as far as Bethany, where he lifted his hands and blessed them. [51]As he blessed them, he left them and was taken up to heaven. [52]They worshipped him and returned to Jerusalem overwhelmed with joy. [53]And they were continuously in the temple praising God.

Primary Hymns and Songs for the Day

"Hail the Day That Sees Him Rise" (Acts, Luke) (O)
    B165, E214, N260, UM312, VU189, W471 (PD)
        H-3   Hbl-72; Chr-50; Desc-69; Org-78
        S-1   #213-14. Transposition with desc.
        S-1   #213. Desc.
"Crown Him with Many Crowns" (Acts)
    B161, C234, E494, EL855, F345, G268, L170, N301, P151,
    UM327 (PD), VU211
        H-3   Hbl-55; Chr-60; Desc-30; Org-27
        S-1   #86-88. Various treatments
"He Is Exalted" (Acts, Pss, Luke, Ascension) (C)
    S2070, SF2070, SP66
"Thine Be the Glory" (Acts, Pss, Luke) (C)
    B163, C218, EL376, F291, G238, L145, N253, P122, UM308,
    VU173 (Fr.)

Additional Hymn Suggestions

"Loving Spirit" (Acts)
    C244, EL397, G293, P323, S2123, VU387
"Wonder of Wonders" (Acts, Baptism)
    C378, G489, N328, P499, S2247
"I'll Fly Away" (Acts, Ascension)
    N595, S2282, SF2282
"Christ the Lord Is Risen Today" (Acts, Luke)
    B159, C216, EL373, F289, G245, L130, N233, P113, UM302
    (PD), VU155/157, W463
"Come, Ye Faithful, Raise the Strain" (Acts, Luke)
    C215, E199, EL363, G234, L132, N230, P115, UM315 (PD),
    VU165, W456
"Christ Jesus Lay in Death's Strong Bands" (Acts, Luke)
    E186, EL370, G237, L134, P110, UM319 (PD)
"Hail Thee, Festival Day" (Acts, Luke)
    E216, EL394, L142, N262, P120, UM324, VU163
"At the Font We Start Our Journey" (Acts, Luke, Baptism)
    N308, S2114, SF2114
"The Trees of the Field" (Pss)
    G80, S2279, SF2279, SP128, VU884
"Hope of the World" (Eph)
    C538, E472, G734, L493, N46, P360, UM178, VU215
"My Hope Is Built" (Eph)
    B406, C537, EL596/597, F92, G353, L293/ 294, N368, P379,
    UM368 (PD)
"For All the Saints" (Eph)
    B355, C637, E287, EL422, F614, G326, L174, N299, P526,
    UM711 (PD), VU705, W705
"There Are Some Things I May Not Know" (Eph)
    N405, S2147, SF2147
"Come, Share the Lord" (Eph, Comm.)
    C408, G510, S2269, SF2269, VU469
"Give Me Jesus" (Eph)
    EL770, N409, WS3140
"Christ the Lord Is Risen Today" (Luke, Ascension)
    B159, C216, EL373, F289, G245, L130, N233, P113, UM302
    (PD), VU155/157, W463
"Sent Out in Jesus' Name" ("*Enviado Soy de Dios*") (Luke) (C)
    EL538, G747, S2184, SF2184
"The Spirit Sends Us Forth to Serve" (Luke) (C)
    EL551, S2241, SF2241

Additional Contemporary Suggestions

"Holy Spirit, Come to Us" (Acts)
    EL406, G281, S2118, SF2118, W473
"Come, Holy Spirit" (Acts)
    SP132, S2125, SF2125, WS3091

"Jesus, We Are Here" ("*Yesu Tawa Pano*") (Acts, Luke)
    EL529, G392, S2273, SF2273
"Holy Spirit, Rain Down" (Acts, Eph)
    M88
"Shout to the Lord" (Pss)
    EL821, M16, S2074, SF2074; V-3 (2) p. 32 Vocal Solo
"Lord, I Lift Your Name on High" (Pss, Ascension)
    AH4071, EL857, M2, S2088, SF2088
"Glory to God in the Highest" (Pss, Eph, Ascension)
    S2276, SF2276
"Forever" (Pss)
    M68, WS3023
"Lord Most High" (Pss, Ascension)
    M120
"Awesome Is the Lord Most High" (Pss, Ascension)
    M234
"Glorious Day" (Pss, Ascension)
    M279
"Open the Eyes of My Heart" (Eph)
    G452, M57, WS3008
"In Christ Alone" (Eph, Ascension)
    M138, WS3105
"Above All" (Eph, Ascension)
    M77; V-3 (2) p. 17 Vocal solo
"Alleluia" (Ascension, Easter)
    G589, S2078, SF2078
"Once Again" (Ascension)
    M78

Vocal solos

"Give Me Jesus" (Eph)
    V-3 (1)   p. 53
    V-8   p. 256
"Rise Again" (Ascension, Easter)
    V-8   p. 31

Anthems

"Hail the Day That Sees Him Rise" (Acts, Luke)
Arr. Dan Forrest; Beckenhorst BP2039
SATB, organ, opt. horn, trumpet, and percussion

"Come, You People, Rise and Sing"
Kenneth Dake; MorningStar MSM-50-2526
SATB, organ

Other Suggestions

Visuals:
    O   Risen Christ, baptism, seven flames, ascension, angels
    P   Clapping, singing, shouting, crown/throne, shields
    E   Open Bible, Christ, right hand, feet, Church
    G   Open Bible, crucifix, Christ, lifted hands
These ideas may be used on May 28 as Ascension Sunday.
Introit: C220, E203, EL386/E387, G235/255, L139, N244, P116
    (PD), UM317, VU170, W447, st. 1. "O Sons and Daughters,
    Let Us Sing" (Luke)
Greeting: Acts 1:8. Receive power from the Holy Spirit
Prayer: UM323 (Ascension, Acts, Luke, Eph)
Song of Preparation: WS3047, st. 3. "God Almighty, We Are
    Waiting" (Luke)

Acts 1:6-14

⁶As a result, those who had gathered together asked Jesus, "Lord, are you going to restore the kingdom to Israel now?"

⁷Jesus replied, "It isn't for you to know the times or seasons that the Father has set by his own authority. ⁸Rather, you will receive power when the Holy Spirit has come upon you, and you will be my witnesses in Jerusalem, in all Judea and Samaria, and to the end of the earth."

⁹After Jesus said these things, as they were watching, he was lifted up and a cloud took him out of their sight. ¹⁰While he was going away and as they were staring toward heaven, suddenly two men in white robes stood next to them. ¹¹They said, "Galileans, why are you standing here, looking toward heaven? This Jesus, who was taken up from you into heaven, will come in the same way that you saw him go into heaven."

¹²Then they returned to Jerusalem from the Mount of Olives, which is near Jerusalem—a sabbath day's journey away. ¹³When they entered the city, they went to the upstairs room where they were staying. Peter, John, James, and Andrew; Philip and Thomas; Bartholomew and Matthew; James, Alphaeus' son; Simon the zealot; and Judas, James' son— ¹⁴all were united in their devotion to prayer, along with some women, including Mary the mother of Jesus, and his brothers.

Psalm 68:1-10 (G55, N664, UM792)

¹Let God rise up; / let his enemies scatter; / let those who hate him / run scared before him! / ²Like smoke is driven away, / drive them away! / Like wax melting before fire, / let the wicked perish before God! / ³But let the righteous be glad / and celebrate before God. / Let them rejoice with gladness! / ⁴Sing to God! Sing praises to his name! / Exalt the one who rides the clouds! / The Lord is his name. / Celebrate before him! / ⁵Father of orphans and defender of widows / is God in his holy habitation. / ⁶God settles the lonely in their homes; / he sets prisoners free with happiness, / but the rebellious dwell in a parched land. / ⁷When you went forth before your people, God, / when you marched through the wasteland, *[Selah]* / ⁸the earth shook! / Yes, heaven poured down / before God, the one from Sinai— / before God, the God of Israel! / ⁹You showered down abundant rain, God; / when your inheritance grew weary, / you restored it yourself, / ¹⁰and your creatures settled in it. / In your goodness, God, / you provided for the poor.

1 Peter 4:12-14; 5:6-11

¹²Dear friends, don't be surprised about the fiery trials that have come among you to test you. These are not strange happenings. ¹³Instead, rejoice as you share Christ's suffering. You share his suffering now so that you may also have overwhelming joy when his glory is revealed. ¹⁴If you are mocked because of Christ's name, you are blessed, for the Spirit of glory—indeed, the Spirit of God—rests on you. . . .

5 . . . ⁶Therefore, humble yourselves under God's power so that he may raise you up in the last day. ⁷Throw all your anxiety onto him, because he cares about you. ⁸Be clear-headed. Keep alert. Your accuser, the devil, is on the prowl like a roaring lion, seeking someone to devour. ⁹Resist him, standing firm in the faith. Do so in the knowledge that your fellow believers are enduring the same suffering throughout the world. ¹⁰After you have suffered for a little while, the God of all grace, the one who called you into his eternal glory in Christ Jesus, will himself restore, empower, strengthen, and establish you. ¹¹To him be power forever and always. Amen.

John 17:1-11

¹When Jesus finished saying these things, he looked up to heaven and said," Father, the time has come. Glorify your Son, so that the Son can glorify you. ²You gave him authority over everyone so that he could give eternal life to everyone you gave him. ³This is eternal life: to know you, the only true God, and Jesus Christ whom you sent. ⁴I have glorified you on earth by finishing the work you gave me to do. ⁵Now, Father, glorify me in your presence with the glory I shared with you before the world was created.

⁶"I have revealed your name to the people you gave me from this world. They were yours and you gave them to me, and they have kept your word. ⁷Now they know that everything you have given me comes from you. ⁸This is because I gave them the words that you gave me, and they received them. They truly understood that I came from you, and they believed that you sent me.

⁹"I'm praying for them. I'm not praying for the world but for those you gave me, because they are yours. ¹⁰Everything that is mine is yours and everything that is yours is mine; I have been glorified in them. ¹¹I'm no longer in the world, but they are in the world, even as I'm coming to you. Holy Father, watch over them in your name, the name you gave me, that they will be one just as we are one."

Primary Hymns and Songs for the Day

"Hail the Day That Sees Him Rise" (Acts) (O)
 B165, E214, N260, UM312, VU189, W471 (PD)
   H-3 Hbl-72; Chr-50; Desc-69; Org-78
   S-1 #213-14. Transposition with desc.
   S-1 #213. Desc.
"Alleluia! Sing to Jesus!" (Heb) (O)
 C233, E460/E461, EL392, G260, L158, N257, P144, W737
   H-3 Hbl-46; Chr-26, 134; Desc-53; Org-56
   S-1 #168-71. Various treatments
"Come, Ye Faithful, Raise the Strain" (Acts)
 C215, E199, EL363, G234, L132, N230, P115, UM315 (PD),
 VU165, W456
"He Is Exalted" (Acts)
 S2070, SF2070, SP66
"How Firm a Foundation" (Pss, 1 Pet) (C)
 B338, C618, E636/637, EL796, F32, G463, L507, N407, P361,
 UM529 (PD), VU660, W585
   H-3 Hbl-27, 69; Chr-102; Desc-41; Org-41
   S-1 #133. Harm.
     #134. Performance note

Additional Hymn Suggestions

"Lo, He Comes with Clouds Descending" (Acts)
 B199, E57/58, EL435, F306, G348, L27, P6, UM718, VU25
"Loving Spirit" (Acts)
 C244, EL397, G293, P323, S2123, VU387
"Wonder of Wonders" (Acts, Baptism)
 C378, G489, N328, P499, S2247
"I'll Fly Away" (Acts)
 N595, S2282, SF2282
"Christ the Lord Is Risen Today" (Acts)
 B159, C216, EL373, F289, G245, L130, N233, P113, UM302
 (PD), VU155/157, W463
"Hail Thee, Festival Day" (Acts)
 E216, EL394, L142, N262, P120, UM324, VU163
"Immortal, Invisible, God only Wise" (Acts, John)
 B6, C66, E423, EL834, F319, G12, L526, N1, P263, UM103
 (PD), VU264, W512
"Christ, Whose Glory Fills the Skies" (Acts, John)
 EL553, F293, G662, L265, P462/463, UM173 (PD), VU336
"I'll Praise My Maker While I've Breath" (Pss)
 B35, C20, E429 (PD), G806, P253, UM60, VU867
"Praise, My Soul, the King of Heaven" (Pss)
 B32, C23, E410, EL864/865, F339, G619/620, L549,
 P478/479, UM66 (PD), VU240, W530
"Joyful, Joyful, We Adore Thee" (Pss, John)
 B7, C2, E376, EL836, F377, G611, L551, N4, P464, UM89
 (PD), VU232, W525
"Lift Every Voice and Sing" (Pss, 1 Pet)
 AH4055, B627, C631, E599, EL841, G339, L562, N593, P563,
 UM519, W641
"Blessed Assurance" (1 Pet)
 B334, C543, EL638, F67, G839, N473, P341, UM369 (PD),
 VU337
"The Trees of the Field" (1 Pet)
 G80, S2279, SF2279, SP128, VU884
"We Cannot Measure How You Heal" (1 Pet)
 G797, VU613, WS3139
"By Gracious Powers" (1 Pet, John)
 E695/696, EL626, G818, N413, P342, UM517, W577
"O Jesus, I Have Promised" (John)
 B276, C612, E655, EL810, F402, G724/725, L503, N493,
 P388/389, UM396 (PD), VU120

Additional Contemporary Suggestions

"Holy Spirit, Come to Us" (Acts)
 EL406, G281, S2118, SF2118, W473
"Come, Holy Spirit" (Acts)
 SP132, S2125, SF2125, WS3091
"Above All" (Acts, Ascension)
 M77
"Holy Spirit, Rain Down" (Acts, Pss)
 M88
"Lord, I Lift Your Name on High" (Pss)
 AH4071, EL857, M2, S2088, SF2088
"Shout to the Lord" (Pss)
 EL821, M16, S2074, SF2074; V-3 (2) p. 32 Vocal Solo
"God Is Good All the Time" (1 Pet)
 AH4010, M45, WS3026
"God Is So Good" (1 Pet)
 B23, G658, S2056, SF2056
"Humble Thyself in the Sight of the Lord" (1 Pet)
 S2131, SF2131, SP223
"Cares Chorus" (1 Pet, John)
 S2215, SF2215, SP221
"Today Is the Day" (1 Pet)
 M223
"Praise You" (John)
 M84, S2003, SF2003
"Lord, Be Glorified" (John)
 B457, EL744, G468, S2150, SF2150, SP196
"Be Glorified" (John)
 M152

Vocal Solos

"Above All" (Acts, Easter, Ascension)
 V-3 (2) p. 17
"My Heart Is Steadfast" (1 Pet, John)
 V-5 (2) p. 40

Anthems

"Fly Away Home" (Acts)
Pepper Choplin; Lorenz 10/4691L
SATB, piano

"Immortal, Invisible" (Acts, John)
Arr. Craig Courtney; Beckenhorst BP1827
SATB, piano, organ, and trumpet

Other Suggestions

Visuals:
 Acts Cloud, ascension, Jesus ascending, angels, prayer
 P Melting candle, music notes, clouds, broken chains, abundant rain
 E Fire, trials, testing, suffering, relief from suffering
 G Jesus ascending, sun, lifted hands
Today may also be celebrated as Ascension Sunday using the ideas for May 25.
Introit: EL529, G392, S2273, SF2273. "Jesus, We Are Here" (*"Yesu Tawa Pano"*) (Acts)
Song of Preparation: WS3047, st. 3. "God Almighty, We Are Waiting" (Acts)
Introit and Sung Benediction: EL412, WS3017, verses 1 and 3. "Come, Join the Dance of Trinity" (Luke)

Acts 2:1-21

[1]When Pentecost Day arrived, they were all together in one place. [2]Suddenly a sound from heaven like the howling of a fierce wind filled the entire house where they were sitting. [3]They saw what seemed to be individual flames of fire alighting on each one of them. [4]They were all filled with the Holy Spirit and began to speak in other languages as the Spirit enabled them to speak.

[5]There were pious Jews from every nation under heaven living in Jerusalem. [6]When they heard this sound, a crowd gathered. They were mystified because everyone heard them speaking in their native languages. [7]They were surprised and amazed, saying, "Look, aren't all the people who are speaking Galileans, every one of them? [8]How then can each of us hear them speaking in our native language? [9]Parthians, Medes, and Elamites; as well as residents of Mesopotamia, Judea, and Cappadocia, Pontus and Asia, [10]Phrygia and Pamphylia, Egypt and the regions of Libya bordering Cyrene; and visitors from Rome (both Jews and converts to Judaism), [11]Cretans and Arabs—we hear them declaring the mighty works of God in our own languages!" [12]They were all surprised and bewildered. Some asked each other, "What does this mean?" [13]Others jeered at them, saying, "They're full of new wine!"

[14]Peter stood with the other eleven apostles. He raised his voice and declared, "Judeans and everyone living in Jerusalem! Know this! Listen carefully to my words! [15]These people aren't drunk, as you suspect; after all, it's only nine o'clock in the morning! [16]Rather, this is what was spoken through the prophet Joel:

[17] In the last days, God says,
　　I will pour out my Spirit on all people.
　　　Your sons and daughters will prophesy.
　　　Your young will see visions.
　　　Your elders will dream dreams.
[18] 　*Even upon my servants, men and women,*
　　　I will pour out my Spirit in those days,
　　　and they will prophesy.
[19] 　*I will cause wonders to occur in the heavens above*
　　　and signs on the earth below,
　　　　blood and fire and a cloud of smoke.
[20] 　*The sun will be changed into darkness,*
　　　and the moon will be changed into blood,
　　　　before the great and spectacular day of the Lord comes.
[21] 　*And everyone who calls on the name of the Lord will be*
　　　saved.

Psalm 104:24-34, 35b (G34, N689, P224, UM826)

[24]Lord, you have done so many things! / You made them all so wisely! / The earth is full of your creations! / [25]And then there's the sea, wide and deep, / with its countless creatures— / living things both small and large. / [26]There go the ships on it, / and Leviathan, which you made, plays in it! / [27]All your creations wait for you / to give them their food on time. / [28]When you give it to them, they gather it up; / when you open your hand, they are filled completely full! / [29]But when you hide your face, they are terrified; / when you take away their breath, / they die and return to dust. / [30]When you let loose your breath, they are created, / and you make the surface of the ground brand-new again.

[31]Let the Lord's glory last forever! / Let the Lord rejoice in all he has made! / [32]He has only to look at the earth, and it shakes. / God just touches the mountains, and they erupt in smoke.

[33]I will sing to the Lord as long as I live; / I will sing praises to my God while I'm still alive. / [34]Let my praise be pleasing to him; / I'm rejoicing in the Lord! . . . . [35b]But let my whole being bless the Lord! / Praise the Lord!

1 Corinthians 12:3b-13

[3]So I want to make it clear to you that no one says, "Jesus is cursed!" when speaking by God's Spirit, and no one can say, "Jesus is Lord," except by the Holy Spirit. [4]There are different spiritual gifts but the same Spirit; [5]and there are different ministries and the same Lord; [6]and there are different activities but the same God who produces all of them in everyone. [7]A demonstration of the Spirit is given to each person for the common good. [8]A word of wisdom is given by the Spirit to one person, a word of knowledge to another according to the same Spirit, [9]faith to still another by the same Spirit, gifts of healing to another in the one Spirit, [10]performance of miracles to another, prophecy to another, the ability to tell spirits apart to another, different kinds of tongues to another, and the interpretation of the tongues to another. [11]All these things are produced by the one and same Spirit who gives what he wants to each person.

[12]Christ is just like the human body—a body is a unit and has many parts; and all the parts of the body are one body, even though there are many. [13]We were all baptized by one Spirit into one body, whether Jew or Greek, or slave or free, and we all were given one Spirit to drink.

John 7:37-39

[37]On the last and most important day of the festival, Jesus stood up and shouted,
　　"All who are thirsty should come to me!
[38] 　All who believe in me should drink!
　　As the scriptures said concerning me,
　　　Rivers of living water will flow out from within him."
[39]Jesus said this concerning the Spirit. Those who believed in him would soon receive the Spirit, but they hadn't experienced the Spirit yet since Jesus hadn't yet been glorified.

Primary Hymns and Songs for the Day

"On Pentecost They Gathered" (Acts) (O)
    C237, G289, N272, P128, VU195
        H-3   Hbl-86; Chr-153; Org-95
        S-1   #243. Harm.
"Spirit of the Living God" (Acts, Pentecost)
    SP131; S-1#212 Vocal Desc. idea
    B244, C259, G288, N283, P322, SP131, UM393, VU376
"Forward Through the Ages" (1 Cor)
    N355, UM555 (PD)
        H-3   Hbl-59; Chr-156; Org-140
"Breathe on Me, Breath of God" (Acts) (C)
    B241, C254, E508, F161, G286, L488, N292, P316, UM420
    (PD), VU382 (Fr.), W725
        H-3   Hbl-49; Chr-45; Desc-101; Org-166

Additional Hymn Suggestions

"Hail Thee, Festival Day" (Acts) (O)
    E225, EL394, L142, N262, UM324, VU163
"Come Down, O Love Divine" (Acts)
    C582, E516, EL804, G282, L508, N289, P313, UM475,
    VU367, W472
"Filled with the Spirit's Power" (Acts)
    L160, N266, UM537, VU194
"Gather Us In" (Acts)
    C284, EL532, G401, S2236, SF2236, W665
"Here, O Lord, Your Servants Gather" (Acts)
    B179, C278, EL530, G311, N72, P465, UM552, VU362
"Holy Spirit, Truth Divine" (Acts)
    C241, EL398, L257, N63, P321, UM465 (PD), VU368
"Wind Who Makes All Winds That Blow" (Acts)
    C236, N271, P131, UM538, VU196
"O Spirit of the Living God" (Acts)
    N263, UM539
"Spirit, Spirit of Gentleness" (Acts, Pentecost)
    C249, EL396, G291, N286, P319, S2120, VU375 (Fr.)
"Loving Spirit" (Acts, Pentecost)
    C244, EL397, G293, P323, S2123, VU387
"In the Midst of New Dimensions" (Acts, Pentecost)
    G315, N391, S2238, SF2238
"Deep in the Shadows of the Past" (Acts, Pentecost)
    G50, N320, P330, S2246
"Praise God for This Holy Ground" (Acts, Pentecost)
    G405, WS3009
"Come, Share the Lord" (Acts, Comm.)
    C408, G510, S2269, SF2269, VU469
"Like the Murmur of the Dove's Song" (Acts, 1 Cor)
    C245, E513, EL403, G285, N270, P314, UM544, VU205
"Many Gifts, One Spirit" (1 Cor)
    N177, UM114
"One Bread, One Body" (1 Cor, Comm.)
    C393, EL496, G530, UM620, VU467
"We All Are One in Mission" (1 Cor)
    EL576, G733, P435, S2243, SF2243
"Source and Sovereign, Rock and Cloud" (John)
    C12, G11, UM113
"Holy Spirit, Come, Confirm Us" (John, Pentecost)
    N264, UM331

Additional Contemporary Suggestions

"Surely the Presence of the Lord" (Acts, Pentecost)
    C263, SP243, UM328; S-2 #200. Stanzas for soloist
"Sweet, Sweet Spirit" (Acts, Pentecost)
    B243, C261, F159, G408, N293, P398, SP136, UM334

"Spirit Song" (Acts, Pentecost)
    C352, SP134, UM347
"Holy, Holy" (Acts, Pentecost)
    B254, F149, P140, S2039, SP141
"God Is Here Today" ("Dios Está Aquí") (Acts)
    G411, S2049, SF2049
"Open Our Eyes, Lord" (Acts)
    B499, S2086, SF2086, SP199
"Where the Spirit of the Lord Is" (Acts, Pentecost)
    C264, S2119, SF2119
"Holy Ground" (Acts)
    B224, C112, G406, S2272, SF2272, SP86
"Open the Eyes of My Heart" (Acts)
    G452, M57, WS3008
"Holy Spirit, Rain Down" (Acts)
    M88
"God of Wonders" (Pss)
    M80, WS3034
"We Are the Body of Christ" (1 Cor)
    G768, S2227, SF2227
"I'm Goin' a Sing When the Spirit Says Sing" (1 Cor, Pentecost)
    AH4073, UM333
"You Who Are Thirsty" (John)
    S2132, SP219
"The River Is Here" (John, Pentecost)
    M5
"Who Can Satisfy My Soul Like You?" (John)
    M28
"All Who Are Thirsty" (John)
    M159
"Dwell" (Pentecost)
    M154

Vocal Solos

"Spirit of Faith Come Down" (Acts, Pentecost)
    V-1   p. 43
"I Feel the Spirit Moving" (Acts, 1 Cor)
    V-3 (1)   p. 22
"One Bread, One Body" (1 Cor)
    V-3 (2)   p. 40

Anthems

"O Thou Who Camest from Above" (Acts)
Philip W. J. Stopford; MorningStar MSM-50-5209
SATB, organ

"The Greater Gifts" (1 Cor)
Paul M. French; MorningStar MSM-50-5018
SATB, organ, opt. brass quartet

Other Suggestions

Visuals:
    O   Wind, tongues of fire, praise, all races
    P   Sea/ships, whales, dove, volcano, quake, Ps 104:35b
    E   Pile of gifts, seven flames, clasped hands, circle,
            baptism, drinking glasses
    G   Water/pitcher/glasses, river fountain
Introit: SP132, S2125, or WS3091. "Come, Holy Spirit" (Acts)
Call to Prayer: EL406, G281, S2118, SF2118, W473. "Holy Spirit,
    Come to Us" (Acts, 1 Cor)
Prayer: UM329 or UM542 (Acts, Pentecost)
Response: WS3183. "As We Go" (Pentecost)

Genesis 1:1–2:4a

[1]When God began to create the heavens and the earth— [2]the earth was without shape or form, it was dark over the deep sea, and God's wind swept over the waters— [3]God said, "Let there be light." And so light appeared. [4]God saw how good the light was. God separated the light from the darkness. [5]God named the light Day and the darkness Night.

There was evening and there was morning: the first day.

[6]God said, "Let there be a dome in the middle of the waters to separate the waters from each other." [7]God made the dome and separated the waters under the dome from the waters above the dome. And it happened in that way. [8]God named the dome Sky.

There was evening and there was morning: the second day.

[9]God said, "Let the waters under the sky come together into one place so that the dry land can appear." And that's what happened. [10]God named the dry land Earth, and he named the gathered waters Seas. God saw how good it was. [11]God said, "Let the earth grow plant life: plants yielding seeds and fruit trees bearing fruit with seeds inside it, each according to its kind throughout the earth." And that's what happened. [12]The earth produced plant life: plants yielding seeds, each according to its kind, and trees bearing fruit with seeds inside it, each according to its kind. God saw how good it was.

[13]There was evening and there was morning: the third day.

[14]God said, "Let there be lights in the dome of the sky to separate the day from the night. They will mark events, sacred seasons, days, and years. [15]They will be lights in the dome of the sky to shine on the earth." And that's what happened. [16]God made the stars and two great lights: the larger light to rule over the day and the smaller light to rule over the night. [17]God put them in the dome of the sky to shine on the earth, [18]to rule over the day and over the night, and to separate the light from the darkness. God saw how good it was.

[19]There was evening and there was morning: the fourth day.

[20]God said, "Let the waters swarm with living things, and let birds fly above the earth up in the dome of the sky." [21]God created the great sea animals and all the tiny living things that swarm in the waters, each according to its kind, and all the winged birds, each according to its kind. God saw how good it was. [22]Then God blessed them: "Be fertile and multiply and fill the waters in the seas, and let the birds multiply on the earth."

[23]There was evening and there was morning: the fifth day.

[24]God said, "Let the earth produce every kind of living thing: livestock, crawling things, and wildlife." And that's what happened. [25]God made every kind of wildlife, every kind of livestock, and every kind of creature that crawls on the ground. God saw how good it was. [26]Then God said, "Let us make humanity in our image to resemble us so that they may take charge of the fish of the sea, the birds of the sky, the livestock, all the earth, and all the crawling things on earth."

[27]God created humanity in God's own image,
in the divine image God created them,
male and female God created them.

[28]God blessed them and said to them, "Be fertile and multiply; fill the earth and master it. Take charge of the fish of the sea, the birds of the sky, and everything crawling on the ground." [29]Then God said, "I now give to you all the plants on the earth that yield seeds and all the trees whose fruit produces its seeds within it. These will be your food. [30]To all wildlife, to all the birds of the sky, and to everything crawling on the ground—to everything that breathes—I give all the green grasses for food." And that's what happened. [31]God saw everything he had made: it was supremely good.

There was evening and there was morning: the sixth day.

2 The heavens and the earth and all who live in them were completed. [2]On the sixth day God completed all the work that he had done, and on the seventh day God rested from all the work that he had done. [3]God blessed the seventh day and made it holy, because on it God rested from all the work of creation. [4]This is the account of the heavens and the earth when they were created.

Psalm 8 (G25, N624, P162/163, UM743)

[1]Lord, our Lord, how majestic / is your name throughout the earth! / You made your glory higher than heaven! / [2]From the mouths of nursing babies / you have laid a strong foundation / because of your foes, / in order to stop vengeful enemies. / [3]When I look up at your skies, / at what your fingers made— / the moon and the stars / that you set firmly in place— / [4]what are human beings / that you think about them; / what are human beings / that you pay attention to them? / [5]You've made them only slightly less than divine, / crowning them with glory and grandeur. / [6]You've let them rule over your handiwork, / putting everything under their feet— / [7]all sheep and all cattle, / the wild animals too, / [8]the birds in the sky, / the fish of the ocean, / everything that travels the pathways of the sea. / [9]Lord, our Lord, how majestic is your name throughout the earth!

2 Corinthians 13:11-13

[11]Finally, brothers and sisters, good-bye. Put things in order, respond to my encouragement, be in harmony with each other, and live in peace—and the God of love and peace will be with you.

[12]Say hello to each other with a holy kiss. All of God's people say hello to you.

[13]The grace of the Lord Jesus Christ, the love of God, and the fellowship of the Holy Spirit be with you all.

Matthew 28:16-20

[16]Now the eleven disciples went to Galilee, to the mountain where Jesus told them to go. [17]When they saw him, they worshipped him, but some doubted. [18]Jesus came near and spoke to them, "I've received all authority in heaven and on earth. [19]Therefore, go and make disciples of all nations, baptizing them in the name of the Father and of the Son and of the Holy Spirit, [20]teaching them to obey everything that I've commanded you. Look, I myself will be with you every day until the end of this present age."

Primary Hymns and Songs for the Day
"All Creatures of Our God and King" (Gen, Pss, Trinity) (O)
  B27, C22, E400, EL835, F347, G15, L527, N17, P455, UM62,
  VU217 (Fr.), W520
    H-3   Hbl-44; Chr-21; Desc-66; Org-73
    S-1   #198-204. Various treatments
"How Majestic Is Your Name" (Pss) (O)
  C63, G613, S2023, SF2023, SP14
"Come, Join the Dance of Trinity" (Gen, Matt, Trinity)
  EL412, WS3017
"Go Ye, Go Ye into the World" (Matt) (C)
  S2239, SF2239
"Go to the World" (Matt) (C)
  G295, VU420, WS3158

Additional Hymn Suggestions
"Morning Has Broken" (Gen)
  B48, C53, E8, EL556, F5, G664, P469, UM145, VU409
"All Things Bright and Beautiful" (Gen)
  C61, E405, G20, N31, P267, UM147 (PD), VU291, W505
"God Created Heaven and Earth" (Gen)
  EL738, N33, P290, UM151, VU251
"Wind Who Makes All Winds That Blow" (Gen)
  C236, N271, P131, UM538, VU196
"O God, We Bear the Imprint of Your Face" (Gen)
  C681, G759, N585, P385
"Womb of Life" (Gen, Trinity, Comm.)
  C14, G3, N274, S2046, SF2046
"Bring Many Names" (Gen,)
  C10, G760, N11, S2047, SF2047, VU268
"Mothering God, You Gave Me Birth" (Gen, Trinity)
  C83, EL735, G7, N467, S2050, SF2050, VU320
"God the Sculptor of the Mountains" (Gen)
  EL736, G5, S2060, SF2060
"Spirit, Spirit of Gentleness" (Gen)
  C249, EL396, G291, N286, P319, S2120, VU375 (Fr.)
"Loving Spirit" (Gen)
  C244, EL397, G293, P323, S2123, VU387
"God Made from One Blood" (Gen)
  C500, N427, S2170, SF2170, VU554
"Touch the Earth Lightly" (Gen)
  C693, EL739, G713, N569, VU307, WS3129
"From All That Dwell below the Skies" (Gen, Pss)
  B13, C49, E380, G327, L550, N27, P229, UM101 (PD)
"I Sing the Almighty Power of God" (Gen, Pss)
  B42, C64, E398, G32, N12, P288, UM152, VU231, W502
"Come, Thou Almighty King" (Pss, Trinity)
  B247, C27, E365, EL408, F341, G2, L522, N275, P139, UM61
  (PD), VU314, W487
"How Great Thou Art" (Pss)
  AH4015, B10, C33, EL856, F2, G625, L532, N35, P467,
  UM77, VU238 (Fr.)
"Lord, You Give the Great Commission" (2 Cor, Matt)
  C459, E528, EL579, G298, P429, UM584, VU512, W470
"Sois la Semilla" ("You Are the Seed") (Matt)
  C478, N528, UM583
"Draw Us in the Spirit's Tether" (Matt, Comm.)
  C392, EL470, G529, N337, P504, UM632, VU479, W731
"Sent Out in Jesus' Name" ("Enviado Soy de Dios") (Matt)
  EL538, G747, S2184, SF2184
"Guide My Feet" (Matt)
  G741, N497, P354, S2208
"We All Are One in Mission" (Matt)
  EL576, G733, P435, S2243, SF2243
"Day of Arising" (Matt, Comm.)
  G252, EL374, WS3086

Additional Contemporary Suggestions
"Thou Art Worthy" (Gen)
  C114, S2041, SF2041, SP5
"Holy Spirit, Come to Us" (Gen)
  EL406, G281, S2118, SF2118, W473
"Come, Holy Spirit" (Gen)
  SP132, S2125, SF2125, WS3091
"How Great Is Our God" (Gen, Pss, Trinity)
  M117, WS3003
"God of Wonders" (Gen, Pss)
  M80, WS3034
"There's a Song" (2 Cor)
  S2141, SF2141
"Make Me a Channel of Your Peace" (2 Cor)
  G753, S2171, SF2171, VU684
"Song of Hope" ("Canto de Esperanza") (2 Cor)
  G765, P432, S2186, VU424
"They'll Know We Are Christians" (2 Cor, Trinity)
  AH4074, C494, G300, S2223, SF2223
"In Christ Alone" (Matt)
  M138, WS3105
"Rising" (Matt)
  M232
"A New Hallelujah" (Matt)
  M269
"Holy, Holy" (Trinity)
  B254, F149, P140, S2039, SP141
"We Were Baptized in Christ Jesus" (Trinity, Baptism)
  EL451, S2251, SF2251

Vocal Solos
"In the Image of God" (Gen)
  V-8   p. 362
"Make Me a Channel of Your Peace" (2 Cor)
  V-3 (2)   p. 25
  V-3 (3)   p. 28

Anthems
"Let the Whole Creation Cry" (SOCB60) (Gen)
Arr. Ferguson/Aspaas; Augsburg 9781451499032
TBB, organ

"Emerald Stream" (Gen)
Seth Houston; Santa Barbara Music SBMP-1046
SATB a cappella

Other Suggestions
Visuals:
  O   Wind, light/dark, sky (evening/morning)
  P   Majesty, earth, infants, sky/stars, people, sheep/ox
  E   Waving, circle (unity), dove/branch, kiss/parting
  G   Jesus, eleven men, Christ candle, worship, globe,
           baptism
  Trinity Sunday: Symbols of the Trinity, 3-wick candle
Introit: B179, C278, EL530, G311, N72, P465, UM552, VU362.
  "Here, O Lord, Your Servants Gather" (2 Cor)
Opening Prayer: N826 or WSL64 (Gen) or N830 (Trinity)
Sung Benediction: WS3183. "As We Go" (Matt)

Genesis 18:1-15, (21:1-7)

[1]The LORD appeared to Abraham at the oaks of Mamre while he sat at the entrance of his tent in the day's heat. [2]He looked up and suddenly saw three men standing near him. As soon as he saw them, he ran from his tent entrance to greet them and bowed deeply. [3]He said, "Sirs, if you would be so kind, don't just pass by your servant. [4]Let a little water be brought so you may wash your feet and refresh yourselves under the tree. [5]Let me offer you a little bread so you will feel stronger, and after that you may leave your servant and go on your way—since you have visited your servant."

They responded, "Fine. Do just as you have said."

[6]So Abraham hurried to Sarah at his tent and said, "Hurry! Knead three seahs of the finest flour and make some baked goods!" [7]Abraham ran to the cattle, took a healthy young calf, and gave it to a young servant, who prepared it quickly. [8]Then Abraham took butter, milk, and the calf that had been prepared, put the food in front of them, and stood under the tree near them as they ate.

[9]They said to him, "Where's your wife Sarah?"

And he said, "Right here in the tent."

[10]Then one of the men said, "I will definitely return to you about this time next year. Then your wife Sarah will have a son!"

Sarah was listening at the tent door behind him. [11]Now Abraham and Sarah were both very old. Sarah was no longer menstruating. [12]So Sarah laughed to herself, thinking, I'm no longer able to have children and my husband's old. [13]The LORD said to Abraham, "Why did Sarah laugh and say, 'Me give birth? At my age?' [14]Is anything too difficult for the LORD? When I return to you about this time next year, Sarah will have a son."

[15]Sarah lied and said, "I didn't laugh," because she was frightened. But he said, "No, you laughed." . . . .

21 The LORD was attentive to Sarah just as he had said, and the LORD carried out just what he had promised her. [2]She became pregnant and gave birth to a son for Abraham when he was old, at the very time God had told him. [3]Abraham named his son—the one Sarah bore him—Isaac. [4]Abraham circumcised his son Isaac when he was eight days old just as God had commanded him. [5]Abraham was 100 years old when his son Isaac was born. [6]Sarah said, "God has given me laughter. Everyone who hears about it will laugh with me." [7]She said, "Who could have told Abraham that Sarah would nurse sons? But now I've given birth to a son when he was old!"

Psalm 116:1-2, 12-19 (G655, N699, P228, UM837)

[1]I love the LORD because he hears / my requests for mercy. / [2]I'll call out to him as long as I live, / because he listens closely to me. . . .

[12]What can I give back to the LORD / for all the good things he has done for me? / [13]I'll lift up the cup of salvation. / I'll call on the LORD's name. / [14]I'll keep the promises I made to the LORD / in the presence of all God's people. / [15]The death of the LORD's faithful / is a costly loss in his eyes.

[16]Oh yes, LORD, I am definitely your servant! / I am your servant and the son of your female servant— / you've freed me from my chains. / [17]So I'll offer a sacrifice of thanksgiving to you, / and I'll call on the LORD's name. / [18]I'll keep the promises I made to the LORD / in the presence of all God's people, / [19]in the courtyards of the LORD's house, / which is in the center of Jerusalem.

Praise the LORD!

Romans 5:1-8

[1]Therefore, since we have been made righteous through his faithfulness, we have peace with God through our Lord Jesus Christ. [2]We have access by faith into this grace in which we stand through him, and we boast in the hope of God's glory. [3]But not only that! We even take pride in our problems, because we know that trouble produces endurance, [4]endurance produces character, and character produces hope. [5]This hope doesn't put us to shame, because the love of God has been poured out in our hearts through the Holy Spirit, who has been given to us.

[6]While we were still weak, at the right moment, Christ died for ungodly people. [7]It isn't often that someone will die for a righteous person, though maybe someone might dare to die for a good person. [8]But God shows his love for us, because while we were still sinners Christ died for us.

Matthew 9:35–10:8, (9-23)

[35]Jesus traveled among all the cities and villages, teaching in their synagogues, announcing the good news of the kingdom, and healing every disease and every sickness. [36]Now when Jesus saw the crowds, he had compassion for them because they were troubled and helpless, like sheep without a shepherd. [37]Then he said to his disciples, "The size of the harvest is bigger than you can imagine, but there are few workers. [38]Therefore, plead with the Lord of the harvest to send out workers for his harvest."

10 He called his twelve disciples and gave them authority over unclean spirits to throw them out and to heal every disease and every sickness. [2]Here are the names of the twelve apostles: first, Simon, who is called Peter; and Andrew his brother; James the son of Zebedee; and John his brother; [3]Philip; and Bartholomew; Thomas; and Matthew the tax collector; James the son of Alphaeus; and Thaddaeus; [4]Simon the Cananaean; and Judas, who betrayed Jesus.

[5]Jesus sent these twelve out and commanded them, "Don't go among the Gentiles or into a Samaritan city. [6]Go instead to the lost sheep, the people of Israel. [7]As you go, make this announcement: 'The kingdom of heaven has come near.' [8]Heal the sick, raise the dead, cleanse those with skin diseases, and throw out demons. You received without having to pay. Therefore, give without demanding payment. [9]Workers deserve to be fed, so don't gather gold or silver or copper coins for your money belts to take on your trips. [10]Don't take a backpack for the road or two shirts or sandals or a walking stick. [11]Whatever city or village you go into, find somebody in it who is worthy and stay there until you go on your way. [12]When you go into a house, say, 'Peace!' [13]If the house is worthy, give it your blessing of peace. But if the house isn't worthy, take back your blessing. [14]If anyone refuses to welcome you or listen to your words, shake the dust off your feet as you leave that house or city. [15]I assure you that it will be more bearable for the land of Sodom and Gomorrah on Judgment Day than it will be for that city.

[16]"Look, I'm sending you as sheep among wolves. Therefore, be wise as snakes and innocent as doves. [17]Watch out for people—because they will hand you over to councils and they will beat you in their synagogues. [18]They will haul you in front of governors and even kings because of me so that you may give your testimony to them and to the Gentiles. [19]Whenever they hand you over, don't worry about how to speak or what you will say, because what you can say will be given to you at that moment. [20]You aren't doing the talking, but the Spirit of my Father is doing the talking through you. [21]Brothers and sisters will hand each other over to be executed. A father will turn his child in. Children will defy their parents and have them executed. [22]Everyone will hate you on account of my name. But whoever stands firm until the end will be saved. [23]Whenever they harass you in one city, escape to the next, because I assure that you will not go through all the cities of Israel before the Human One comes."

Primary Hymns and Songs for the Day
"The God of Abraham Praise" (Gen) (O)
  B34, C24, E401, EL831, F332, G49, L544, N24, P488, UM116
  (PD), VU255, W537
    H-3 Hbl-62, 95; Chr-59; Org-77
    S-1 #211. Harm.
"I Love the Lord" (Pss)
  G799, P362, N511, VU617, WS3142
"When I Survey the Wondrous Cross" (Rom)
  B144, C195, E803, F258, G223, N224, P101, UM298
    H-3 Hbl-6, 102; Chr-213; Desc-49; Org-49
    S-1 #155. Desc.
"The Summons" ("Will You Come and Follow Me") (Matt)
  EL798, G726, S2130, SF2130, VU567
"Go to the World" (Matt) (C)
  G295, VU420, WS3158
    H-3 Hbl-58; Chr-65; Org-152
    S-1 #314-18. Various treatments
"Sent Forth by God's Blessing" (Pss, Matt) (C)
  EL547, L221, N76, UM664, VU481
    H-3 Chr-125; Org-9
    S-1 #327. Desc.
    N76 Desc.

Additional Hymn Suggestions
"Deep in the Shadows of the Past" (Gen)
  G50, N320, P330, S2246
"We Walk by Faith" (Gen, Rom)
  E209, EL635, G817, N256, P399, S2196, SF2196, W572
"Come, Holy Spirit, Heavenly Dove" (Rom)
  C248, E510, G279, N281, P126
"In the Cross of Christ I Glory" (Rom)
  B554, C207, E441, EL324, F251, G213, L104, N193, P84,
  UM295
"When I Survey the Wondrous Cross" (Rom)
  E474, L482, G224, P100, UM299 (PD), VU149 (Fr.)
"Blessed Assurance" (Rom)
  B334, C543, EL638, F67, G839, N473, P341, UM369 (PD),
  VU337
"Standing on the Promises" (Rom)
  AH4057, B335, C552, F69, G838, UM374 (PD)
"Open My Eyes, That I May See" (Rom)
  B502, C586, F486, G451, P324, UM454, VU371
"O Love That Wilt Not Let Me Go" (Rom)
  B292, C540, G833, L324, N485, P384, UM480 (PD), VU658
"Spirit of God, Descend upon My Heart" (Rom)
  B245, C265, EL800, F147, G688, L486, N290, P326, UM500
  (PD), VU378
"O For a Thousand Tongues to Sing" (Rom, Matt)
  B216, C5, E493, EL886, F349, G610, L559, N42, P466, UM57
  (PD), VU326 (See also WS3001)
"Gather Us In" (Matt) (O)
  C284, EL532, G401, S2236, SF2236, W665
"To God Be the Glory" (Matt)
  B4, C72, F363, G634, P485, UM98 (PD)
"Come, Labor On" (Matt)
  E541, G719, N532, P415
"Jesus Shall Reign" (Matt)
  B587, C95, E544, EL434, F238, G265, L530, N157, P423,
  UM157 (PD), VU330, W492
"Where Cross the Crowded Ways of Life" (Matt)
  C665, E609, EL719, F665, G343, L429, N543, P408, UM427
  (PD), VU681
"We All Are One in Mission" (Matt)
  EL576, G733, P435, S2243, SF2243

"Sent Out in Jesus' Name" ("*Enviado Soy de Dios*") (Matt)
  EL538, G747, S2184, SF2184
"In Remembrance of Me" (Matt, Comm.)
  B365, C403, G521, S2254
"Lord, You Give the Great Commission" (Matt) (C)
  C459, E528, EL579, G298, P429, UM584, VU512, W470
"Loving Spirit" (Father's Day)
  C244, EL397, G293, P323, S2123, VU387

Additional Contemporary Suggestions
"Falling on My Knees" (Gen, Pss)
  M155, WS3099
"I Will Call upon the Lord" (Pss)
  G621, S2002, SF2002, SP224
"We Bring the Sacrifice of Praise" (Pss)
  S2031, SF2031, SP1
"I Love You, Lord" (Pss)
  B212, G627, S2068, SF2068, SP72
"I Could Sing of Your Love Forever" (Pss, Rom)
  M63
"I Stand Amazed" (Pss, Rom)
  M79
"I Will Not Forget You" (Ps, Rom, Matt)
  M211
"O How He Loves You and Me!" (Rom)
  B146, F622, S2108, SF2108, SP113
"God Is Good All the Time" (Rom)
  AH4010, M45, WS3026
"Grace Like Rain" (Rom)
  M251
"The King of Glory Comes" (Matt)
  B127, S2091, SF2091, W501
"I'm Gonna Live So God Can Use Me" (Matt)
  C614, G700, P369, S2153, VU575

Vocal Solos
"O For a Thousand Tongues to Sing" (Rom, Matt)
  V-1   p. 32
"Here I Am" (Matt)
  V-11   p. 19

Anthems
"The God of Abraham Praise" (Gen)
Arr. David Giardiniere; Augsburg 0-8006-2025-9
SATB, organ

"In Remembrance" (Matt, Comm.)
Red/Arr. Lloyd Larson; Hope C-5899
SSA, piano, two flutes; SATB C-5565

Other Suggestions
Visuals:
  O   Oaks, tent, noon, three men eating, old man/woman/
      laugh
  P   Prayer, raised cup, recent dead, open manacles, praise
  E   Crucifix, suffering, pouring
  G   Jesus, lost/helpless, one sheep, harvest, few working,
      prayer, twelve disciples, Matt. 10:7b, 8b
Response: B474, F488, N500, UM418, st. 3-4. "We Are Climbing
  Jacob's Ladder" (Rom, Matt)
Alternate Lessons (see p. 4): Exod 19:2-8a; Ps 100

Genesis 21:8-21

[8]The boy grew and stopped nursing. On the day he stopped nursing, Abraham prepared a huge banquet. [9]Sarah saw Hagar's son laughing, the one Hagar the Egyptian had borne to Abraham. [10]So she said to Abraham, "Send this servant away with her son! This servant's son won't share the inheritance with my son Isaac."

[11]This upset Abraham terribly because the boy was his son. [12]God said to Abraham, "Don't be upset about the boy and your servant. Do everything Sarah tells you to do because your descendants will be traced through Isaac. [13]But I will make of your servant's son a great nation too, because he is also your descendant." [14]Abraham got up early in the morning, took some bread and a flask of water, and gave it to Hagar. He put the boy in her shoulder sling and sent her away.

She left and wandered through the desert near Beer-sheba. [15]Finally the water in the flask ran out, and she put the boy down under one of the desert shrubs. [16]She walked away from him about as far as a bow shot and sat down, telling herself, I can't bear to see the boy die. She sat at a distance, cried out in grief, and wept.

[17]God heard the boy's cries, and God's messenger called to Hagar from heaven and said to her, "Hagar! What's wrong? Don't be afraid. God has heard the boy's cries over there. [18]Get up, pick up the boy, and take him by the hand because I will make of him a great nation." [19]Then God opened her eyes, and she saw a well. She went over, filled the water flask, and gave the boy a drink. [20]God remained with the boy; he grew up, lived in the desert, and became an expert archer. [21]He lived in the Paran desert, and his mother found him an Egyptian wife.

Psalm 86:1-10, 16-17 (G844, N677)

[1]LORD, listen closely to me and answer me, / because I am poor and in need. / [2]Guard my life because I am faithful. / Save your servant who trusts in you—you! My God! / [3]Have mercy on me, Lord, / because I cry out to you all day long. / [4]Make your servant's life happy again / because, my Lord, I offer my life to you, / [5]because, my Lord, you are good and forgiving, / full of faithful love for all those who cry out to you. / [6]Listen closely to my prayer, LORD; / pay close attention to the sound of my requests for mercy. / [7]Whenever I am in trouble, I cry out to you, / because you will answer me. / [8]My Lord! There is no one like you among the gods! / There is nothing that can compare to your works! / [9]All the nations that you've made will come / and bow down before you, Lord; / they will glorify your name, / [10]because you are awesome / and a wonder-worker. / You are God. Just you. . . .

[16]Come back to me! Have mercy on me! / Give your servant your strength; / save this child of your servant! / [17]Show me a sign of your goodness / so that those who hate me will see it and be put to shame— / show a sign that you, LORD, / have helped me and comforted me.

Romans 6:1b-11

[1b]Should we continue sinning so grace will multiply? [2]Absolutely not! All of us died to sin. How can we still live in it? [3]Or don't you know that all who were baptized into Christ Jesus were baptized into his death? [4]Therefore, we were buried together with him through baptism into his death, so that just as Christ was raised from the dead through the glory of the Father, we too can walk in newness of life. [5]If we were united together in a death like his, we will also be united together in a resurrection like his. [6]This is what we know: the person that we used to be was crucified with him in order to get rid of the corpse that had been controlled by sin. That way we wouldn't be slaves to sin anymore, [7]because a person who has died has been freed from sin's power. [8]But if we died with Christ, we have faith that we will also live with him. [9]We know that Christ has been raised from the dead and he will never die again. Death no longer has power over him. [10]He died to sin once and for all with his death, but he lives for God with his life. [11]In the same way, you also should consider yourselves dead to sin but alive for God in Christ Jesus.

Matthew 10:24-39

[24]"Disciples aren't greater than their teacher, and slaves aren't greater than their master. [25]It's enough for disciples to be like their teacher and slaves like their master. If they have called the head of the house Beelzebul, it's certain that they will call the members of his household by even worse names.

[26]"Therefore, don't be afraid of those people because nothing is hidden that won't be revealed, and nothing secret that won't be brought out into the open. [27]What I say to you in the darkness, tell in the light; and what you hear whispered, announce from the rooftops. [28]Don't be afraid of those who kill the body but can't kill the soul. Instead, be afraid of the one who can destroy both body and soul in hell. [29]Aren't two sparrows sold for a small coin? But not one of them will fall to the ground without your Father knowing about it already. [30]Even the hairs of your head are all counted. [31]Don't be afraid. You are worth more than many sparrows.

[32]"Therefore, everyone who acknowledges me before people, I also will acknowledge before my Father who is in heaven. [33]But everyone who denies me before people, I also will deny before my Father who is in heaven.

[34]"Don't think that I've come to bring peace to the earth. I haven't come to bring peace but a sword. [35]I've come to turn a man *against his father, a daughter against her mother, and a daughter-in-law against her mother-in-law.* [36]*People's enemies are members of their own households.*

[37]"Those who love father or mother more than me aren't worthy of me. Those who love son or daughter more than me aren't worthy of me. [38]Those who don't pick up their crosses and follow me aren't worthy of me. [39]Those who find their lives will lose them, and those who lose their lives because of me will find them."

Primary Hymns and Songs for the Day

"Give to the Winds Thy Fears" (Gen, Matt) (O)
  G815, N404, P286, UM129 (PD), VU636
    H-3   Chr-71; Desc-39; Org-39
    S-1   #129. Desc.
"Children of the Heavenly Father" (Gen, Matt)
  B55, EL781, F89, L474, N487, UM141
    H-3   Chr-46; Desc-102
    S-2   #180-85. Various treatments
"Take Up Thy Cross" (Matt)
  B494, E675, EL667, G718, L398, N204, P393, UM415, VU561,
  W634
"I Have Decided to Follow Jesus" (Matt)
  B305, C344, S2129, SF2129
"We Know That Christ Is Raised" (Rom, Baptism) (C)
  E296, EL449, G485, L189, P495, UM610, VU448, W721
    H-3   Hbl-100; Chr-214; Desc- ; Org-37
    S-1   #118-27. Various treatments

Additional Hymn Suggestions

"The God of Abraham Praise" (Gen)
  B34, C24, E401, EL831, F332, G49, L544, N24, P488, UM116
  (PD), VU255, W537
"Saranam, Saranam" ("Refuge") (Gen)
  G789, UM523
"Deep in the Shadows of the Past" (Gen)
  G50, N320, P330, S2246
"I Need Thee Every Hour" (Gen, Pss)
  B450, C578, F443, G735, N517, UM397 (PD), VU671
"O Master, Let Me Walk with Thee" (Gen, Pss)
  B279, C602, E659/E660, EL818, F442, G738, L492, N503,
  P357, UM430 (PD), VU560
"Hear My Prayer, O God" (Gen, Pss)
  G782, WS3131
"His Eye Is on the Sparrow" (Gen, Matt)
  C82, G661, N475, S2146, SF2146
"Alleluia, Alleluia" (Rom)
  B170, E178, G240, P106, UM162, VU179, W441
"Amazing Grace" (Rom)
  AH4091, B330, C546, E671, EL779, F107, G649, L448, N547
  and N548, P280, UM378 (PD), VU266 (Fr.), W583
"Nearer, My God, to Thee" (Rom)
  B458, C577, N606, UM528 (PD), VU497 (Fr.)
"Baptized in Water" (Rom, Baptism)
  B362, EL456, G482, P492, S2248, W720
"It Is Well with My Soul" (Rom, Matt)
  B410, C561, EL785, F495, G840, L346, N438, UM377
"Blessed Quietness" (Rom, Matt)
  F145, C267, N284, S2142, SF2142
"God Will Take Care of You" (Matt)
  B64, F56, N460, UM130 (PD)
"Swiftly Pass the Clouds of Glory" (Matt)
  G190, P73, S2102
"You, Lord, Are Both Lamb and Shepherd" (Matt)
  G274, SF2102, VU210, WS3043

Additional Contemporary Suggestions

"Falling on My Knees" (Gen)
  M155, WS3099
"Came to My Rescue" (Gen, Pss)
  M257
"I Will Call upon the Lord" (Pss)
  G621, S2002, SF2002, SP224
"Glorify Thy Name" (Pss)
  B249, S2016, SF2016, SP19

"Lord, Listen to Your Children" (Pss)
  EL752, S2207, SF2207
"Grace Alone" (Rom)
  M100, S2162, SF2162
"God Is Good All the Time" (Rom)
  AH4010, M45, WS3026
"Amazing Grace" ("My Chains Are Gone") (Rom)
  M205, WS3104
"We Fall Down" (Rom)
  G368, M66, WS3187
"Stronger" (Rom)
  M228
"Salvation Is Here" (Rom)
  M242
"Grace Like Rain" (Rom)
  M251
"I've Got Peace Like a River" (Rom, Matt)
  B418, C530, G623, N478, P368, S2145, VU577
"Let It Be Said of Us" (Matt)
  M53
"Every Move I Make" (Matt)
  M122
"Everyday" (Matt)
  M150
"One Way" (Matt)
  M248
"We Will Follow" ("Somlandela") (Matt)
  WS3160
"The Family Prayer Song" (Father's Day)
  M54, S2188, SF2188

Vocal Solos

"His Eye Is on the Sparrow" (Gen, Matt)
  V-8   p. 166
"And Can It Be That I Should Gain" (Rom)
  V-1   p. 29
"Amazing Grace" (Rom)
  V-8   p. 56
"Lead Me to Calvary" (Matt)
  V-8   p. 226

Anthems

"Children of the Heavenly Father" (Gen, Matt)
Arr. Dan Forrest; Beckenhorst BP1920
SATB, piano, opt. flute, cello, and handbells

Concertato on "We Know that Christ Is Raised" (Rom, Baptism)
Arr. Hal Hopson; Alfred GCMR03566
SATB, organ, opt. brass and handbells

Other Suggestions

Visuals:
  O   Toddler/woman, bread/waterbag, wilderness, well,
       bow
  P   Praying hands, people bowing, Ps 86:9
  E   Baptism, crucifix, open manacles
  G   Cross for each, light, housetop, two sparrows/penny,
       hair, sword
Response: EL814, G698, WS3119. "Take, O Take Me As I Am"
  (Rom)
Alternate Lessons (see p. 4): Jer 20:7-13; Ps 69:7-10 (11-15), 16-18

Genesis 22:1-14

[1]After these events, God tested Abraham and said to him, "Abraham!"

Abraham answered, "I'm here."

[2]God said, "Take your son, your only son whom you love, Isaac, and go to the land of Moriah. Offer him up as an entirely burned offering there on one of the mountains that I will show you." [3]Abraham got up early in the morning, harnessed his donkey, and took two of his young men with him, together with his son Isaac. He split the wood for the entirely burned offering, set out, and went to the place God had described to him.

[4]On the third day, Abraham looked up and saw the place at a distance. [5]Abraham said to his servants, "Stay here with the donkey. The boy and I will walk up there, worship, and then come back to you."

[6]Abraham took the wood for the entirely burned offering and laid it on his son Isaac. He took the fire and the knife in his hand, and the two of them walked on together. [7]Isaac said to his father Abraham, "My father?"

Abraham said, "I'm here, my son."

Isaac said, "Here is the fire and the wood, but where is the lamb for the entirely burned offering?"

[8]Abraham said, "The lamb for the entirely burned offering? God will see to it, my son." The two of them walked on together.

[9]They arrived at the place God had described to him. Abraham built an altar there and arranged the wood on it. He tied up his son Isaac and laid him on the altar on top of the wood. [10]Then Abraham stretched out his hand and took the knife to kill his son as a sacrifice. [11]But the Lord's messenger called out to Abraham from heaven, "Abraham? Abraham?"

Abraham said, "I'm here."

[12]The messenger said, "Don't stretch out your hand against the young man, and don't do anything to him. I now know that you revere God and didn't hold back your son, your only son, from me." [13]Abraham looked up and saw a single ram caught by its horns in the dense underbrush. Abraham went over, took the ram, and offered it as an entirely burned offering instead of his son. [14]Abraham named that place "the Lord sees." That is the reason people today say, "On this mountain the Lord is seen."

Psalm 13 (G777, N626, UM746)

[1]How long will you forget me, Lord? Forever? / How long will you hide your face from me? / [2]How long will I be left to my own wits, / agony filling my heart? Daily? / How long will my enemy keep defeating me? / [3]Look at me! / Answer me, Lord my God! / Restore sight to my eyes! / Otherwise, I'll sleep the sleep of death, / [4]and my enemy will say, "I won!" / My foes will rejoice over my downfall. / [5]But I have trusted in your faithful love. / My heart will rejoice in your salvation. / [6]Yes, I will sing to the Lord / because he has been good to me.

Romans 6:12-23

[12]So then, don't let sin rule your body, so that you do what it wants. [13]Don't offer parts of your body to sin, to be used as weapons to do wrong. Instead, present yourselves to God as people who have been brought back to life from the dead, and offer all the parts of your body to God to be used as weapons to do right. [14]Sin will have no power over you, because you aren't under Law but under grace.

[15]So what? Should we sin because we aren't under Law but under grace? Absolutely not! [16]Don't you know that if you offer yourselves to someone as obedient slaves, that you are slaves of the one whom you obey? That's true whether you serve as slaves of sin, which leads to death, or as slaves of the kind of obedience that leads to righteousness. [17]But thank God that although you used to be slaves of sin, you gave wholehearted obedience to the teaching that was handed down to you, which provides a pattern. [18]Now that you have been set free from sin, you have become slaves of righteousness. [19](I'm speaking with ordinary metaphors because of your limitations.) Once, you offered the parts of your body to be used as slaves to impurity and to lawless behavior that leads to still more lawless behavior. Now, you should present the parts of your body as slaves to righteousness, which makes your lives holy. [20]When you were slaves of sin, you were free from the control of righteousness. [21]What consequences did you get from doing things that you are now ashamed of? The outcome of those things is death. [22]But now that you have been set free from sin and become slaves to God, you have the consequence of a holy life, and the outcome is eternal life. [23]The wages that sin pays are death, but God's gift is eternal life in Christ Jesus our Lord.

Matthew 10:40-42

[40]"Those who receive you are also receiving me, and those who receive me are receiving the one who sent me. [41]Those who receive a prophet as a prophet will receive a prophet's reward. Those who receive a righteous person as a righteous person will receive a righteous person's reward. [42]I assure you that everybody who gives even a cup of cold water to these little ones because they are my disciples will certainly be rewarded."

Primary Hymns and Songs for the Day

"The God of Abraham Praise" (Gen) (O)
B34, C24, E401, EL831, F332, G49, L544, N24, P488, UM116
(PD), VU255, W537
"Breathe on Me, Breath of God" (Rom)
B241, C254, E508, F161, G286, L488, N292, P316, UM420
(PD), VU382 (Fr.), W725
> H-3   Hbl-49; Chr-45; Desc-101; Org-166

"The Spirit Sends Us Forth to Serve" (Matt) (C)
EL551, S2241, SF2241
> H-3   Hbl-129; Chr-106; Desc-65; Org-72
> S-2   #105. Flute/violin desc.
>   #106. Harm.

Additional Hymn Suggestions

"Here I Am, Lord" (Gen)
C452, EL574, G69, P525, UM593, VU509
"We Walk by Faith" (Gen)
E209, EL635, G817, N256, P399, S2196, SF2196, W572
"Why Stand so Far Away, My God?" (Gen, Pss)
C671, G786, S2180, SF2180
"By Gracious Powers" (Gen, Pss)
E695/696, EL626, G818, N413, P342, UM517, W577
"Rock of Ages" (Gen, Rom) (C)
B342, C214, E685, EL623, F108, G438, L327, N596, UM361
"If Thou But Suffer God to Guide Thee" (Pss)
B57, C565, E635, EL769, G816, L453, N410, P282, UM142
(PD), VU285 (Fr.) and VU286
"Out of the Depths I Cry to You" (Pss)
EL600, G424, L295, N483, P240, UM515
"Be Still, My Soul" (Pss)
C566, F77, G819, N488, UM534, VU652
"How Long, O Lord" (Pss)
G777, S2209, SF2209
"Ye Servants of God" (Rom)
B589, C110, E535, EL825 (PD), F360, G299, N305, P477,
UM181 (PD), VU342
"Amazing Grace" (Rom)
AH4091, B330, C546, E671, EL779, F107, G649, L448, N547
and N548, P280, UM378 (PD), VU266 (Fr.), W583
"O Jesus, I Have Promised" (Rom)
B276, C612, E655, EL810, F402, G724/725, L503, N493,
P388/389, UM396 (PD), VU120
"Take My Life, and Let It Be" (Rom)
B277/B283, C609, E707, EL583/EL685, G697, L406, P391,
N448, UM399 (PD), VU506
"I Am Thine, O Lord" (Rom)
AH4087, B290, C601, F455, N455, UM419 (PD)
"Where Cross the Crowded Ways of Life" (Rom, Matt)
C665, E609, EL719, F665, G343, L429, N543, P408, UM427
(PD), VU681
"*Jesu, Jesu*" (Rom, Matt)
B501, C600, E602, EL708, G203, N498, P367, UM432,
VU593, W431, S-1 #63. Vocal part
"There's a Spirit in the Air" (Matt)
B393, C257, P433, N294, UM192, VU582, W531
"O Master, Let Me Walk with Thee" (Matt)
B279, C602, E659/E660, EL818, F442, G738, L492, N503,
P357, UM430 (PD), VU560
"*Cuando el Pobre*" ("When the Poor Ones") (Matt)
C662, EL725, G762, P407, UM434, VU702
"God Made from One Blood" (Matt)
C500, N427, S2170, SF2170, VU554
"Together We Serve" (Matt)
G767, S2175, SF2175

"Let Us Build a House Where Love Can Dwell"
EL641, G301 (See also WS3152)
"In Remembrance of Me" (Matt, Comm.)
B365, C403, G521, S2254
"As We Gather at Your Table" (Matt, Comm.)
EL522, N332, S2268, SF2268, VU457
"This Is My Song" (Independence Day)
C722, EL887, G340, N591, UM437

Additional Contemporary Suggestions

"We Fall Down" (Gen, Rom)
G368, M66, WS3187
"Falling on My Knees" (Gen, Pss)
M155, WS3099
"Your Love, Oh Lord" (Gen, Pss)
M189
"I Will Call upon the Lord" (Pss)
G621, S2002, SF2002, SP224
"How Great Are You, Lord" (Pss, Rom)
M103
"Grace Alone" (Rom)
M100, S2162, SF2162
"In the Lord I'll Be Ever Thankful" (Rom)
G654, S2195, SF2195
"I Am Crucified with Christ" (Rom)
SP208
"Amazing Grace" ("My Chains Are Gone") (Rom)
M205, WS3104
"Stronger" (Rom)
M228
"Grace Like Rain" (Rom)
M251
"Make Me a Servant" (Matt)
S2176, SF2176, SP193
"People Need the Lord" (Matt)
B557, S2244, SF2244

Vocal Solos

"And Can It Be That I Should Gain" (Rom)
> V-1   p. 29

"Take My Life" ("Consecration") (Rom, Matt)
> V-8   p. 262

Anthems

"The Lamb" (Gen)
Ron Barnett; MorningStar MSM-50-3102
Unison, piano

"Be Still and Know" (Pss)
Michael John Trotta; MorningStar MSM-50-6415
SATB, keyboard

Other Suggestions

Visuals:
> **O**   Gen 22:1c, mountain, dawn, donkey, man/boy, wood/
>   knife, altar, angel. ram
> **P**   Praying hands, eyes/sleep, joy, singing
> **E**   Baptism, manacles, Rom. 6:23
> **G**   Welcome, cup of water offered

Greeting: N819 (Gen, Pss) or N816 (Matt) or N824 (Rom)
Alternate Lessons (see p. 4): Jer 28:5-9, Ps 89:1-4, 15-18

Genesis 24:34-38, 42-49, 58-67

[34]The man said, "I am Abraham's servant." [35]The LORD has richly blessed my master, has made him a great man, and has given him flocks, cattle, silver, gold, men servants, women servants, camels, and donkeys. [36]My master's wife Sarah gave birth to a son for my master in her old age, and he's given him everything he owns. [37]My master made me give him my word: 'Don't choose a wife for my son from the Canaanite women, in whose land I'm living. [38]No, instead, go to my father's household and to my relatives and choose a wife for my son.' . . .

[42]"Today I arrived at the spring, and I said, 'LORD, God of my master Abraham, if you wish to make the trip I'm taking successful, [43]when I'm standing by the spring and the young woman who comes out to draw water and to whom I say, "Please give me a little drink of water from your jar," [44]and she responds to me, "Drink, and I will draw water for your camels too," may she be the woman the LORD has selected for my master's son.' [45]Before I finished saying this to myself, Rebekah came out with her water jar on her shoulder and went down to the spring to draw water. And I said to her, 'Please give me something to drink.' [46]She immediately lowered her water jar and said, 'Drink, and I will give your camels something to drink too.' So I drank and she also gave water to the camels. [47]Then I asked her, 'Whose daughter are you?' And she said, 'The daughter of Bethuel, Nahor's son whom Milcah bore him.' I put a ring in her nose and bracelets on her arms. [48]I bowed and worshipped the LORD and blessed the LORD, the God of my master Abraham, who led me in the right direction to choose the granddaughter of my master's brother for his son. [49]Now if you're loyal and faithful to my master, tell me. If not, tell me so I will know where I stand either way." . . .

[58]They called Rebekah and said to her, "Will you go with this man?"

She said, "I will go."

[59]So they sent off their sister Rebekah, her nurse, Abraham's servant, and his men. [60]And they blessed Rebekah, saying to her,

"May you, our sister, become
  thousands of ten thousand;
  may your children possess
  their enemies' cities."

[61]Rebekah and her young women got up, mounted the camels, and followed the man. So the servant took Rebekah and left.

[62]Now Isaac had come from the region of Beer-lahai-roi and had settled in the arid southern plain. [63]One evening, Isaac went out to inspect the pasture, and while staring he saw camels approaching. [64]Rebekah stared at Isaac. She got down from the camel [65]and said to the servant, "Who is this man walking through the pasture to meet us?"

The servant said, "He's my master." So she took her headscarf and covered herself. [66]The servant told Isaac everything that had happened. [67]Isaac brought Rebekah into his mother Sarah's tent. He married Rebekah and loved her. So Isaac found comfort after his mother's death.

Psalm 45:10-17 (G333, N650)

[10]Listen, daughter; pay attention, and listen closely! / Forget your people and your father's house. / [11]Let the king desire your beauty. / Because he is your master, bow down to him now. / [12]The city of Tyre, the wealthiest of all, / will seek your favor with gifts, [13]with riches of every sort / for the royal princess, dressed in pearls, / her robe embroidered with gold. / [14]In robes of many colors, she is led to the king. / Her attendants, the young women servants following her, / are presented to you as well. / [15]As they enter the king's palace, / they are led in with celebration and joy. / [16]Your sons, great king, will succeed your fathers; / you will appoint them as princes throughout the land. / [17]I will perpetuate your name from one generation to the next / so the peoples will praise you forever and always.

Romans 7:15-25a

[15]I don't know what I'm doing, because I don't do what I want to do. Instead, I do the thing that I hate. [16]But if I'm doing the thing that I don't want to do, I'm agreeing that the Law is right. [17]But now I'm not the one doing it anymore. Instead, it's sin that lives in me. [18]I know that good doesn't live in me—that is, in my body. The desire to do good is inside of me, but I can't do it. [19]I don't do the good that I want to do, but I do the evil that I don't want to do. [20]But if I do the very thing that I don't want to do, then I'm not the one doing it anymore. Instead, it is sin that lives in me that is doing it.

[21]So I find that, as a rule, when I want to do what is good, evil is right there with me. [22]I gladly agree with the Law on the inside, [23]but I see a different law at work in my body. It wages a war against the law of my mind and takes me prisoner with the law of sin that is in my body. [24]I'm a miserable human being. Who will deliver me from this dead corpse? [25a]Thank God through Jesus Christ our Lord!

Matthew 11:16-19, 25-30

[16]"To what will I compare this generation? It is like a child sitting in the marketplaces calling out to others, [17]'We played the flute for you and you didn't dance. We sang a funeral song and you didn't mourn.' [18]For John came neither eating nor drinking, and they say, 'He has a demon.' [19]Yet the Human One came eating and drinking, and they say, 'Look, a glutton and a drunk, a friend of tax collectors and sinners.' But wisdom is proved to be right by her works." . . .

[25]At that time Jesus said, "I praise you, Father, Lord of heaven and earth, because you've hidden these things from the wise and intelligent and have shown them to babies. [26]Indeed, Father, this brings you happiness.

[27]"My Father has handed all things over to me. No one knows the Son except the Father. And nobody knows the Father except the Son and anyone to whom the Son wants to reveal him.

[28]"Come to me, all you who are struggling hard and carrying heavy loads, and I will give you rest. [29]Put on my yoke, and learn from me. I'm gentle and humble. And you will find rest for yourselves. [30]My yoke is easy to bear, and my burden is light."

Primary Hymns and Songs for the Day

"Love Divine, All Loves Excelling" (Rom) (O)
B208, C517, E657, EL631, F21, G366, N43, P376, UM384
(PD), VU333, W588
>   H-3   Chr-134; Desc-18; Org-13
>   S-1   #41-42. Desc. and harm.

"Lord, I Want to Be a Christian" (Rom)
B489, C589, F421, G729, N454, P372 (PD), UM402
>   H-3   Chr-130

"Come, Thou Fount of Every Blessing" (Rom, Matt, Comm.)
AH4086, B15/18, C16, E686, EL807, F318, G475, L499,
N459, P356, UM400 (PD), VU559
>   H-3   Chr-57; Desc-79; Org-96
>   S-1   #244. Desc.

"Just a Closer Walk with Thee" (Rom, Matt)
B448, C557, EL697, F591, G835, S2158, SF2158

"How Firm a Foundation" (Rom, Matt) (C)
B338, C618, E636/637, EL796, F32, G463, L507, N407, P361,
UM529 (PD), VU660, W585
>   H-3   Hbl-27, 69; Chr-102; Desc-41; Org-41
>   S-1   #133. Harm.
>   #134. Performance note

Additional Hymn Suggestions

"When Love Is Found" (Gen, Pss, Comm.)
C499, N362, UM643, VU489, W745

"Your Love, O God, Has Called Us Here" (Gen, Pss)
B509, E353, N361, UM647

"O Morning Star, How Fair and Bright" (Pss)
C105, E497, EL308, G827, L76, N158, P69, UM247, VU98

"Taste and See" (Pss, Comm.)
EL493, G520, S2267, SF2267

"To God Be the Glory" (Rom)
B4, C72, F363, G634, P485, UM98 (PD)

"*Camina, Pueblo de Dios*" ("Walk On, O People of God") (Rom)
N614, P296, UM305

"Spirit of God, Descend upon My Heart" (Rom)
B245, C265, EL800, F147, G688, L486, N290, P326, UM500
(PD), VU378

"Blessed Jesus, at Thy Word" (Rom)
E440, EL520, G395, N74, P454, UM596 (PD), VU500

"If Thou But Suffer God to Guide Thee" (Rom, Matt)
B57, C565, E635, EL769, G816, L453, N410, P282, UM142
(PD), VU285 (Fr.) and VU286

"O Love, How Deep" (Rom, Matt)
E448/449, EL322, G618, L88, N209, P83, UM267, VU348

"Come, Ye Sinners, Poor and Needy" (Rom, Matt)
B323 (PD), G415, UM340, W756

"Jesus Loves Me" (Matt)
B344 (PD), C113, EL595 (PD), F226, G188, N327, P304,
UM191, VU365

"Be Thou My Vision" (Matt)
B60, C595, E488, EL793, G450, N451, P339, UM451, VU642

"What a Friend We Have in Jesus" (Matt)
B182, C585, EL742, F466, G465, L439, N506, P403, UM526
(PD), VU661

"Blessed Quietness" (Matt)
F145, C267, N284, S2142, SF2142

"You Are Mine" (Matt)
EL581, G177, S2218, SF2218

"Feed Us, Lord" (Matt, Comm.)
G501, WS3167

Additional Contemporary Suggestions

"I Could Sing of Your Love Forever" (Pss, Matt)
M63

"I Love You, Lord" (Pss)
B212, G627, S2068, SF2068, SP72

"In the Lord I'll Be Ever Thankful" (Rom)
G654, S2195, SF2195

"Thank You, Lord" (Rom)
AH4081, C531, UM84

"My Tribute" (Rom)
B153, C39, F365, N14, SP118, UM99; V-8 p. 5 Vocal solo

"Thy Word Is a Lamp" (Rom)
C326, G458, SP183, UM601

"Counting on God" (Rom)
M226

"Give Thanks" (Rom, Matt)
C528, G647, S2036, SF2036, SP170

"You Who Are Thirsty" (Matt)
S2132, SP219

"Cares Chorus" (Matt)
S2215, SF2215, SP221

"Fill My Cup, Lord" (Matt, Comm.)
C351, F481, UM641 (refrain only), WS3093

"Still" (Matt)
M216, WS3134

"Come to the Table of Grace" (Matt, Comm.)
G507, WS3168

"Holy and Anointed One" (Matt)
M32

"My Redeemer Lives" (Matt)
M73

Vocal Solos

"A Song of Joy" (Pss, Matt)
>   V-11   p. 2

"Just a Closer Walk with Thee" (Rom, Matt)
>   V-5 (2)   p. 31
>   V-8   p. 323

"I Will Sing of Thy Great Mercies" (Matt)
>   V-4   p. 43

Anthems

"Jesus Loves Me" (SOCM42) (Matt)
Arr. Christopher Aspaas; Augsburg 9781451499032
TTBB, piano

"Tune My Heart to Sing God's Praise!" (Rom, Matt, Comm.)
Arr. Lloyd Larson; Beckenhorst Press BP1962
SATB, keyboard

Other Suggestions

Visuals:
>   O   Spring, water jar, nose ring, bracelets, ring
>   P   Many-colored/gold robes, joy, bride/maids
>   E   Open Bible, manacles (closed/open), Christ
>   G   Children playing, marketplace, flute, John, Jesus,
>   eating/drinking, infants, burdens, yoke

Additional Hymn Suggestions: N361–64 (Gen, Pss)
Call to Prayer: WS3094. "Come to Me" (Matt)
Sung Confession: WS3138. "Confession" (Rom)
Alternate Lessons (see p. 4): Zech 9:9-12, Ps 145:8-14

Genesis 25:19-34

[19]These are the descendants of Isaac, Abraham's son. Abraham became the father of Isaac. [20]Isaac was 40 years old when he married Rebekah the daughter of Bethuel the Aramean and the sister of Laban the Aramean, from Paddan-aram. [21]Isaac prayed to the LORD for his wife, since she was unable to have children. The LORD was moved by his prayer, and his wife Rebekah became pregnant. [22]But the boys pushed against each other inside of her, and she said, "If this is what it's like, why did it happen to me?"

So she went to ask the LORD. [23]And the LORD said to her,

"Two nations are in your womb;
 two different peoples will emerge from your body.
One people will be stronger than the other;
 the older will serve the younger."

[24]When she reached the end of her pregnancy, she discovered that she had twins. [25]The first came out red all over, clothed with hair, and she named him Esau. [26]Immediately afterward, his brother came out gripping Esau's heel, and she named him Jacob. Isaac was 60 years old when they were born.

[27]When the young men grew up, Esau became an outdoorsman who knew how to hunt, and Jacob became a quiet man who stayed at home. [28]Isaac loved Esau because he enjoyed eating game, but Rebekah loved Jacob. [29]Once when Jacob was boiling stew, Esau came in from the field hungry [30]and said to Jacob, "I'm starving! Let me devour some of this red stuff." That's why his name is Edom.

[31]Jacob said, "Sell me your birthright today."

[32]Esau said, "Since I'm going to die anyway, what good is my birthright to me?"

[33]Jacob said, "Give me your word today." And he did. He sold his birthright to Jacob. [34]So Jacob gave Esau bread and lentil stew. He ate, drank, got up, and left, showing just how little he thought of his birthright.

Psalm 119:105-112 (G64, N701, UM840)

[105]Your word is a lamp before my feet / and a light for my journey./ [106]I have sworn, and I fully mean it: / I will keep your righteous rules. / [107]I have been suffering so much— / LORD, make me live again according to your promise. / [108]Please, LORD, accept my spontaneous gifts of praise. / Teach me your rules! / [109]Though my life is constantly in danger, / I won't forget your Instruction. / [110]Though the wicked have set a trap for me, / I won't stray from your precepts. / [111]Your laws are my possession forever / because they are my heart's joy. / [112]I have decided to keep your statutes forever, every last one.

Romans 8:1-11

[1]So now there isn't any condemnation for those who are in Christ Jesus. [2]The law of the Spirit of life in Christ Jesus has set you free from the law of sin and death. [3]God has done what was impossible for the Law, since it was weak because of selfishness. God condemned sin in the body by sending his own Son to deal with sin in the same body as humans, who are controlled by sin. [4]He did this so that the righteous requirement of the Law might be fulfilled in us. Now the way we live is based on the Spirit, not based on selfishness. [5]People whose lives are based on selfishness think about selfish things, but people whose lives are based on the Spirit think about things that are related to the Spirit. [6]The attitude that comes from selfishness leads to death, but the attitude that comes from the Spirit leads to life and peace. [7]So the attitude that comes from selfishness is hostile to God. It doesn't submit to God's Law, because it can't. [8]People who are self-centered aren't able to please God.

[9]But you aren't self-centered. Instead you are in the Spirit, if in fact God's Spirit lives in you. If anyone doesn't have the Spirit of Christ, they don't belong to him. [10]If Christ is in you, the Spirit is your life because of God's righteousness, but the body is dead because of sin. [11]If the Spirit of the one who raised Jesus from the dead lives in you, the one who raised Christ from the dead will give life to your human bodies also, through his Spirit that lives in you.

Matthew 13:1-9, 18-23

[1]That day Jesus went out of the house and sat down beside the lake. [2]Such large crowds gathered around him that he climbed into a boat and sat down. The whole crowd was standing on the shore.

[3]He said many things to them in parables: "A farmer went out to scatter seed. [4]As he was scattering seed, some fell on the path, and birds came and ate it. [5]Other seed fell on rocky ground where the soil was shallow. They sprouted immediately because the soil wasn't deep. [6]But when the sun came up, it scorched the plants, and they dried up because they had no roots. [7]Other seed fell among thorny plants. The thorny plants grew and choked them. [8]Other seed fell on good soil and bore fruit, in one case a yield of one hundred to one, in another case a yield of sixty to one, and in another case a yield of thirty to one. [9]Everyone who has ears should pay attention." . . .

[18]"Consider then the parable of the farmer. [19]Whenever people hear the word about the kingdom and don't understand it, the evil one comes and carries off what was planted in their hearts. This is the seed that was sown on the path. [20]As for the seed that was spread on rocky ground, this refers to people who hear the word and immediately receive it joyfully. [21]Because they have no roots, they last for only a little while. When they experience distress or abuse because of the word, they immediately fall away. [22]As for the seed that was spread among thorny plants, this refers to those who hear the word, but the worries of this life and the false appeal of wealth choke the word, and it bears no fruit. [23]As for what was planted on good soil, this refers to those who hear and understand, and bear fruit and produce—in one case a yield of one hundred to one, in another case a yield of sixty to one, and in another case a yield of thirty to one."

Primary Hymns and Songs for the Day
"Spirit of the Living God" (Rom) (O)
  B244, C259, G288, N283, P322, SP131, UM393, VU376
    S-1   #212 Vocal desc. idea
"Thy Word Is a Lamp" (Pss, Matt)
  C326, G458, SP183, UM601
"*Sois la Semilla*" ("You Are the Seed") (Matt)
  C478, N528, UM583
"O Blessed Spring" (Matt)
  EL447, S2076, SF2076, VU632
    H-3   Chr-200; Org-45
"Hymn of Promise" (Matt) (C)
  C638, G250. N433, UM707, VU703
    H-3   Chr-112; Org-117
    S-1   #270. Desc.

Additional Hymn Suggestions
"The God of Abraham Praise" (Gen)
  B34, C24, E401, EL831, F332, G49, L544, N24, P488, UM116 (PD), VU255, W537
"Where Cross the Crowded Ways of Life" (Gen)
  C665, E609, EL719, F665, G343, L429, N543, P408, UM427 (PD), VU681
"For the Healing of the Nations" (Gen)
  C668, G346, N576, UM428, VU678, W643
"Out of the Depths" (Gen)
  C510, N554, S2136, SF2136, VU611
"God Made from One Blood" (Gen)
  C500, N427, S2170, SF2170, VU554
"Come Down, O Love Divine" (Gen, Rom)
  C582, E516, EL804, G282, L508, N289, P313, UM475, VU367, W472
"Lead Me, Lord" (Pss)
  C593, N774, UM473 (PD), VU662
"Blessed Jesus, at Thy Word" (Pss, Matt)
  E440, EL520, G395, N74, P454, UM596 (PD), VU500
"O Word of God Incarnate" (Pss, Matt)
  C322, E632, EL514, G459, L231, N315, P327, UM598 (PD), VU499
"Wonderful Words of Life" (Pss, Matt)
  B261, C323, F29, N319, UM600 (PD)
"Be Thou My Vision" (Pss, Rom)
  B60, C595, E488, EL793, G450, N451, P339, UM451, VU642
"Just a Closer Walk with Thee" (Pss, Rom)
  B448, C557, EL697, F591, G835, S2158, SF2158
"Lead Me, Guide Me" (Pss, Rom)
  C583, EL768, G740, S2214, SF2214
"O For a Thousand Tongues to Sing" (Rom)
  B216, C5, E493, EL886, F349, G610, L559, N42, P466, UM57 (PD), VU326 (See also WS3001)
"To God Be the Glory" (Rom)
  B4, C72, F363, G634, P485, UM98 (PD)
"Alas! And Did My Savior Bleed" (Rom)
  AH4067, B139/145, C204, EL337, F274, G212, L98, N199/N200, P78, UM294/UM359
"Every Time I Feel the Spirit" (Rom)
  C592, G66, N282, P315, UM404
"Breathe on Me, Breath of God" (Rom, Matt)
  B241, C254, E508, F161, G286, L488, N292, P316, UM420 (PD), VU382 (Fr.), W725
"Holy Spirit, Truth Divine" (Rom, Matt)
  C241, EL398, L257, N63, P321, UM465 (PD), VU368
"Come, Ye Thankful People, Come" (Matt) (O)
  B637, C718, E290, EL693, F392, G367, L407, N422, P551, UM694 (PD), VU516, W759

"Come, We That Love the Lord" (Matt) (C)
  B525, E392, N379, UM732, VU715, W552
"Marching to Zion" (Matt) (C)
  AH4153, B524, C707, EL625, F550, N382, UM733 (PD), VU714
"Creating God, Your Fingers Trace" (Matt)
  C335, E394/394, EL684, N462, P134, UM109, VU265
"Lord, Dismiss Us with Thy Blessing" (Matt)
  C439, E344, EL545, F520, G546, L259, N77, P538, UM671 (PD), VU425
"When God Restored Our Common Life" (Matt)
  G74, S2182, SF2182
"Come to Tend God's Garden (Matt)
  N586
"Mothering God, You Gave Me Birth" (Matt, Comm.)
  C83, EL735, G7, N467, S2050, SF2050, VU320

Additional Contemporary Suggestions
"The Family Prayer Song" (Gen)
  M54, S2188, SF2188
"Cry of My Heart" (Pss)
  M39, S2165, SF2165
"Jesus, the Light of the World" (Pss)
  WS3056 (See also AH4038, G127, N160)
"Breathe" (Pss, Rom)
  M61, WS3112
"More Precious than Silver" (Pss, Rom)
  S2065, SF2065, SP99
"My Tribute" (Rom)
  B153, C39, F365, N14, SP118, UM99; V-8 p. 5

Vocal Solo
"Spirit Song" (Rom)
  C352, SP134, UM347
"Stronger" (Rom)
  M228
"Step by Step" (Matt)
  G743, M51, WS3004

Vocal Solos
"Just a Closer Walk with Thee" (Pss, Rom, Matt)
  V-5 (2)   p. 31
  V-8   p. 323
"Keep A-Inchin' Along" (Rom, Matt)
  V-7   p. 32

Anthems
"Just a Closer Walk with Thee" (Pss, Rom, Matt)
Arr. Graham Farrell; Hinshaw HPC7099
SATB, organ and trumpet solo

"The Best of Rooms" (Matt)
Z. Randall Stroope; MorningStar MSM-50-5808
SATB, organ

Other Suggestions
Visuals:
  O   Wedding, prayer, newborn twins, birth certificate
  P   Open Bible, lamp, path, open hand, snare, Ps 119:11
  E   Open manacles, Spirit symbols, open/closed Bibles
  G   Boat/sea, sower/seed, birds/sun/thorns, soil/grain
Alternate Lessons (see p. 4): Isa 55:10-13, Ps 65:(1-8), 9-13
Response: N608. "Christ will Come Again" (Matt)

Genesis 28:10-19a

[10]Jacob left Beer-sheba and set out for Haran. [11]He reached a certain place and spent the night there. When the sun had set, he took one of the stones at that place and put it near his head. Then he lay down there. [12]He dreamed and saw a raised staircase, its foundation on earth and its top touching the sky, and God's messengers were ascending and descending on it. [13]Suddenly the LORD was standing on it and saying, "I am the LORD, the God of your father Abraham and the God of Isaac. I will give you and your descendants the land on which you are lying. [14]Your descendants will become like the dust of the earth; you will spread out to the west, east, north, and south. Every family of earth will be blessed because of you and your descendants. [15]I am with you now, I will protect you everywhere you go, and I will bring you back to this land. I will not leave you until I have done everything that I have promised you."

[16]When Jacob woke from his sleep, he thought to himself, The LORD is definitely in this place, but I didn't know it. [17]He was terrified and thought, This sacred place is awesome. It's none other than God's house and the entrance to heaven. [18]After Jacob got up early in the morning, he took the stone that he had put near his head, set it up as a sacred pillar, and poured oil on the top of it. [19a]He named that sacred place Bethel.

Psalm 139:1-12, 23-24 (G28/29/426, N715, P248, UM854)

[1]LORD, you have examined me. / You know me. / [2]You know when I sit down and when I stand up. / Even from far away, you comprehend my plans. / [3]You study my traveling and resting. / You are thoroughly familiar with all my ways. / [4]There isn't a word on my tongue, LORD, / that you don't already know completely. / [5]You surround me—front and back. / You put your hand on me. / [6]That kind of knowledge is too much for me; / it's so high above me that I can't fathom it. / [7]Where could I go to get away from your spirit? / Where could I go to escape your presence? / [8]If I went up to heaven, you would be there. / If I went down to the grave, you would be there too! / [9]If I could fly on the wings of dawn, / stopping to rest only on the far side of the ocean— / [10]even there your hand would guide me; / even there your strong hand would hold me tight! / [11]If I said, "The darkness will definitely hide me; / the light will become night around me," / [12]even then the darkness isn't too dark for you! / Nighttime would shine bright as day, / because darkness is the same as light to you! . . . .

[23]Examine me, God! Look at my heart! / Put me to the test! Know my anxious thoughts! / [24]Look to see if there is any idolatrous way in me, / then lead me on the eternal path!

Romans 8:12-25

[12]So then, brothers and sisters, we have an obligation, but it isn't an obligation to ourselves to live our lives on the basis of selfishness. [13]If you live on the basis of selfishness, you are going to die. But if you put to death the actions of the body with the Spirit, you will live. [14]All who are led by God's Spirit are God's sons and daughters. [15]You didn't receive a spirit of slavery to lead you back again into fear, but you received a Spirit that shows you are adopted as his children. With this Spirit, we cry, "Abba, Father." [16]The same Spirit agrees with our spirit, that we are God's children. [17]But if we are children, we are also heirs. We are God's heirs and fellow heirs with Christ, if we really suffer with him so that we can also be glorified with him.

[18]I believe that the present suffering is nothing compared to the coming glory that is going to be revealed to us. [19]The whole creation waits breathless with anticipation for the revelation of God's sons and daughters. [20]Creation was subjected to frustration, not by its own choice—it was the choice of the one who subjected it—but in the hope [21]that the creation itself will be set free from slavery to decay and brought into the glorious freedom of God's children. [22]We know that the whole creation is groaning together and suffering labor pains up until now. [23]And it's not only the creation. We ourselves who have the Spirit as the first crop of the harvest also groan inside as we wait to be adopted and for our bodies to be set free. [24]We were saved in hope. If we see what we hope for, that isn't hope. Who hopes for what they already see? [25]But if we hope for what we don't see, we wait for it with patience.

Matthew 13:24-30, 36-43

[24]Jesus told them another parable: "The kingdom of heaven is like someone who planted good seed in his field. [25]While people were sleeping, an enemy came and planted weeds among the wheat and went away. [26]When the stalks sprouted and bore grain, then the weeds also appeared.

[27]"The servants of the landowner came and said to him, 'Master, didn't you plant good seed in your field? Then how is it that it has weeds?'

[28]"'An enemy has done this,' he answered.

"The servants said to him, 'Do you want us to go and gather them?'

[29]"But the landowner said, 'No, because if you gather the weeds, you'll pull up the wheat along with them. [30]Let both grow side by side until the harvest. And at harvesttime I'll say to the harvesters, "First gather the weeds and tie them together in bundles to be burned. But bring the wheat into my barn." ' " . . .

[36]Jesus left the crowds and went into the house. His disciples came to him and said, "Explain to us the parable of the weeds in the field."

[37]Jesus replied, "The one who plants the good seed is the Human One. [38]The field is the world. And the good seeds are the followers of the kingdom. But the weeds are the followers of the evil one. [39]The enemy who planted them is the devil. The harvest is the end of the present age. The harvesters are the angels. [40]Just as people gather weeds and burn them in the fire, so it will be at the end of the present age. [41]The Human One will send his angels, and they will gather out of his kingdom all things that cause people to fall away and all people who sin. [42]He will throw them into a burning furnace. People there will be weeping and grinding their teeth. [43]Then the righteous will shine like the sun in their Father's kingdom. Those who have ears should hear."

Primary Hymns and Songs for the Day

"Come, Ye Thankful People, Come" (Matt) (O)
   B637, C718, E290, EL693, F392, G367, L407, N422, P551,
   UM694 (PD), VU516, W759
         H-3   Hbl-54; Chr-58; Desc-94; Org-137
         S-1   #302-303. Harm. with desc.
"We Are Climbing Jacob's Ladder" (Gen)
   B474, F488, N500, UM418
         H-3   Chr-205
         S-1   #187. Choral arr.
"Nearer, My God, to Thee" (Gen)
   B458, C577, N606, UM528 (PD), VU497 (Fr.)
"Bring Forth the Kingdom" (Matt)
   S2190, SF2190
"Love Divine, All Loves Excelling" (Rom) (C)
   B208, C517, E657, EL631, F21, G366, N43, P376, UM384
   (PD), VU333, W588

Additional Hymn Suggestions

"Touch the Earth Lightly" (Gen)
   C693, EL739, G713, N569, VU307, WS3129
"Feed Us, Lord" (Gen, Comm.)
   G501, WS3167
"Guide My Feet" (Gen, Pss)
   G741, N497, P354, S2208
"Lead Me, Guide Me" (Gen, Pss)
   C583, EL768, G740, S2214, SF2214
"Creating God, Your Fingers Trace" (Pss)
   C335, E394/394, EL684, N462, P134, UM109, VU265
"Praise to the Lord, the Almighty" (Pss)
   B14, C25, E390, EL858 (PD) and 859, F337, G35, L543, N22,
   P482, UM139, VU220 (Fr.) and VU221, W547
"I Want to Walk as a Child of the Light" (Pss)
   E490, EL815, G377, UM206, W510
"Savior, Again to Thy Dear Name" (Pss)
   E345, EL534, F519, L262, N80, P539, UM663 (PD), VU426
"I Was There to Hear Your Borning Cry" (Pss, Bapt.)
   C75, EL732, G488, N351, S2051, SF2051, VU644
"We Are Called" (Pss)
   EL720, G749, S2172, SF2172
"Womb of Life" (Pss, Rom, Comm.)
   C14, G3, N274, S2046, SF2046
"Mothering God, You Gave Me Birth" (Pss, Rom)
   C83, EL735, G7, N467, S2050, SF2050, VU320
"Loving Spirit" (Pss, Rom)
   C244, EL397, G293, P323, S2123, VU387
"Gather Us In" (Pss, Matt)
   C284, EL532, G401, S2236, SF2236, W665
"Every Time I Feel the Spirit" (Rom)
   C592, G66, N282, P315, UM404
"We Shall Overcome" (Rom)
   AH4047/4048, C630, G379, N570, UM533
"The Church's One Foundation" (Rom)
   B350, C272, E525, EL654, F547, G321, L369, N386, P442,
   UM545/546, VU332 (Fr.)
"Holy" ("Santo") (Rom)
   EL762, G594, S2019, SF2019
"O Holy Spirit, Root of Life" (Rom)
   C251, EL399, N57, S2121, SF2121, VU379
"Baptized in Water" (Rom, Baptism)
   B362, EL456, G482, P492, S2248, W720
"Sois la Semilla" ("You Are the Seed") (Matt)
   C478, N528, UM583
"God the Sculptor of the Mountains" (Matt)
   EL736, G5, S2060, SF2060

"We All Are One in Mission" (Matt)
   EL576, G733, P435, S2243, SF2243
"Come to Tend God's Garden" (Matt)
   N586
"Christ Will Come Again" (Matt)
   N608

Additional Contemporary Suggestions

"Surely the Presence of the Lord" (Gen)
   C263, SP243, UM328; S-2 #200. Stanzas for soloist
"He Who Began a Good Work in You" (Gen)
   S2163, SF2163, SP180
"Holy Ground" (Gen)
   B224, C112, G406, S2272, SF2272, SP86
"Shout to the North" (Gen)
   G319, M99, WS3042
"How Great Is Our God" (Gen, Pss)
   M117, WS3003
"Lead Me, Lord" (Gen, Pss)
   M108
"He Knows My Name" (Gen, Pss)
   M109
"God of Wonders" (Pss)
   M80, WS3034
"Spirit of the Living God" (Rom)
   B244, C259, G288, N283, P322, SP131, UM393, VU376
"Holy" ("Santo") (Rom)
   EL762, G594, S2019, SF2019
"Holy, Holy" (Rom)
   B254, F149, P140, S2039, SP141
"On Eagle's Wings" (Matt)
   B71, C77, EL787, G43, N775, UM143, VU807/808, S-2 #143
   Stanzas for soloist
"Days of Elijah" (Matt)
   M139, WS3186

Vocal Solos

"Sing a Song of Joy" (Gen, Pss)
   V-4   p. 2
"I Am His, and He Is Mine" (Gen, Rom)
   V-8   p. 348

Anthems

"Jacob's Ladder" (Gen)
Arr. John Carter; Beckenhorst BP1378
SATB, organ

"The Kingdom of God" (Matt)
Robert J. Powell; Paraclete Press PPMO1036
SATB, organ

Other Suggestions

Visuals:
   O   Night, stone, ladder, angels, dust, gate, oil
   P   Sit/stand, path, bed, hand, wings, sea, light/dark
   E   Children, fear, adoption papers, will, fruit, labor
   G   Seed, bundle of weeds/wheat, scythe, harvest/field,
           angels, fire, Matt 13:43, sun
Opening Prayer: N828 or N831 (Rom., Matt.)
Sung Prayer: WS3115. "Covenant Prayer" (Rom)
Alternate Lessons (see p. 4): Wis 12:13, 16-19 or Isa 44:6-8, Ps 86:11-17

Genesis 29:15-28

¹⁵Laban said to Jacob, "You shouldn't have to work for free just because you are my relative. Tell me what you would like to be paid."

¹⁶Now Laban had two daughters: the older was named Leah and the younger Rachel. ¹⁷Leah had delicate eyes, but Rachel had a beautiful figure and was good-looking. ¹⁸Jacob loved Rachel and said, "I will work for you for seven years for Rachel, your younger daughter."

¹⁹Laban said, "I'd rather give her to you than to another man. Stay with me."

²⁰Jacob worked for Rachel for seven years, but it seemed like a few days because he loved her. ²¹Jacob said to Laban, "The time has come. Give me my wife so that I may sleep with her." ²²So Laban invited all the people of that place and prepared a banquet. ²³However, in the evening, he took his daughter Leah and brought her to Jacob, and he slept with her. ²⁴Laban had given his servant Zilpah to his daughter Leah as her servant. ²⁵In the morning, there she was—Leah! Jacob said to Laban, "What have you done to me? Didn't I work for you to have Rachel? Why did you betray me?"

²⁶Laban said, "Where we live, we don't give the younger woman before the oldest. ²⁷Complete the celebratory week with this woman. Then I will give you this other woman too for your work, if you work for me seven more years." ²⁸So that is what Jacob did. He completed the celebratory week with this woman, and then Laban gave him his daughter Rachel as his wife.

Psalm 105:1-11, 45b (G59, N691, UM828)

¹Give thanks to the Lord; / call upon his name; / make his deeds known to all people! / ²Sing to God; / sing praises to the Lord; / dwell on all his wondrous works! / ³Give praise to God's holy name! / Let the hearts rejoice of all those seeking the Lord! / ⁴Pursue the Lord and his strength; / seek his face always! / ⁵Remember the wondrous works he has done, / all his marvelous works, and the justice he declared— / ⁶you who are the offspring of Abraham, his servant, / and the children of Jacob, his chosen ones. / ⁷The Lord—he is our God. / His justice is everywhere throughout the whole world. / ⁸God remembers his covenant forever, / the word he commanded to a thousand generations, / ⁹which he made with Abraham, / the solemn pledge he swore to Isaac. / ¹⁰God set it up as binding law for Jacob, / as an eternal covenant for Israel, / ¹¹promising, "I hereby give you the land of Canaan / as your allotted inheritance." . . .

⁴⁵ᵇPraise the Lord!

Romans 8:26-39

²⁶In the same way, the Spirit comes to help our weakness. We don't know what we should pray, but the Spirit himself pleads our case with unexpressed groans. ²⁷The one who searches hearts knows how the Spirit thinks, because he pleads for the saints, consistent with God's will. ²⁸We know that God works all things together for good for the ones who love God, for those who are called according to his purpose. ²⁹We know this because God knew them in advance, and he decided in advance that they would be conformed to the image of his Son. That way his Son would be the first of many brothers and sisters. ³⁰Those who God decided in advance would be conformed to his Son, he also called. Those whom he called, he also made righteous. Those whom he made righteous, he also glorified.

³¹So what are we going to say about these things? If God is for us, who is against us? ³²He didn't spare his own Son but gave him up for us all. Won't he also freely give us all things with him?

³³Who will bring a charge against God's elect people? It is God who acquits them. ³⁴Who is going to convict them? It is Christ Jesus who died, even more, who was raised, and who also is at God's right side. It is Christ Jesus who also pleads our case for us.

³⁵Who will separate us from Christ's love? Will we be separated by trouble, or distress, or harassment, or famine, or nakedness, or danger, or sword? ³⁶As it is written,

We are being put to death all day long for your sake.
We are treated like sheep for slaughter.

³⁷But in all these things we win a sweeping victory through the one who loved us. ³⁸I'm convinced that nothing can separate us from God's love in Christ Jesus our Lord: not death or life, not angels or rulers, not present things or future things, not powers ³⁹or height or depth, or any other thing that is created.

Matthew 13:31-33, 44-52

³¹He told another parable to them: "The kingdom of heaven is like a mustard seed that someone took and planted in his field. ³²It's the smallest of all seeds. But when it's grown, it's the largest of all vegetable plants. It becomes a tree so that the birds in the sky come and nest in its branches."

³³He told them another parable: "The kingdom of heaven is like yeast, which a woman took and hid in a bushel of wheat flour until the yeast had worked its way through all the dough." . . .

⁴⁴"The kingdom of heaven is like a treasure that somebody hid in a field, which someone else found and covered up. Full of joy, the finder sold everything and bought that field.

⁴⁵"Again, the kingdom of heaven is like a merchant in search of fine pearls. ⁴⁶When he found one very precious pearl, he went and sold all that he owned and bought it.

⁴⁷"Again, the kingdom of heaven is like a net that people threw into the lake and gathered all kinds of fish. ⁴⁸When it was full, they pulled it to the shore, where they sat down and put the good fish together into containers. But the bad fish they threw away. ⁴⁹That's the way it will be at the end of the present age. The angels will go out and separate the evil people from the righteous people, ⁵⁰and will throw the evil ones into a burning furnace. People there will be weeping and grinding their teeth.

⁵¹"Have you understood all these things?" Jesus asked.

They said to him, "Yes."

⁵²Then he said to them, "Therefore, every legal expert who has been trained as a disciple for the kingdom of heaven is like the head of a household who brings old and new things out of their treasure chest."

Primary Hymns and Songs for the Day

"I Love Thy Kingdom, Lord" (Matt) (O)
  B354, C274, E524, F545, G310, L368, N312, P441, UM540
          H-3   Hbl-53; Chr-167; Desc-97; Org-147
          S-1   #311. Desc. and harm.
"Bring Forth the Kingdom" (Matt)
  S2190, SF2190
"Seek Ye First" (Matt)
  B478, C354, E711, G175, P333, UM405, SP182, VU356
"O Day of God, Draw Nigh" (Matt, Pss) (C)
  B623, C700, E601, N611, P452, UM730 (PD), VU688 and
  VU689 (Fr.)
          H-3   Hbl-79; Chr-141; Desc-95; Org-143
          S-1   #306-308. Various treatments

Additional Hymn Suggestions

"When Love Is Found" (Gen)
  C499, N362, UM643, VU489, W745
"We Sing to You, O God" (Pss)
  EL791, N9, S2001, SF2001
"Praise Our God Above" (Pss, Matt)
  N424, P480, S2061
"Holy God, We Praise Thy Name" (Rom)
  E366, F385, EL414 (PD), G4, L535, N276, P460, UM79,
  VU894 (Fr.), W524
"Children of the Heavenly Father" (Rom)
  B55, EL781, F89, L474, N487, UM141
"Hope of the World" (Rom)
  C538, E472, G734, L493, N46, P360, UM178, VU215
"I Am Thine, O Lord" (Rom)
  AH4087, B290, C601, F455, N455, UM419 (PD)
"O Love That Wilt Not Let Me Go" (Rom)
  B292, C540, G833, L324, N485, P384, UM480 (PD), VU658
"Prayer Is the Soul's Sincere Desire" (Rom)
  F446 (PD), N508, UM492
"By Gracious Powers" (Rom)
  E695/696, EL626, G818, N413, P342, UM517, W577
"Like the Murmur of the Dove's Song" (Rom)
  C245, E513, EL403, G285, N270, P314, UM544, VU205
"O Holy Spirit, Root of Life" (Rom)
  C251, EL399, N57, S2121, SF2121, VU379
"Jesus, Priceless Treasure" (Matt)
  E701, EL775, F277, G830, L457, N480 P365, UM532 (PD),
  VU667 and VU668 (Fr.)
"*Sois la Semilla*" ("You Are the Seed") (Matt)
  C478, N528, UM583
"Come, Ye Thankful People, Come" (Matt)
  B637, C718, E290, EL693, F392, G367, L407, N422, P551,
  UM694 (PD), VU516, W759
"We All Are One in Mission" (Matt)
  EL576, G733, P435, S2243, SF2243
"Enter in the Realm of God" (Matt)
  N615

Additional Contemporary Suggestions

"You Never Let Go" (Gen, Rom)
  M258
"How Great Is Our God" (Pss)
  M117, WS3003
"You Are Good" (Pss)
  AH4018, M124, WS3014
"I'm Goin' a Sing When the Spirit Says Sing" (Rom)
  AH4073, UM333
"Change My Heart, O God" (Rom)
  EL801, G695, S2152, SF2152, SP195,

"Cry of My Heart" (Rom)
  M39, S2165, SF2165
"In His Time" (Rom)
  B53, S2203, SF2203, SP39
"Hallelujah" ("Your Love Is Amazing") (Rom)
  M118, WS3027
"Shout to the North" (Rom)
  G319, M99, WS3042
"Your Grace Is Enough" (Rom)
  M191, WS3106
"No Greater Love" (Rom)
  M25
"I Could Sing of Your Love Forever" (Rom)
  M63
"Show Me Your Ways" (Rom)
  M107
"Good to Me" (Rom)
  M164
"In Christ Alone" (Rom)
  M138, WS3105
"You Are My All in All" (Rom, Matt)
  G519, SP220, WS3040
"More Precious than Silver" (Matt)
  S2065, SF2065, SP99
"Fill My Cup, Lord" (Matt) *See esp. st. 2–3*
  C351, F481, UM641 (refrain only), WS3093
"Days of Elijah" (Matt)
  M139, WS3186
"Jesus, You Are My Life" (Matt)
  M33
"When It's All Been Said and Done" (Matt)
  M115
"Forever Reign" (Matt)
  M256

Vocal Solos

"If God Be For Us" (Rom)
  V-2
"Who Shall Separate Us?" (Rom)
  V-8   p. 265

Anthems

"By Gracious Powers" (Rom)
Russell Schulz-Widmar, Augsburg Fortress 9781451451573
SATB, organ

"The Kingdom" (Matt)
Andre Thomas; Hinshaw HMC-1307
SATB, keyboard

Other Suggestions

Visuals:
  O   Young lovers, "7", feast, engagement
  P   Singing, hearts, covenant, praise
  E   Prayer, Spirit, heart, Rom 8:28, 31, 38, Jesus, newborn,
            cross, disaster, love
  G   Mustard seed/shrub, birds/nest, yeast/flour, treasure,
            pearl, net/fish/baskets, fire, new/old
Call to Prayer: N521. "In Solitude" (Rom.)
Litany: F50 God Is For Us or F90 Hope (Rom.)
Affirmation of Faith: UM887, WSL76 or WSL77 (Rom.)
Alternate Lessons (see p. 4): 1 Kgs 3:5-12, Ps 119:129-136

Genesis 32:22-31

[22]Jacob got up during the night, took his two wives, his two women servants, and his eleven sons, and crossed the Jabbok River's shallow water. [23]He took them and everything that belonged to him, and he helped them cross the river. [24]But Jacob stayed apart by himself, and a man wrestled with him until dawn broke. [25]When the man saw that he couldn't defeat Jacob, he grabbed Jacob's thigh and tore a muscle in Jacob's thigh as he wrestled with him. [26]The man said, "Let me go because the dawn is breaking."

But Jacob said, "I won't let you go until you bless me."

[27]He said to Jacob, "What's your name?" and he said, "Jacob." [28]Then he said, "Your name won't be Jacob any longer, but Israel, because you struggled with God and with men and won."

[29]Jacob also asked and said, "Tell me your name."

But he said, "Why do you ask for my name?" and he blessed Jacob there. [30]Jacob named the place Peniel, "because I've seen God face-to-face, and my life has been saved." [31]The sun rose as Jacob passed Penuel, limping because of his thigh.

Psalm 17:1-7, 15 (G211, N629, UM749)

[1]Listen to what's right, Lord; / pay attention to my cry! / Listen closely to my prayer; / it's spoken by lips that don't lie! / [2]My justice comes from you; / let your eyes see what is right! / [3]You have examined my heart, / testing me at night. / You've looked me over closely, / but haven't found anything wrong. / My mouth doesn't sin. / [4]But these other people's deeds? / I have avoided such violent ways / by the command from your lips. / [5]My steps are set firmly on your paths; / my feet haven't slipped. / [6]I cry out to you because you answer me. / So tilt your ears toward me now— / listen to what I'm saying! / [7]Manifest your faithful love in amazing ways / because you are the one / who saves those who take refuge in you, / saving them from their attackers / by your strong hand. . . .

[15]But me? I will see your face in righteousness; / when I awake, I will be filled full by seeing your image.

Romans 9:1-5

[1]I'm speaking the truth in Christ—I'm not lying, as my conscience assures me with the Holy Spirit: [2]I have great sadness and constant pain in my heart. [3]I wish I could be cursed, cut off from Christ if it helped my brothers and sisters, who are my flesh-and-blood relatives. [4]They are Israelites. The adoption as God's children, the glory, the covenants, the giving of the Law, the worship, and the promises belong to them. [5]The Jewish ancestors are theirs, and the Christ descended from those ancestors. He is the one who rules over all things, who is God, and who is blessed forever. Amen.

Matthew 14:13-21

[13]When Jesus heard about John, he withdrew in a boat to a deserted place by himself. When the crowds learned this, they followed him on foot from the cities. [14]When Jesus arrived and saw a large crowd, he had compassion for them and healed those who were sick. [15]That evening his disciples came and said to him, "This is an isolated place and it's getting late. Send the crowds away so they can go into the villages and buy food for themselves."

[16]But Jesus said to them, "There's no need to send them away. You give them something to eat."

[17]They replied, "We have nothing here except five loaves of bread and two fish."

[18]He said, "Bring them here to me." [19]He ordered the crowds to sit down on the grass. He took the five loaves of bread and the two fish, looked up to heaven, blessed them and broke the loaves apart and gave them to his disciples. Then the disciples gave them to the crowds. [20]Everyone ate until they were full, and they filled twelve baskets with the leftovers. [21]About five thousand men plus women and children had eaten.

Primary Hymns and Songs for the Day

"When Morning Gilds the Skies" (Gen) (O)
  B221, C100, E427, EL853 (PD), F322, G667, L546, N86,
  P487, UM185, VU339 (Fr.), W675
"O Love That Wilt Not Let Me Go" (Gen)
  B292, C540, G833, L324, N485, P384, UM480 (PD), VU658
    H-3   Chr-146; Org-142
"Break Thou the Bread of Life" (Matt, Comm.)
  B263, C321, EL515, F30, G460, L235, N321, P329, UM599
  (PD), VU501
    H-3   Chr-44; Org-15
"Here, O My Lord, I See Thee" (Gen, Comm.) (C)
  C416, E318, G517, L211, N336, P520, UM623, VU459

Additional Hymn Suggestions

"Source and Sovereign, Rock and Cloud" (Gen)
  C12, G11, UM113
"The God of Abraham Praise" (Gen)
  B34, C24, E401, EL831, F332, G49, L544, N24, P488, UM116
  (PD), VU255, W537
"Be Thou My Vision" (Gen) (O)
  B60, C595, E488, EL793, G450, N451, P339, UM451, VU642
"We Walk by Faith" (Gen)
  E209, EL635, G817, N256, P399, S2196, SF2196, W572
"Praise God for This Holy Ground" (Gen)
  G405, WS3009
"Jesus, Lover of My Soul" (Gen, Pss)
  B180 (PD), C542, E699, G440, N546, P303, UM479, VU669
"Sweet Hour of Prayer" (Gen, Matt)
  B445, C570, F439, N505, UM496 (PD)
"God Be with You till We Meet Again" (Gen, Matt) (C)
  C434, EL536, F523, G541/542, N81, P540, UM672/673,
  VU422/423
"All My Hope Is Firmly Grounded" (Pss, Rom)
  C88, E665, EL757, N408, UM132, VU654/655
"If Thou But Suffer God to Guide Thee" (Rom)
  B57, C565, E635, EL769, G816, L453, N410, P282, UM142
  (PD), VU285 (Fr.) and VU286
"Standing on the Promises" (Rom)
  AH4057, B335, C552, F69, G838, UM374 (PD)
"Holy Spirit, Truth Divine" (Rom)
  C241, EL398, L257, N63, P321, UM465 (PD), VU368
"The Church of Christ in Every Age" (Rom)
  B402, C475, EL729, G320, L433, N306, P421, UM589,
  VU601, W626
"*Tú Has Venido a la Orilla*" ("Lord, You Have Come to the
  Lakeshore") (Matt)
  C342, EL817, G721, N173, P377, UM344, VU563
"Softly and Tenderly, Jesus Is Calling" (Matt)
  B312, C340, EL608 (PD), F432, G418, N449, UM348
"Dear Lord and Father of Mankind" (Matt)
  (Alternate Text: "Parent of Us All")
  B267, C594, E652/563, F422, G169, L506, N502, P345,
  UM358 (PD), VU608
"Let Us Break Bread Together" (Matt, Comm.)
  B366, C425, EL471 (PD), F564, G525, L212, N330, P513,
  UM618, VU480, W727
"Bread of the World" (Matt, Comm.)
  C387, E301, G499, N346, P502, UM624, VU461
"All Who Hunger" (Matt, Comm.)
  C419, EL461, G509, S2126, SF2126, VU460
"Come, Share the Lord" (Matt, Comm.)
  C408, G510, S2269, SF2269, VU469

Additional Contemporary Suggestions

"Surely the Presence of the Lord" (Gen)
  SP243; S-2, #200 Stanzas for soloist
  C263, SP243, UM328; S-2 #200. Stanzas for soloist
"Spirit of the Living God" (Gen)
  B244, C259, G288, N283, P322, SP131, UM393, VU376
"Seek Ye First" (Gen)
  B478, C354, E711, G175, P333, UM405, SP182, VU356
"Holy Ground" (Gen)
  B224, C112, G406, S2272, SF2272, SP86
"How Great Is Our God" (Gen, Pss)
  M117, WS3003
"He Knows My Name" (Gen, Pss)
  M109
"The Steadfast Love of the Lord" (Gen, Pss)
  SP185
"Your Love, Oh Lord" (Gen, Pss)
  M189
"I Will Call upon the Lord" (Pss)
  G621, S2002, SF2002, SP224
"O Lord, Hear My Prayer" (Pss)
  EL751, G471, S2200, SF2200
"Hallelujah" ("Your Love Is Amazing") (Pss)
  M118, WS3027
"Forever" (Pss. Rom)
  M68, WS3023
"Above All" (Rom)
  M77; V-3 (2) p. 17 Vocal Solo
"Jesus, We Are Here" (Matt)
  EL529, G392, S2273, SF2273
"You Are" (Matt)
  M243
"You Who Are Thirsty" (Matt, Comm.)
  S2132, SF2132, SP219
"Spirit Song" (Matt, Comm.)
  C352, SP134, UM347

Vocal Solos

"Come, O Thou Traveler Unknown" (Gen)
  V-1   p. 21
  V-9   p. 44
"Softly and Tenderly" (Matt)
  V-5 (3)   p. 52

Anthems

"Come O Thou Traveler Unknown" (Gen)
David Mennicke, MorningStar MSM-50-8109
SATB, two-part or unison, piano, opt. C instruments

"The Hour of Banquet and of Song" (Matt, Comm.)
Arr. Howard Helvey; Hinshaw Music HMC2440
SATB, organ

Other Suggestions
Visuals:
  O   River ford, wrestling, hip, cane, Gen 32:26b, name
  P   Prayer, heart, night, feet/path, listening
  E   Broken heart, salvation history, Christ
  G   Boat, healing, loaves, two fish, twelve baskets, 5,000
Reading: F25. God, Thou Art Love (Gen.)
Poem: UM387. "Come, O Thou Traveler Unknown" (Gen)
Alternate Lessons (see p. 4): Isa 55:1-5, Ps 145:8-9, 14-21

Genesis 37:1-4, 12-28

¹Jacob lived in the land of Canaan where his father was an immigrant. ²This is the account of Jacob's descendants. Joseph was 17 years old and tended the flock with his brothers. While he was helping the sons of Bilhah and Zilpah, his father's wives, Joseph told their father unflattering things about them. ³Now Israel loved Joseph more than any of his other sons because he was born when Jacob was old. Jacob had made for him a long robe. ⁴When his brothers saw that their father loved him more than any of his brothers, they hated him and couldn't even talk nicely to him. . . .

¹²Joseph's brothers went to tend their father's flocks near Shechem. ¹³Israel said to Joseph, "Aren't your brothers tending the sheep near Shechem? Come, I'll send you to them."

And he said, "I'm ready."

¹⁴Jacob said to him, "Go! Find out how your brothers are and how the flock is, and report back to me."

So Jacob sent him from the Hebron Valley. When he approached Shechem, ¹⁵a man found him wandering in the field and asked him, "What are you looking for?"

¹⁶Joseph said, "I'm looking for my brothers. Tell me, where are they tending the sheep?"

¹⁷The man said, "They left here. I heard them saying, 'Let's go to Dothan.'" So Joseph went after his brothers and found them in Dothan.

¹⁸They saw Joseph in the distance before he got close to them, and they plotted to kill him. ¹⁹The brothers said to each other, "Here comes the big dreamer. ²⁰Come on now, let's kill him and throw him into one of the cisterns, and we'll say a wild animal devoured him. Then we will see what becomes of his dreams!"

²¹When Reuben heard what they said, he saved him from them, telling them, "Let's not take his life." ²²Reuben said to them, "Don't spill his blood! Throw him into this desert cistern, but don't lay a hand on him." He intended to save Joseph from them and take him back to his father.

²³When Joseph reached his brothers, they stripped off Joseph's long robe, ²⁴took him, and threw him into the cistern, an empty cistern with no water in it. ²⁵When they sat down to eat, they looked up and saw a caravan of Ishmaelites coming from Gilead, with camels carrying sweet resin, medicinal resin, and fragrant resin on their way down to Egypt. ²⁶Judah said to his brothers, "What do we gain if we kill our brother and hide his blood? ²⁷Come on, let's sell him to the Ishmaelites. Let's not harm him because he's our brother; he's family." His brothers agreed. ²⁸When some Midianite traders passed by, they pulled Joseph up out of the cistern. They sold him to the Ishmaelites for twenty pieces of silver, and they brought Joseph to Egypt.

Psalm 105:1-6, 16-22, 45b (G59, N691, UM828)

¹Give thanks to the LORD; / call upon his name; / make his deeds known to all people! / ²Sing to God; / sing praises to the Lord; / dwell on all his wondrous works! / ³Give praise to God's holy name! / Let the hearts rejoice of all those seeking the LORD! / ⁴Pursue the LORD and his strength; / seek his face always! / ⁵Remember the wondrous works he has done, / all his marvelous works, and the justice he declared— / ⁶you who are the offspring of Abraham, his servant, / and the children of Jacob, his chosen ones. . . .

¹⁶When God called for a famine in the land, / destroying every source of food, / ¹⁷he sent a man ahead of them, / who was sold as a slave: it was Joseph. / ¹⁸Joseph's feet hurt in his shackles; / his neck was in an iron collar, / ¹⁹until what he predicted actually happened, / until what the LORD had said proved him true. / ²⁰The king sent for Joseph and set him free; / the ruler of many people released him. / ²¹The king made Joseph master of his house and ruler over everything he owned, / ²²to make sure his princes acted according to his will, / and to teach wisdom to his advisors. . . .

⁴⁵ᵇPraise the LORD!

Romans 10:5-15

⁵Moses writes about the righteousness that comes from the Law: *The person who does these things will live by them.* ⁶But the righteousness that comes from faith talks like this: *Don't say in your heart, "Who will go up into heaven?"* (that is, to bring Christ down) ⁷or *"Who will go down into the region below?"* (that is, to bring Christ up from the dead). ⁸But what does it say? *The word is near you, in your mouth and in your heart* (that is, the message of faith that we preach). ⁹Because if you confess with your mouth "Jesus is Lord" and in your heart you have faith that God raised him from the dead, you will be saved. ¹⁰Trusting with the heart leads to righteousness, and confessing with the mouth leads to salvation. ¹¹The scripture says, *All who have faith in him won't be put to shame.* ¹²There is no distinction between Jew and Greek, because the same Lord is Lord of all, who gives richly to all who call on him. ¹³*All who call on the Lord's name will be saved.*

¹⁴So how can they call on someone they don't have faith in? And how can they have faith in someone they haven't heard of? And how can they hear without a preacher? ¹⁵And how can they preach unless they are sent? As it is written, *How beautiful are the feet of those who announce the good news.*

Matthew 14:22-33

²²Right then, Jesus made the disciples get into the boat and go ahead to the other side of the lake while he dismissed the crowds. ²³When he sent them away, he went up onto a mountain by himself to pray. Evening came and he was alone. ²⁴Meanwhile, the boat, fighting a strong headwind, was being battered by the waves and was already far away from land. ²⁵Very early in the morning he came to his disciples, walking on the lake. ²⁶When the disciples saw him walking on the lake, they were terrified and said, "It's a ghost!" They were so frightened they screamed.

²⁷Just then Jesus spoke to them, "Be encouraged! It's me. Don't be afraid."

²⁸Peter replied, "Lord, if it's you, order me to come to you on the water."

²⁹And Jesus said, "Come."

Then Peter got out of the boat and was walking on the water toward Jesus. ³⁰But when Peter saw the strong wind, he became frightened. As he began to sink, he shouted, "Lord, rescue me!"

³¹Jesus immediately reached out and grabbed him, saying, "You man of weak faith! Why did you begin to have doubts?" ³²When they got into the boat, the wind settled down.

³³Then those in the boat worshipped Jesus and said, "You must be God's Son!"

Primary Hymns and Songs for the Day

"Guide Me, O Thou Great Jehovah" (Gen) (O)
  B56, C622, E690, EL618, F608, G65, L343, N18/19, P281,
  UM127 (PD), VU651 (Fr.)
        H-3   Hbl-25, 51, 58; Chr-89; Desc-26; Org-23
        S-1   #76-77. Desc. and harm.
"Children of the Heavenly Father" (Gen, Pss)
  B55, EL781, F89, L474, N487, UM141
        H-3   Chr-46; Desc-102
        S-2   #180-85. Various treatments
"Holy" ("*Santo*") (Rom)
  EL762, G594, S2019, SF2019
"Here I Am, Lord" (Gen, Matt, Rom) (C)
  C452, EL574, G69, P525, UM593, VU509
        H-3   Chr-97; Org-54

Additional Hymn Suggestions

"We Shall Overcome" (Gen)
  AH4047/4048, C630, G379, N570, UM533
"Praise to the Lord, the Almighty" (Gen, Pss)
  B14, C25, E390, EL858 (PD) and 859, F337, G35, L543, N22,
  P482, UM139, VU220 (Fr.) and VU221, W547
"Many Gifts, One Spirit" (Rom)
  N177, UM114
"I Love to Tell the Story" (Rom)
  B572, C480, EL661, G462, L390, N522, UM156, VU343
"At the Name of Jesus" (Rom)
  B198, E435, EL416, F351, G264, L179, P148, UM168, VU335,
  W499
"Here, O Lord, Your Servants Gather" (Rom, Comm.)
  B179, C278, EL530, G311, N72, P465, UM552, VU362
"Just As I Am" (Rom)
  B303/307, C339, E693, EL592, F417, G442, L296, N207,
  P370, UM357 (PD), VU508
"We Walk by Faith" (Rom, Matt)
  E209, EL635, G817, N256, P399, S2196, SF2196, W572
"Take, O Take Me As I Am" (Rom, Matt)
  EL814, G698, WS3119
"How Firm a Foundation" (Rom, Matt)
  B338, C618, E636/637, EL796, F32, G463, L507, N407, P361,
  UM529 (PD), VU660, W585
"Give to the Winds Thy Fears" (Matt)
  G815, N404, P286, UM129 (PD), VU636
"I Sing the Almighty Power of God" (Matt)
  B42, C64, E398, G32, N12, P288, UM152, VU231, W502
"O Sing a Song of Bethlehem" (Matt)
  B120, F208, G159, N51, P308, UM179 (PD)
"Dear Lord and Father of Mankind" (Matt)
  (Alternate Text: "Parent of Us All")
  B267, C594, E652/563, F422, G169, L506, N502, P345,
  UM358 (PD), VU608
"Jesus, Lover of My Soul" (Matt)
  B180 (PD), C542, E699, G440, N546, P303, UM479, VU669
"Jesus, Savior, Pilot Me" (Matt)
  EL755, L334, N441, UM509 (PD), VU637
"I'm So Glad Jesus Lifted Me" (Matt)
  C529, EL860 (PD), N474, S2151, SF2151
"My Life Flows On" (Matt)
  C619, EL763, G821, N476, S2212, SF2212, VU716
"You Are Mine" (Matt)
  EL581, G177, S2218, SF2218

Additional Contemporary Suggestions

"Give Thanks" (Pss)
  C528, G647, S2036, SF2036, SP170
"In the Lord I'll Be Ever Thankful" (Pss)
  G654, S2195, SF2195
"How Great Is Our God" (Pss)
  M117, WS3003
"Step by Step" (Pss. Matt)
  G743, M51, WS3004
"Forever" (Pss, Matt)
  M68, WS3023
"Came to My Rescue" (Pss, Matt)
  M257
"He Is Lord" (Rom)
  B178, C117, F234, SP122, UM177
"God Is So Good" (Rom)
  B23, G658, S2056, SF2056
"God Is Good All the Time" (Rom)
  AH4010, M45, WS3026
"Come, Now Is the Time to Worship" (Rom)
  M56, WS3176
"The Heavens Shall Declare" (Rom)
  M111
"We Will Dance" (Rom)
  M140
"One Bread, One Body" (Rom, Comm.)
  C393, EL496, G530, UM620, VU467
"I Will Call upon the Lord" (Rom, Matt)
  G621, S2002, SF2002, SP224
"Cares Chorus" (Matt)
  S2215, SF2215, SP221
"In Christ Alone" (Matt)
  M138, WS3105
"You Never Let Go" (Matt)
  M258

Vocal Solos

"Here I Am" (Gen)
  V-11   p. 19
"Jesus, Lover of My Soul" (Matt)
  V-1   p. 37

Anthems

"Here I Am, Lord" (Gen, Matt, Rom)
Arr. Craig Courtney; Beckenhorst BP1403
SATB, piano, opt. flute

"O Lord Increase My Faith" (Matt)
Orlando Gibbons; E.C. Schirmer #375
SATB a cappella

Other Suggestions

Visuals:
  O   Staff, colorful robe, pit, caravan, twenty coins, Egypt
  P   Singing, hearts, famine, open manacles, iron collar
  E   Christ, heart, speaking, Rom. 10:8b, 13, 15b, feet
  G   Boat, mountain, prayer, storm/sea, Jesus/Peter/water,
            Matt. 14:30b, 31b, 33b
Opening Prayer: N828 (Matt.)
Medley: "Take This Moment, Sign, and Space" (WS3118) and
  "Take, O Take Me As I Am" (EL814, G698, WS3119) (John)
Litany: B556. Evangelism and Missions (Rom.)
Alternate Lessons (see p. 4): 1 Kgs 19:9-18, Ps 85:8-13

Genesis 45:1-15

[1]Joseph could no longer control himself in front of all his attendants, so he declared, "Everyone, leave now!" So no one stayed with him when he revealed his identity to his brothers. [2]He wept so loudly that the Egyptians and Pharaoh's household heard him. [3]Joseph said to his brothers, "I'm Joseph! Is my father really still alive?" His brothers couldn't respond because they were terrified before him.

[4]Joseph said to his brothers, "Come closer to me," and they moved closer. He said, "I'm your brother Joseph! The one you sold to Egypt. [5]Now, don't be upset and don't be angry with yourselves that you sold me here. Actually, God sent me before you to save lives. [6]We've already had two years of famine in the land, and there are five years left without planting or harvesting. [7]God sent me before you to make sure you'd survive and to rescue your lives in this amazing way. [8]You didn't send me here; it was God who made me a father to Pharaoh, master of his entire household, and ruler of the whole land of Egypt.

[9]"Hurry! Go back to your father. Tell him this is what your son Joseph says: 'God has made me master of all of Egypt. Come down to me. Don't delay. [10]You may live in the land of Goshen, so you will be near me, your children, your grandchildren, your flocks, your herds, and everyone with you. [11]I will support you there, so you, your household, and everyone with you won't starve, since the famine will still last five years.' [12]You and my brother Benjamin have seen with your own eyes that I'm speaking to you. [13]Tell my father about my power in Egypt and about everything you've seen. Hurry and bring my father down here." [14]He threw his arms around his brother Benjamin's neck and wept, and Benjamin wept on his shoulder. [15]He kissed all of his brothers and wept, embracing them. After that, his brothers were finally able to talk to him.

Psalm 133 (G397/398, N712, P241, UM850)

[1]Look at how good and pleasing it is / when families live together as one! / [2]It is like expensive oil poured over the head, / running down onto the beard— / Aaron's beard!— / which extended over the collar of his robes. / [3]It is like the dew on Mount Hermon / streaming down onto the mountains of Zion, / because it is there that the LORD has commanded the blessing: / everlasting life.

Romans 11:1-2a, 29-32

[1]So I ask you, has God rejected his people? Absolutely not! I'm an Israelite, a descendant of Abraham, from the tribe of Benjamin. [2a]God hasn't rejected his people, whom he knew in advance. . . .

[29]God's gifts and calling can't be taken back. [30]Once you were disobedient to God, but now you have mercy because they were disobedient. [31]In the same way, they have also been disobedient because of the mercy that you received, so now they can receive mercy too. [32]God has locked up all people in disobedience, in order to have mercy on all of them.

Matthew 15:(10-20), 21-28

[10]Jesus called the crowd near and said to them, "Listen and understand. [11]It's not what goes into the mouth that contaminates a person in God's sight. It's what comes out of the mouth that contaminates the person."

[12]Then the disciples came and said to him, "Do you know that the Pharisees were offended by what you just said?"

[13]Jesus replied, "Every plant that my heavenly Father didn't plant will be pulled up. [14]Leave the Pharisees alone. They are blind people who are guides to blind people. But if a blind person leads another blind person, they will both fall into a ditch."

[15]Then Peter spoke up, "Explain this riddle to us."

[16]Jesus said, "Don't you understand yet? [17]Don't you know that everything that goes into the mouth enters the stomach and goes out into the sewer? [18]But what goes out of the mouth comes from the heart. And that's what contaminates a person in God's sight. [19]Out of the heart come evil thoughts, murders, adultery, sexual sins, thefts, false testimonies, and insults. [20]These contaminate a person in God's sight. But eating without washing hands doesn't contaminate in God's sight."

[21]From there, Jesus went to the regions of Tyre and Sidon. [22]A Canaanite woman from those territories came out and shouted, "Show me mercy, Son of David. My daughter is suffering terribly from demon possession." [23]But he didn't respond to her at all.

His disciples came and urged him, "Send her away; she keeps shouting out after us."

[24]Jesus replied, "I've been sent only to the lost sheep, the people of Israel."

[25]But she knelt before him and said, "Lord, help me."

[26]He replied, "It is not good to take the children's bread and toss it to dogs."

[27]She said, "Yes, Lord. But even the dogs eat the crumbs that fall off their masters' table."

[28]Jesus answered, "Woman, you have great faith. It will be just as you wish." And right then her daughter was healed.

Primary Hymns and Songs for the Day

"My Faith Looks Up to Thee" (Matt) (O)
    B416, C576, E691, EL759, G829, L479, P383, UM452, VU663
        H-3   Hbl-77; Chr-138; Org-108
        S-2   #142. Flute/violin desc.
"Where Charity and Love Prevail" (Gen, Pss)
    E581, EL359, G316, L126, N396, UM549
        S-2   #162. Harm.
"Bind Us Together" (Gen, Pss)
    S2226, SF2226, SP140
"This Is a Day of New Beginnings" (Gen, Matt) (C)
    B370, C518, N417, UM383, W661
        H-3   Chr-196

Additional Hymn Suggestions

"Great Is Thy Faithfulness" (Gen) (O)
    B54, C86, EL733, F98, G39, N423, P276, UM140, VU288
"Forgive Our Sins as We Forgive" (Gen)
    E674, EL605, G444, L307, P347, UM390, VU364
"Forgive Us, Lord" ("*Perdón, Señor*") (Gen)
    G431, S2134, SF2134
"God, How Can We Forgive" (Gen)
    G445, S2169, SF2169
"Come, Share the Lord" (Gen, Comm.)
    C408, G510, S2269, SF2269, VU469
"Draw Us in the Spirit's Tether" (Gen, Comm.)
    C392, EL470, G529, N337, P504, UM632, VU479, W731
"Help Us Accept Each Other" (Gen, Pss)
    C487, G754, N388, P358, UM560, W656
"God Made from One Blood" (Gen, Pss)
    C500, N427, S2170, SF2170, VU554
"Rock of Ages, Cleft for Me" (Gen, Matt) (C)
    B342, C214, E685, EL623, F108, G438, L327, N596, UM361
"When God Restored Our Common Life" (Gen, Matt)
    G74, S2182, SF2182
"Blest Be the Tie That Binds" (Pss)
    B387, C433, EL656, F560, G306, L370, N393, P438, UM557
    (PD), VU602
"In Christ There Is No East or West" (Pss, Rom)
    B385, C687, E529, EL650 (PD), F685, G317/318, L359,
    N394/N395, P439/P440, UM548, VU606, W659
"There's a Wideness in God's Mercy" (Rom, Matt)
    B25, C73, E470, EL587/88F115, F115, G435, L290, N23,
    P298, UM121, VU271, W595
"O Christ, the Healer" (Rom, Matt)
    C503. EL610, G793, L360, N175, P380, UM265, W747
"Standing on the Promises" (Rom, Matt)
    AH4057, B335, C552, F69, G838, UM374 (PD)
"O Spirit of the Living God" (Rom, Matt)
    N263, UM539
"O For a Thousand Tongues to Sing" (Matt)
    B216, C5, E493, EL886, F349, G610, L559, N42, P466, UM57
    (PD), VU326 (See also WS3001)
"I'll Praise My Maker While I've Breath" (Matt)
    B35, C20, E429 (PD), G806, P253, UM60, VU867
"All Hail the Power of Jesus' Name" (Matt)
    B200/B201/B202, C91/C92, E450/E451, EL634, F325/
    F326/F327, G263, L328/L329, N304, P142/P143, UM154/
    UM155, VU334, W494
"Jesus Shall Reign" (Matt)
    B587, C95, E544, EL434, F238, G265, L530, N157, P423,
    UM157 (PD), VU330, W492
"Silence, Frenzied, Unclean Spirit" (Matt)
    C186, G180/G181, N176, UM264, VU620, W751
    Alternate Tunes: EBENEZER or BEACH SPRING

"My Hope Is Built" (Matt)
    B406, C537, EL596/597, F92, G353, L293/ 294, N368, P379,
    UM368 (PD)
"Lord, I Want to Be a Christian" (Matt)
    B489, C589, F421, G729, N454, P372 (PD), UM402
"We Walk by Faith" (Matt)
    E209, EL635, G817, N256, P399, S2196, SF2196, W572
"Healer of Our Every Ill" (Matt)
    C506, EL612, G795, S2213, SF2213, VU619
"Lord, Have Mercy" (Matt)
    C299, G576, S2277, SF2277

Additional Contemporary Suggestions

"Make Me a Channel of Your Peace" (Gen)
    G753, S2171, SF2171, VU684
"Make Us One" (Gen, Pss)
    AH4142, S2224, SF2224, SP137
"People Need the Lord" (Gen, Matt)
    B557, S2244, SF2244
"Mighty to Save" (Gen, Matt)
    M246, WS3038
"Your Grace Is Enough (Gen, Matt)
    M191, WS3106
"*Ubi Caritas*" ("Live in Charity") (Pss)
    C523, EL642, G205, S2179, SF2179, W604
"O Look and Wonder" ("*¡Miren Qué Bueno!*") (Pss, Rom)
    C292, EL649, G397, S2231, SF2231, VU856
"Oh, I Know the Lord's Laid His Hands on Me" (Matt)
    S2139, SF2139
"I'm So Glad Jesus Lifted Me" (Matt)
    C529, EL860 (PD), N474, S2151, SF2151
"Lord, Listen to Your Children" (Matt)
    C305, G469, S2193, SF2193, VU400

Vocal Solos

"Make Me a Channel of Your Peace" (Gen)
    V-3 (2)   p. 25
    V-3 (3)   p. 28
"I Heard About a Man" (Matt)
    V-8   p. 72

Anthems

"Christ Has Broken Down the Wall" (Gen, Matt)
Mark Miller, Choristers Guild CGA-1224
SATB, piano

"*Hine Mah Tov*" (Pss)
Simon Sargon; Transcontinental Music 991250
SATB, flute and keyboard

Other Suggestions

Visuals:
    O   Weeping, remnant, famine, Gen 45:5c, 8, men
             hugging
    P   Unity, Ps 133:1, oil, robe, dew, mountain
    E   No/Yes, Rom 11:29, 32, gifts, calling, prison/manacles
    G   Woman shouting, Jesus, dogs/crumbs, girl healed
Call to Prayer: UM371, st. 1. "I Stand Amazed" (Matt)
Prayer: C483. For a Renewed Sense of Compassion (Gen)
Alternate Lessons (see p. 4): Isa 56:1, 6-8, Ps 67

Exodus 1:8–2:10

[8]Now a new king came to power in Egypt who didn't know Joseph. [9]He said to his people, "The Israelite people are now larger in number and stronger than we are. [10]Come on, let's be smart and deal with them. Otherwise, they will only grow in number. And if war breaks out, they will join our enemies, fight against us, and then escape from the land." [11]As a result, the Egyptians put foremen of forced work gangs over the Israelites to harass them with hard work. They had to build storage cities named Pithom and Rameses for Pharaoh. [12]But the more they were oppressed, the more they grew and spread, so much so that the Egyptians started to look at the Israelites with disgust and dread. [13]So the Egyptians enslaved the Israelites. [14]They made their lives miserable with hard labor, making mortar and bricks, doing field work, and by forcing them to do all kinds of other cruel work.

[15]The king of Egypt spoke to two Hebrew midwives named Shiphrah and Puah: [16]"When you are helping the Hebrew women give birth and you see the baby being born, if it's a boy, kill him. But if it's a girl, you can let her live." [17]Now the two midwives respected God so they didn't obey the Egyptian king's order. Instead, they let the baby boys live.

[18]So the king of Egypt called the two midwives and said to them, "Why are you doing this? Why are you letting the baby boys live?"

[19]The two midwives said to Pharaoh, "Because Hebrew women aren't like Egyptian women. They're much stronger and give birth before any midwives can get to them." [20]So God treated the midwives well, and the people kept on multiplying and became very strong. [21]And because the midwives respected God, God gave them households of their own.

[22]Then Pharaoh gave an order to all his people: "Throw every baby boy born to the Hebrews into the Nile River, but you can let all the girls live."

2 Now a man from Levi's household married a Levite woman. [2]The woman became pregnant and gave birth to a son. She saw that the baby was healthy and beautiful, so she hid him for three months. [3]When she couldn't hide him any longer, she took a reed basket and sealed it up with black tar. She put the child in the basket and set the basket among the reeds at the riverbank. [4]The baby's older sister stood watch nearby to see what would happen to him.

[5]Pharaoh's daughter came down to bathe in the river, while her women servants walked along beside the river. She saw the basket among the reeds, and she sent one of her servants to bring it to her. [6]When she opened it, she saw the child. The boy was crying, and she felt sorry for him. She said, "This must be one of the Hebrews' children."

[7]Then the baby's sister said to Pharaoh's daughter, "Would you like me to go and find one of the Hebrew women to nurse the child for you?"

[8]Pharaoh's daughter agreed, "Yes, do that." So the girl went and called the child's mother. [9]Pharaoh's daughter said to her, "Take this child and nurse it for me, and I'll pay you for your work." So the woman took the child and nursed it. [10]After the child had grown up, she brought him back to Pharaoh's daughter, who adopted him as her son. She named him Moses, "because," she said, "I pulled him out of the water."

Psalm 124 (G330, N706, P236, UM846)

[1]If the LORD hadn't been for us— / let Israel now repeat!— / [2]if the LORD hadn't been for us, / when those people attacked us / [3]then they would have swallowed us up whole / with their rage burning against us! / [4]Then the waters would have drowned us; / the torrent would have come over our necks; / [5]then the raging waters would have come over our necks! / [6]Bless the LORD / because he didn't hand us over / like food for our enemies' teeth! / [7]We escaped like a bird from the hunters' trap; / the trap was broken so we escaped! / [8]Our help is in the name of the LORD, / the maker of heaven and earth. /

Romans 12:1-8

[1]So, brothers and sisters, because of God's mercies, I encourage you to present your bodies as a living sacrifice that is holy and pleasing to God. This is your appropriate priestly service. [2]Don't be conformed to the patterns of this world, but be transformed by the renewing of your minds so that you can figure out what God's will is—what is good and pleasing and mature.

[3]Because of the grace that God gave me, I can say to each one of you: don't think of yourself more highly than you ought to think. Instead, be reasonable since God has measured out a portion of faith to each one of you. [4]We have many parts in one body, but the parts don't all have the same function. [5]In the same way, though there are many of us, we are one body in Christ, and individually we belong to each other. [6]We have different gifts that are consistent with God's grace that has been given to us. If your gift is prophecy, you should prophesy in proportion to your faith. [7]If your gift is service, devote yourself to serving. If your gift is teaching, devote yourself to teaching. [8]If your gift is encouragement, devote yourself to encouraging. The one giving should do it with no strings attached. The leader should lead with passion. The one showing mercy should be cheerful.

Matthew 16:13-20

[13]Now when Jesus came to the area of Caesarea Philippi, he asked his disciples, "Who do people say the Human One is?"

[14]They replied, "Some say John the Baptist, others Elijah, and still others Jeremiah or one of the other prophets."

[15]He said, "And what about you? Who do you say that I am?"

[16]Simon Peter said, "You are the Christ, the Son of the living God."

[17]Then Jesus replied, "Happy are you, Simon son of Jonah, because no human has shown this to you. Rather my Father who is in heaven has shown you. [18]I tell you that you are Peter. And I'll build my church on this rock. The gates of the underworld won't be able to stand against it. [19]I'll give you the keys of the kingdom of heaven. Anything you fasten on earth will be fastened in heaven. Anything you loosen on earth will be loosened in heaven." [20]Then he ordered the disciples not to tell anybody that he was the Christ.

Primary Hymns and Songs for the Day

"Guide Me, O Thou Great Jehovah" (Exod) (O)
    B56, C622, E690, EL618, F608, G65, L343, N18/19, P281,
    UM127 (PD), VU651 (Fr.)
        H-3   Hbl-25, 51, 58; Chr-89; Desc-26; Org-23
        S-1   #76-77. Desc. and harm.
"Forward Through the Ages" (Matt) (O)
    N355, UM555 (PD)
        H-3   Hbl-59; Chr-156; Org-140
"Many Gifts, One Spirit" (Rom)
    N177, UM114
"Take My Life, and Let It Be" (Rom) (C)
    B277/B283, C609, E707, EL583/EL685, G697, L406, P391,
    N448, UM399 (PD), VU506

Additional Hymn Suggestions

"O God Our Help in Ages Past" (Exod)
    B74, C67, E680, EL632, F370, G687, L320, N25, P210,
    UM117 (PD), VU806, W579
"God Will Take Care of You" (Exod)
    B64, F56, N460, UM130 (PD)
"Jesus, Lover of My Soul" (Exod)
    B180 (PD), C542, E699, G440, N546, P303, UM479, VU669
"Spirit, Spirit of Gentleness" (Exod)
    C249, EL396, G291, N286, P319, S2120, VU375 (Fr.)
"Why Stand so Far Away, My God?" (Exod)
    C671, G786, S2180, SF2180
"Glorious Things of Thee Are Spoken" (Exod, Pss, Matt)
    B398, C709, E522 (or 523), EL647, F376, G81, L358, N307,
    P446, UM731 (PD)
"Deep in the Shadows of the Past" (Exod, Pss)
    G50, N320, P330, S2246
"Come, Thou Fount of Every Blessing" (Exod, Rom)
    AH4086, B15/18, C16, E686, EL807, F318, G475, L499,
    N459, P356, UM400 (PD), VU559
"Great Is Thy Faithfulness" (Pss)
    B54, C86, EL733, F98, G39, N423, P276, UM140, VU288
"Rock of Ages" (Pss, Matt)
    B342, C214, E685, EL623, F108, G438, L327, N596, UM361
"I Am Thine, O Lord" (Rom)
    AH4087, B290, C601, F455, N455, UM419 (PD)
"Like the Murmur of the Dove's Song" (Rom)
    C245, E513, EL403, G285, N270, P314, UM544, VU205
"I Come with Joy" (Rom, Comm.)
    B371, C420, E304, EL482, G515, N349, P507, UM617,
    VU477, W726
"Draw Us in the Spirit's Tether" (Rom, Comm.)
    C392, EL470, G529, N337, P504, UM632, VU479, W731
"Una Espiga" ("Sheaves of Summer") (Rom, Comm.)
    C396, G532, N338, UM637
"I'm Gonna Live so God Can Use Me" (Rom)
    C614, G700, P369, S2153, VU575
"The Church's One Foundation" (Rom, Matt)
    B350, C272, E525, EL654, F547, G321, L369, N386, P442,
    UM545/546, VU332 (Fr.)
"Christ Is Made the Sure Foundation" (Rom, Matt)
    B356 (PD), C275, E518, EL645, F557, G394, L367, N400,
    P416/417, UM559 (PD), VU325, W617
"Here I Am, Lord" (Rom, Matt)
    C452, EL574, G69, P525, UM593, VU509
"We Would Be Building" (Rom, Matt)
    N607
"Jesus, the Very Thought of Thee" (Matt)
    C102, E642, EL754, G629, L316, N507, P310, UM175
"My Hope Is Built" (Matt)
    B406, C537, EL596/597, F92, G353, L293/ 294, N368, P379,
    UM368 (PD)
"The Church of Christ, in Every Age" (Matt)
    B402, C475, EL729, G320, L433, N306, P421, UM589,
    VU601, W626
"I'm So Glad Jesus Lifted Me" (Matt)
    C529, EL860 (PD), N474, S2151, SF2151

Additional Contemporary Suggestions

"Freedom Is Coming" (Exod)
    G359, S2192, SF2192
"Grace Like Rain" (Exod)
    M251
"If It Had Not Been for the Lord" (Pss)
    S2053, SF2053
"Blessed Be the Name of the Lord" (Pss)
    M12, S2034, SF2034, UM63
"One Bread, One Body" (Rom, Comm.)
    C393, EL496, G530, UM620, VU467
"Grace Alone" (Rom)
    M100, S2162, SF2162
"Sanctuary" (Rom)
    G701, M52, S2164, SF2164
"Bind Us Together" (Rom)
    S2226, SF2226, SP140
"Take This Life" (Rom)
    M98
"I Will Not Forget You" (Rom)
    M211
"I'm So Glad Jesus Lifted Me" (Matt)
    C529, EL860 (PD), N474, S2151, SF2151
"Amazing Grace" ("My Chains Are Gone") (Matt)
    M205, WS3104

Vocal Solos

"Oh, Freedom" (Exod)
    V-7   p. 10
"Take My Life" ("Consecration") (Rom)
    V-8   p. 262
"A Covenant Prayer" (Rom)
    V-11   p. 6

Anthems

"Come, Thou Fount of Every Blessing" (Exod, Rom)
Arr. Michael Larkin; MorningStar MSM-50-0051
SATB, piano

"Tu es Petrus" (Matt)
David M. Cherwien; MorningStar 50-6512
SATB, organ

Other Suggestions

Visuals:
    O   Bricks/mortar, birthstool, newborn, basket/reeds/
         river
    P   Enemies, flood/torrent/water, bird/broken snare, Ps
         124:8
    E   Transformer, dance, offering plate, seven gifts
    G   Jesus teaching, Peter, large rock/keys, Matt 16:15, 16
Reading: N574. "In Egypt Under Pharaoh" (Exod)
Litany: F243. Who Is This Man? (Matt)
Alternate Lessons (see p. 4): Isa 51:1-6, Ps 138

INDEX OF SCRIPTURES REFERENCED

New Testament

NOTES

WORSHIP PLANNING SHEET 1

Date: _____ Color:_____

Preacher: _____

Liturgist: _____

Selected Scripture: _____

Selected Hymns	No.	Placement

Psalter #_____

Keyboard Selections

Title	Composer	Placement

Anthems

Title	Choir	Composer	Placement

Vocal Solos

Title	Singer	Composer	Placement

Other Ideas:

Acolytes: _____

Head Usher: _____

Altar Guild Contact: _____

Other Participants: _____

_____

WORSHIP PLANNING SHEET 2

Date: _____ Sunday: _____ Color: _____

Preacher: _____

Liturgist: _____

Opening Voluntary   Composer

_____

_____

Hymn   Tune Name   No.

_____

Opening Prayer: _____

Prayer for Illumination: _____

First Lesson: _____

Psalter: _____

Second Lesson: _____

Gospel Lesson: _____

Hymn   Tune Name   No.

_____

Response to the Word: _____

Prayers of the People: _____

Offertory   Composer

_____

Communion Setting: _____

Communion Hymns   Tune Name   No.

_____

_____

Closing Hymn   Tune Name   No.

_____

Benediction: _____

Closing Voluntary   Composer

_____

CONTEMPORARY WORSHIP PLANNING SHEET

Because of the diversity in orders of worship, you will want to adjust this planning sheet to meet the needs of your worship planning team. A common order used would consist of three to four opening praise choruses and lively hymns, a time of informal prayers of the congregation along with songs of prayer, reading of the primary scripture for the day, a drama or video to illustrate the day's theme, a message from the preacher, a testimony on the theme for the day (if a drama or video was not presented earlier), followed by closing songs appropriate to the mood of the service and the message. Any offering would usually be taken early in the service, and Holy Communion would normally take place following the message. Special music (solos, duets, instrumental music) can be used wherever it best expresses the theme of the service.

Date: _____ Sunday: _____

Thematic Emphasis or Topic: _____

Color: _____ Visual Focus: _____

Opening Songs:
_____
_____

Prayer Songs:
_____

Scripture Selection(s):
_____

Drama or Video:
_____

Message Title:
_____

Testimony: _____

Special Music:
_____

Closing Songs:
_____

Preacher: _____ Music Leader: _____

Worship Facilitator: _____ Prayer Leader: _____

2016–2017 Lectionary Calendar

Lectionary verses and worship suggestions in this edition of *The UM Planner* relate to the unshaded dates in the calendar below.

Lectionary Year C: September 4, 2016–November 24, 2016

Lectionary Year A: November 27, 2016–August 27, 2017

2016

JANUARY 2016

S	M	T	W	T	F	S
					1	2
3	4	5	6	7	8	9
10	11	12	13	14	15	16
17	18	19	20	21	22	23
24	25	26	27	28	29	30
31						

FEBRUARY 2016

S	M	T	W	T	F	S
	1	2	3	4	5	6
7	8	9	10	11	12	13
14	15	16	17	18	19	20
21	22	23	24	25	26	27
28	29					

MARCH 2016

S	M	T	W	T	F	S
		1	2	3	4	5
6	7	8	9	10	11	12
13	14	15	16	17	18	19
20	21	22	23	24	25	26
27	28	29	30	31		

APRIL 2016

S	M	T	W	T	F	S
					1	2
3	4	5	6	7	8	9
10	11	12	13	14	15	16
17	18	19	20	21	22	23
24	25	26	27	28	29	30

MAY 2016

S	M	T	W	T	F	S
1	2	3	4	5	6	7
8	9	10	11	12	13	14
15	16	17	18	19	20	21
22	23	24	25	26	27	28
29	30	31				

JUNE 2016

S	M	T	W	T	F	S
			1	2	3	4
5	6	7	8	9	10	11
12	13	14	15	16	17	18
19	20	21	22	23	24	25
26	27	28	29	30		

JULY 2016

S	M	T	W	T	F	S
					1	2
3	4	5	6	7	8	9
10	11	12	13	14	15	16
17	18	19	20	21	22	23
24	25	26	27	28	29	30
31						

AUGUST 2016

S	M	T	W	T	F	S
	1	2	3	4	5	6
7	8	9	10	11	12	13
14	15	16	17	18	19	20
21	22	23	24	25	26	27
28	29	30	31			

SEPTEMBER 2016

S	M	T	W	T	F	S
				1	2	3
4	5	6	7	8	9	10
11	12	13	14	15	16	17
18	19	20	21	22	23	24
25	26	27	28	29	30	

OCTOBER 2016

S	M	T	W	T	F	S
						1
2	3	4	5	6	7	8
9	10	11	12	13	14	15
16	17	18	19	20	21	22
23	24	25	26	27	28	29
30	31					

NOVEMBER 2016

S	M	T	W	T	F	S
		1	2	3	4	5
6	7	8	9	10	11	12
13	14	15	16	17	18	19
20	21	22	23	24	25	26
27	28	29	30			

DECEMBER 2016

S	M	T	W	T	F	S
				1	2	3
4	5	6	7	8	9	10
11	12	13	14	15	16	17
18	19	20	21	22	23	24
25	26	27	28	29	30	31

2017

JANUARY 2017

S	M	T	W	T	F	S
1	2	3	4	5	6	7
8	9	10	11	12	13	14
15	16	17	18	19	20	21
22	23	24	25	26	27	28
29	30	31				

FEBRUARY 2017

S	M	T	W	T	F	S
			1	2	3	4
5	6	7	8	9	10	11
12	13	14	15	16	17	18
19	20	21	22	23	24	25
26	27	28				

MARCH 2017

S	M	T	W	T	F	S
			1	2	3	4
5	6	7	8	9	10	11
12	13	14	15	16	17	18
19	20	21	22	23	24	25
26	27	28	29	30	31	

APRIL 2017

S	M	T	W	T	F	S
						1
2	3	4	5	6	7	8
9	10	11	12	13	14	15
16	17	18	19	20	21	22
23	24	25	26	27	28	29
30						

MAY 2017

S	M	T	W	T	F	S
	1	2	3	4	5	6
7	8	9	10	11	12	13
14	15	16	17	18	19	20
21	22	23	24	25	26	27
28	29	30	31			

JUNE 2017

S	M	T	W	T	F	S
				1	2	3
4	5	6	7	8	9	10
11	12	13	14	15	16	17
18	19	20	21	22	23	24
25	26	27	28	29	30	

JULY 2017

S	M	T	W	T	F	S
						1
2	3	4	5	6	7	8
9	10	11	12	13	14	15
16	17	18	19	20	21	22
23	24	25	26	27	28	29
30	31					

AUGUST 2017

S	M	T	W	T	F	S
		1	2	3	4	5
6	7	8	9	10	11	12
13	14	15	16	17	18	19
20	21	22	23	24	25	26
27	28	29	30	31		

SEPTEMBER 2017

S	M	T	W	T	F	S
					1	2
3	4	5	6	7	8	9
10	11	12	13	14	15	16
17	18	19	20	21	22	23
24	25	26	27	28	29	30

OCTOBER 2017

S	M	T	W	T	F	S
1	2	3	4	5	6	7
8	9	10	11	12	13	14
15	16	17	18	19	20	21
22	23	24	25	26	27	28
29	30	31				

NOVEMBER 2017

S	M	T	W	T	F	S
			1	2	3	4
5	6	7	8	9	10	11
12	13	14	15	16	17	18
19	20	21	22	23	24	25
26	27	28	29	30		

DECEMBER 2017

S	M	T	W	T	F	S
					1	2
3	4	5	6	7	8	9
10	11	12	13	14	15	16
17	18	19	20	21	22	23
24	25	26	27	28	29	30
31						